# Short Fellow

To Gina and Pat

First published in 1995 by Marino Books, an imprint of Mercier Press
16 Hume Street Dublin 2
e.mail: books@marino.ie
Tel: (01) 661 5299; Fax: 661 8583

Trade enquiries to CMD Distribution, 55A Spruce Avenue, Stillorgan Industrial Park, Blackrock, Co Dublin.
Tel: 294 2556; Fax: 294 2556
e.mail: cmd@columba.ie



ISBN 1 86023 100 4

10 9 8 7 6 5 4 3 2 1

A CIP record for this title is available from the British Library

Cover design by Penhouse Design
Cover photo courtesy of Colman Doyle
Author photo courtesy fo Kevin Coleman
Printed in Ireland by ColourBooks, Baldoyle Industrial Estate, Dublin 13

# Short Fellow

## A Biography of Charles J. Haughey

# Contents

# Introduction

One Sunday afternoon in 1974 I was having dinner with my great-aunt Gerty at her regular table just inside the door of the Mount Brandon Hotel in Tralee when Charlie Haughey walked in. He stood there looking for somebody, possibly his friend John Byrne, one of the principal owners of the hotel.

'There's your friend,' I whispered to my aunt, a staunch Fianna Fáil supporter.

She turned and looked at Haughey, who was standing only a few feet from her. 'Who is he?' she asked me, in a normal voice that he obviously could hear.

Suddenly I regretted having said anything. Aunt Gerty was a big, bossy type of woman who terrorised her contemporaries but was loved by the younger generations of the family.

'That's Charlie Haughey!' I whispered.

She sat bolt upright and turned her body towards him. She, sitting down, was almost as tall as he was standing. She looked him up and down. He seemed a little uneasy at being inspected. 'My God!' she exclaimed, with a gasp of surprise. 'He's awful insignificant-looking.'

She was actually being complimentary in her own peculiar way. After all, he was one of the strong men of Fianna Fáil, the party founded by her hero, Éamon de Valera. He was the long fellow, with what she used to call 'strong artistocratic features'. It came as a shock to her system that Charlie Haughey, the man with the larger-than-life reputation, was actually rather a short fellow.

Twenty-two years later, while sitting in the RTÉ television studio in Tralee waiting to take part in a *Prime Time* programme devoted to Charles Haughey, I heard the other guests being ushered into the studio in Dublin. Miriam O'Callaghan told them that I would be appearing on a link-up and one of them exclaimed, 'He's a fierce Charlie supporter.'

I had already written *Charlie,* an interim biography of Haughey that was published in 1987. When I began research for that book I had a very hostile view of Haughey but was determined to be fair to him. The end product was certainly more favourable to Haughey than I had initially envisaged, but it was far from uncritical because even at that stage Haughey had a mixed record.

His career is the story of a lust for power and, some may argue, an affirmation of Lord Acton's famous dictum that 'Power tends to corrupt, and absolute power tends to corrupt absolutely.' But Haughey never achieved absolute political power. He was blocked by the electorate, who were influenced by a combination of his opponents within Fianna Fáil, the Opposition and the media. Now his perennial critics are contending that they were right all along, but if they were so perceptive why did they get things so wrong for so long? If Haughey was a malignant ogre who never achieved anything worthwhile politically, why was he so popular with so many people?

During his first two stints as Taoiseach, his performance was little short of disastrous, which was disappointing because he had performed admirably in other posts. Even one of his most determined opponents, Peter Berry, a senior civil servant in the Department of Justice, credited him with being the most able and efficient Minister for Justice of the fourteen under whom he had served. James Dillon, the Fine Gael leader, described Haughey as 'an extremely good Minister for Agriculture', and he was also extolled as a brilliant Minister for Finance and a highly successful Minister for Health. During his third spell as Taoiseach he led a government that is generally credited with having achieved a virtual economic miracle in turning Ireland's near-bankrupt economy around in the late 1980s.

Some will argue that he had to institute the changes because of the attitude of the International Monetary Fund, and others will contend, probably correctly, that the reforms were greatly facilitated by the attitude of Alan Dukes, who provided Fine Gael support. Haughey admitted that there was no choice and readers will have to determine for themselves how the credit should be shared for turning things around.

Haughey was often depicted as a bitter and vicious politician, but Conor Cruise O'Brien and Dick Spring, two of his most outspoken political opponents, have both stated that he was never other than polite to them. Haughey was invariably polite to his opponents; it was members of Fianna Fáil who had to watch out, according to Cruise O'Brien.

Throughout the bulk of his political career Haughey helped create an aura of success around himself by exhibiting the trappings of wealth. He lived in regal opulence in a magnificent mansion set in palatial grounds. He affected the studied gestures of Napoleon and frequently behaved in an imperious manner towards those around him. He courted publicity by a variety of means, as he clearly loved the limelight. Haughey entertained lavishly and often threw money around, with the result that he gained a reputation for being generous to the point of profligacy; he was known as a soft touch for hard-luck cases. He was involved in horse racing, the 'sport of kings', as both an owner and a breeder. He owned his own yacht as well as an island off the coast of Kerry, and he helped set his son up in the helicopter business. 'Every aspect of his character attracts curiosity,' Bruce

Arnold declared in his largely hostile, though highly readable, biography of Haughey. 'No man so dominated his period, in and out of power,' Arnold noted.

In time it would become apparent that much of his money was borrowed and bummed. Those who saw his wealth as the proof of his success would ultimately be disappointed: this success would prove fleeting, and those people now see him as a great failure. But if such things are to be considered the measure of success or failure, it should be realised that Haughey was in good company. Daniel O'Connell – arguably the most famous and influential Irishman of all time – lived beyond his means for much of his life.

O'Connell was reared by a rich uncle who was none too pleased at his nephew's extravagance. 'The main indications he has given of a liberal mind in the expenditure of money has left a vacuum in my purse, as well as an impression on my mind, not easily eradicated,' his guardian uncle wrote to his mother. O'Connell lived extravagantly, in the confident expectation that he would inherit his uncle's fortune, but the uncle lived to the ripe old age of ninety-seven. After entering politics in the 1820s O'Connell gave up his practice at the Bar and financed his lavish lifestyle with the help of national subscriptions from ordinary people. These subscriptions amounted to an average of about £13,000 a year, but in one year shortly before the outbreak of the Famine they totalled around £50,000. Unlike Haughey, who got much of his money from the fabulously wealthy, O'Connell accepted his from people who were living in a state of virtual subsistence. O'Connell was mercilessly ridiculed in his lifetime over the state of his financial affairs.

It was not just Haughey's lifestyle which attracted curiosity and attention. He was involved in three scandals of Watergate proportions: the Arms Crisis in the 1970s, the telephone-tapping controversy in the 1980s and then a series of financial scandals that have persisted throughout the 1990s, and that have been or still are the subject of various tribunals of enquiry established by the Dáil. While it is too early to say what will emerge from the current tribunals, nobody got to the bottom of either of the two earlier scandals.

No one was ever convicted of any wrongdoing in these two scandals. There was obvious perjury at the Arms Trial and the subsequent inquiry by the Dáil's Committee of Public Accounts, but nobody was ever charged with an offence in relation to the case, and the Taoiseach of the day was never even questioned about it.

There was no real investigation into the telephone-tapping scandal either, because if there had been it would have been just as embarrassing for the government of the day as the Arms Trial. The innocent public paid dearly through legal settlements, but the events surrounding the Beef Tribunal were literally a thousand times more costly. While the Beef Tribunal was still sitting Haughey was finally ousted as Taoiseach, even though he was replaced, ironically, by a man whose political judgement in relation to those matters was more suspect than Haughey's had been.

Normally before an interview, his aide, P. J. Mara, would warn the interviewer not to ask 'the Boss' questions about his private business affairs or the arms crisis. As Mara graphically put it to one interviewer, 'No oul' Arms Trial shite, now!'

This is the story of Charles J. Haughey, 'Arms Trial shite', telephone-tapping, money-cadging and all.

*TRD*

*Tralee, November 1999*

# 1

## 'COWBOY FILMS WERE THE BIG DEAL'
## EARLY YEARS, 1925–1957

Charles James Haughey was born in Castlebar, County Mayo, on 16 September 1925, the second son of Commandant Johnny Haughey. Both his father and mother, the former Sarah McWilliams, were from Swartragh, County Derry, in what became Northern Ireland. Both of them were active in the republican movement during the War of Independence.

Although a staunch republican, Johnny Haughey followed Michael Collins and served in the Free State Army during the Civil War of 1922–3. Over the years it would be conveniently forgotten by many people that the Treaty split, which divided the independence movement and led to the Civil War, had little to do with the partition issue.

The British had resorted to partition rather than confront the armed minority concentrated in the Six Counties, and Collins was prepared to emulate the unionists by arming Northern nationalists so that Westminster would agree to re-partition rather than confront the armed minority in Northern Ireland. As the forces under him had British weapons, Collins secretly sent these weapons to republicans in the Six Counties. He also sent some 400 British rifles to Donegal with instructions for General Joseph Sweeney to hold them for an emissary. This emissary, who turned out to be Johnny Haughey, then brought the guns over the border.

Followers of Collins who placed a high priority on ending partition became disillusioned as his successors virtually ignored the question after his death. Johnny Haughey quit the army in 1928 and moved to Sutton, County Dublin, before buying a farm in the vicinity of Dunshaughlin, County Meath, where Charlie, or Cathal as he was known to his family, began school.

While farming, however, Johnny developed multiple sclerosis and sold the farm. The family moved to Belton Park Road, Dublin, in the early 1930s. With Johnny sick and the family dependent on his army pension, supplemented by a small IRA pension awarded to his wife, things could not have been easy for the large family. Charlie had three brothers, Sean, Eoghan and Pádraig (Jock), and three sisters, Maureen, Peggy, and Sheila.

After moving to Dublin, Charlie attended Scoil Mhuire National School in Marino, where he demonstrated great academic and athletic talents. He played on the school's football and hurling teams and finished in first place in Dublin Corporation's scholarship examination. His memories of those early years were of playing football and hurling, collecting birds' eggs and going to movies – when he had the money.

'Cowboy films were the big deal,' he recalled. 'People like Gene Autry and things like that.' He spent 'a lot of his summer holidays' with his grandmother in Northern Ireland. 'It was a small farm and I got a very good insight there of life on a small farm and of the social life and economics of small farming,' he explained. 'And I also got a very clear impression of the community situation in Northern Ireland – how the Catholic small farmers viewed their Protestant neighbours and how they lived with them.'

From Scoil Mhuire he went on to St Joseph's Christian Brothers School, Fairview, where he was again a brilliant student and an outstanding athlete. He mastered subjects with apparent ease and was usually first in his class in every subject. His classmates included Harry Boland, with whom he later went into business, and George Colley, with whom he would eventually develop a bitter political rivalry. In his final year at St Joseph's he won a county council scholarship to University College Dublin and also achieved the distinction of being selected to represent the Leinster colleges in both football and hurling.

'I liked school,' he recalled. 'By and large the games at school made up for the less attractive side of it. If you did something awful or outrageous, you got the leather, but it certainly left no scars on me.'

Haughey's teenage years fell during a particularly turbulent period on the international scene. The Second World War erupted when he was thirteen years old and did not end until the month before his twentieth birthday.

'When I was a teenager, the war was on, so the whole environment was totally different,' he recalled. 'The whole country was down to subsistence level.' There was extensive rationing, and private motor cars virtually vanished from the roads, with the result that movement was severely restricted and opportunities for foreign travel were practically eliminated. 'The big thing,' he noted, 'was the number of one's friends that went off to join the British Army because there was no work. You either joined the Irish Army or the British Army.'

Haughey never had any interest in joining the British Army, which was hardly surprising, given his family background. One of his uncles, Pat McWilliams, was interned in Northern Ireland for the duration of the war.

Towards the end of his first year at UCD, Haughey was involved in an incident which received international publicity. The incident occurred on 7 May 1945 following the announcement that Germany would formally surrender the next day.

Celebrating the news, a group of students at Trinity College, which was still widely identified as an Anglophile institution, began flying the Allied flags from the flagpole on the roof of the entrance to the college, in the heart of the city. When people on the street took exception to the Irish tricolour being flown below the other flags, the students responded by taking down the Irish flag and trying to burn it.

On hearing what had happened, a group of UCD students organised a counter-demonstration. With some students carrying Nazi flags, the demonstrators marched on Trinity College. Outside the entrance, the scene of the earlier incident, Haughey produced a Union Jack and he and a colleague proceeded to burn it. What had started out in fairly good humour turned very ugly, and a riot ensued as the police baton-charged the gathering. Some of the crowd broke away and later stoned the residence of the British Representative and the offices of the US Consul General.

During his time at UCD Haughey took an active part in student affairs and the social life of the college. Among the girls he dated were Maureen Lemass, whom he married in 1951, and Joan O'Farrell, who later married a fellow student of Haughey's, Garret Fitzgerald. The two young men knew each other in college but were never friends.

Two of Haughey's fairly close friends at the time were Harry Boland and George Colley, both sons of Fianna Fáil deputies. Haughey was apparently attracted to the party, but he did not join it until the year after his father's death in 1947.

After receiving a Bachelor of Commerce degree Haughey went to work for the accounting firm of Boland Burke and Company, along with Harry Boland, who was a brother of one of the principals of the firm. Haughey got his accountancy examinations at the first attempt and studied for the Bar at

King's Inns. Although he was called to the Bar in 1949, he never practised. Instead, he set up the accountancy firm Haughey Boland and Company Ltd in partnership with Harry Boland in 1951.

Haughey kept irregular hours at the office, as he concentrated on drumming up business for the firm with some free-spending socialising. He was particularly active in the Gaelic Athletic Association. He was an accomplished club footballer, normally playing in the half-forward line, where he was noted for his tenacious play and quick temper. On one occasion he was suspended for a year for striking a linesman. He won a Dublin county championship football medal with Parnells, while his brother Pádraig (Jock) was a member of the famous Dublin football team of the 1950s.

Haughey first became involved with Fianna Fáil in helping with postering for the Boland and Colley families in the general election of 1948. He formally joined the party that year and was elected secretary of the Fairview branch. He stood as a Fianna Fáil candidate for the Dáil in the 1951 general election but finished last of the party's four candidates.

At the age of twenty-seven he was co-opted to fill a Fianna Fáil vacancy on Dublin Corporation, but he again failed miserably in an election, losing his deposit when he ran for the Dáil in the 1954 general election. In the aftermath of the Fianna Fáil defeat in this election, his father-in-law Sean Lemass was given the task of reorganising the party, and he picked Haughey and a number of active young men like George Colley, Brian Lenihan and Eoin Ryan to visit party clubs throughout the country.

In 1956 Haughey got the Fianna Fáil nomination to contest the by-election to fill a vacancy caused by the death of the colourful independent Alfie Byrne. This time he lost out to

Byrne's son Patrick, but as his party's only standard-bearer he made a credible showing and finally won election to the Dáil at his fourth attempt, in the general election of 1957, when Fianna Fáil enjoyed a landslide victory.

In his early years in the Dáil, Haughey had a high public profile and enjoyed a good press, but he was quiet about his private life and especially his business dealings. He appeared to amass a considerable fortune at a time when politics was not a particularly well-paid profession. Haughey was engaged in a number of outside interests. He was involved with Donogh O'Malley in Reema (Ireland) Ltd, a property company of which O'Malley was chief executive and Haughey was secretary. Reema bought up property around Limerick on the road to Shannon Airport. At the time, questions were asked about him and O'Malley basing these purchases on inside knowledge. Haughey was very mysterious when it came to money. He bought a farm in Ashbourne, County Meath, and a chicken hatchery. He was rapidly moving up in the world.

After the marriage of Charles Haughey and Maureen Lemass in 1951, the Haugheys initially lived in a semi-detached house in a Raheny housing estate, but in 1957 they moved to Grangemore, a large Victorian mansion on a forty-five acre site in Raheny. The builder Matt Gallagher advised Haughey to splash out £13,000 to buy the house in Raheny, with the promise that, when the time was right and planning permission had been secured to build houses on the site, Gallagher would buy it from him. Gallagher did so two years later, paying over £200,000 for the property.

With this money, Haughey bought Abbeville in Kinsealy, County Dublin. This fine eighteenth-century mansion had served as the summer home for several Lord Lieutenants of Ireland prior to the government's acquisition of the Viceregal

Lodge (now Áras an Uachtaráin). Abbeville was designed by the renowned architect James Gandon, whose more famous works included the Customs House and the Four Courts in Dublin. Haughey, his wife and their four children, Eimear, Conor, Ciarán, and Sean, who were all born between 1955 and 1961, moved into the house. The 250-acre estate included some of the finest gardens in the Dublin area, and Haughey sought to develop part of the property into a wildlife reserve and set up a stud farm on the grounds.

By then, Haughey's political career had taken off. In 1959 Sean Lemass took over as Taoiseach, and Haughey, as his son-in-law, was quickly singled out as a likely successor. He therefore became the victim of what one admirer would later describe as 'the Fine Gael rumour machine'. An endless stream of unflattering rumours began to flow about Haughey's private life and business dealings.

He lived in ostentatious opulence, flaunting his wealth as the trappings of his success in much the same way as businessmen drive expensive cars to generate an aura of achievement. But Haughey did not just have an expensive car; he also had a yacht, a plane, his son's helicopter firm and a holiday home on his own island — Innishvicillaun, one of the Blasket Islands, off the coast of Kerry. He dabbled in horse racing and bred his own racehorses.

Questions were repeatedly asked about how he could afford his expensive livestyle, but it was not until after he had retired from politics in the 1990s that the real answers to these questions began to emerge. He was being financed by large 'gifts' of money from various wealthy acquaintances from the world of business.

'Haughey was financed in order to create the environment which the Anglo-Irish had enjoyed and that we as a people could never aspire to,' as Matt Gallagher's son Patrick explained.

'To be a wealthy politician was the sin of the day – and

Charlie Haughey was indecently wealthy,' according to the columnist John Healy. 'If a pub changed hands, Haughey was the secret buyer.'

At one point he supposedly owned about five public houses on both the north and south sides of Dublin. His amorous activities, both real and imagined, were also the subject of much public speculation. 'There were enough rumours about him to form a legend of sorts,' says Conor Cruise O'Brien.

In ancient Celtic folk tales, the hero was a man of great sexual prowess. Daniel O'Connell was reputed to have had a voracious sexual appitite. It used to be said that one could not throw a stone over a workhouse wall without hitting one of O'Connell's bastards. In reality he had a loving relationship with his wife, Mary, and there is no evidence that he had an affair with anyone before her death, but he never seemed to be unduly troubled by the rumours to the contrary.

Later in the century Charles Stewart Parnell had a long-standing relationship with a married woman, Kitty O'Shea. This affair was well known at the time, but it was only after the whole thing was dragged into the public domain – when her husband sued for divorce and cited Parnell as a co-respondent – that it essentially wrecked his career. He had become a victim of the hypocrisy of British society, in the eyes of his Irish followers at any rate.

Haughey was the subject of numerous rumours and, like the old Gaelic chieftains, he seemed to encourage them. His affair with journalist Terry Keane must have been the worst-kept secret in Ireland. Haughey publicly stated that his own great regret in life was that he had been born too early for the permissive era. 'To my dying day,' he said, 'I'll regret that I was too late for the free society. We missed out on that! It came too late for my generation.'

His daughter Eimear grew up to take charge of his stud, his eldest son, Conor, qualified as a mining engineer, Ciarán took over the Celtic Helicopter firm and the youngest child, Sean, went into politics. Haughey frequently took his holidays on Innishvicillaun, where he got away from the hustle and bustle of politics and city life.

Over the years he has assiduously patronised the arts, both by introducing legislation to help writers and artists and by adorning his home and grounds with sculptures and paintings by Irish artists. 'He was an aristocrat in the proper sense of the word; not a nobleman or even a gentleman, but one who believed in the right of the best people to rule, and that he himself was the best of the best people,' Cruise O'Brien wrote in 1972, at a particularly low point in Haughey's political career. The writer's use of the past tense betrayed a rather premature tendency to write off the political career of the man from Kinsealy.

'People liked him,' Cruise O'Brien continued, 'not for the possession of any of the more obviously likeable qualities but for lending some colour to life in a particularly drab period.' Opponents often accused him of arrogance and even incompetence, but nobody ever accused him of being dull. By the end of the sixties he was unquestionably one of the most influential politicians in the country. Things turned sour in 1970, however. He was dismissed from the government and subsequently charged with conspiring to import arms illegally for the use of the IRA in Northern Ireland. Although he was acquitted of the charges in court, he had an uphill struggle to regain his political standing. In the circumstances it was an achievement for Haughey just to survive politically, but he did much more than that. By 1977 he was back in government, as Minister for Health and Social Welfare, even though public-opinion polls indicated that he was deeply distrusted. The front-bench members of his own party rated him as the person they would least like to see as Taoiseach. Nonetheless, a little over two years later he became Taoiseach.

'Coming to terms with Charlie Haughey is like making your confirmation or losing your virginity,' wrote *Sunday Independent* journalist Anne Harris, who described him as 'the acceptable face of fantasy'. Over the years he has provided inspiration for Irish people wishing to fantasise about money, power and the good life.

'Haughey is all things to all women without necessarily having to do anything to any of them,' Harris continued. 'He has a way with women. Young women and matrons alike ache for him.' His taste for champagne and his passion for power commanded awe.

Haughey is a man with charisma in the true sense; this should not be confused with charm or popularity. An essential dimension of charismatic political leadership is the belief among followers that their leader has superhuman qualities. Probably only three Irish politicians in the twentieth century could therefore be described as possessing real charisma – Éamon de Valera, Michael Collins and Charles Haughey. In Haughey's case, the elusive 'superhuman' quality has been his extraordinary ability to survive a plethora of political crises.

Before his election to the Dáil in 1957 he had to survive two dismal showings in general elections, his failure to retain the seat to which he had been co-opted on the Dublin Corporation and a by-election defeat. He overcame a near-mutiny among the Gardaí in 1961, when he was Minister for Justice, and survived a virtual revolt by farmers in 1966, when he was Minister for Agriculture. He overcame his dismissal as Minister for Finance in 1970 and beat gun-running charges in court before staging a dramatic political recovery which culminated in his election as Taoiseach before the end of the decade. In the early 1980s he survived three different challenges to his leadership of Fianna Fáil. On the third occasion he was written off by virtually the whole media. The *Irish Press* took the extraordinary step of publishing what amounted to his political obituary, and bookmakers made the mistake of offering odds on the selection of his successor without taking the possibility of his survival into account. Yet he again survived. Afterwards, one writer noted that Haughey's critics would probably wait for three days after the Taoiseach's death before reporting the event – just in case!

Haughey admitted that he was fascinated by politics and had been lured into political life by two different considerations – his wish to get things done and what he called, using a sporting term, 'the roar of the crowd'. 'I have no sympathy for the person who wants political office for the sake of the office and even less for the person who wants political office for the trappings,' Haughey said. 'I think it's only worthwhile and can only justify all the disadvantages and the unpleasantness if you can positively achieve things and have a say, a real say, in the world around you – to improve things, and certainly to achieve economic development. What politics should be about is making the world a better place for those you serve.'

One of the things that can be said with absolute certainty about Charles Haughey is that, as the *Irish Times* noted in a 1969 profile, 'He is a man who wants power. He has everything else.' But he pursued his ambition with such single-mindedness that many people found his quest for power disconcerting. 'Ambition,' the *Irish Times* continued, 'is a trait we admire in people. Yet when we isolate it in a politician and recognise it, we tend to resent it as an indecency.'

Haughey candidly admitted that he sought election to the

Dáil because the power to shape things was to be found there. The primary duty of deputies is to legislate, and in this area he has excelled. He has enjoyed the cut and thrust of debate, and possesses the tactical skill required to steer bills through the Oireachtas.

As Minister for Justice, Haughey introduced a phenomenal amount of legislation as part of his attempt to update the country's legal system. This required a great deal of patience, especially from a man renowned for his short temper.

This is only one of the many contradictions in Haughey's character: he is held up by some as a prototype of the uncaring capitalist but has demonstrated a real social concern in the various departments in which he has served. He explained that he wished 'to make sure that whatever progress was achieved was distributed to the greatest possible extent and as fairly as possible to those who needed it'. Having grown up in a family that was dependent on his father's pension, he has introduced some imaginative schemes to help pensioners, including free travel, free electricity and free telephones.

Tending to dismiss such measures as gimmicks to curry popularity, some critics have charged that he would do almost anything to win votes. 'No one will dispute,' the playwright Hugh Leonard once wrote, 'that to catch a vote Mr Haughey would unhesitatingly roller skate backwards into a nunnery, naked from the waist down and singing "Kevin Barry" in Swahili.' Yet for Haughey, pleasing the people was the very essence of representative democracy.

He was prepared to help people and be generous even when there was no political advantage to be gained from doing so. For instance, after learning that a German crew had spent some days on Innishvicillaun following the crash of their bomber off the island in November 1940, he traced the five airmen, invited them to the island and gave them his house for a fortnight in the summer of 1980. There was certainly no political advantage to be gained from this, as their visit was never publicised.

This side of Haughey's character helps explain his enormous popularity amongst his own constituents. Despite his early difficulties in getting elected to the Dáil, he was returned at the head of the poll in every other general election he contested.

'I have a perfectly good relationship with my people, my constituency,' he explained to one interviewer. 'They know me, I know they trust me and I think they like me. They don't think I'm a bad person or am out to do anything detrimental to them or their interests. And that's what matters. That is the compensation for when you read something in the paper that you know is unfair – grossly unfair – and wrong. And when that happens you're inclined to get outraged and angry and upset about it.'

Those people that Haughey likes get sworn at ribaldly with no expletives deleted. His loyalty to friends often left him open to the charge of appointing people to offices for which they were unsuited. 'I am perhaps a little sentimental or romantic in my loyalties to people,' he admitted. But in return he demanded an unwavering personal loyalty, and he has tended to regard any questioning of his motives or actions as betrayal.

At times Haughey seemed almost paranoid in his suspicion of the media. On occasions he would make unguarded comments, such as in the autumn of 1982, when a reporter from the *Irish Times* tried to question him in the street and Haughey expressed his annoyance at some recent editorials.

'Who writes the *Irish Times* editorials, anyway?' Haughey asked, betraying a gnawing resentment at some recent editorials. 'They read like they have been done by an old woman sitting in a bath with the water getting cold around her fanny!'

# 2

## 'Too many people are making insufficient profits'
## Backbencher, 1957–1962

When Haughey entered the Dáil, the leadership of Fianna Fáil was still heavily dominated by the old guard of the party. The Taoiseach, Éamon de Valera, and eight of his eleven ministers had been founding members thirty years earlier. The ministers who had not been founding members of the party were Jack Lynch, Neil Blaney and Kevin Boland. It was a party where bright young men would soon be given opportunities; the old guard could not last for ever.

Following his election, Haughey promptly adopted a professional approach towards the media. He tried using his own personal public-relations man. He approached the society columnist Terry O'Sullivan, and when O'Sullivan declined, Tony Grey of the *Irish Times* accepted the job.

Clearly in a hurry to make his mark in politics, Haughey waited less than two months to deliver his maiden speech in the Dáil, during the debate on the new government's first budget. He suggested that the government should follow the example of Northern Ireland in constructing factory buildings to lease to industrialists. This plan, which would help both to promote the establishment of new factories and to assist the recovery of the heavily depressed building industry, foreshadowed the practice later adopted by the Industrial Development Authority.

Haughey was unambiguously capitalistic in outlook. Profit motivation formed the central theme of his economic philosophy. 'The trouble with this country is that too many people are making insufficient profits,' he told the Dáil in his maiden address. 'It would be well for this country from every point of view – and particularly from the point of view of the weaker sections of the community – if our industrialists were put in a position where they could make adequate profits, which would ensure their continuation in business and their being able to finance further expansion.' His message was simple: enhanced profits would give industry the incentive to expand, thereby providing employment for the less-well-off in society.

He was not a monetarist, content to leave everything to market forces. He advocated state involvement and state investment, especially to modernise native industries like agriculture and fisheries. In only his second address to the Dáil, for example, he complained about the state's 'very pathetic investment' in fisheries, which he believed were 'capable of giving such a tremendous return'. He suggested that An Bord Iascaigh Mhara should expand its involvement to research, education and training because virtually everything – with the exception of engines – needed for the fishing industry could be provided from within Ireland. As there was a plentiful supply of fish off the coast, modernisation of the fishing industry would provide employment in boat building, harbour reconstruction, and fish processing. Hence he called for the formulation of a 'long-term plan to contemplate a far greater volume of investment in the industry'.

He admitted to knowing 'very little about agriculture', but this did not stop him speaking out on the subject. In the debate on the bill to establish the Agricultural Institute, for instance, he talked forcefully about the need for agricultural research, which he said should 'be broadened to include market research on a worldwide scale for Irish agriculture'.

Haughey stood out amidst the ageing members of the Fianna Fáil hierarchy. Young, highly educated and enthusiastic, he attracted attention as a man of the future. By repeatedly calling for more research and development, he was basically advocating change and modernisation, and this set him apart from the conservative orthodoxy of his party elders. Yet profit was still the basic motivation behind the policies he advocated.

'Once and for all, let us get rid of this cant that there is something illegal, immoral or wrong in profits,' he declared. Research and development could be encouraged by exempting from income tax the royalties earned by inventors, he suggested. Complaining that the Finance Bill of 1959 allowed inventors to spread their earning over only six years, he called for a total tax exemption for these people.

'In the state of our economy, one of the things we need today is to encourage productivity in every possible way,' he explained. 'We should be trying to encourage inventors, people who have technical skill and know-how, to bring forth inventions which will help our industry.' Arguing that the amount of money involved would be insubstantial and would 'not be of any significance' in relation to the overall revenue needed by the government, he called on the Minister for Finance to adopt his suggestion. Haughey's comments foreshadowed his own conduct as Minister for Finance in the following decade.

'Possibly the biggest problem facing Irish agriculture and our national economy,' he contended, 'is not so much the necessity for an increase in agricultural production as the means to sell that production when it is produced.' In short, a proper profit incentive did not exist. 'It has always been clear to me that if the Irish farmer is given a price for his products, he will embarrass you with his production.'

Haughey spoke in the Dáil with all the confidence and brashness of youth, as he took on opposition spokesmen and even dared to advise ministers from his own party. But from his earliest days in the Dáil, he exhibited a characteristic which did not diminish with age: a habit of becoming personal when challenged. On one occasion he challenged figures cited by the Fine Gael leader, James Dillon, whom he accused of being a better orator than he was a mathematician. 'It is not for me to suggest that the deputy may have gone a little senile,' Haughey responded, after Dillon had referred to his long years of experience in the Dáil.

Although an inexperienced backbencher, Haughey was not afraid to debate with Dillon, who was one of the greatest orators ever to sit in Dáil Éireann. He not only took on Dillon but sometimes got the better of him – and obviously won the respect of the Fine Gael leader, at least for a time.

During a debate in June 1957, for instance, Dillon admitted that, as Minister for Agriculture and Fisheries a few years earlier, he had been advised to scrap some boats. Even though he knew this would be the best course, he decided against it because Fianna Fáil would make political capital out of his decision.

'It was a lack of moral courage on your part,' Haughey interjected. His sarcastic sense of humour often provoked a bitter response from across the floor and, in turn, exposed not only his own inability to accept criticism gracefully but also a viperish ability to strike back.

One early incident involved veiled aspersions from the Fine Gael benches about his character and friends. This occurred in April 1959 during a debate on estimates for the Department of Justice. The Fine Gael deputy, Oliver J. Flanagan, was complaining about some unsolved murders that had been committed in his constituency.

'Maybe you did them yourself,' Haughey interjected, sarcastically.

'I will leave that to Deputy Haughey's friends,' Flanagan replied. 'He does not have to go outside a very wide circle.'

Some exchanges followed Flanagan's assertion that 'political crime is one thing; cold-blooded murder and robbery is another'. Haughey argued that this implied condoning political murder, and the two men accused each other of advocating mob rule.

'I should be glad,' Flanagan said, 'if Deputy Haughey would get up and let us hear the speech he would make in favour of the robbers, thieves and plunderers.'

'And perjurers,' Haughey added, pointedly. Some years earlier Flanagan had been cited for perjury in the report of a judicial tribunal examining the Locke Distillery affair of the late 1940s.

'I have got a sense of humour, but sometimes my sense of humour is inclined to explode,' an indignant Flanagan responded. 'I know Deputy Haughey and members of his family maybe a little too well to say the things I might be provoked to say, but, if I say them in the course of the debate, no matter how hurtful they may be, I hope Deputy Haughey will accept them in the spirit in which I accept the ugly remarks he made now. I shall show the deputy if he opens his mouth again; I shall tell him something he and his family will not like to hear.'

The acting speaker, who had already called Haughey to order a number of times during these exchanges, intervened again, this time to point out that Haughey's family had nothing to do with the business of the house, and the unseemly exchanges were mercifully concluded.

In his Dáil contributions Haughey also revealed a competence which belied his parliamentary inexperience. When it came to some new measures for income-tax relief in the budget of 1959, for instance, Finance Minister James Ryan admitted Haughey had a 'better grip of it' than he did himself. It was not long therefore before he was being considered for higher office. The fact that his father-in-law, Sean Lemass, succeeded de Valera as Taoiseach in 1959 certainly did not hurt Haughey's political prospects.

Minister for Justice Oscar Traynor – in his mid-seventies and the oldest member of the government – was ailing and no longer able to keep up with the full workload of his department. As a result, Lemass suggested that the cabinet appoint a parliamentary secretary to assist him. Traynor submitted a list of four potential candidates who had been suggested by his department. The first of those, Sean Flanagan, refused the job, and the other three were rejected by the Taoiseach. Haughey was nominated instead.

There is confusion over who actually suggested Haughey. According to some accounts it was Lemass, but others contend that the idea came from within the cabinet and that the Taoiseach only reluctantly agreed to offer the post to his son-in-law. Whoever made the suggeation, Traynor was bitterly opposed to it. He and Haughey were from the same constituency, and their election rivalry had clearly cut very deeply. Traynor told Peter Berry, then Assistant Secretary of the Department of Justice, that the Taoiseach had predicted that Haughey would probably reject the post because it would interfere with efforts to build up his expanding practice as a chartered accountant. According to Haughey, Lemass actually advised him not to take the post.

'As Taoiseach,' Lemass said to him, 'it is my duty to offer you the post of parliamentary secretary, and as your father-in-law I am advising you not to take it.'

'I was an accountant at the time and doing fairly well, and I think he was sounding a warning,' Haughey recalled. He thought the Taoiseach was saying to him, 'Look, politics is a most uncertain career and if you want to look after my daughter the way she should be looked after you'd better stick to your accountancy.'

But there was no doubt in Haughey's mind about what he should do. 'I never had any hesitation about taking the job,' he explained. 'I think I told him I'd think it over, but I came back next day and said I'd take it.'

Ever since entering politics, he had been determined to make a career of it, so he was not about to turn down an opportunity of advancement. 'A parliamentary secretary in those days was not a very important office,' he admitted, but it was a step closer to real power.

Oscar Traynor was particularly unhappy about the appointment. 'If he had had the remotest idea that he would be saddled with Deputy Haughey he would have turned down the offer in the first instance', according to Berry. But there seemed to be no legitimate grounds for opposing the selection of Haughey. 'I knew from mutual acquaintances,' Berry wrote, 'that he was regarded as of first-class intelligence, with initiative, application and tenacity.'

The Minister for Justice was unable to refer to specific reasons why Haughey should not be appointed, but he clearly harboured deep reservations about Haughey's suitability for higher office. Such reservations, which were shared by others at the time, would be expressed repeatedly throughout Haughey's career, but no specific reasons for them, other than murky insinuations about his character or friends, were given.

'Mr Traynor told me,' Berry wrote, 'that his misgivings were shared by my former minister, Mr Gerald Boland, and other senior ministers.' Gerry Boland – whose son, Harry, was still in partnership with Haughey in the accounting firm – expressed his personal disapproval to Berry 'more than once in earlier years'.

Lemass announced Haughey's appointment in the Dáil on 9 May 1960. It would undoubtedly have been the subject of debate had not the standing rules of the House precluded discussion on the appointment of parliamentary secretaries. The Fine Gael leader meekly accepted the decision when the speaker ruled out any debate. Thus Haughey's initial elevation into government passed without Dáil comment.

During his tenure as parliamentary secretary, he sought work which he could process without referring to Traynor, who was reluctant to hand over such responsibility. This led to some friction.

'Throughout 1961,' Berry recalled, 'the minister expressed uneasiness about his working arrangements with the parliamentary secretary, whom he felt was undermining him both in his constituency and in the parliamentary party.' Basically Haughey took over Traynor's duties in piloting legislation through the Dáil, while the minister concentrated on administrative matters connected with the Department of Justice.

In accordance with parliamentary procedure, the first stage in the enactment of legislation consisted of securing permission to introduce a bill, which would then be published without debate. A general debate on the bill would ensue at the second stage, at which point Haughey would outline the measure in a general way, emphasising its important features. Other deputies would then have the chance to comment on it, and he would wind up the discussion, usually by responding to some of the general points made by the other deputies. The third step, or committee stage, involved a detailed examination, in which Haughey would take the House through every aspect of the bill, piece by piece. At this stage, deputies could make specific suggestions to improve the bill. Frequently their suggestions would just be changes in wording, which Haughey could accept without resorting to a formal vote of the House. Other suggestions might be taken under advice. The Dáil would then await any Senate amendments, which would be taken up at the fourth – or report – stage. Unless the bill had to be referred to the Senate again, it would clear the House with the completion of the report stage, and the bill would be deemed an act once it had been signed into law by the President.

At the time of Haughey's appointment, some bills had already been introduced and had had their first reading but had not been taken any further. Thus the new parliamentary secretary piloted five different bills from the second stage right through to their enactment. These were the Charities Bill, 1957; the Solicitors (Amendment) Bill, 1960; the Rent Restrictions Bill, 1960; the Civil Liability Bill, 1960; and the Defamation Bill, 1961.

Some of those bills were very complicated pieces of legislation, while others were fairly straightforward and uncontentious. For instance, the Defamation Bill, the second stage of which was moved only on 3 May 1961, was passed into law before the summer recess. It was largely a composite bill, in which various old acts of the Westminster Parliament – such as the Libel Acts of 1843 and 1845, the Law of Libel Amendment Act of 1888 and the Slander of Women Act of 1891 – were re-enacted in a single Irish statute with only very slight modifications. John A. Costello, the former Taoiseach, voiced his 'complete approval' of the bill. Consequently it had an easy passage through the Oireachtas, as did the Solicitors (Amendment) Bill. The Rent Restrictions Bill, on the other hand, was highly technical and very complicated. One deputy noted that only lawyers participated in the debate on this bill 'because no one else could understand it'.

The most important feature of the bill was a provision

allowing landlords to increase controlled rents by 12.5 per cent. These rents, which had remained static since 1926, were seen as a disincentive to providing rented accommodation. If rent increases were allowed, Haughey argued, the profit incentive would encourage landlords to make flats in old houses and thereby provide much-needed rental accommodation. The legislation, which he emphasised was designed 'to procure the maximum amount of decontrol, consistent with the avoidance of any hardship to tenants', contributed to Haughey's growing reputation as a friend of the property developers.

When Declan Costello tried to have houses of less than a certain valuation exempted from the increase in order to protect the poor, Haughey rejected the move by contending that it would be better to cope with this under social legislation, such as an increase in the old-age pension. Haughey also rejected a Fine Gael suggestion calling for fair-rent courts, which he argued would simply create a lawyers' paradise.

Although a qualified lawyer himself, Haughey could never be charged with complicating the legal system for the benefit of his legal contemporaries. Instead, he worked to simplify it, especially after he became Minister for Justice in 1961. This desire for simplification was already evident while he was a parliamentary secretary.

The Civil Liability Bill, for instance, was another piece of complicated legislation which was largely aimed at simplifying legal procedures in order to cut down on the amount of litigation. It aimed to achieve this by ensuring that 'all matters of liability' arising out of a particular case would be heard in one action, except in very unusual cases.

The Charities Bill of 1957 was equally complicated. First drafted back in 1954, it ran into difficulty over its definition of 'charitable purposes'. A new bill was drafted, omitting any definition of 'charitable purposes', and was introduced in the Dáil in July 1957. This bill lay dormant until being rescued by Haughey, who moved its second stage in November 1960. From the political standpoint, the bill was not very contentious because it had basically been drafted during the life of the previous coalition government. Thus the Opposition was largely responsible for it and could hardly be very critical of it. Nevertheless, Dillon and Haughey argued over the retention of the existing practice of allowing a member of the Commissioners of Charitable Donations and Bequests to sit on the bench. After all, Haughey noted, this practice had been followed for a hundred years.

'Is that not a lovely comment from a young Lochinvar come out of the west?' Dillon asked. 'It lasted for a hundred years.'

'Without complaint,' interjected Haughey.

'Without complaint!' Dillon exclaimed, sarcastically. 'Sin has existed since the world began but the world is not better off for its survival. If it is wrong now, the fact that it has been wrong for a hundred years does not make it any better.'

In the course of his legislative duties, the parliamentary secretary would clash with Dillon on a number of occasions, but the Fine Gael leader developed a real regard for Haughey's industry and legislative skill. When the Dáil continued to sit into August 1961, it was obvious that the backlog of legislation was being cleared in order to facilitate an early general election. Dillon complained that the legislation was being rushed, but he was at pains not to hold Haughey responsible for this.

'I do not blame the parliamentary secretary,' the Fine Gael leader explained. 'On the contrary, I compliment him on the skill with which he has had recourse to his brief. He has read out to the House learned discourses on various aspects of this legislation which, I have no doubt, will be quoted from the Official Reports hereafter as evidence of his exceptional and outstanding ability.' Referring to Haughey's 'carefully prepared briefs' as testimony to 'his extraordinary erudition', Dillon hoped to be as well briefed himself when his own party came to power. 'Indeed,' he continued, 'I hope I shall make half as good use of the brief.' This was a significant tribute – from the leader of another party just before an election – and was all the more extraordinary when compared to later remarks by Fine Gael leaders, including Dillon himself.

When Oscar Traynor decided to retire, Haughey was presented with the relatively easy task of retaining his seat in the ensuing election. In fact, he more than doubled his vote, to head the poll with 8,566 votes. In the process he helped Fianna Fáil gain a seat in the constituency: the party took three of the five seats overall. His two successful colleagues were his friend and future critic George Colley and Eugene Timmons, who finally made it to the Dáil, on his third attempt. The increase in Haughey's vote was particularly notable given that the party's vote dropped nationally and it lost its overall majority in the Dáil. Charlie Haughey had become a political force to be reckoned with.

# 3

## 'THERE ARE SOME QUARE FILES IN MY OFFICE'
## MINISTER FOR JUSTICE, 1961–1964

Although Fianna Fáil was five seats short of an overall majority, Sean Lemass was again proposed as Taoiseach when the Dáil reconvened on 11 October 1961. Two of the independent deputies stated that they would be supporting the nomination of Lemass on the grounds that he had a better chance of forming a stable government than anyone else, and another independent deputy indicated he would be abstaining, so Lemass was assured of victory. But before the voting began Lemass made it clear that he had made no deals with any of those people for their support.

'I have not asked any deputy in this House, outside the members of my own party, to support the motion, either by their vote or by their abstention,' he said. 'If I should be elected Taoiseach, it would be my intention to implement the programme of my party in all respects.'

Following his re-election, Lemass renominated twelve of his outgoing cabinet, the one change in personnel being necessitated by the retirement of Oscar Traynor. Most ministers retained their old posts. The last man nominated – and the only new appointment to the cabinet – was Haughey, as Minister for Justice. He had clearly earned his promotion by doing an effective job as parliamentary secretary. Now he took over full responsibility for the Department of Justice.

Fine Gael deputies were strongly critical of the Lemass team, but only two deputies mentioned Haughey's appointment, and both of them actually spoke of it in favourable terms. For instance, Michael J. O'Higgins was quite caustic about the 'dull, unenterprising and unimaginative' cabinet being appointed, but he singled out Haughey as an exception to this. 'I sincerely congratulate the Taoiseach,' he said, 'on the new appointment he has proposed, the appointment of Deputy Haughey as minister. I have no doubt it will improve the team which the Taoiseach is suggesting to the House.' Although such treatment was not unprecedented for a new minister, this was the last time Haughey was appointed to any ministerial portfolio without being subjected to severe criticism, especially from the Fine Gael benches.

His new duties were wide-ranging. The Department of Justice was responsible for the conditions under which the country's courts functioned, matters relating to the police force and the administration of the prison service, the Land Registry Office, Registry of Deeds Office, and Public Records Office, as well as the interpretation of a large number of statutes connected with the control of aliens, the granting of citizenship and the adoption of children. In addition, the censorship of books and films was conducted under the aegis of his department, which was also responsible for drafting a broad range of legislation. In fact, on the first day of the new Dáil two pieces of legislation, the Coroners Bill and the Garda Síochána Bill – for which Haughey would have responsibility – were introduced. The Dáil then adjourned until 15 November 1961.

During the recess the need for reform of the Gardaí became particularly apparent when there was a near-mutiny within the force, which had become demoralised as a result of low pay, poor promotional prospects and a feeling that its leadership was out of touch with the problems of the rank and file. When a request from the Garda Representative Body for a pay increase was turned down, some discontented elements began holding meetings in Dublin Garda stations. These were banned by the commissioner, Daniel Costigan, under the force's Disciplinary Code, so a meeting was arranged for the Macushla Ballroom in Dublin on 5 November 1961. At Haughey's direction gardaí were forbidden to attend this meeting, and some senior officers, who were stationed outside, took the names of 167 of the 815 members who showed up. The 'Macushla Revolt', as the incident became known, took on added significance when the young guards decided on a 'go slow' campaign.

Dublin traffic was thrown into near-chaos as Gardaí stopped directing traffic and refused to give out parking tickets. On 8 November the commissioner responded by asking that Haughey summarily dismiss eleven of the ringleaders of the revolt. The minister duly complied but at the same time issued a statement emphasising his willingness to enquire into Garda grievances 'on receiving an assurance from the commissioner that discipline had been fully restored throughout the force'. A crisis within the force seemed imminent, but Haughey secretly turned for help to the Catholic Archbishop of Dublin, John Charles McQuaid, with whom he formed a special relationship.

The archbishop recognised Haughey to be 'a young man who would go far', and Haughey, of course, recognised McQuaid to be one of the most powerful and influential men in the country. Haughey had a secret late-night meeting with the archbishop to get him to intervene in the dispute. No mention was made of their meeting. McQuaid merely announced that he was sure that discipline would be restored if Garda grievances were investigated by the Department of Justice.

On 13 November Haughey announced that the requested review would be undertaken. 'The fact that the guarantee has been given by the Archbishop is good enough for me,' he said. 'I am satisfied that full discipline has now been restored to the force, and the commissioner agrees with me.'

The eleven dismissed men were reinstated and proceedings were dropped against others for attending secret meetings, contrary to Garda regulations. Haughey also assured the Dáil that there would be no victimisation of those who had taken part in the affair. In the end the whole thing turned out to be little more than a storm in a teacup. 'But it had a vital significance for the development of the force over the next decade,' according to Garda historian Conor Brady. The authorities were 'thoroughly shaken by the realisation that the force could not be relied upon unquestioningly'. This led to a tightening in discipline that was to have some repercussions, but at the same time the standing and influence of the Garda Representative Body – which was broken up into three separate units representing superintendents and chief superintendents, sergeants and inspectors, and ordinary Gardaí – was considerably strengthened.

Haughey got on well with his staff at the Department of Justice. Peter Berry, who had taken over as permanent secretary of the department in February 1961, had a good, though sometimes stormy, working relationship with the new minister.

'Haughey was a dynamic minister,' Berry recalled years later. 'He was a joy to work with, and the longer he stayed the better he got.' Haughey was quick to master the bureaucratic mysteries of the department and the way in which policies were formulated and implemented. Berry, who had served in the department under fourteen different ministers, beginning with Kevin O'Higgins back in the 1920s, noted that 'Haughey learned fast and was in complete control of his department from the outset.' In fact, he rated him 'the ablest' of all the ministers under whom he had served. 'He did not interfere in minor details,' Berry explained, 'but where political kudos or political disadvantage might arise he was sharp as a razor.'

In his first month in office Haughey drew up a ten-point programme that he wanted implemented. His first goal was to crush the IRA's border campaign, which had been going on since 1956.

The IRA had clearly lost most of the sympathy it had enjoyed at the start of the campaign. Back in 1957 Sinn Féin had won four seats in the Dáil, but now, four years later, the party fared dismally. None of the twenty-one candidates fielded in 1961 were successful – fourteen actually lost their deposits as the party secured only 3 per cent of the vote. It was clearly a disaster for the party and was recognised as such, even by republicans themselves.

'The all-too-public denial of support at the polls had badly damaged morale,' according to historian J. Bowyer Bell. 'There had been no spectacular operation in the North. Public and private pressure to call off the campaign was growing. The Army Council agreed that a big effort must be made to rectify the situation but that they might have to quit.'

On 12 November the IRA ambushed an RUC patrol near Jonesboro, County Armagh, killing one of the constables. He was the sixth policeman to be killed in the campaign. The ambush was a last-gasp effort on the part of the IRA.

The Dublin government responded decisively. On 22 November Haughey announced the reactivation of the Special Criminal Court, which had been dormant since the end of the Second World War. It quickly began handing down severe sentences. For instance, men found guilty of the possession of firearms were being sentenced to six months in jail in the district courts, while those convicted in the Special Criminal Court were sentenced to an average of five years each. One man who had been sentenced to six months in 1959 following an abortive ambush was now sentenced to eight years in jail. In the following weeks thirty-one people were sentenced to stiff prison terms.

While implementing this policy of the stick, Haughey also began holding forth a carrot: in early February he offered an amnesty to IRA members who surrendered their weapons. Of course, by then he knew that the IRA leadership had already secretly decided to quit because the campaign had run aground on the rocks of public hostility and indifference. The amnesty offer should therefore be seen both as a means of facilitating the IRA's desire to end hostilities and as a ploy to score political points for the government in general and the Minister for Justice in particular.

'I offered an arms amnesty, with good results,' Haughey explained. The facts seemed to support him, because the IRA publicly announced it was calling off the campaign within a month. 'Because of the effective action we took, they actually called it off publicly. I think it's about the only time in history the IRA publicly renounced a campaign,' he contended.

The suspension of previous IRA campaigns had been followed by public agitation to free republican prisoners, but this time Haughey moved quickly to prevent the question becoming a major political issue. During March he announced that the government was again disbanding the Special Criminal Court, and all those held in custody under the Offences Against the State Act were released.

The border campaign was over. In comparison with the troubles of the following decade, the five-year campaign, which claimed a total of nineteen lives, seemed like little more than a series of skirmishes. Haughey arrived on the scene when the writing was on the wall, but he deserves credit for turning the screw at the right psychological moment. He thereby helped end the campaign and clear up its loose ends with competence and dispatch.

'I know,' he told the Dáil, 'that it is the wish of every right-thinking person that we are finished, finally, with this kind of unlawful activity and that all those who have supported it will realise that they have been out of touch with the realities of our time.'

Reviewing the events of his first year in office, Haughey described the ending of the border campaign as his department's 'most important single achievement, from the point of view of law and order'. He was also able to point to a modest drop in the overall crime rate and an increase in detection rates, though violent crimes and house break-ins had increased. While the investigation of crimes came under the aegis of the Department of Justice, the Attorney-General, Aindrias O'Keeffe, was responsible for the actual prosecution of those charged with offences. Hence Haughey distanced himself from involvement in the debacle surrounding the prosecution of Paul Singer of Shanahan Stamps Limited. Singer was arrested in 1959 and convicted of fraud involving more than £700,000 almost two years later, but the conviction was overturned and a new trial ordered after it was disclosed that the foreman of the convicting jury was an investor in the company. The second trial, which began on 3 November 1961 and continued until 24 January 1962, was the longest in the country's history. Much to the embarrassment of the government, the proceedings culminated in the judge directing the jury to find Singer not guilty. The defendant was therefore freed, and he promptly vanished, leaving hundreds of thousands of pounds unaccounted for. As a result, the entire judicial system came in for some criticism.

Prior to Haughey's appointment as Minister for Justice, charges against prominent politicians or their friends for matters such as drunk-driving would never get to court, but Haughey adopted a different approach. Those who approached him were told that they would have to go to court and face the music but that he was ready to help them by ensuring the case would not be reported in the press.

As all district justices were political appointees, a friendly justice, who was willing to rise at 5 o'clock in the evening and go to his rooms, could always be found. Journalists would naturally leave for the evening, thinking that their work was done for the day, and the judge would then return and hear the case. The politician would plead guilty and accept his punishment, and that would be the end of the matter.

In this way the needs of justice were served without subjecting the accused to damaging publicity. Haughey was satisfied, and in fairness to him, he had some justification. At least it was better than fixing the case so that the accused got off scot-free.

'He didn't see his secret courts as a piece of smart-assery in which he exploited the known habits of the court reporters or that he ran his secret courts at the professional expense of the reporters,' one Dublin editor later wrote. 'In any public challenge in the Dáil the reply would make the media look, at worst, as accomplices who might have taken a backhander to kill the case or, at best, people who were slovenly and lacked basic contacts in the building in which they had worked for half a lifetime. As far as Haughey was concerned, it was a just a case of helping someone in trouble.'

'As editor of a Sunday paper,' the late John Healy recalled, 'I had heard three of four instances where Fianna Fáil bigwigs dodged the press punishment by way of extra early or extra late sittings by obliging district justices.' These went unreported until one of the accused got a bit too greedy and tried to fight a case. As a result, the case was postponed and the press were ready when it reconvened.

That should have been the end of the so-called 'secret courts', but of course it wasn't. 'When the next one was held,' Healy noted, 'I was editing the *Evening Mail.* I got a tip from the courts. Charlie had pulled the wool over our eyes again.'

Donogh O'Malley, parliamentary secretary to the Minister for Finance, had been quietly prosecuted for drunk-driving the previous evening. He had pleaded guilty and was fined and banned from driving for six months.

'I remember the sense of frustration of the morning,' Healy wrote, more than thirty years later. The board of the *Irish Times* had just informed him that it was closing the *Evening Mail.* He assigned a reporter to investigate the O'Malley case, and the reporter came back with the story, which Healy passed to a sub-editor with instructions to put it 'on page one, where people will see it'.

'I was still in the boardroom working out details of the funeral of the paper when the first edition was brought down to me,' he continued. 'We spread the drunk-driving charge, which was not even the day's news, across the front page as a lead story. In the shoulder, under the banner head, was a single column saying the *Mail* was going to die.'

'It was so wrong,' he went on. 'You rarely lead an evening paper with a drunk-driving court case. A strong single column would have done it. To make it worse it looked as if we were, in our death throes, trying to bring down a politician with us.'

'Are you the fucker that crucified me in the *Mail*?' O'Malley asked Healy when they next met. The editor said he was unapologetic. 'We weren't crucifying O'Malley,' he told Haughey, 'we were crucifying you and your secret courts.' According to Healy that 'was the end of the *Mail* – and the end of Charlie's secret courts'.

It made a fascinating story, but unfortunately Healy had

embellished the tale to such an extent that it was changed beyond all recognition. Healy was friendly with both Haughey and O'Malley, and he possibly liked to think that he had broken the story, but the banner headline on the front page that evening actually read, 'Mail Publication Will Be Suspended'. The story about O'Malley's arrest and the secret-court hearing were true all right, but the *Evening Mail* did not report them in that edition – or in any other edition before it finally folded, for that matter.

John Healy may have been confusing the 'secret court' story with the 'Backbencher' column, which he started, along with Ted Nealon, in the *Mail*'s sister paper, the *Sunday Review*. The following Sunday, 'Backbencher' reported that the Fine Gael knives were out for Haughey. 'I cannot see the minister, with all his resourcefulness, coming out unscathed,' he continued.

The case took a particularly unseemly turn shortly afterwards, when James Travers, the Garda who had arrested O'Malley, was transferred to new duties. Contending that his transfer amounted to victimisation, the Garda – a six-year veteran – refused to move. He was then given the option of resigning voluntarily or being dismissed from the force. In the circumstances he resigned.

The issue was raised in the Dáil when Richie Ryan of Fine Gael accused the government of conducting 'a reign of terror' within the Garda Síochána and the Department of Justice. Haughey replied to this charge, accusing the opposition of political scavenging, much to the irritation of Gerard Sweetman, the deputy leader of Fine Gael. He threatened to ask embarrassing questions about 'an amazing coincidence' concerning another Garda who had also been asked to resign recently.

'There are some quare files in my office, too,' Haughey warned. It seemed like a threat to reveal information that would be embarrassing to Fine Gael.

'Let us not be pushed too far,' James Dillon, the Fine Gael leader, cautioned, but he and his colleagues did not dare pursue the Garda's case any further. 'This ended the discussion,' the *Irish Times* noted, with a certain finality.

In his book *Ireland Since the Rising*, Tim Pat Coogan, who became editor of the *Irish Press,* concluded that those Fine Gael deputies who had been 'unsporting enough to enquire into the strange happenings that befell the policeman' were intimidated into silence by Haughey simply 'alluding to files in his office at the Department of Justice'. Those files were believed to contain damaging information about Fine Gael deputies. If those deputies were intimidated in this manner, it did not reflect favourably either on their courage or character, but it reflected even less well on those in the media who were not prepared to follow up the story.

During 1961 juvenile crime reached its highest level since the foundation of the state. Haughey responded by having a special crime unit set up, and he introduced a juvenile liaison scheme that had been operating with some success in Britain.

'The task of this Garda unit,' he explained, 'will be, with the cooperation of parents, teachers, clergy, youth leaders and other persons and organisations interested in youth welfare, to guide young boys into channels of activity leading to good citizenship.' Under the scheme, juvenile offenders could be placed under police supervision without being committed to any penal institution. 'It was an idea which, if developed, could have revolutionised the whole concept of policing in Ireland,' according to Conor Brady. 'Unfortunately its potential was not realised either by subsequent commissioners or ministers.'

There was an after-care institution for young people which had been set up by Archbishop John Charles McQuaid. 'This institution represented, in Haughey's view, 'a really important and significant development,' Bruce Arnold noted in his book *Haughey: His Life and Unlucky Deeds*. 'Into the bargain, it was free. 'The fact that it is being provided on a voluntary basis without any cost to the state is something at which, in these modern times, we can only marvel.' Unfortunately, in time it would become apparent that sexual abuse was rampant in the institutions run by the Catholic Church, where children were preyed upon by paedophile priests and Christian Brothers.

Haughey was credited at the time with demonstrating an enlightened outlook towards penal reform. 'Prison is not, and is not intended to be, a home from home, and it will always be a place of punishment,' Haughey contended, 'but it seems to me that our prisons nowadays must to an increasing extent become places of rehabilitation as well.'

On retiring as governor of Mountjoy Prison in 1970, Sean Kavanagh credited Haughey – who was then ironically facing a possible prison sentence himself – with reforming the prison service. 'Since 1962,' Kavanagh explained, 'some excellent schemes for the reform and rehabilitation of prisoners have been initiated, notably by Mr Charles J. Haughey while Minister for Justice.' These reforms included the establishment of a corrective training unit as well as the building of a hostel to accommodate prisoners who would be granted daily release to outside employment obtained for them through a new prison welfare service. A full-time welfare officer was appointed to Mountjoy in order to assist in the work of rehabilitation and to help prisoners with personal problems. Such schemes had been in operation as part of modern prison treatment in England, Sweden and other countries for several years. 'But before 1962,' Kavanagh noted, 'little or no interest in them was taken by our Department of Justice, especially where the extra cost of putting them into effect became obvious.'

Expressions of Haughey's desire for penal reform were to be found more in debate than in actual legislation. Despite the amount of legislation that he piloted through the Oireachtas, he did not introduce any important bills affecting the country's prison system. Haughey's performance was in that regard probably handicapped by a lack of vision on the part of those most closely associated with the prison service.

Of course, Haughey did not reform every aspect of his department during the two and a half years that he was Minister for Justice, but it would be unrealistic to think that anyone could have done so in such a short time. Bruce Arnold blamed Haughey not only for what he failed to achieve in the area of prison reform but also for the failings of his successors in the same area over the next thirty years. This was grossly unfair.

For instance, Arnold accused Haughey of taking 'the easy way out' in 1964 when he ordered the release of a travelling woman who had been sentenced to jail for begging in Galway, even though she was a mother of twelve and expecting her thirteenth child at the time. It is unclear whether the author was blaming Haughey for the fact that the woman and her family would not have personally benefited from her serving her full prison sentence. He may have been accusing him of not implementing the social reforms which would have prevented her being sent to jail in the first place. If the latter was the case, this is an absurd accusation, because Haughey was the youngest and least experienced member of the government – and was Minister for Justice and not Minister for Social Welfare.

Prior to Haughey's appointment the Department of Justice had often been frustrated in its schemes by lack of money. 'At the time of his becoming Minister for Justice,' Peter Berry recalled, 'the Department had been bogged down for quite some time, primarily through lack of adequate finance. Successive

Ministers for Justice had failed to get the necessary monies from the Department of Finance, but Mr Haughey proved very adroit at extracting the necessary financial support.' He was a good man to cut through red tape.

Haughey worked long hours – ten hours a day on average – and prided himself on efficiency and getting things done. He could be a good listener, but he became irritable when people became long-winded. He sought to emulate the capacity of his father-in-law to make quick, considered decisions without agonising interminably over the pros and cons, as had been the practice in de Valera's government. Haughey's telephone conversations were short and to the point, and his notes to civil servants working under him were characteristically brief – often consisting of no more than the word 'OK' written in the margin of their memoranda to him.

The Secretary of the Department had also been keenly interested in prison reform. 'Berry was a very, very dedicated, devoted civil servant,' according to Haughey, but there were a few problems between them because the secretary tended to be rather set in some of his ideas. 'He needed to be under the control, guidance and direction of a minister who could take a much broader view of things,' Haughey contended.

Berry recalled two incidents in which he clashed with Haughey. The first took place shortly after the new minister took office. As parliamentary secretary he had promised a minor appointment with a small capitation grant to someone, unaware that Traynor had already made the appointment. On becoming minister, Haughey could have removed his predecessor's appointee. This would have been resented by the deputies who had approached Traynor in the first place, however, so he decided to let Traynor's appointment stand while at the same time appointing his own man. This would have required a second grant, which Berry, as the department's accounting officer, refused to sanction.

'I told Mr Haughey,' Berry wrote, 'that I couldn't make payment, and when he insisted I said that, of course, I would obey his direction but that I was requested under the Rules to report the matter to the Minister for Finance and to the Committee of Public Accounts.' With that, the matter was dropped, and Berry, who was about to go on holiday, made sure it could not be revived in his absence. He informed the assistant secretary of the department of the details of the matter.

'On my return,' Berry continued, 'the assistant secretary told me that he had received a ministerial directive to appoint the second man to the post, that he had informed the minister that he was aware of the accounting officer's refusal earlier and that the minister would be liable to personal surcharge. He said that the minister was furious with me, not only for my refusal but also for forewarning the assistant secretary, thus causing the minister to lose face.'

The second incident centred on Haughey's desire to have a certain individual appointed immigration officer at Cork Airport. He explained to Berry that Jack Lynch had made representations on behalf of a man already based in Cork. The Garda commissioner, who had the responsibility of making recommendations, set up a board, which ranked the person backed by Lynch and Haughey only fourth in order of merit.

Having been appointed by the government, Berry had no intention of acting 'as a rubber stamp for the minister in official matters'. He believed he had a duty to advise the minister, whether or not the minister wanted that advice. Berry therefore objected to the appointment and warned Haughey that he would be open to 'grave criticism' if he disregarded the advice of the commissioner and the board.

'And,' Berry added, 'I could not lend my support to it.'

Haughey was furious. 'Well,' he said, 'I have appointed Number 4.' He then threw the file at Berry, who walked out, leaving the papers strewn on the floor.

'It would make for chaos in administration and would not serve government or parliament if senior civil servants were not free to brief their ministers and government according to conscience and their specialised knowledge and judgements,' the secretary later argued. 'There were occasions in the years to come where I and my colleagues were subjected to this kind of pressure but I always encouraged my colleagues by word and example to record their true arguments without in any way questioning the minister's authority to make the final decisions.'

The second incident was undoubtedly complicated by Haughey's inability to accept criticism gracefully – a difficulty which would surface again and again throughout his political career. Berry had a valid point when he contended that departmental secretaries should advise their ministers but that the latter should be free to disregard that advice without being lectured about their responsibilities, no matter how experienced the secretary. Quite often recommendations from people on the ground turn out to be much better than those from departmental heads and interview boards. Haughey was charged with making the appointment, and the ultimate responsibility for it was his. From the tone of Berry's own account of the incident, it would appear that he not only lectured Haughey on his ministerial duties but went beyond the bounds of propriety by asking the Garda Commissioner to 'spread the word that I was not a party to the minister's decision.'

Haughey's greatest impact as Minister for Justice was in the field of legislation. He piloted through the Oireachtas an enormous number of bills. On occasions he had as many as five different bills going through the Dáil. He spent a tremendous amount of time on this aspect of his work. Listing the bills gives some idea of the amount of work involved, especially when one realises that Dáil and Seanad reports provide only a glimpse of the amount of work involved. 'Parliamentary bills are like icebergs in that less than one-fifth of the work put into their structure appears above the surface,' Haughey explained. 'A great deal of consultation goes on between the promoting department and the various interests involved, with experts on points of law at issue, and then the minister and government in turn have to immerse themselves in the intricacies and decide on policy and major issues.'

In preparing the legislation, the new minister worked closely with Roger Hayes, whom he found 'passionately committed to law reform. For the first time ever,' Haughey said, 'he found, in me, somebody who could give expression to his desire for law reform.' In January 1962 the department published a white paper outlining the measures Haughey hoped to introduce.

By then Haughey had already introduced the Coroners Bill, Garda Síochána Bill, Criminal Justice (Legal Aid) Bill and Short Titles Bill. In the next two and a half years he introduced the Official Secrets Bill, Courts (Supplemental Provisions Amendment) Bill, Street and House-to-House Collections Bill, Intoxicating Liquor Bill, Statute Law Revision (Pre-Union Irish Statutes) Bill, Hotel Proprietors Bill, Adoption Bill, Firearms Bill, Criminal Justice (Abolition of Capital Punishment) Bill, Registration of Titles Bill, Funds of Suitors Bill, Courts Bill (1963), Guardianship of Infants Bill, Pawnbrokers Bill, Extradition Bill, Civil Liberties (Amendment) Bill and Succession Bill.

These bills covered a very wide area of legislation, extending from family law to international law. Some were essentially new measures, while others amended or simply re-enacted laws dating as far back as the fourteenth century. According to Haughey, for instance, the Statute Law Revision (Pre-Union Irish Statutes) Bill, which dealt with legislation passed before 1800, was introduced to remove from the statute book a 'great mass of obsolete legislation' so that an updated index could be produced 'to the whole of statute law in force in the State'.

The state was only forty years old, and all laws in force at the time of independence remained on the statute books unless they had been formally repealed or amended since then. As a result, some of the legislation was obsolete. For instance, the Act of Union of 1800 had been effectively repealed by the Constitution of 1937 but still remained on the statute book because it had never been formally repealed. Thus the new Minister for Justice was trying to start the modernisation of the country's whole legal system. 'It is desirable,' he contended, 'that so far as possible our law should be contained in modern statutes passed by the Oireachtas and it should be our ultimate aim to get ourselves into a position where that would apply to all our statute law.'

The Criminal Justice Bill of 1963 sought to abolish the death penalty for all except certain specified crimes like treason and the murder of a Garda or an ambassador. 'Very shortly after becoming Minister for Justice,' Haughey later recalled, 'I went up to Mountjoy to see the condemned cell, and I was so revolted by the whole atmosphere that I resolved to do away with the death penalty. Afterwards he was sorry he had not abolished capital punishment completely, but at the time the remaining capital crimes 'seemed to be so remote and academic that they were not of practical importance.'

Some of the minor bills were to cause as much trouble as complicated ones, especially in the uncertain political climate prevailing, in which the government was unable to depend on majority support in the Dáil. There were vociferous objections to the Intoxicating Liquor Bill of 1962, which extended opening hours only in some minor respects – the most notable being slightly earlier opening and later closing times on Sundays. The Courts (Supplemental Provisions Amendment) Act also came in for strong criticism because it contained substantial salary increases for members of the judiciary. Haughey contended that the measure was necessary to ensure that the best and most capable people were on the bench.

'It is a natural tenendency to be envious of highly paid people and I accuse the Opposition of playing on that simple human emotion and trying to make political capital out of it,' he told the Dáil. 'A man who is only earning £9 or £10 per week is going to resent an already highly paid member of the judiciary getting an increase. It is difficult to explain to such a man why this is necessary, and the Opposition are doing their best to make sure that the people will be as envious as possible.'

'Do we not all know that a man's work or value is judged by what he earns?' he asked, on introducing that bill. 'It is a human and natural thing and it is something which is very common here – to look down on a man who does not earn as much as you do. I think it applies to all levels of our society.'

While that kind of thinking may have been fundamental to Haughey's philosophy it had no appeal whatever to a socialist like Noel Browne. 'I do not agree with that at all,' Browne said. 'I think the complete contrary is true.' People like the Little Sisters of the Poor or the Carmelite Fathers earn very little, but this did not mean that society placed more value on the services of a brothel-keeper just because he was paid more money, Browne argued.

'I do not know anything about them. I leave them to the deputy,' Haughey replied, adding that Browne would know more about pimps than he would.

There was little empathy between Browne and Haughey, whose proposed legislation showed little concern for the needs of the poor or underprivileged. Instead the Minister for Justice seemed more concerned with facilitating the legal profession and catering to the comforts of the well-to-do. The Street and House-to-House Collections Act, for instance, sought to eliminate begging by regulating public collections, while the Funds of Suitor Bill of 1963 was introduced to provide a £50,000 grant towards the building of Cork Opera House.

Although the Criminal Justice (Legal Aid) Act provided for free legal aid, this was restricted to cases in which the court thought it 'essential in the interest of justice'. Haughey admitted the measure was rather restrictive; he would have liked to make free legal aid as widely available as possible, but the measure was new and experimental.

Of course, legislation relating to welfare matters had practically nothing to do with the Department of Justice. Presumably Haughey was so busy with his own enormous workload that he did not have time to concern himself with other matters. In the Dáil he generally confined himself to matters relating to his own department. When he did digress, it was usually to speak on financial issues like the budget. Here his remarks foreshadowed the compassionate approach he would later adopt as Minister for Finance. For instance, he strongly supported the introduction of the controversial turnover tax in the 1963 budget by arguing that it would provide the government with the extra money required to increase children's allowances and social welfare benefits.

'We are not political fools,' Haughey explained, on deputising for the Minister for Finance during the committee stage of the Finance Bill. 'We do not do unpopular things for the fun of it. We made up our minds on the improvements which had to be brought about in our social welfare arrangements, health services and so on, and we satisfied ourselves beyond any shadow of doubt that the money required could not be provided by any of the conventional methods.' Hence the government decided to introduce this sales tax as 'the fairest, the most effective and the cheapest way of raising the money required for our plans,' he added.

Noel Browne objected that the new tax would hurt the poor more than the rich because both would have to pay it equally. His criticism led to some rather unseemly exchanges, in which Haughey charged that Browne had 'difficulty proving he is not a communist'.

A few days later *Time* magazine described Haughey as 'the shrewd, hard-knuckled Minister for Justice, who is tipped as a potential Prime Minister'. Haughey seemed to confirm the hard-knuckled nature to which the article referred by promptly getting involved in another ugly row with Browne.

'Oh, shut up,' Haughey snapped, when Browne tried to question him in the Dáil on 11 July 1963.

'The Minister will not shut me up with his puppyish tactics,' Browne replied. Later the same day Browne had his chance to tell Haughey to be quiet. He was complaining that there would be an exemption of turnover tax for medicine for animals but not for medicine for humans. Charlie tried to explain, but Browne cut him off.

'I am not finished,' Browne snapped. 'Do not interrupt me.'

'Do not be so dictatorial,' Haughey replied.

'Do not be so damned imperious,' Browne retorted.

'This is arrogance indeed. I was only trying to be helpful.'

'Do not be supercilious,' Browne continued. 'Sit down and behave yourself.'

'This is the communist mentality,' Haughey said.

Browne appealed to the chair to order that the remark be

withdrawn on the grounds that he was being accused of being a communist.

'It is not,' Haughey insisted. 'It is an indication of the communist mentality.'

'I do not see any indication that the deputy is a communist,' the acting Speaker ruled.

'I say that the minister's behaviour is the behaviour of a fascist,' Browne retorted.

'That rubs off me much more lightly,' Haughey replied.

By squabbling with Browne, a recognised champion of the poor and underprivileged, Haughey was inevitably seen as a friend of the rich, and his ostentatious lifestyle exacerbated the impression. Fianna Fáil had once been proud that it consisted of the men with the cloth caps, but the Minister for Justice was representative of a new breed in the party. A wealthy businessman who owned racehorses and rode with the hunt, he came to be classified as one of the men in the mohair suits. He enjoyed his prosperity and flaunted it, with the result that he soon became the subject of gossip and colourful rumours. Most of these rumours – including the one that he was 'seen running naked after a woman during a ball attended by Princess Grace in Enniskerry' – were probably untrue.

The *Sunday Independent* provoked Haughey's wrath by publishing a cartoon depicting him in the midst of a group of drunken people in evening dress being offloaded from a paddy-wagon outside a Garda station, with a Garda saying, 'Come on out, you tally-hoing, hunt-balling pack . . . Oh sorry, Mr Minister, I didn't see you in there.' Although this was mild in comparison to some later cartoons, Haughey threatened legal action; the *Sunday Independent* settled by making a contribution to a charity of his choice.

Some of the bills introduced by the Minister for Justice were designed to protect children. The Firearms Act regulated the use of air guns, while the Adoption Act extended the age at which children could be adopted from seven to nine years and dropped the stipulation that the adopting parents had to be Irish citizens. The Guardianship of Infants Act consolidated previous legislation and amended it to the extent that, henceforth, the child's welfare would be the first and paramount consideration. The act also strengthened the rights of the mother by stipulating for the first time that each of the parents had equal rights to guardianship and custody.

Shortly before the summer recess in 1964 Haughey introduced the Succession Bill – a fairly novel piece of legislation that sought to ensure that testators provided adequately for their dependants in their wills. One of the main aims of the bill was to prevent a man leaving his family destitute while all his money was left for something like the saying of Masses for the repose of his soul. The bill was an extremely complicated piece of legislation and had some serious defects, but before the Dáil could discuss these Haughey was moved from the Department of Justice.

In early October Paddy Smith, the Minister for Agriculture, resigned in protest over aspects of the government's economic policies. This placed Lemass in a tricky situation because Smith's resignation could easily have led to a political crisis and brought down the minority government. As a result he had to move fast, but he could not appoint a replacement from outside the cabinet without the approval of the Dáil. He therefore took over the justice portfolio himself and appointed Haughey Minister for Agriculture.

'Lemass was a great politician,' Haughey later argued. 'He had a great capacity to anticipate things, to be ahead of the developments, not having to react to them. On that occasion he had the new appointment made before the general public were aware of the resignation. He didn't allow any atmosphere to build up; it was all over and done with before most people knew what was happening.'

Haughey's new appointment was clearly a promotion. This fact might well have led to charges of nepotism under different circumstances, because at first glance he seemed one of the most unlikely people to become Minister for Agriculture.

'Dublin was agog last night with speculation about Mr Haughey's chances of making a go of Agriculture,' one *Irish Times* reporter wrote, following the announcement. The newspaper itself noted in an editorial that the new minister's aptitude for agriculture was an unknown quantity. 'His urban and urbane background, his knowledge of law and accountancy, and even horses and horsemanship, do not seem at first glance to fit him for the post,' the leader contended. 'We can only wait and see whether he can sufficiently adapt his considerable talents to a new and challenging position.'

# 4

## IN TROUBLE WITH THE COWBOYS
## MINISTER FOR AGRICULTURE AND FISHERIES, 1964–1966

The appointment of Haughey as Minister for Agriculture raised many eyebrows. Some farmers had already been complaining that the government was out of touch with the problems of the agricultural community, and the Taoiseach's son-in-law could only have increased that perception. After all, Haughey, who was generally seen as the prototype of the modern urban politician, had already told the Dáil that he knew nothing about agriculture.

Haughey had generally been tight-lipped about his business dealings, but following his new appointment he disclosed that he owned a farm in County Meath and had already gone in for farming in a modern, progressive way. This reflected what was happening in Irish farming as a whole. Previously, for instance, Irish egg production had been largely a sideline, in which the wives of farmers kept free-range hens as a means of earning extra income, but now the market was being flooded with cheap eggs following the advent of the battery hen. When Michael Pat Murphy of the Labour Party complained in the Dáil that prices had fallen so drastically that nobody could make money keeping chickens, Haughey announced that he owned a profitable poultry farm.

'I have 2,000 hens,' he said, and I made £874 net profit out of them in twelve months. I can show the deputy audited accounts to prove it.' Haughey's motives in making the disclosure were transparent. He was obviously trying to dispel the notion of those who, as Murphy noted, 'felt that the minister knew nothing about agriculture'.

Haughey's duties in the Ministry of Agriculture were largely administrative, in marked contrast to his period at the Justice Department, where he was involved in piloting a great deal of legislation through the Oireachtas. Now his Dáil functions were restricted mainly to answering questions about the administrative functions of the Department of Agriculture and justifying the necessary legislation to finance the department's activities.

One of Haughey's earliest acts in his new post was to introduce a supplementary estimate to cover cost overruns due largely to his predecessor's failure to gauge the likely response to the calf-heifer scheme, which had been introduced in January in an attempt to build up the national herd by giving a grant for every heifer-in-calf. The scheme was so successful that cattle numbers reached their targeted figure for 1968 by the end of the first year. As a result, costs soared, and the first year of the scheme cost more than seven times the £405,000 originally estimated.

Haughey was taking over the agricultural portfolio at a challenging time. Ireland was moving towards membership of the EEC, and he realised that all aspects of the economy needed to be modernised. 'We know that free trade is coming,' he told the Dáil in 1963, 'and we must prepare the country for the conditions of free trade and the keener competition that will arise in those conditions. We must gear the economy to meet the challenge.' The economy of the country had been gradually coming out of the recession of the 1950s. The recovery was most apparent in the industrial sector, which had been seriously depressed, while the improvement in agriculture was less dramatic and more gradual. In 1964 and 1965, however, there were considerable advances in this area.

'All indications are that 1964 was one of the best years ever for Irish agriculture,' Haughey told the Dáil in his review of the year. He noted that cattle exports were up. There was an 11 per cent increase in store-cattle exports and a 66.6 per cent increase in exports of fat cattle. Cattle exports to the continent almost quadrupled in value, from £3.3 million to £12.7 million. As a result, the average farm income rose by a phenomenal 20 per cent.

In keeping with his modern, progressive image, Haughey enthusiastically supported a wide range of modernisation and incentive schemes. In view of the success of the calf-heifer scheme, he introduced a farrow-sow scheme to build up pig numbers and a hogget-ewe scheme to do the same for the sheep population. He was also enthusiastic about the promotion of disease eradication. He claimed that great strides had been made in the eradication of bovine tuberculosis, and he introduced legislation aimed at brucellosis eradication, measures to eliminate sheep scab and a scheme to improve livestock breeds by importing Charolais and Friesian bulls and heifers, texel sheep from Holland and pigs from Scandinavia. He also announced plans for veterinary laboratories at Cork, Limerick, Athlone and Sligo to supplement the existing one at Abbotstown, County Dublin.

'The view was once common that one did not need any training to farm successfully,' Haughey explained. 'Fortunately that view is losing ground in recent years, but there is still a lot to be done.' Recent departmental studies 'showed in a very striking way that education is very closely associated with success in farming and that the possession of both post-primary and agricultural education bettered one's chances of being in the group of highly successful farmers,' he declared.

Survey teams of experts were set up to examine the different facets of agriculture, including horse breeding and the glasshouse industry, with a view to suggesting adjustment measures to enable Ireland to adapt to international trade in the event of the country entering the EEC. Haughey also established a committee to consider and recommend desirable ways of improving the quality, handling and marketing of Irish wool.

By the time of his second annual review of the agricultural scene, which he gave on 11 May 1966, Haughey was still painting an optimistic picture. 'I am convinced,' he said, 'that the prospects for the agricultural industry were never better.' There had been a disquieting drop in tillage, which he attributed partly to bad weather conditions, but the calf-heifer scheme continued to be a runaway success. The national herd rose to 1,535,000 head, the number of pigs delivered to bacon factories rose by 14.8 per cent and poultry numbers rose by 15 per cent. He was also able to declare that the whole country had been tested for bovine tuberculosis. In fact, he stated rather rashly that the disease had been almost eradicated. 'From now on,' he said, 'there is very little excuse for an outbreak of bovine tuberculosis in a herd.'

Despite the marked increase in production in many agricultural sectors, Haughey realised that this did not guarantee an increased income for farmers. In 1965 they received an average rise in income of about 5 per cent, which he contended was slightly higher than the average rise in industrial wages. He failed to mention, however, that these advances were partly the result of a drift from the land, which meant that agricultural earnings were being distributed among fewer people. Between 1964 and 1966, for instance, the number employed in the agricultural sector dropped by 45,000 people. The minister warned of some ominous indications, as 'food surpluses were appearing everywhere'. In particular, he noted that the highly protective nature of the EEC's Common Agricultural Policy was rapidly curtailing the opportunities for Irish expansion and that even the countries of the European Free Trade Association, of which Ireland was a member, had been 'steadily pursuing their own protectionist agricultural policies'.

Haughey later explained that, on becoming Minister for Agriculture, he had been struck by the fact that 'we were planning for major increases in our agricultural production and exports while the markets in which we could dispose of them were becoming more and more restricted.' As a result, he enthusiastically welcomed the agricultural aspects of the Anglo-Irish Free Trade Agreement, which were due to come into effect in June. He noted that the country's quotas for butter exports to Britain had been doubled and that Irish store cattle were being given free access to the British market. 'It is,' he said, 'impossible to exaggerate the importance of the breakthrough represented by the fact that the agreement provides for the extension of the British agricultural support price system to our finished products – 25,000 tons of carcass beef and 5,550 tons of carcass lamb.'

One of the most important aspects of the the agreement, as far as he was concerned, was the fact that it provided a safeguard for Irish produce in the event of restrictions in the British market. 'It is true that it is difficult to estimate in accounting terms the value of the agreement to Irish agriculture and fisheries. In the long term, the value will be enormous if we make full use of the opportunities now available.' He estimated it would be worth £10 million a year at the outset.

The accord was 'an agreement of opportunity', according to Haughey. 'It will be the aim of my department, with the assistance of the advisory services, the Agricultural Institute, the co-operative movement and the colleges and universities, to help the farmer in every way to meet this great, new, challenging opportunity,' he explained. 'If we work together, united and agreed on the objective to be achieved, then this agreement will surely mark the beginning of a period of development and progress in Irish agriculture unparalleled in our history.' Haughey's optimistic projection for agriculture would begin to haunt him even before the end of the month, however, as he ran into difficulties with the main farming organisations, the Irish Creamery Milk Suppliers Association (ICMSA) and National Farmers Association (NFA).

In late spring the ICMSA became quite militant in demanding higher milk prices: it advocated the introduction of a new two-tier price system, in accordance with which all farmers would receive an extra 4 pence per gallon for the first 7,000 gallons of milk they produced annually and 2 pence per gallon for any milk above that quota. Since the average milk delivery was only around 3,600 gallons per year, this meant that almost all dairy farmers would enjoy the full benefits of such an increase. Only the very largest farmers, who were more likely to be members of the rival NFA, would exceed the quota.

Under the leadership of its president, John Feely, the ICMSA placed a picket outside Leinster House on 27 April 1966. The government responded, in a rather high-handed manner, by having the twenty-eight picketers arrested under the Offences Against the State Act. Feely defiantly announced that the picket would remain in place until his organisation's demands were met. Seventy-eight farmers were arrested while picketing next day and a further eighty were arrested the following day, as the dispute escalated.

At the outset Haughey seemed to adopt a firmer approach to the ICMSA protest than he had to the Macushla Revolt in the Garda Síochána in his previous ministry. As with the controversy involving the Gardaí, Haughey refused to negotiate while the protesters were acting illegally. This time, though, in contrast with the earlier dispute, he made it clear that he would not concede to the protesters' demands in any event. He said he would like to help the farmers by conceding the price increase being sought but asserted that the government simply could not afford to do so because it would cost £6 million, or more than 15 per cent of the annual agricultural budget at the time. While the minister closed the question of a milk-price increase, he nevertheless offered to discuss 'other ways in which the income of the dairy farmer can be increased'.

The ICMSA removed its picket for a time so that discussions could be held between its leaders and the minister on 4 May, but there was no progress. 'They gave me to understand clearly that they were only interested in and would accept nothing less than their original two-tier price system,' Haughey later told the Dáil. He had strong objections to this two-tier system, from both the philosophical and administrative standpoints. For one thing, the reduced price for milk above the quota would be 'a disincentive to increased production' and would thus stunt progress. 'It would be bad economics,' he said, 'to discourage more efficient and more large-scale production'. Moreover, such a plan would be an administrative nightmare because it would be impossible to prevent abuses by farmers producing more than the quota. They would simply have their surpluses delivered in the name of a friend or another member of their family.

Prompted by his own capitalist instincts, Haughey also had serious reservations about granting any price increase under such circumstances for fear that this would lead to socialised agriculture. 'There is a danger that agitation directed only to getting higher prices may develop a kind of dole mentality, which would eventually make agriculture subservient to the state,' he contended.

'What I want to achieve is a self-reliant, independent and progressive agriculture, fully backed by, but not utterly dependent on, the state.'

Before the end of the month, however, Haughey was sounding a more sombre note, compared with his exuberant optimism of April. 'The task which confronts me, indeed any Minister for Agriculture,' he told the Dáil on 26 May 1966, 'is of such vast proportions and the problems are so intractable that I do not think it is possible ever to be enthusiastic about the progress which is being achieved at any given moment compared with what still remains to be done.' He then proceeded to back down on the milk-price issue by announcing an immediate increase of 2 pence per gallon, with a further penny per gallon for quality milk after 1 April 1967. Counting the one penny per gallon extra previously given for quality milk, this meant that farmers who produced milk with an insufficiently high cream content would in fact get the requested 4 pence per gallon extra within twelve months if they brought their milk up to the desired quality.

In view of the strong, reasoned stand taken by Haughey against any increase only weeks earlier, questions must be asked about why he virtually capitulated on the issue in the end. There was no doubt in the minds of many people, especially in Opposition circles, that the concessions were related to the presidential election campaign being conducted at the time. The Fine Gael candidate, T. F. O'Higgins, was running very well in Dublin and other urban areas, so President de Valera needed his party's traditional rural support if he was going to win a second term. This support would obviously be endangered if the Fianna Fáil government was still at odds with farmers over the price of milk. As a result, Haughey, who was de Valera's national director of elections, pulled a political stroke and shored up the President's rural support by conceding the milk-price increase. In view of the narrowness of de Valera's subsequent victory, the price concessions may well have made the difference between victory and defeat. It appeared that Haughey had backed down for political reasons under ICMSA pressure; he would pay for this dearly before the year was out.

Haughey was flying high at this time, which was the start of a particularly crucial period, with Sean Lemass indicating his intention to retire as Taoiseach within the next twelve months. Lemass's son-in-law, who had never made any secret of his aspirations for the office, was clearly in a good position to succeed him. As Minister for Agriculture, Haughey was in one of the most influential posts in the government, and his comparative youth was a decided advantage: on his next birthday he would be the same age as John F. Kennedy was when he became America's youngest president ever. Kennedy had made a profound impression on the Irish people, and Haughey never seemed averse to being compared with the late president. Moreover, the comparisons between the two men extended beyond the political arena.

Much of Haughey's success was due to his own ability to sell himself. Now he was trying to convince people he was a success as Minister for Agriculture. If he could do this – thereby securing a rural base – he would almost certainly become the next Taoiseach: notwithstanding his short temper and vindictive reputation, he was already widely seen as the prototype of the young, suave, highly educated, articulate, urban politician.

Having talked so favourably about the prospects for Irish agriculture and boasted about the success of the calf-heifer scheme in building up the national herd, Haughey came in for particular criticism when the bottom virtually fell out of the cattle market during the summer. The problems, which were the result of a series of external factors, were really beyond his control. On average, about 80 per cent of Irish cattle and beef was exported, and there was little the Department of Agriculture could do to control overseas markets.

In April 1966 the EEC virtually closed its doors to Irish cattle by introducing a prohibitive tariff on all beef imports from outside the community. Irish farmers therefore had to turn to the British market to sell their surplus cattle, and they ran into serious difficulties here too. A strike by seamen initially blocked imports, and then, when this dispute had been settled, a glut developed as the backlog was dumped on the market. This situation was then complicated by a credit squeeze, which impaired the ability of British importers to keep Irish cattle for the two months necessary to claim a subsidy from their government. As a result, the demand for Irish cattle dropped.

As prices tumbled, Haughey came in for criticism. Inasmuch as the events were beyond his control, the criticism was unfair, but he had left himself wide open to censure by his failure to prepare farmers for the slump, which became inevitable following the closure of EEC markets in April. Of course, apprising the farmers at that stage would have meant giving them bad news just before the presidential election, and that was not Haughey's way of doing things. Instead, having already said it was 'impossible to exaggerate' the importance of British subsidies for Irish cattle under the Anglo-Irish Free Trade Agreement, due to come into force in June, he proceeded to say that the prospects for Irish agriculture were 'never better'.

At the annual general meeting of the NFA in August, Rickard Deasy, the organisation's president, criticised the minister's handling of events. Haughey, who was highly sensitive to criticism at the best of times, responded by cancelling a planned meeting with NFA leaders. This was a crucial stage in the run-up to the selection of a new Taoiseach, and Haughey was apparently overreacting. Indeed, his problems were compounded by his own arrogance as he got into a controversy with the media over the whole affair.

On 29 September, as the cattle prices continued to fall, he told the Dáil that farmers should hold on to their animals to await better prices. The NFA responded by advising them to sell as soon as possible because prices would continue to drop. That night RTÉ, on its nightly television news, reported the minister's statement, followed by the NFA's contradictory advice. Haughey immediately telephoned the news department to protest.

'I felt compelled in the public interest to protest that the NFA statement should be carried immediately after mine,' Haughey explained. 'I gave specific advice to farmers in reply to questions from deputies in the Dáil as the responsible minister, and I felt that to have my advice followed by a contradiction from an organisation could only lead to confusion and damage the industry.'

The deputy news editor telephoned the head of news at his home, and the item was dropped from further broadcasts, but the *Sunday Independent* broke the story. As a result, questions were asked in the Dáil, and Haughey came across as rather arrogant, arguing that RTÉ had been wrong to air advice that contradicted him as minister. 'I think it was a very unwise thing, to say the least of it, for Radio Telefis Éireann to follow that solemn advice of mine given as Minister for Agriculture with a contradiction by one organisation,' he said. 'I pointed this out to the newsroom of Telefis Éireann and I think I was absolutely right in doing so.'

The NFA described the RTÉ affair not only as an attempt 'to hinder the democratic right of freedom of speech' but also as 'one further example of the arrogance of Mr Haughey'. The minister suddenly found himself embroiled in a controversy over the freedom of broadcasting.

RTÉ journalists had been uneasy for some months over the station's role in the recent presidential-election campaign. In his mid-eighties and almost totally blind, de Valera was unable to wage a campaign to match his younger opponent, so it was decided that he would not campaign at all. As his director of elections, Haughey sought to minimise the Fine Gael candidate's physical advantages by persuading RTÉ not to cover the campaign. Haughey contended that the President would not campaign as he was above politics and that RTÉ should consequently ignore his opponent's campaign in the interest of fairness. RTÉ's news department accepted the argument, which was unfair to de Valera's opponent, Tom O'Higgins. Unlike the President, O'Higgins campaigned actively but got practically no news coverage, whereas the various government ministers that Haughey dispatched to rallies around the country were able to secure publicity for de Valera's campaign by using their own official positions to make supposedly newsworthy pronouncements. Although Haughey had pulled another political stroke, the pent-up frustrations of RTÉ journalists were now suddenly released following the controversy over the minister's protest to RTÉ about the NFA's statement.

Matters were compounded when Haughey withdrew from a scheduled television appearance on the current-affairs programme *Divisions,* on which he was supposed to debate the cattle situation with Deasy. RTÉ decided to go ahead with the programme anyway, using one of its own reporters, Ted Nealon, to put forward the minister's case.

Haughey protested against this decision. He made it clear that, while he had no reservations about Nealon's integrity or professional competence, he took exception to the reporter being allowed to put forward government policy. 'I emphatically reject the right of any person not authorised by me to do so to purport to outline the policy of this department,' Haughey declared. The programme went ahead in spite of his objections. No doubt those objections would have been even stronger if he could have foreseen that Nealon would one day be elected to the Dáil as a Fine Gael deputy and would be Minister of State to the future Taoiseach, Garret Fitzgerald.

With the Minister for Agriculture refusing to meet the NFA leadership, the latter decided to exert pressure by enlisting public support for a protest march. On 7 October Deasy set out on foot with other members of the NFA to walk the 210 miles to Dublin; the protesters planned to hold a rally outside Leinster House in Merrion Square on 19 October. In the next few days, other marchers set out from different centres to join with those coming from Bantry, and the various marches gathered support as they made their way to the capital. By the time they reached Merrion Square on the appointed date, there were several thousand protesters. After the rally, Deasy and eight other leaders went over to the Department of Agriculture and asked to meet Haughey, but he refused the request.

Deasy and his colleagues had walked a long way, so the minister's refusal to meet them seemed churlish – at least to NFA members, if not to the general public. It would quickly become apparent that Haughey had made a tactical blunder, because the farmers' leaders set about dramatising his refusal in a novel way. Deasy promptly vowed that he and his colleagues would wait outside the Department of Agriculture – for 'a bloody month', if necessary – until the minister met them. The nine of them thereupon camped outside the front door of the department for the next three weeks, while the quest to find a successor to Lemass reached its climax within Leinster House.

Haughey travelled to the Continent and tried frantically to

find a market for Irish cattle. He was actually depicted as a cowboy driving cattle to the ends of the earth on the cover of the next issue of *Dublin Opinion* magazine. The only firm concession he secured, however, was a German promise to purchase 2,000 head. He promptly announced this to the Dáil, much to the embarrassment of the Germans, who had not had time to clear the matter with their European partners.

Haughey and George Colley were initially seen as the main contenders to succeed Lemass, while others, including Jack Lynch, Donogh O'Malley, Neil Blaney, and Paddy Hillery, were mentioned only as outsiders. 'Almost all agreed that Mr Colley starts with an advantage as the first choice of the Taoiseach at the present time,' wrote Michael McInerney, the political correspondent of the *Irish Times*, 'but there is great appreciation of the sheer ability of Mr Haughey in the Dáil, in the party and in the government. The only snag, it is generally agreed, is that his public image is not favourable.'

Haughey's image was not being enhanced either by the RTÉ controversy or by his refusal to meet the farmers camped on the doorstep of his office. When he went to Athlone for a party meeting on 21 October, his car was attacked by a mob of protesting farmers. Four days later the same thing happened outside the Intercontinental Hotel in Dublin.

'Rat, rat, come out of your sewer, sewer rat,' many of the 200 farmers chanted, as they tried to prevent his car entering the hotel grounds. Later they tried to prevent him from leaving by standing in front of the car and pounding on it.

'Go on, go on,' an elegantly dressed woman shouted from the sidelines. 'I hate him.'

Such scenes were not helping Haughey's leadership chances, though the Taoiseach came to his aid by endorsing the minister's actions. In the course of a blistering denunciation of the intimidatory tactics being used against Haughey, Lemass contended that the farmers were challenging the elementary principles of democracy. 'In these circumstances,' he added, 'it would be a matter for the government, and not the minister, to decide when and in what manner discussions with the National Farmers Association representatives would be resumed.'

George Colley was in the United States when he suddenly cut short his mission. He had been called home by the Taoiseach, who disclosed his intention of resigning within a week.

There is a certain amount of confusion about the role Lemass played in the succession drama. He led some correspondents to believe he was supporting Colley, but it has been argued that this was a deliberate ploy to help Haughey by discouraging others from entering the fray. Colley, with the backing of senior party figures like Frank Aiken and Sean MacEntee, was seen as the candidate of party traditionalists in the mould of de Valera, who was more concerned with the revival of the Gaelic language than with economic matters. Like Oscar Traynor and Gerry Boland before them, Aiken and MacEntee both detested Haughey and were convinced that he would destroy Fianna Fáil if he became leader. On the other hand, Haughey's support came largely from those interested in a more pragmatic, business-minded approach to politics.

According to Tim Pat Coogan, Haughey was 'the epitome of the men in the mohair suits' who were changing the face of Fianna Fáil. The Minister for Agriculture and his cabinet colleagues Donogh O'Malley and Brian Lenihan were urban realists with little time for the pastoral idealism which inspired de Valera's dream of comely maidens dancing at the crossroads. Instead, they hung out at the Russell Hotel in company with self-made men, speculators, builders and architects, the very people who were destroying the pastoral dream with their concrete jungles. Haughey, O'Malley and Lenihan were known as the three musketeers.

These three men strove to modernise Ireland by zealously encouraging change. Lenihan, who succeeded Haughey at the Department of Justice, reformed the country's draconian system of censorship, which had become notorious for having banned the works of some of the country's most famous writers. O'Malley caused a sensation by proposing free secondary education for all children.

Haughey carefully identified himself with the ideas of economic progress and development that were associated with his father-in-law. He was not afraid to take up a challenge and tackle the task with energy, dynamism and a strong intellectual grasp of what was required. He worked very hard but also played hard, and he became the subject of an elaborate mythology of rumours, many of which were ribald and vicious. His bon vivant lifestyle, with its aristocratic trappings, commanded attention – though not always the approval of those he seemed to be imitating. Among many of the staid, county set, he was despised as nouveau riche. This rejection hurt Haughey, but he was able to overcome the pain by immersing himself in both work and play. Others, some probably jealous of his successful rise, questioned how, in a relatively short time, he had made enough money to live in such opulence, especially when much of his career was in public life, whose practitioners were not particularly well-paid. Haughey was secretive about his business dealings, so the unanswered questions led to speculation and created a situation that could easily be exploited by his enemies, who spread some extremely scurrilous, defamatory rumours about him.

Of course, given the country's strong libel laws, which Haughey had rewritten himself, the rumours were not published.

He had already shown, in the case of the *Sunday Independent* cartoon in August 1964, that he was not afraid to threaten legal action. He could do little or nothing, however, about the rumours circulating in Leinster House, where the succession contest would be decided.

All agreed the contest would be close. By coincidence, Frank Aiken and Sean MacEntee were both in the United States at the same time as Colley, who was seen by many as the likely winner of any contest with Haughey alone, even though Colley had been a member of the cabinet for less than two years. Aiken obviously thought that this lack of experience would be a handicap, because he pleaded with Lemass to remain Taoiseach for another couple of years.

'As I see it, George would be the most acceptable to the party but he could do with another couple of years' experience,' Aiken wrote. 'He would also need time and opportunity to become better known to the country so that he could lead Fianna Fáil to victory in the next election.'

Lemass, who had never been very close to Aiken, was not influenced by the appeal. He was determined to step down. 'My decision to relinquish office is purely a political decision, uninfluenced by any personal considerations,' he told a press conference. 'I am convinced it is in the interests of the country, the government and the Fianna Fáil party that responsibility should now pass to a younger man.'

This was only the second time in forty years that a Fianna Fáil leader had stepped down. On the previous occasion, de Valera had prepared the way for Lemass to take over. Now, in contrast, Lemass believed that he should remain aloof – a particularly understandable decision given that his son-in-law was one of the main contenders to take his place. 'The most damaging thing you could do with a party is to give the impression among the members that everything is cut and dried behind closed doors and that they have no choice or say in the matter at all,' Lemass told Michael Mills.

The intense suspicion of Haughey was exacerbated by his ongoing disputes with the farmers and RTÉ. Many of the provincial deputies were distinctly uneasy at the choice being offered to the party. Deputies like Tom McEllistrim of Kerry and Eugene Gilbride of Sligo began putting pressure on Lynch to run, but he persisted with his decision not to do so. Although the *Irish Times* described Haughey as 'far and away the strongest candidate', the political correspondent of the *Cork Examiner* believed that Colley was virtually certain to win a contest between just the two of them because Haughey was so unpopular at the time. Donogh O'Malley, Haughey's campaign manager, obviously shared this conviction, because when Kevin Boland announced on 3 November that he would be nominating Neil Blaney, O'Malley promptly switched his support to Blaney, who indicated that he would stand if Lynch could be persuaded not to run. O'Malley apparently defected from his friend Haughey because he concluded that Colley would win in a straight contest between them. With that, Haughey's chances evaporated. James Dillon later recalled seeing him that night.

'I took one look at his face, white as parchment, and I said: "Haughey is down the sink".'

With the entry of Blaney into the race, Lemass finally moved and put pressure on Lynch to stand. Lynch agreed to reconsider, and, after discussing the matter with his wife, Máirín, decided to stand. 'This was the greatest decision I have had to make in my life,' he explained some hours later. 'I only allowed my name to go forward after prolonged and insistent pressure.'

Once Lynch had agreed to stand, Lemass called in the other candidates and informed them that he would be backing Lynch and that he wanted the rest of them to withdraw. Colley told him that he would first have to consult his wife, Mary.

'What kind of people have I got when one man has to get his wife's permission to run and the other has to get his wife's permission to withdraw?' Lemass reportedly remarked. His own wife told the press at the time that he had simply come home and told her that he had announced that he was about to resign as Taoiseach; that was his way of doing things.

As his chances had already been fatally wounded by the defection of Donogh O'Malley, Haughey immediately agreed to withdraw and even offered to nominate Lynch. 'I'm glad someone can give me a straight answer around here,' Lemass remarked.

The Taoiseach then called in Blaney and told him the news. 'What are you doing?' he asked.

'What are George and Charlie doing?' responded Blaney.

'Charlie is no problem,' Lemass replied.

'What about George?'

'George is going out to ask Mary to allow him to withdraw.' With that, Blaney agreed to stand down.

Brian Lenihan told the press that Lynch's election was certain. Colley decided to stand anyway, but the outcome was seen as a foregone conclusion.

On the eve of the crucial meeting with the NFA, Lemass patched up a deal ending the dispute with the farmers. He invited the NFA leaders to meet himself and Haughey, and the farmers called off the protest outside the Department of Agriculture. At the ensuing meeting it was agreed that there would be further discussions with the incoming government.

No doubt the fact that the Taoiseach was standing down strengthened Haughey's hand, especially since the leadership moves had shifted the national spotlight from the farmers. Moreover, there was little likelihood of the spotlight returning to the dispute with the farmers now that attention would inevitably be given to the new government in the following days.

At the crucial parliamentary-party meeting on 9 November, Lemass began by expressing the hope that no sympathetic speeches would be made about his retirement and that the decision on his successor could be made swiftly. Lynch was undoubtedly one of the most popular politicians in Leinster House, and Colley had indicated beforehand that he would have no problems supporting the Corkman if he became leader of the party.

Although everything seemed set for an amicable contest, Sean MacEntee threw a spanner in the works with a deperate effort to prevent the inevitable. There had always been an intense rivalry between himself and Lemass, but they had been able to keep their differences within the cabinet. Now, however, with Lemass standing down, MacEntee launched into a scathing attack based on his view that the party was 'at its lowest ebb' and that the Taoiseach 'could not have chosen a worse time' to stand down. There was little doubt that MacEntee himself could not have chosen a worse moment for his own attack.

'Responsibility for this situation in my view rests mainly on the Taoiseach,' MacEntee declared. 'The devious course which he has pursued, not only in relation to his leadership and on the succession, but to other questions as well, has confounded the members of our organisation so that none of them knows where we stand on any issue.'

'It is astonishing and unjustifiable that the Taoiseach, at this precise moment, should propose, by resigning, to wash his hands of responsibility for the country's affairs,' MacEntee continued. 'Only reasons of the utmost gravity, on the borderline, so to speak, between life and death, could justify such a step on the part of a leader.' De Valera had passed on a great Fianna Fáil heritage, but Lemass had squandered it, in MacEntee's opinion. 'Sometimes in recent years it seemed as if it were being dealt with like a personal possession,' he said. 'The state was tottering towards anarchy.'

What the Taoiseach was doing was tantamount to 'deserting in the face of the enemy,' MacEntee contended, and he insisted that Lemass should stay in office for a further two years. 'Is he so weary, so unnerved, that he baulks at the task which he will leave to his successor?'

Members sat in stunned silence. It was not the time for such a tirade. After forty years on the front line of Fianna Fáil, Lemass had every right to retire then without having his patriotism questioned. MacEntee's contribution was as absurd as it was outrageous. At one point in his speech, for instance, he cited Franciso Franco of Spain and Antonio Salazar of Portugal as the prototypes of proper leadership. He could hardly have picked two more inappropriate world leaders for the leader of a democracy to emulate: both Franco and Salazar were quasi-fascist dictators who had shown consistent contempt for democracy.

Dick Grogan promptly took issue with MacEntee's contribution, but rather than allow a debate to develop on that speech, Tom McEllistrim rose to nominate Lynch, who was seconded by Eugene Gilbride of Sligo.

Frank Aiken nominated Colley and in the process denounced the way that Lynch had been selected, expressing his detestation of the tyranny of consensus. He was seconded by Bobby Molloy, who called for strong leadership rather than a *via media.* Another veteran, Paddy Smith, also supported Colley, but MacEntee announced that he was supporting Lynch. Of course, after his untimely tirade against Lemass, his support was likely to be only a liability for whichever candidate he chose; this possibly explains why he openly declared himself for Lynch.

The vote for party leader was a secret ballot. An old shoebox was used to collect the votes; Lemass described this box as 'a queer receptacle for such a momentuous decision'. The vote was a decisive victory for Lynch, by fifty-two votes to nineteen. Afterwards, Colley pledged his loyalty and support to Lynch and professed that he was happy with his own showing.

Unlike thirteen years later, when Haughey was elected to succeed him, Lynch's victory was widely welcomed, even in Opposition circles. Even his most trenchant critic, Noel Browne, admitted that 'personally Mr Lynch is the nicest politician in Leinster House.' There was obvious relief in Opposition circles that Haughey had not become party leader.

James Dillon, who had confidently predicted back in July that Lynch would succeed Lemass, now rejoiced openly, forecasting that Haughey would never be Taoiseach. 'Remember,' Dillon told the Dáil, 'when he failed to land his fish last Wednesday night, he will never land it. He is finished. He stinks – politically, of course.'

Having backed Lynch in the end, Haughey was rewarded with a prestigious promotion: he was appointed Minister for Finance.

# 5

## 'Some people in high places appear to have low standards'
## Minister for Finance, 1966-1970

As Minister for Finance, Haughey had landed what was probably the second most powerful job in government. Moreover, he could hardly have secured the position at a better time, because the country was in the midst of an economic boom and the new Taoiseach gave the members of his cabinet an enormous amount of freedom.

After his appointment as Minister for Finance, Jack Lynch had never really exerted his authority over his ministerial colleagues in financial matters. He had already been in office for more than a year when Donogh O'Malley announced, in September 1966, his intention to introduce free secondary education for all. He had done this without first securing the approval of the cabinet or even consulting Lynch as Minister for Finance. This demonstrated a degree of contempt by O'Malley for the Corkman that was in fact shared by both Haughey and Brian Lenihan. While there may be some doubt as to whether Lemass had quietly encouraged O'Malley to take this initiative, there was no doubt that Lynch had essentially been ignored and that the government was effectively committed to an extremely costly course of action.

Yet free secondary education was a very popular venture. O'Malley had demonstrated that a way of making a name for himself in politics was merely to announce a popular scheme: the government would then be forced to implement it regardless of the cost. As Taoiseach, Lynch initially showed no more inclination to assert his authority, with the result that his cabinet quickly took on the appearance of 'a coalition between the various strong-headed ministers, each bent on the achievement of particular ambitions,' according to *Hibernia* magazine.

To have so many ministers harbouring such naked ambition might well have destabilised a Taoiseach with less confidence in his own position, but Lynch seemed to welcome the ambitions of his colleagues as a healthy political phenomenon. He was quite prepared to allow them to shine, in the same way as he would have welcomed the stellar performances of team-mates in the hurling championship.

'When a deputy is elected to the Dáil, I take it as a natural ambition for him to become a minister, and a natural progression of that ambition is that the deputy, having become a minister, would look to the day when he might become Taoiseach,' Lynch told John O'Sullivan during his first year in office. 'I am ten years older than many of my colleagues and it would only be natural, certainly among the younger ones, that they would look to the day when they might become Taoiseach, and therefore they will have the incentive to perform their particular duties well, to make themselves seen to be performing them well, so that when the time for the appointment of a successor to me comes they will have projected themselves.'

Of course, it suited his more ambitious colleagues to think that Lynch was just an interim Taoiseach, and he had contributed to the perception that he was acting as a caretaker until circumstances were more favourable for somebody like Haughey to take over. Nonetheless, now that he had the job, Lynch was determined to hold on to it.

Haughey's new post accorded him real scope, especially in the prevailing economic climate. The figures for the financial year to 31 March 1967 showed an annual surplus of £800,000, as opposed to a deficit of ten times that amount for the previous year. He therefore announced that his first budget would reverse his predecessor's deflationary course. He was not going to raise taxation on any capital items. Instead he hoped to raise the money needed either domestically or by 'foreign borrowing if necessary'.

Haughey boasted about increasing government spending on a wide range of programmes, including local-authority housing, where almost a quarter of the allocated £12.5 million was being spent on the Ballymun project in Dublin. Although there had been an increase in unemployment, he attributed this to a 60 per cent drop in emigration, compared with the previous year, due to problems in the British economy.

In each of the budgets introduced by Haughey, there were increases in the duty on drink, tobacco and petrol. He made no apologies for these increases, because consumption continued to rise, as did the state's revenues from each. 'As long as they continue to come up smiling,' he said, 'they cannot expect to escape the attention of any Minister of Finance.'

These price rises were cleverly hidden by strokes of political genius that involved imaginative yet comparatively cheap give-aways. In the budget of 1967, for instance, Haughey announced that old-age pensioners would be given a hundred free units of electricity every two months and that they would allowed to travel free on public buses and trains during off-peak hours. The Electricity Supply Board and Irish Transport Authority would then be compensated for these concessions by the exchequer.

Other measures designed to help the needy included welfare and pension increases which more than offset the previous year's inflation. As Minister for Agriculture, Haughey had been appalled by the poverty he had seen in the west of Ireland, and he took steps to help the poorer members of the farming community by announcing a complete derogation from rates on holdings of poorer agricultural land. He also announced that 10,000 small farmers could henceforth draw unemployment assistance between March and October.

Opposition deputies saw these measures as Haughey's way of repairing his damaged relations with the farming community in general. The Opposition in fact accused Haughey of using such measures as 'a political smokescreen' to obscure Fianna Fáil's dealings with property developers.

Fianna Fáil had been adopting American methods. Haughey asked his friend Des Greevy to set up a Ways and Means Committee to raise funds for Fianna Fáil. The minister helped draw up the blueprint for *Taca*, a support group made up mostly of businessmen, who were invited to join for £100 a year. The money was deposited in a bank until election time, and the interest was used to fund lavish dinners at which members of *Taca* could mix with cabinet ministers.

*Taca*, which is Irish for 'support', was 'a fairly innocent concept', according to Haughey. 'Insofar as it had any particular motivation, it was to make the party independent of big business and try to spread the level of financial support right across a much wider spectrum of the community.' Some members had previously been subscribing 'substantially more' to the party at election time than the £500 that would accumulate in *Taca* subscriptions if the Dáil ran its full five-year term, he contended.

Although Haughey was the politician most closely associated in the public mind with *Taca*, the idea for the organisation had come from somebody else, and he had no control over its funds. Nonetheless, he embraced the scheme with enthusiasm and organised the first dinner – a particularly lavish affair attended by the whole cabinet.

'We were all organised by Haughey and sent to different tables around the room,' Kevin Boland recalled. 'The extraordinary thing about my table was that everybody at it was in some way or other connected with the construction industry.'

Opposition deputies promptly questioned the propriety of such fraternisation between property developers and members of the government. In particular, there were questions about the selection of property being rented by government departments and agencies as they mushroomed in the midst of the unprecedented economic growth.

Boland insisted that he 'never did a thing' within his department for any member of *Taca*, but he admitted that other ministers might have been 'susceptible'. A cloud of suspicion was cast over the operations of *Taca,* and Boland's remark 'unfortunately provided a basis for political attack which,' Haughey said, 'did us a lot of damage at the time.'

Suspicions of corruption were widespread, and these were fuelled in May 1967 when George Colley urged those attending a Fianna Fáil youth conference in Galway not to be 'dispirited if some people in high places appear to have low standards'. It was widely assumed that he was alluding to Haughey in particular, in view of the intensity of their rivalry over the party leadership some months earlier, but Colley rather disingenuously denied that this was the case. He said he was referring to the Opposition leaders.

On 11 May 1967 Ireland formally applied for membership of the EEC, and a delegation was selected for bilateral talks with the leaders of each of the EEC's six member states. The delegation consisted of Lynch, Haughey and two senior civil servants, T. K. Whitaker, the Secretary of the Department of

Finance, and Hugh J. McCann, the Secretary of the Department of External Affairs.

From the outset, the fate of the Irish application was bound up with a similar British request. If Britain joined, Ireland could not afford to stay out because the Irish economy was so heavily dependent on trade with Britain. Ireland had no choice economically, Haughey admitted to the Dáil, but he argued that it was wrong, in psychological terms, to argue this way. He advocated speaking forcefully about the benefits of membership.

One of the more attractive aspects of membership of the EEC, he explained, was the budgetary freedom it would provide by relieving the national exchequer 'of the burden of supplementing the export of agricultural surpluses'. At the time, over 26 per cent of the agricultural budget went on export subsidies. Removing this burden from the exchequer would, he said, provide 'very great scope for the development of social services, health services and education services to European levels'.

'We believe that the possibility of membership of the Community offers us an opportunity unparalleled in our history,' Haughey continued. 'Inside that new Europe I think we could feel a great deal more secure in this troubled world because this new united Europe would be a potent influence in world affairs in the promotion of international peace in our time.' He left no doubt that the country's avowed policy of neutrality should not be allowed to prevent involvement in the military alignment which was then seen as an inevitable aspect of EEC membership, given that all six members were also members of the North Atlantic Treaty Organisation.

President Charles de Gaulle of France effectively vetoed Britain's application for EEC membership in the summer of 1967, so the Irish application had to be postponed until after de Gaulle's departure from the political scene, which took place a couple of years later. The extent of Ireland's economic dependence on Britain was highlighted on 14 November 1967 by the Dublin government's decision to devalue the Irish currency by 14.3 per cent, in line with a similar devaluation announced simultaneously in London.

Despite the devaluation, Haughey was able to contend in his next budget address, on 23 April 1968, that the cost of living had risen by only 2 per cent. The devaluation had not yet had time to make its way through the system, however, and he either underestimated or underplayed its true impact. This miscalculation would necessitate a mini-budget later in the year.

Some of Haughey's new financial proposals went down very well with all sides of the House. He introduced legislation to provide pensions for the widows of deputies and senators. The Dáil's Committee on Procedures and Privilege also asked him to give a £500 salary increase to deputies, who were being paid £1,500 per annum at the time. His reaction was to offer them double the raise requested. He reasoned that he would get just as much political stick from the public for proposing either increase. Ministerial salaries were also raised by a similar proportion.

As Minister for Local Government, Kevin Boland was charged with overseeing the regular revision of constituency boundaries. Like Lynch, he had been appointed to the cabinet in 1957, but, unlike Lynch, he was elected to the Dáil for the first time that year. He obviously owed his position to his father, Gerry Boland, who had been one of de Valera's chief lieutenants in the formation of Fianna Fáil. During the war years, Gerry Boland had served as Minister for Justice when internment without trial was implemented; six members of the IRA had been executed and four others were allowed to die on hunger strike.

De Valera had eased Gerry Boland out of his cabinet in 1957 by appointing his son Kevin as Minister for Defence instead. As dour and dull as he was determined, Kevin Boland was described as 'one of the most tortuous personalities in the cabinet'. He neither smoked nor drank, but he was prone to lose his temper. He was accused of redrawing the constituency boundaries in a way which was likely to favour Fianna Fáil. At the time, the redrawing of the boundaries was called 'Boland's gerrymander'.

Boland was particularly determined to reverse Fianna Fáil's failure to abolish the multi-seat constituencies in favour of the British first-past-the-post system of voting. He took the 1959 referendum defeat badly and was determined to have another crack at a referendum in 1968. Liam Cosgrave, the leader of Fine Gael, personally favoured the change as well. If Cosgrave had been able to carry his party with him, the referendum would undoubtedly have passed. Most members of Fine Gael, however, were more concerned with embarrassing Fianna Fáil than with reforming the system.

In neither of his two general elections as Taoiseach had Lemass been able to lead Fianna Fáil to an overall majority – and those elections had been held in the most favourable political circumstances. Under Lynch's leadership, by contrast, Fianna Fáil had secured an overall majority by winning four consecutive by-elections in his first year of office. Nonetheless, there was a genuine feeling that the days of majority government were numbered and that the system of proportional representation would lead to almost continual coalition governments.

Haughey was appointed national director of the Fianna Fáil referendum campaign. If Lynch had been seen as a principal exponent of the constitutional amendment, it might have been possible to sell the idea as something that was in the national interest, but in the hands of people like Boland and Haughey the concept was seen as a cynical attempt by Fianna Fáil to preserve its grip on power.

Haughey realised early on that the amendment was in deep trouble and he privately expressed fears that he would be blamed for the setback. Following a car accident in County Wicklow on 20 September 1968, however, he was hospitalised for the final weeks of the campaign. There followed rumours that he had insisted on driving his ministerial car back from the election rally. Thereafter all ministerial drivers were ordered not to allow their respective ministers – or anyone else – to drive their cars. As Haughey had been seriously injured in the accident, the Opposition did not press the matter on this occasion.

In a way, the accident turned out to be a blessing in disguise because it meant that Haughey missed out on the referendum's ignominious conclusion, with the government's proposal being roundly rejected at the polls. He also missed out on the Taoiseach introducing the mini-budget, which had the immediate effect of causing unpopular price rises. As a result, he was 'relatively untainted by the odium of recent setbacks', according to the magazine *Hibernia*.

The corrective measures proved successful, at least as far as Haughey was concerned. He proudly declared that '1968 was the best year in our economic history'. Industrial production increased by 11 per cent, to reach a record level, and 'the value and volume' of agricultural output also 'broke all previous records'. As a result, farm income increased by 16 per cent.

In 1969 the budget was clearly devised with one eye on the forthcoming general election, which was then less than six weeks away. As usual Haughey included some give-aways, for which he had received extensive publicity. His most celebrated stroke in the 1969 budget was his proposal to grant income-tax exemptions to writers and artists. This measure secured international publicity for Haughey as a patron of the arts.

In the same budget address, he announced that disabled drivers would henceforth be permitted to buy up to 350 gallons of duty-free petrol annually. The cheap-fuel scheme was extended to cover the months of October and April, and children's allowances were increased. Haughey also announced that the exchequer would pay £100 to parents in the event of them having triplets and £150 to those who had quadruplets.

'The Minister is the best gimmick-raiser in the business,' Paddy Donegan of Fine Gael exclaimed, in reaction to the grants for triplets and quadruplets. The whole thing would not cost even £1,000 because very few triplets were born in any given year and at that point no quads had ever been born in Ireland. Describing the whole thing as 'typical of the minister's approach to life and politics,' Donegan noted that Haughey was so anxious to please voters that he 'would chase a vote from where he lives right across the city to Dun Laoghaire'.

This, of course, was the art of politics, as far as Haughey was concerned. Whether they were gimmicks or not, such measures distracted attention from the more unpalatable aspects of the economic situation. Compared with the previous year's surplus, there had been a swing of £35 million into the red, which Haughey conveniently glossed over by saying that the deficit was not as high as had been projected.

He was making no apologies for his policy of borrowing. 'The public capital programme of investment by the government in desirable social and economic projects has been increasing year by year,' he explained. 'We have been borrowing money to finance that programme and we are very proud to be able to do that. The public capital programme this year is the highest on record.'

Haughey was again National Director of Elections for Fianna Fáil in the June general election, which was Jack Lynch's first as Taoiseach. Haughey sought to exploit Lynch's popularity with an American presidential-style campaign, in which the party leader visited each constituency in the country. At one point Lynch travelled from Donegal to Dublin by helicopter for a television appearance and then flew to Ballina afterwards. It was the first time a party leader had used a helicopter for campaigning in the Republic. The Taoiseach's rallies were well attended, and the party conducted an extensive newspaper-advertising campaign. National newspapers ran full-page advertisements that used red-scare tactics, stating that there were really two Labour parties. 'One is made of the traditional Labour supporters,' the advertisement explained. 'The other is a group of extreme left-wing socialists who are preaching class warfare and who want state control and all that goes with it.'

Following the referendum setback, Fianna Fáil's days in power looked distinctly numbered. Lynch had called the general election for June 1969. It was a brilliant piece of timing. The civil-rights campaign had begun in Northern Ireland and civil unrest was growing in the area; this unrest would soon explode into widespread violence – but not until after the general election.

The Opposition parties were confident of doing well. The plethora of small parties from the 1940s and 1950s had disappeared, and the Labour Party had persuaded a number of high-profile candidates to stand in the election. These included intellectuals like Conor Cruise O'Brien, the former Irish and United Nations diplomat, who was lecturing at the University of New York at the time; Dr Justin Keating of UCD; Dr David Thornley of Trinity College, who was also a presenter of current-affairs programmes on RTÉ television; and Dr Noel Browne. In addition, Rickard Deasy, the former head of the National

Farmers Association, was selected to stand as a Labour candidate in Tipperary, and the party was endorsed by former General Michael J. Costello, managing director of the highly successful Irish Sugar Company.

Brendan Corish, the leader of the Labour Party, proudly proclaimed that the 'seventies will be socialist'. The party nominated the highest number of candidates in its history for the general election, as did Fine Gael, which nominated even more candidates than Fianna Fáil. The Labour Party, however, which was apparently content to stay out of government, refused to conclude any kind of pre-election pact with Fine Gael, but it did indicate that it was prepared to back a minority government, provided that such a government implemented Labour's policies.

During the campaign Lynch cleverly exploited the divisions between Fine Gael and Labour. The two previous coalitions had ended in political grief, but the Taoiseach warned 'that a captive minority government would be even worse', with the Labour Party capable of bringing down the government whenever it wished. 'Such an exercise of power without responsibility could only mean the end of any effective leadership in the country's effort to achieve economic and social betterment,' Lynch warned.

Some of Lynch's cabinet colleagues were even more critical than he was of a number of the Labour Party candidates. Neil Blaney denounced them as 'the new Irish Marxists', accusing them of promoting the false doctrines which preceded the downfall of democracy in Russia, Cuba, North Korea and North Vietnam. He did not bother to explain the kind of democracy that supposedly existed in these countries before the communists came to power there. Instead he argued that Corish was being driven along the road of self-destruction by merry Marxists with their pseudo-intellectual twaddle.

'He tells us about Nero fiddling while Rome burns, but he

fiddles with dangerous imported doctrines while a triumvirate battles over control of agriculture,' Blaney said. 'It used to be honest Mickey Pat Murphy from west Cork who spoke for the party on agriculture. Now, the newcomer Dr Keating is catching the headlines, while the irrepressible Mr Deasy, the new Mussolini of the rural scene, aspires to the same post.'

In the midst of the mud-slinging, Haughey soon found himself implicated in controversy. This controversy centred on a sensational report in the *Evening Herald* on the sale of Haughey's Raheny home, which the newspaper stated was sold to his developer friend Matt Gallagher for over £200,000 earlier in the year, after the area had been rezoned for housing.

'I object to my private affairs being used in this way,' Haughey declared. None of the figures involved could be reported with certainty, because he did not give details of them to any journalist. 'It is a private matter between myself and the purchaser,' he said.

'I don't mind being weighed, assessed on my public performance as a politician,' he told a televised news conference. 'I am prepared to be criticised, evaluated, praised – if you like, blamed as a public person in my public office. I resent very much my private and personal affairs being the subject of a political campaign. If this is to be so, then let us look at everybody's personal affairs.'

Gerard Sweetman of Fine Gael charged that Haughey might have acted improperly by not explaining to the Dáil that he stood to benefit personally from legislation that he had introduced himself. It was suggested that he might have been liable for income tax on the sale of his land if part of the 1965 Finance Act had not been repealed recently.

Fianna Fáil had started throwing mud at the Labour Party, and now Haughey's private business dealings were an election issue. 'Because he [Sweetman] has impugned my reputation,' Haughey explained, 'I have felt obliged to refer the matter to the Revenue Commissioners, under whose care and management are placed all taxes and duties imposed by the Finance Act, 1965.'

The Revenue Commissioners promptly reported 'that no liability to income tax or surtax would have arisen' under any provision of the 1965 act. Although this should have killed the issue, one of his opponents in his Dublin North Central constituency – the Labour Party candidate Conor Cruise O'Brien – raked up the issue repeatedly during the campaign in an effort to expose what he described as 'the Fianna Fáil speculator-orientated oligarchy'.

Fianna Fáil ended the campaign with a massive eve-of-election rally in Cork. About a hundred people marched down Patrick Street carrying republican banners and chanting slogans. They then lined up in front of the speaking platform. An egg was thrown at the Taoiseach, and the republican element gave the Nazi salute, shouting '*Sieg Heil!*' This incident of course played very much into the hands of the moderate Lynch, who was essentially campaigning against the supposed alien philosophies of Fianna Fáil's opponents and seeking to highlight the differences between Fine Gael and the Labour Party.

Some members of the Opposition claimed that Kevin Boland was redrawing constituency boundaries in a manner that favoured Fianna Fáil, but there is little doubt that the divisions between Fine Gael and Labour prevented the two opposition parties from maximising the number of seats they could secure. Fianna Fáil's first-preference votes dropped by 2 per cent nationally, but the party actually gained two seats, to win an overall majority. Lynch had become the first party leader in the history of the state to lead his party to an overall majority in his first general election as leader – and Haughey had been his director of elections.

# 6

## 'Get Kelly to do it'
## The Arms Crisis, 1969–1970

When Lynch formed his new government, Haughey was again appointed Minister for Finance. During this stint in office, however, he would be best remembered for other events, especially in connection with developments in Northern Ireland, where things began to go horribly wrong at the close of the 1960s.

To understand what happened one must go back to events surrounding the serious violence which erupted in Derry following the Apprentice Boys parade on 12 August 1969. The parade was attacked by nationalist protesters. The police, supported by unionist thugs, then besieged the nationalist area of the city. The conflict, which became known as the Battle of the Bogside, quickly spread to other nationalist areas of Northern Ireland, which seemed on the brink of full-scale civil war.

Amid the escalating violence, the cabinet met in Dublin. Lynch arrived with a draft speech which he intended to deliver during a television address that evening. Haughey, Neil Blaney, Kevin Boland, Jim Gibbons, Brian Lenihan and Sean Flanagan all called for something stronger than the speech which Lynch had prepared, however, so a new address was drawn up at the cabinet meeting.

'The Stormont government evidently is no longer in control of the situation, which is the inevitable outcome of policies pursued for decades by them,' Lynch told the nation that evening. 'The government of Ireland can no longer stand by.'

The statement had an electrifying impact on the situation in the North. The besieged nationalists in the Bogside concluded that the Republic was going to come to their aid militarily, while the unionist population – blinded by an almost irrational fear of the South – reacted hysterically, in the belief that Northern Ireland was about to be invaded. Lynch's speech had extremely unfortunate consequences, because he never had any intention of ordering an invasion of the North.

The Irish army was woefully unprepared. Even Kevin Boland, one of the cabinet's most outspoken proponents of assisting the Northern nationalists, believed it would be 'disastrous' for the army to become involved in the conflict. 'Places contiguous to the border could obviously be assisted effectively,' he contended, 'but to do so would mean the wholesale slaughter of nationalists (or Catholics) in other areas where there was no defence available. I feel reasonably certain that the others also saw this and that none of them visualised an actual incursion.'

Faced with the irrational frenzy of the heavily armed unionist community, Northern nationalists were extremely vulnerable. They had few arms, while the unionists apparently had at their disposal the armed Royal Ulster Constabulary and the dreaded paramilitary police reserve, the B-Specials. Defence committees were established in nationalist areas and their representatives came south to Dublin for help. All carried the same message – they needed arms to protect themselves. Even renowned moderates were among those asking for guns.

Dublin launched a propaganda campaign to enlist international sympathy for the nationalist position, but there was little the government could do in practical terms. 'There was a feeling among the government, and among the community as a whole, that we could not do a great deal to help the people of the North,' Haughey explained. 'We knew that a lot of people were suffering very severe hardship and distress and the government decided to be generous in coming to their aid. I was appointed as the person to see that this aid was given as freely and generously as possible.'

The actual terms of the cabinet decision were that 'a sum of money – the amount and the channel of disbursement of which would be determined by the Minister for Finance – should be made available from the exchequer to provide aid for the victims of the current unrest in the Six Counties.'

'There was no sum of money specified,' according to Haughey. 'I was instructed by the government to make money available on a generous scale to whatever extent we required.' In short, he was given virtual carte blanche to help the nationalists financially.

'In my experience,' Charles H. Murray, the Secretary of the Department of Finance, said, 'I have never seen a government decision that was drafted in such wide terms.'

A committee consisting of Haughey, Blaney, Pádraig Faulkner and Joe Brennan was set up to advise the government on Northern Ireland because of the lack of reliable information about what was happening there. 'We were given the instruction that we should develop the maximum possible contacts with persons inside the Six Counties and try to inform ourselves as fully as possible on events and on political and other types of developments in the Six-County area,' Haughey later testified.

It was decided that contingency plans should be drawn up in case the government later decided to intervene militarily in Northern Ireland. Jim Gibbons, the Minister for Defence, was supposed to get the army to prepare these plans. As the army had been starved of money for years, Haughey and Gibbons were charged with ensuring that the forces were equipped with the best resources the state could afford.

'It was an amazingly irresponsible thing to do,' according to Kevin Boland. Haughey and Gibbons had been advocating a hardline policy, with which Lynch did not agree. The Taoiseach should have seen the danger signs within a week. On 20 August 1969 Peter Berry, the Secretary of the Department of Justice, gave Michael Moran, the Minister for Justice, a seven-page document outlining, among other things, details of a meeting between an unnamed cabinet minister and the IRA Chief of Staff, Cathal Goulding. According to the report, the minister promised that the authorities would not interfere with IRA operations planned for Northern Ireland if the IRA called off all its activities south of the border. Moran read out this document at the next cabinet meeting.

'That could have been me,' Haughey volunteered. 'I was asked to see someone casually and it transpired to be this person. There was nothing to it, it was entirely casual.'

On hearing this, Berry 'was completely reassured' because he remembered that Haughey had taken such a strong stand against the IRA on becoming Minister for Justice in 1961. Now it seemed inconceivable that he would act in collusion with the IRA, especially when the organisation was controlled by radical socialists. The security people, however, were not reassured at all. 'They repeated that their sources had proved reliable in the past,' Berry noted. Moreover, they subsequently reported that Haughey had supposedly promised Goulding £50,000 at the meeting.

There were also some disturbing reports about the activities of Haughey's brother, Pádraig (Jock), who had been selected by the Minister for Finance to go to Britain as part of an official team to galvanise 'those disposed to be friendly' to help relieve the distress in Northern Ireland. While in London, Special Branch reported that Jock Haughey engaged in negotiations to purchase arms.

The unarmed nationalists in the Six Counties were undoubtedly suffering from mental strain, as they lived in dread of armed, hostile thugs. In this situation, providing arms for defensive purposes could be seen as a legitimate means of relieving distress. Jock Haughey and John Kelly opened negotiations with one Captain M. Randall, who was in fact an undercover British agent. Sensing that something was wrong, the two Irishmen returned home and invited Randall for further talks in Dublin, where the Englishman betrayed himself by trying to recruit a republican as a British agent. At that point Randall might well have been murdered, had it not been for the intervention of an Irish Military Intelligence officer, Captain James J. Kelly, who was soon to play a central role in the developing drama.

Captain Kelly was in Derry on holiday when the Battle of the Bogside began, in August 1969. On returning to Dublin he wrote a report of his impressions of events for the Director of Military Intelligence, Colonel Michael Hefferon, who was delighted to get the report. Hefferon instructed Kelly to maintain his Northern contacts, and the captain made another visit to the North in the first half of September, along with Seamus Brady, a journalist working on the government's propaganda campaign.

Kelly had a meeting at the Belfast home of a prominent nationalist politician, who pleaded with him that 'it was of paramount importance to get in arms immediately.' Next day Kelly wrote a secret report of the meeting; this report was sent to the Minister for Defence.

On returning to Dublin, Brady suggested to Haughey the idea of establishing a newspaper and a pirate radio station to direct propaganda into the Six Counties in order 'to maintain the newfound morale of the minority and to keep pressure up against the unionist authorities'.

'I brought the idea to Charles Haughey for a preliminary discussion because I valued his judgement,' Brady wrote. Haughey endorsed the newspaper idea and even suggested it be called the *Voice of Ireland* – an idea which was partially adopted when Brady launched the *Voice of the North* a few weeks later.

Haughey was having difficulty selecting reliable people to ensure that relief money would get to the right people in the North. Initially it had been envisioned that most of the money would be distributed by the Irish Red Cross, but this organisation was refused permission to function in Northern Ireland by its British counterpart. Haughey therefore turned to Military Intelligence for help.

'About the end of September,' Colonel Hefferon recalled, 'I was asked by Mr Haughey to see him at his residence and to bring Captain Kelly along.' The Minister for Finance was looking for advice in establishing a committee of reputable individuals who would oversee the distribution of financial relief in Northern Ireland. Captain Kelly briefed him on the situation there.

'At this stage,' Captain Kelly later explained, 'there were delegations coming down to see government members, and primarily the conversation was about the members of these delegations: any of them I had met, what information I had concerning them and so on.' He told Haughey of arrangements to meet between fifteen and twenty representatives from the various defence committees in nine days' time at a hotel in Bailieboro, County Cavan, but he needed money to cover his expenses. On Haughey's instructions, the Department of Finance provided £500.

Captain Kelly's activities had already aroused the suspicion of Special Branch. Berry was in hospital for tests when he learned that Kelly was in Bailieboro for a meeting with leading members of the IRA, including Goulding. Believing that the information was of critical national importance, he felt he had to warn a member of the cabinet as soon as possible, but he was unable to contact either the Minister for Justice or the Taoiseach, as neither was at home. He therefore telephoned Haughey, who promptly called to the hospital.

'I told him of Captain Kelly's goings-on and of the visit planned for Bailieboro,' Berry noted. 'He did not seem unduly perturbed about Captain Kelly but was quite inquisitive about what I knew of Goulding. I felt reassured.'

Berry had no idea that Haughey had provided money to cover the expenses of the Bailieboro meeting, and the short fellow made no effort to enlighten him. This meeting was the genesis of the Arms Crisis itself. Berry had confided in Haughey, but the latter had not reciprocated.

It was only a matter of time before Special Branch learnt of Haughey's involvement, and Berry undoubtedly felt a sense of betrayal. It was Berry who then did most to frustrate the gun-running plans hatched at the Bailieboro meeting. It was largely because of the stand Berry took that the whole thing was eventually called off at the eleventh hour, and Berry's personal attitude towards Haughey was clearly a factor in his determination to ensure that the whole affair was not hushed up.

Despite Berry's warning, Haughey was so confident that he was on top of the situation that he had 'no hesitation in receiving assistance from Captain Kelly in briefing me on the situation in the North of Ireland and letting me know who the different groups were and all that sort of thing'. With the captain's help, Haughey selected a committee of three Northern nationalists to administer the government's relief funds following the Bailieboro meeting. A bank account was opened under their joint control in Clones, and Haughey personally telephoned the Secretary

General of the Irish Red Cross to deposit £5,000 in the account. Thereafter, Haughey's personal secretary, Anthony Fagan, transferred money to the Red Cross with instructions that it be forwarded to the relief account.

The Irish Red Cross was essentially being used to launder the money: the committee could pretend its funds had nothing to do with the Dublin government. 'If there were any questions in the North then they could say, "We got it from the Irish Red Cross",' Fagan explained. 'In other words, it was a ruse, if you like, but a deliberate one to protect these people.'

Anxious to insulate his department from any apparent involvement in Northern Ireland, Haughey ordered his staff to ensure 'that no communication should go north of the border which indicates that we are interested in helping out these people'. Captain Kelly acted as an unofficial liaison between the Minister for Finance and the Northern nationalists. Whenever Haughey wanted information or wished to pass on a message about the North, he would call on the captain.

'Get Kelly to do it,' he would tell Fagan.

When money was needed, Captain Kelly would go to Fagan, who would forward a note that read something like the following:

> Minister, Kelly wants another £3,500 from the bank
> a/c in the usual way. Is this OK please?

Haughey would simply write 'OK' on the note. A few times he baulked temporarily at such requests. 'This cannot go on forever,' he said to Fagan. Nonetheless, he authorised payment – after discussing the matter with Captain Kelly – each time it was requested.

When Berry learned the details of what had happened at the Bailieboro meeting, he was unable to get in touch with Moran.

As a result he telephoned Lynch, who called at the hospital on the morning of 18 October 1969 as Berry was undergoing tests. Although 'a bit muzzy' at the time, Berry was certain he told the Taoiseach of Captain Kelly's activities.

'I told him of Captain Kelly's prominent part in the Bailieboro meeting with known members of the IRA, of his possession of a wad of money, of his standing drinks and of the sum of money – £50,000 – that would be available for the purchase of arms.'

Although Lynch later denied that the conversation had ever taken place, he told Gibbons about Berry's report, and the Minister for Defence in turn questioned Colonel Hefferon. That was apparently the end of the matter. When this information came out many years later, Gibbons admitted that as of 'October–November 1969' he informed the Taoiseach 'that there were questionable activities on the part of certain members of the government making contact with people they should not make contact with'.

The *United Irishman*, the mouthpiece for the IRA, accused Haughey and Blaney of promising help to nationalists in order to undermine the standing of the IRA north of the border. Some people later contended that those two men were responsible for the split that led to the establishment of the Provisional IRA.

In the last week of December 1969 there was a curious incident following the arrest of some Derrymen with weapons near the border. Moran told Berry the Taoiseach wanted 'to throw the book' at those arrested. Charges were brought against the men.

'Twenty-four hours later Mr Haughey was on to me, furiously inquiring who had given the Gardaí the stupid direction to arrest the men,' Berry wrote. 'I told him that the decision came from the very top.'

'Do you mean the Taoiseach?' Haughey asked.

'Yes.'

Berry explained what had happened but said the charges would be thrown out if the men recognised the court. Otherwise he said they would be committed for contempt. Haughey remained furious. 'His language,' according to Berry, 'was not the kind usually heard in church. He said that he would ensure that there would be no contempt.'

As a result of all of this Berry concluded that the arrests were the Taoiseach's way of publicly dissociating himself from such conduct. But at the same time his failure to make 'any more than a cursory enquiry' about the Bailieboro meeting led Berry to believe that Lynch 'was not thankful' for being told of the plot to import arms. In short, Berry suspected that the Taoiseach wished to turn a blind eye to the planned gun-running, and this assessment was shared by more than one member of the cabinet.

There had already been persistent rumours about an earlier importation of a quantity of small arms destined for Northern Ireland, and members of the government were certain the gun-running had occurred. Consequently, when nothing effective was done about Berry's warning, Kevin Boland concluded that the Taoiseach privately approved of smuggling arms. 'As far as I could see,' Boland explained, 'everyone assumed everyone else knew, and the matter was spoken of as if it was a case of the government assisting in the only way a government could assist without a diplomatic breach.' Nevertheless, he believed that Lynch would veto any gun-running if the subject was brought up in cabinet. Whatever about the Taoiseach turning a blind eye to the gun-running plans, there can be little doubt that his wishes were deliberately circumvented by Haughey on the question of financing *Voice of the North*.

Brady thought the Government Information Bureau wanted him to publish the *Voice of the North,* but the bureau refused to give him any financial support. He therefore turned to the Minister for Finance for help. 'He came to me,' Haughey said, 'and indicated that he had put £650 of his own money into the publication and he was now in difficulty with the Government Information Bureau because they were not prepared to pay up.'

Haughey talked to the Taoiseach about the matter, but Lynch was adamant 'that public moneys were not to be used for this publication'. Nevertheless, more than £5,000 of public funds, allocated for relief of distress in Northern Ireland, was secretly given to Brady to support the publication in the following weeks.

Initially the funds from the Department of Finance were laundered simply to protect the committee supervising the account, but some twists were soon added to the laundering procedure. On 7 November Captain Kelly made arrangements to transfer most of the money from the Clones bank account to a new account at the Munster & Leinster Bank in Baggot Street, Dublin. This time the three people supposedly controlling the account were listed under assumed names. A further twist was added to the laundering system a couple of days later, when two other accounts were opened at the same bank in the names of George Dixon and Ann O'Brien.

Relief money allocated by the Department of Finance was sent to the Red Cross with instructions that it be transferred to the relief account in Baggot Street. The money was then transferred to the Ann O'Brien account, from where the payments were made to Brady. Other transfers were made to the George Dixon account, from which the money used to purchase arms was withdrawn.

During February and March 1970 Captain Kelly visited Germany, where he purchased a variety of machine-guns, grenades and pistols, as well as flak jackets and ammunition. It was planned that the arms would be shipped from Antwerp on the

*City of Dublin*, which set sail on 19 March and docked in Dublin six days later.

As Minister for Finance, Haughey gave instructions for the cargo to be cleared through customs without being inspected. It emerged, however, that the weapons had not been loaded because the papers for them were not in order. British Intelligence was already aware of the scheme and had apparently frustrated it.

Captain Kelly went to the Continent to have the cargo transferred to Trieste for shipment to Ireland, but while it was en route he had it offloaded in Vienna so that it could be flown directly to Ireland on a chartered plane. Special Branch, however, staked out the airport, with the aim of seizing the cargo.

Haughey learned that Special Branch were at the airport with instructions to seize the incoming cargo unless someone in authority told them to do otherwise. He therefore telephoned Berry.

'You know about the cargo that is coming into Dublin Airport on Sunday?' Haughey asked.

'Yes, minister.'

'Can it be let through on a guarantee that it will go direct to the North?'

'No.'

'I think that is a bad decision,' Haughey said. 'Does the man from Mayo know?' This was an obvious reference to Michael Moran, the Minister for Justice, who was from Mayo.

'Yes.'

'What will happen to it when it arrives?'

'It will be grabbed,' replied Berry.

'I had better have it called off,' Charlie said, and then he hung up.

'I made notes there and then in my personal diary as to what

Mr Haughey said,' Berry later explained.

Berry thus found himself in a tricky position. He was supposed to report to the Minister for Justice, but Moran was by this stage drinking heavily, and Berry felt that he could not depend on him to pass on his warning to the government. Although Special Branch had been on top of matters for the past few months, the government had done nothing about the warnings Special Branch had given.

Moran, for his part, complained to at least one colleague that he had been trying to get Lynch to act on the matter. The Taoiseach would do nothing. Berry had suspected that this might be the case.

'All this could not have gone on for several months without the knowledge of the Taoiseach unless he was wilfully turning the blind eye,' he concluded. He therefore decided that the time had come to get in touch with President de Valera in order to force Lynch's hand.

Berry did not give de Valera any details of the affair; he simply asked the President what he should do about some information 'of national concern' when he was not sure the information would get to the Taoiseach through normal channels. He knew de Valera would tell him to go directly to Lynch.

'By consulting the President, and telling the Taoiseach that I had consulted the President,' Berry wrote, 'I would be pushing the Taoiseach towards an enforcement of the rule of law.' On the morning of 20 April 1970 Berry told the Taoiseach what had happened. Lynch immediately instructed him to have the whole matter investigated thoroughly and to report again the following morning, when Berry confirmed that Haughey and Blaney had been involved in the plot.

Lynch decided he would interview the two ministers the following day, but the next morning Haughey was hospitalised after a serious accident. It was probably the most famous fall since Dick Francis came to grief while in the lead on Devon Loch near the winning post in the 1956 Grand National. Francis retired as a jockey shortly afterwards to become a famous thriller-writer.

What happened in this country in late April 1970 had all the ingredients of a thriller. Haughey had gone out riding before eight o'clock that morning and had returned about thirty minutes later. As a nineteen-year-old groom, Ruth Young, was taking the horse, Haughey had sought to lift himself off the horse by reaching for a gutter above the stable door. The gutter had given way under his weight, however. The loud crack of the gutter giving way had startled the horse, and Haughey had been thrown heavily to the ground. He had banged his head and fractured his skull. In the process his right eardrum had been torn and he had been bleeding from his ear. He had also broken his right collarbone and chipped a bone in his back.

The day of Haughey's accident was not only the day that Lynch had decided to question him; it was budget day.

'There was a hushed silence as Mr Haughey rose from his usual seat and walked across to the Taoiseach's place on the front bench to open his briefcase,' the *Evening Herald* reported on its front page on 22 April 1970. 'The minister, who began his budget speech earlier than usual because of the small number of queries during question time, started off with a review of the economy in general.'

This was a piece of reckless 'reporting' written in advance. The Minister for Finance usually began his budget speech with a short generalised review of the economy. The prepared address for this occasion did indeed have such a review – highlighting the fact that during the previous year the value of industrial exports had surpassed that of agricultural exports for the first time in the history of the state – but it was the Taoiseach, not Haughey, who rose in the Dáil that afternoon.

'Before leaving his home this morning the Minister for Finance met with an accident which has resulted in concussion,' the Taoiseach announced. 'He is now in hospital and has been ordered to remain under medical observation for some days. Therefore, I will introduce the financial statement myself.'

The most fantastic rumours were circulating in the capital about Haughey's 'riding accident'. The Garda Commissioner phoned Berry 'to say that a strange rumour was circulating in north County Dublin that Mr Haughey's accident occurred on a licensed premises on the previous night'.

'Oh no, not that, too!' a distraught Lynch exclaimed, when Berry had told him the story. Lynch 'was emphatic' that there should be no investigation. 'I conveyed the Taoiseach's view to the commissioner,' Berry noted.

'Within a couple of days there were all sorts of rumours in golf clubs, in political circles, etc, as to how the accident occurred, with various husbands, fathers, brothers or lovers having struck the blow in any one of a dozen pubs around Dublin,' Berry noted.

It was a full week before Lynch was allowed to visit Haughey in hospital. 'I ultimately got the doctor's permission and I decided to interview Deputy Haughey in hospital on Wednesday 29 April,' Lynch explained to the Dáil. Before the meeting, the Taoiseach was very agitated.

'What will I do, what will I do?' he kept muttering, as he paced about his office.

'Well, if I were you,' Berry said, 'I'd sack the pair of them and I would tell the British immediately, making a virtue of necessity, as the British are bound to know, anyway, all that is going on.'

But Lynch had not been looking for advice. He was just talking to himself, and he abused Berry for having had the impertinence to advise him.

The Taoiseach spoke to Blaney first and then went to the hospital to speak to Haughey. Each denied instigating 'in any way the attempted importation of arms,' Lynch told the Dáil. 'They asked me for time to consider their position. I agreed to do so.'

At this point Lynch apparently hoped that the whole thing could be swept under the carpet. He told Berry that the two ministers had assured him that there would be no repetition of events, and he therefore considered the matter closed. Berry was stunned.

'Does that mean Mr Haughey remains Minister for Finance?' he asked, incredulously. 'What will my position be? He knows that I have told you of his conversation with me on 18 April and of the earlier police information.'

'I will protect you,' Lynch replied.

Next day the Taoiseach told his cabinet that he had decided to accept the denials of the two ministers. According to Boland, however, he warned 'that henceforth no minister should take any action in regard to requests for assistance from the Six Counties without approval'.

Boland went straight to Haughey and told him the news. Although Boland thought the crisis was over, it was really only beginning. The story had been leaked to Liam Cosgrave, the Fine Gael leader. He tried to interest the *Sunday Independent* and the *Irish Independent* in the matter, but their editors thought it too hot to handle.

On 5 May 1970 Lynch announced the resignation of Michael Moran as Minister for Justice on the grounds of ill-health. Although rumours were already circulating about the arms plot, the Taoiseach managed to skirt questions about possible further resignations. At eight o'clock that evening, however, Cosgrave confronted Lynch with the story.

'I considered it my duty in the national interest to inform the Taoiseach of information I had received which indicates a situation of such gravity for the nation that it is without parallel in this country since the foundation of the state,' Cosgrave told the Dáil.

That night Lynch demanded the resignations of Haughey and Blaney, but both refused. He therefore requested President de Valera to remove them from office in accordance with the Constitution. At about three o'clock on the morning of 6 May 1970 the Taoiseach issued a statement to the press that he had 'requested the resignation of members of the government, Mr Neil T. Blaney, Minister for Agriculture, and Mr C. J. Haughey, Minister for Finance, because I am satisfied that they do not subscribe fully to government policy in relation to the present situation in the Six Counties as stated by me at the Fianna Fáil ard-fheis in January last.'

On learning of the Taoiseach's decision, Kevin Boland resigned as Minister for Local Government and Social Welfare in protest, and his parliamentary secretary, Paudge Brennan, did likewise. The country was suddenly awash with rumours that the Taoiseach had discovered plans for a *coup d'état*. This was undoubtedly the most serious political crisis since the Civil War.

# 7

—

## 'NOT EVEN THE SLIGHTEST SUSPICION'
## THE ARMS TRIAL, 1970

It was not until some hours later that Lynch explained to the Dáil that he had acted because security forces had informed him 'about an alleged attempt to unlawfully import arms from the continent'. As these reports involved the two cabinet ministers, he said he had asked them to resign on the basis 'that not even the slightest suspicion should attach to any member of the government in a matter of this nature'.

At a meeting of the Fianna Fáil parliamentary party the following afternoon, Haughey joined Blaney and the other members of the party in unanimously upholding the Taoiseach's right to remove the two ministers. The Dáil then began a continuous sitting – that was to last for over thirty-seven hours – to debate the crisis. Tension was running so high that scuffles broke out in the lobbies. 'It was not clear who was directly involved, but some deputies had to restrain others,' the *Irish Independent* reported.

Haughey did not take part in the debate but he voted with the government, as did Blaney and Boland. Members of Fianna Fáil seemed preoccupied with retaining power.

'The necessity to keep the Fianna Fáil government in power at all costs was the overriding consideration,' Berry concluded. 'What was happening in the Lynch regime would have been unthinkable under Mr Lemass or Mr de Valera. The naked face of self-interest in ministerial circles was on exhibition, without any attempts at concealment from the serving civil servants.'

Following the Dáil vote, Haughey issued a statement denying having 'taken part in any illegal importation or attempted importation of arms into this country'. He repeated this assertion on 25 May in a further statement, in which he endorsed the Taoiseach's view that 'not even the slightest suspicion should attach to any member of the government'.

'I have fully accepted the Taoiseach's decision, as I believe that the unity of the Fianna Fáil party is of greater importance to the welfare of the nation than my political career,' Haughey emphasised. He was facing possible criminal charges, and this was a desperate appeal to Fianna Fáil's traditional solidarity. The appeal was in vain, however: three days later he was arrested and taken from his home in a police car.

Although the media were slow to question Lynch's motives in dismissing Haughey and Blaney from the cabinet, there can be little doubt that political considerations played a major part in determining the timing of the arrest of the two men on 28 May 1970. As both still enjoyed support within the parliamentary party, there was a danger that their supporters might react emotionally and bring down the government in a fit of pique.

The Dáil broke up early that day for the bank-holiday weekend; it would not reconvene until the following Wednesday. This gave deputies an opportunity to get over their initial shock; they also had time to ponder the consequences of bringing down the government.

The charge of conspiring to import arms illegally was subsequently dropped against Blaney, but Haughey was returned for trial, along with three others – Captain James Kelly; John Kelly, a Belfast republican; and Albert Luykx, a Belgian businessman.

On 9 September 1970, shortly before the trial began, the Minister for Justice, Des O'Malley, had an extraordinary private meeting with Haughey in Leinster House. Afterwards, O'Malley told Berry that the conversation had concentrated on the evidence that Berry was likely to give at the trial.

'He said that Mr Haughey's principal worry was over my evidence and that he had asked if I could be "induced", "directed" or "intimidated" into not giving evidence or changing my evidence,' Berry recalled. When he asked if 'induced' meant 'bribed', O'Malley did not answer.

'The whole nature of the meeting,' Berry added, 'left me in no doubt that he [O'Malley] was pretending to Mr Haughey that he was a friend. It gave me a touch of nausea.' Of course, O'Malley later flatly rejected any suggestion of impropriety surrounding the meeting.

'I thought it quite appropriate at the time,' he later explained. 'I had told Mr Berry beforehand that I was meeting Mr Haughey, and I told him afterwards what had transpired. But unfortunately the connotation is put on it that I made some kind of request to him, which I certainly didn't. I factually reported what had happened because I thought it was appropriate that he should know.'

The trial began on 22 September 1970. In his opening statement the chief prosecutor appeared to sensationalise the forthcoming testimony for the benefit of the media by quoting what Peter Berry would have to say about his telephone call from Haughey on 18 April. It was obvious, one observer concluded, that the prosecution's tactics were to 'gut Haughey and gut him fast'.

The defendants stood indicted of having 'conspired together and with other persons unknown to import arms and ammunition illegally into the State' between 1 March and 24 April 1970. To prove the case against Haughey, the state was depending on the testimony of three prosecution witnesses: Jim Gibbons, Peter Berry and Anthony Fagan.

Fagan was the first to testify. He told the court that Captain Kelly had come to see Haughey on 19 March. As the minister had been engaged, the captain had told Fagan that the unspecified cargo, about which he had told Haughey the previous month, would be arriving on the *City of Dublin* on 25 March. Kelly had asked whether customs could be instructed to admit the consignment without inspecting it. Haughey, certain that he had the authority to do so, had given the necessary instructions.

Berry told the court of his telephone conversation with Haughey on 18 April. He read a verbatim account of the conversation from notes made in his diary just after the call. He related how Haughey had said that he would call the whole thing off when Berry indicated that the consignment would not be let in even with a guarantee that it would be sent directly to the North.

Jim Gibbons, who took the witness stand on the third day of the trial, testified that he had been uneasy about what Captain Kelly was doing and had therefore asked Haughey to find another job for him in March 1970.

'We'll make a pig-smuggling-prevention officer of him,' Haughey suggested.

Gibbons went on to testify that Haughey had told him in early April that he was not aware of any conspiracy to import guns. They both agreed at this meeting that collective government action was the only way of proceeding 'in matters of this kind'.

Later that month the two men had had a further conversation, according to Gibbons, who was not sure whether the conversation took place on 17 or 20 April. In his statement in the book of evidence, Gibbons described their discussion as a telephone conversation, but he corrected this on the witness stand. He had telephoned Haughey to arrange an urgent meeting, and they had then got together in Haughey's office.

'I told him of certain telephone calls that had come to the Department of Defence concerning the shipment of weapons and ammunition into the country,' Gibbons testified, 'and I asked him if he knew this, and he said, "The dogs in the street are barking it." I asked him if he were in a position to stop it, and he said, "I'll stop it for a month", or words to that effect. I said, "For God's sake, stop it altogether."'

Although the prosecutor had amassed impressive evidence about Haughey's involvement in the whole affair, the State's overall case was already in deep trouble. In order to make the charges against any of the accused stick, the prosecution had to prove beyond reasonable doubt that the Minister for Defence – Gibbons – had not authorised importation of the arms. Gibbons had the power to authorise the importation and, if he had done so, the whole thing was legal and there was no basis for the conspiracy charge.

While on the witness stand, Gibbons admitted that Captain Kelly had told him at their first private meeting that he intended to help the Northern people who were looking for guns. The captain had given him details of the *City of Dublin* fiasco and the fact that he had another plan to bring in the guns.

'I seem to have a recollection of Captain Kelly mentioning the possibility of having them shipped through a port in the Adriatic because I asked him whether that port might be Trieste?' Gibbons testified. He admitted that he did not even suggest that Captain Kelly should have nothing to do with the planned gun-running.

By the time Gibbons had left the stand, on the fifth day of the trial, the prosecution's case was clearly in trouble. It received a further damaging setback later the same day, when the State called Colonel Michael Hefferon to the stand. Hefferon had retired from the army just before the Arms Crisis after almost eight years as Director of Military Intelligence.

Hefferon's testimony was devastating. He established that Captain Kelly had not acted independently but with the knowledge and approval of Hefferon himself. Moreover, he added that, as Director of Military Intelligence, he had reported directly to the Minister for Defence on a regular basis and had kept Gibbons fully briefed on Captain Kelly's activities. Indeed Hefferon testified that he had told Gibbons that Kelly was going to Frankfurt in February 1970 to make enquiries about purchasing weapons.

'From what Captain Kelly said to you, who were these arms to be for?' Hefferon was asked.

'They were to be for the Northern defence committees, in the event that a situation would arise where the government would agree to them going to them,' he explained. He said that, in order to keep the whole thing as secret as possible, he had told Captain Kelly to see Haughey about having the arms cleared through customs without inspection.

Hefferon admitted that, on his retirement from the army, he did not inform his successor about what had been happening. 'I felt that the whole project of importing arms was one of very great secrecy, in which some government ministers, to my mind acting for the government, were involved, and I felt that it should more properly be communicated to him by the Minister for Defence.'

'Were you satisfied at that time that the Minister for Defence had full knowledge of the activities of Captain Kelly?'

'Yes,' Hefferon replied, emphatically.

The State's case was in shambles by the time Hefferon left

the stand the next day, but very shortly the whole proceedings were in disarray when the judge, Aindrias O'Keeffe, the President of the High Court, declared a mistrial after having been accused by one of the defence counsel of conducting the proceedings in an unfair manner.

Haughey was understandably livid. 'Resign from the front bench!' he shouted at the judge.

Afterwards, outside the court, a member of the jury told Captain Kelly that he 'had the case won'. The various defence teams had not even begun to present their defence, but the juror had already made up his mind. 'It was not a guilty verdict, even at this stage,' he explained.

'As the trial went on,' *Private Eye* noted, 'it became clear that if Mr Haughey and his co-defendants were guilty of importing arms into Ireland, so was the entire Irish cabinet.'

There was a lot of speculation about O'Keefe's motives in declaring a mistrial. 'Was it that, having heard the critical evidence, he did not want to have to direct the jury?' Kevin Boland later asked. Many people thought the judge was simply giving the State an opportunity to drop the case without having to suffer the indignity of losing it in open court.

A new trial began on 6 October 1970, with Justice Seamus Henchy presiding. At the outset there was controversy over the status of Hefferon, with the prosecution indicating that it would not be calling him as a witness. Counsel for the defendants naturally objected: they were anxious to cross-examine him, so they did not want to call him as their witness.

The controversy was eventually resolved by the judge calling Hefferon as his witness so that the State and the defence could cross-examine him. The former Director of Military Intelligence again turned out to be a very effective witness for the defence, as did Captain Kelly, who chose to take the witness stand in his own defence.

The two army officers had been very credible witnesses. 'No one in Dublin with whom I discussed the case – and I discussed it with many people of widely different views,' Conor Cruise O'Brien wrote, 'had any hesitation in believing Captain Kelly and Colonel Hefferon.'

At this point Haughey did not need to testify at all, but he was anxious to play down his role in the affair. Captain Kelly's testimony had hardened the evidence of Haughey's involvement, because Kelly had testified that he told the Minister for Finance about the plans to bring in guns; these plans were financed using the money provided by the Department of Finance for relief of distress in Northern Ireland.

On the stand Haughey gave an added twist to his own defence. Like the others, he contended that what had been done was legal because it had the approval of the Minister for Defence, but he added that he did not know that there were arms in the consignment. He said he had authorised customs clearance without knowing or caring about the actual nature of the cargo, which he had assumed was something 'needed by the army to fulfill the contingency plans' to help the people in Northern Ireland. It would have made no difference, he added, if he had been told that guns were involved.

'If you had known that they were intended for possible ultimate distribution to civilians in the North, would that have made any difference?' his counsel, Niall McCarthy, asked.

'No, not really,' he replied, 'provided, of course, that a government decision intervened. I would have regarded it as a very normal part of army preparations in pursuance of the contingency plans that they would provide themselves with, and store here on this side of the border, arms which might ultimately, if the government said so, be distributed to other persons.'

Haughey said he had no reason whatever to suspect Captain Kelly. He had suggested making Kelly a special customs officer to deal with pig smuggling because he believed Gibbons was afraid the British might be aware of the captain's activities.

'My view of the situation was that Captain Kelly was a very valuable intelligence officer,' Haughey explained. 'I never heard any suggestion that he did not have Mr Gibbons's complete confidence.'

While that seemed plausible enough, Haughey was not as convincing when he said he did not know the exact nature of the shipment. Fagan and Berry had testified that they each talked to Haughey on the telephone about the shipment. They knew it was an arms cargo and each of them assumed Haughey also knew, but neither of them actually said that arms were involved.

'Did you ask Mr Fagan any questions as to what this consignment consisted of?' Haughey was asked.

'No,' he replied. 'We were speaking on the phone, and, as far as I can recollect, Mr Fagan told me he had already been in touch with Colonel Hefferon. I had no doubt in my mind that this was a consignment which was coming in as a result of the direction which we had given in pursuance of the contingency plans.'

'Did you appreciate that it was arms and ammunition?'

'No. I did not appreciate or know at that point of time, and even when I spoke to Mr Berry, the words "arms and ammunition" were never used.'

In testifying about his telephone conversation of 18 April with Berry, Haughey tried to give the impression of having a very vivid memory of the discussion. For instance, Berry had said that he had answered the telephone himself, whereas Haughey contended that a child had answered it first.

To remember a small point like that, which had absolutely

no bearing on the subsequent conversation, would indicate a clear recollection of the call. Berry was later adamant on this point, however. He had been preparing for a sauna when the telephone began to ring, and he had hoped somebody else would answer it. When nobody did, he had answered it himself, in the nude.

Haughey said that Berry had omitted a number of things from his account of the call. For instance, he said that Berry had asked at the outset whether Haughey had a scrambler and had mentioned that the consignment weighed 'seven or eight tons'. According to Haughey, Berry had also said that 'it was the most stupidly handled affair he had ever known in his civil-service days'. None of those points were important, except that, if true, they would indicate that, even without contemporary notes, Haughey's recollection of the conversation was better than Berry's. All of this was significant because Haughey had categorically contradicted Berry's testimony on two vital points. Firstly, he had contended that he had never said anything about guaranteeing that the consignment would be sent directly to the North, and secondly, he had stated that Berry had missed his concluding words. Haughey had stated that, after saying that 'it had better be called off,' he had added, 'whatever it is.'

Haughey said he had called off the shipment in order to avoid bad publicity. 'It was made clear to me,' he explained, 'that Special Branch wished this cargo to come, and wished to seize it. I was quite certain in my mind that evening that something had gone wrong and that Army Intelligence was clearly at cross purposes with Special Branch, and there was a grave danger of an unfortunate incident occurring at Dublin Airport, with, as I said, all the attendant publicity.' Yet he said that, throughout all this, he still had not known that a cargo of arms was involved.

Haughey contended that he had not asked Berry because they

had been speaking on an unsecured telephone line without a scrambler. Such confusion might have been understandable in the circumstances, but this does not explain why Haughey did not ask Gibbons what the whole thing was about when they met privately afterwards.

'Do you tell us that a conversation took place with your colleague the Minister for Defence, in the privacy of your office – with nobody else present – and you decided between you to call off the importation of a certain consignment, and that that conversation began and ended without you knowing what the consignment was?' Haughey was asked.

'Yes,' he replied. 'Nor did he mention what the consignment was.'

'Did you not ask him what it was?'

'No. It did not arise. In my mind was present the fact that this was a consignment being brought in by Army Intelligence in pursuance of their own operations.'

'As a matter of simple curiosity, were you not interested at that stage in finding out what the cargo was that all the hullabaloo was about?'

'No,' Haughey replied. 'The important thing was that the army and Special Branch were at cross purposes and that it had better be stopped. I don't rule out the possibility that it could well have been in my mind that it could have been arms and ammunition – but it could have been a lot of other things.'

'If your evidence is correct,' the prosecutor said, 'I suggest that when Mr Gibbons came to see you on Monday your reaction would have been, 'I have already called this off for you but now, please, tell me what it's all about.'

'That's not what happened,' Haughey maintained. 'It may be what you think should have happened – but it did not happen.'

In his opening address the prosecutor had stated 'that Mr

Haughey's involvement – while of a lesser degree, because he was only there briefly – was of a vital nature because it was he who had given directions to Mr Fagan that this consignment was to be cleared without customs examination.' In his closing statement Haughey's counsel contended that the defendant had merely facilitated a legitimate request from Army Intelligence, given that it was actually Colonel Hefferon who had suggested that Captain Kelly should approach Haughey over the matter in the first place.

Niall McCarthy tried to dismiss the damaging evidence given by Gibbons by contending that the Minister for Defence was claiming to have been opposed to importing the arms even though he had never so much as suggested to Captain Kelly that the whole thing should be called off. 'I think,' he continued, 'it is hard to find anywhere – and I mean anywhere – in the evidence of Mr Gibbons anything convincing in his action and in his deeds consistent with what he now says was his view of what was happening at the time.'

'But, gentlemen,' Haughey's counsel said to the jury, 'if Mr Gibbons's attitude to what was happening was as he now declares it to be, surely he would there and then have said, "Captain Kelly, you cannot go on with this – this must stop." But Gibbons did nothing. He left the captain go out of his office without a reprimand, a rebuke or a warning.'

Delivering his summation to the jury, the prosecutor challenged Haughey's testimony. 'For the purpose of establishing the case made by Mr Haughey in his defence, it is necessary,' he said, 'to disbelieve the evidence of four other witnesses: Captain Kelly, Mr Fagan, Mr Berry and Mr Gibbons.' He then outlined some of the discrepancies.

Captain Kelly had testified that he had told Haughey of the nature of the consignment. Moreover, there was 'one piece of evidence which is crucial to the case, crucial in the sense that a verdict in favour of Mr Haughey cannot be reconciled with this piece of evidence,' the prosecutor continued. 'Mr Berry said that Mr Haughey said on the telephone, could the consignment be let through if a guarantee was given that it would go direct to the North?'

'Gentlemen,' the prosecutor added, 'if it was just Mr Haughey and just Mr Berry, or just Mr Haughey and just Mr Fagan, or just Mr Haughey and just Mr Gibbons, or just Mr Haughey and just Captain Kelly, nobody could quarrel with the decision that you are not prepared to reject Mr Haughey's account. But I think you have to consider the cumulative effect of the evidence: is he right, and all they wrong? Because you, gentlemen, have got to hold that they are all wrong.'

In his charge to the jury on the final day of the trial, 23 October 1970, the judge spent some time on the conflict between Haughey's testimony and that of Berry and Gibbons. In each instance, he contended, one of them had committed perjury.

'Either Mr Gibbons concocted this and has come to court and perjured himself, or it happened,' the judge said. 'There does not seem to me to be any way of avoiding a total conflict on this issue between Mr Haughey and Mr Gibbons.' The discrepancies were so great that he did not think they could be attributed to a simple failure of memory on the part of one of the participants.

'I would like to be able to suggest some way you can avoid holding there is perjury in this case,' Justice Henchy continued. 'You have a solemn and serious responsibility to decide in this case, firstly, whether Mr Gibbons's conversation took place or not, and secondly, whether Mr Berry's conversation took place or not. I shall not give any opinion on these crucial matters because, were I to do so, I might be thought to be constituting myself the jury.'

As far as the conspiracy charge went, however, all this would be important only if Captain Kelly were found guilty. If Haughey's testimony were believed, he could be found not guilty while all the others could be convicted. Thus the crucial issue was whether Gibbons had authorised the importation. If he had, then the operation was legal. Henchy told the jury that they could conclude that when the Minister for Defence had been informed of the planned importation and 'did not say "no" in categorical terms, Captain Kelly was entitled to presume that Mr Gibbons was saying "yes". That is a view that is open to you.'

The verdict was a foregone conclusion. The Taoiseach had conveniently gone to New York for a meeting of the United Nations. Everyone who attended the final session of the trial had clearly 'come to cheer the inevitable result,' Kevin Boland wrote. It took the jury less than a hour to reach a verdict: 'not guilty' on all counts. The court immediately erupted into a wild scene of cheering and shaking hands. Outside in the foyer, Haughey's supporters were ecstatic.

'We want Haughey,' they shouted. 'Lynch must go.'

Haughey was apparently gripped by the mood. 'I was never in any doubt that it was a political trial,' he declared, at a press conference immediately afterwards. 'I think those who were responsible for this debacle have no alternative but to take the honourable course that is open to them.'

'What is that?'

'I think that is pretty evident,' he replied. 'There is some dissatisfaction with the Taoiseach at the moment.'

When asked if he would be a candidate for Taoiseach himself, he said he was 'not ruling out anything'.

His remarks were unanimously interpreted as a challenge to the Taoiseach. But Lynch was confident of coping with any challenge to his leadership.

'If the issue is raised,' he told newsmen in New York, 'I look forward to the outcome with confidence.'

Lynch's supporters were ready for a showdown. As a test of strength they called on all members of the parliamentary party to show their loyalty to the Taoiseach by going to Dublin Airport to welcome him home from the United States. 'Everyone had to be there unless he or she had a doctor's cert,' according to Boland. As a result, an overwhelming majority turned out, and Haughey's challenge promptly evaporated.

# 8

## 'Nobody asked me questions'
## Backbench and Front Bench, 1970–1977

Haughey had been acquitted in court, but it took a long struggle for him to regain his standing within Fianna Fáil. He kept a low profile and quickly showed that he was prepared to toe the party line by dutifully voting with the government, even in the vote of confidence in Jim Gibbons as a member of the government. This Fine Gael motion, which was clearly designed to embarrass Fianna Fáil in general and Haughey in particular, was a blatant effort to widen the rift within the governing party.

On dismissing Haughey and Blaney, back in May the Taoiseach had said that there could not be 'even the slightest suspicion' about the activities of a minister. He then seemed to apply a different standard to Gibbons.

If the latter's testimony about not having approved the importation of arms had been accepted by the jury, it is difficult to see how all the defendants could have been acquitted, so their acquittal at least raised the spectre of a reasonable doubt, or, to put it another way, the acquittal cast 'the slightest suspicion' on his role in the controversial events. Moreover, during the trial Gibbons had appeared to admit that he had deliberately lied to the Dáil back in May, when he had denied having any knowledge of an attempt by Captain Kelly to import arms.

'I wish emphatically to deny any such knowledge,' he told the Dáil in May 1970. Yet in court he not only admitted that

Captain Kelly had already informed him but lamely tried to excuse his deception of the Dáil by implying that a different degree of veracity was required in Leinster House.

Rather than vote confidence in the Minister for Agriculture, Boland took the extraordinary step of resigning from the Dáil. In the circumstances, all eyes were on Haughey, but he dutifully voted with the government, thereby giving his critics another opportunity to slate him.

'Whatever charisma attached to the name of C. J. Haughey,' *Hibernia* noted, 'was very seriously, perhaps irrevocably, tarnished by his decision to vote with the government on the Gibbons censure. For a man who so terribly badly wanted to be leader, his epitaph may well read that he tried too hard.'

After resigning from Fianna Fáil rather than vote confidence in Jim Gibbons as a minister, Boland went on to found a new party, Aontacht Éireann. Having stood by Haughey, he had hoped that Haughey would join him, but the latter refused.

'I went to Haughey and tried to persuade him that even if he did succeed in taking over Fianna Fáil, he would be dealing with people who were incompetent, inadequate and unreliable,' Boland recalled. 'But he didn't see it that way.'

Haughey was determined to re-establish himself within Fianna Fáil instead, but there were still some questions to be answered. Captain Kelly's testimony at the Arms Trial had raised a new issue concerning the public money used to purchase arms. Haughey had been ultimately responsible for ensuring that this money was spent properly.

The Dáil decided that the Committee of Public Accounts should investigate the whole affair in order to determine whether money allocated for relief of distress in the North had been misappropriated. Legislation was passed by the Oireachtas allowing a select twelve-man committee to subpoena witnesses to testify under oath. Members of the committee included Ray MacSharry, Jim Tunney, Ben Briscoe and Sylvester Barrett of Fianna Fáil, Garret Fitzgerald, Dick Burke and Eddie Collins of Fine Gael and Justin Keating and Sean Tracy of the Labour Party.

Most of the witnesses at the Arms Trial were called, and the hearings inevitably covered much of the same ground. Some of the witnesses were actually cross-examined on testimony they had given at the trial. Court rules did not apply during the committee hearings, however, so witnesses were able to give hearsay testimony that would have been inadmissible in court. For instance, Chief Superintendent Fleming of Special Branch admitted at the outset that all the pertinent information he possessed he had got second-hand 'from confidential sources' whom he was not at liberty to name. He then proceeded to make some sensational disclosures.

'I know,' Fleming declared at one point, 'that Mr Haughey had a meeting with one of the leading members of the IRA' and promised him £50,000.

'For what purpose?' the committee chairman asked.

'For the IRA, for the North.'

But when asked for further details of this alleged meeting, the chief superintendent explained that he was 'not sure of the date or the place' of the meeting. All he could say was that it had taken place somewhere in Dublin in either August or September 1969. Later he was asked whether he thought Haughey had had any more meetings.

'I am not sure about further meetings,' he replied. 'I know his brother, Pádraig, was deeply involved.' In fact, the chief superintendent said that he believed Pádraig (Jock) Haughey was George Dixon.

Charlie Haughey was suddenly back in the eye of the storm.

He vehemently denied having either met the IRA leader or promised to pay him money. 'No such meeting ever took place, and no such promise was ever made by me,' Haughey declared, in an open letter to the committee chairman.

'Chief Superintendent Fleming's evidence, if one may properly so call it,' he continued, 'included such phrases as "I had other confidential information", "I take it that", "I am not sure but", "I would imagine", "as far as my impression goes" and "as far as I am aware" – all, plainly, indications that his "evidence" was based on rumour, reports, and other hearsay. No court would ever permit such an abuse of privilege, quite apart from the fact that such "evidence" would be inadmissible.'

When Haughey appeared before the committee to testify on 2 March 1971, he explained that it was impossible to give a full and proper accounting for the expenditure. 'None of us ever envisaged that any such accountability would ever be required,' he explained. 'We administered this particular money more or less along the same lines as we would administer the Secret Service vote.' In short, he felt this was like money voted for famine relief in Biafra, about which few questions would be asked once the money was handed over for others to administer. Indeed, when the Dáil formally authorised the expenditure in March 1970, it did so without comment. 'Nobody asked me questions,' Haughey said, 'and it went through without any discussion whatsoever.'

It is important to remember that the events in question took place before the first British soldier had been shot in Northern Ireland. At the time the British Army was generally being welcomed as a protector of the nationalist people. It was also before the establishment of the Provisional IRA. Indeed, as of October 1969 the *United Irishman*, the mouthpiece of the IRA, accused Haughey and Blaney of promising help to nationalists in order to undermine the standing of the IRA north of the border. Southern politicians lost whatever influence they had over the situation following the Arms Crisis.

The money voted by the Dáil was intended for relief of distress in Northern Ireland. A valid case could have been made for arguing that certain propaganda activities or the provision of arms were each a means of relieving mental distress, but Haughey did not argue on these lines. Instead, he accepted that using money for such purposes was 'absolutely' out of order and irregular. 'Public funds were misapproriated,' he declared. 'That is a criminal offence.'

There were doubts about the validity of expenditures in four areas: the funds for the visit of Jock Haughey and others to London in August 1969, the money which Captain Kelly used for the Balieboro meeting, the funds from the Ann O'Brien account used to finance the *Voice of the North* and the money from the Dixon account used to purchase the arms.

Haughey admitted that his brother and three others were selected to go to Britain by himself. 'The purpose of the visits,' he explained, 'was to mobilise assistance over there for relief of distress in the North'. He added that he knew nothing of Fleming's allegations that his brother had engaged in talks relating to arms. 'If the evidence which Chief Superintendant Fleming gave to this committee about my brother is as false and misleading as it is about me,' the former Minister for Finance said, 'then I think the committee should throw it into the waste-paper basket.'

The money used by Captain Kelly for the Bailieboro meeting had in fact been paid to Colonel Hefferon by the Department of Finance. The captain had asked for the money, so the two army officers had believed the £500 was for the Balieboro meeting, but Haughey, who had instructed the department to give the money to Hefferon, said that he had believed the funds were just part of payments made to Colonel Hefferon to fund an office to help Northern refugees.

The circumstances surrounding the financing of the *Voice of the North*, however, were more complicated. Brady had submitted a bill to the Bureau of Information which was forwarded to the Department of Finance. Haughey thought the Taoiseach's Department should look after the bill, so he instructed Fagan to enquire into the matter. The Taoiseach's Department, under which the Bureau of Information functioned, refused to have anything to do with the bill, however.

'I felt Mr Brady was unfairly treated,' Haughey told the committee. 'Mr Brady understood that the Government Information Bureau wished him to publish this newspaper. Whether he was right or wrong, or did not understand it, I cannot say.' But Brady 'certainly' thought he was being wronged, Haughey continued. 'He came to me and indicated that he had put £650 of his own money into the publication and he was now in difficulty with the Government Information Bureau because they were not prepared to pay up,' Haughey continued. 'I went to the Taoiseach on the matter. The Taoiseach gave me a direction and a ruling that public moneys were not to be used for the publication.'

Although there was no hope of Lynch agreeing to spend public money on the project, Haughey had indicated that he would personally make sure Brady would not be out of pocket on what had already been spent, but he had said it might be necessary to suspend publication for the time being. 'You had better hold it,' Haughey had said. 'I myself will see you all right with what you have spent if it comes to that.'

Brady had then gone over and told Captain Kelly that the *Voice of the North* would have 'to fold, as no money was coming in for it'. But within a couple of days Captain Kelly had come back to him with financial support in the form of a cheque drawn on the Ann O'Brien account. Brady said that he had had no idea that this was government money.

Fagan told the committee that shortly afterwards he had seen Brady's original bill on Haughey's desk. 'What is being done about this?' he had asked.

'Oh, that is being looked after,' the minister had replied. 'Ask Kelly how Brady's affairs stand.'

Fagan had duly contacted the captain, who had told him to 'tell the minister he is OK.' Thus, contrary to the specific direction of the Taoiseach, government funds had been used to support the *Voice of the North*, but Haughey swore that he did not know who had helped Brady out. He also testified that he knew nothing about the O'Brien account or indeed any of the three accounts opened at the Munster & Leinster Bank in Baggot Street. The first he had heard of them, he said, was during the Arms Trial.

Two of the witesses felt Haughey must have known about the main account in Baggot Street, but neither witness was certain on this point. For instance, Captain Kelly testified that he 'certainly' told Fagan about this account. And,' he added, 'I should imagine Mr Haughey would know too. I cannot see any reason why not.' Fagan thought it 'inconceivable' that he would not have told the minister but added that he could 'not honestly recall' mentioning it at any specific time. 'It is possible,' Fagan said, 'that on one or more occasions Baggot Street might have come into our discussions, but I do not specifically recall that.'

Haughey explained that he had selected the three Northern nationalists to distribute the relief money in Northern Ireland when it became apparent that the Irish Red Cross could not operate there. He had been aware of the bank account opened in Clones but had not known – or, for that matter, cared – that the money had been transferred to Baggot Street. 'If they nominated someone else to administer the fund, that was not really any particular concern of mine,' he argued. 'We were not concerned with the mechanics of the payments.'

He forcefully denied knowing that any of the relief money had been spent on buying weapons. 'I have no knowledge whatever,' he emphasised, 'that any of these moneys, any halfpenny of these moneys, went for the procurement of arms.'

'I have no personal knowledge of this,' he continued, 'but I am informed that it can be proved beyond any doubt that my brother Pádraig was not George Dixon.'

'You are satisfied that he was not?' Ray MacSharry asked.

'He has so informed me and I accept his word.'

Jock Haughey had by then told the committee under oath that he had never used 'the name of George Dixon in any connection with any financial or banking dealings,' but he had then refused to answer any questions. 'I am advised,' he explained, 'that by giving evidence before this committee I might be liable in civil law and under the laws of the land for any answer I might make.' In American parlance, he was taking the Fifth Amendment, but the United States Constitution did not operate in Ireland, so Pádraig Haughey was cited for contempt and sentenced to six months in jail by the High Court. He appealed successfully to the Supreme Court, which overturned the conviction on constitutional grounds.

'This judgement deprived the committee,' in the estimation of its own members, 'of any effective powers in the event of a witness refusing to attend, to produce documents or to answer questions.' Opposition members of the committee wanted to ask the Oireachtas for the necessary powers to remedy this situation, but this was blocked by Fianna Fáil members, with the result that the hearings sputtered to a rather ineffective conclusion with the presentation of the committee's final report on 13 July 1972.

The report was incomplete; the committee was able only to conclude 'definitely' that a little over £29,000 was 'expended on or in connection with the relief of distress' in Northern Ireland. It found that a further £31,150 may have been spent in the same way but that over £39,000 had, in effect, been misappropriated. There was no definitive conclusion on who was directly responsible for the misappropriations, but the committee was specifically critical of Haughey on two counts. Firstly, it concluded that 'the misappropriation of part of the money which is now known to have been spent on arms might have been avoided' if either Haughey, Blaney or Gibbons had 'passed on to the Taoiseach their suspicion or knowledge of the proposed arms importation'. Secondly, the commitee was 'not satisfied' that Haughey's actions in connection with the £500 given to Captain Kelly for the Bailieboro meeting 'was justified under the terms of the fund'.

Meanwhile, Haughey had begun the long struggle to re-establish himself within the party, going to all party meetings to which he was invited around the country. Three or four nights a week he and a colleague would set off to meetings around the country in a V12 Jaguar. Haughey would drive to the venue and P. J. Mara would usually drive back. Other drivers included party activists like Owen Patten, Dick Murnane and Liam Lawlor.

'You had to do a day's work first,' Mara recalled, 'finish up at 6 pm and head off to, say, Tipperary, Cork or Kerry. And we always came back the same night. That was the rule. We often drove back to Dublin from a function in Bandon in West Cork that would have finished at two in the morning.'

Although Haughey was 'a consummate politician, he was not consumed by politics,' according to Terry Keane, a journalist who began an affair with him at about this time. 'I viewed Charlie as a bit of a wide boy, with a terrible reputation as a womaniser,' she wrote. 'There was a whole series of Charlie stories, some true, some false and some frankly lurid.' She began her affair with him on 17 January 1972 at Club Elizabeth, a nightclub in Leeson Street that was frequented by politicians. At the time she was the fashion editor of the *Sunday Press*; she was in her early thirties and was temporarily separated from her lawyer husband.

At the nightclub she was in the company of Haughey, whom she teased and generally treated rather contemptuously. 'I don't have to put up with this,' he finally snapped in exasperation. 'I'm going home.'

'Don't go,' Keane responded. 'I'll dance with you instead.'

'There was some sort of empathy,' she later explained. 'I felt that I would also be like that if I wasn't the centre of attention. I suddenly thought, "He's attractive." He oozed sex appeal and had the most beautiful mouth of anybody I'd ever seen.'

After that night he invited her to London, where they stayed in an apartment owned by his friend John Byrne, a property developer. That was the first of a number of foreign trips they took together. During one of their early trips to London he introduced her to Cristal champagne. As the waiter was returning with a bottle of the incredibly expensive drink, a customer checked the vintage, much to the indignation of Haughey. 'Who's that fucker and what is he doing with my champagne?' he snapped.

'I couldn't stop laughing: the façade of sophistication demolished at a stroke,' Keane recalled. 'But that's Charlie.' That was the side of him that those with old money sneered at, denigrating him as one of the nouveaux riches.

At the time Haughey was at the nadir of his political career and was being shunned by politicians he had previously considered his friends. He was venomous about the Arms Crisis, feeling that he had been victimised, and much of that venom was reserved for Lynch. There was little doubt that Lynch had turned a blind eye to the affair and then made Haughey the scapegoat, dismissing him from the cabinet while he was still in hospital after his riding accident. 'He didn't even have the decency to wait until I was back on my feet,' Haughey would often complain.

Haughey still had a firm conviction that he would be Taoiseach one day, and he talked to Keane for hours about how he was going to make his way back, this time to the very top. She found him exciting and great fun to be with.

'We were waltzing off to London and Paris all the time for trysts,' she wrote. France was Haughey's favourite. Napoleon, the little emperor who upended all of Europe, was 'his hero and inspiration,' according to her. Haughey loved French things: wines, restaurants, clothes, architecture and history. In the coming years he and Keane would stay in various places in France and Germany without being concerned about publicity, but Haughey was leery of London because of the danger of the affair being outed by the tabloid press. He and Keane were not discreet about their relationship, especially in Dublin, where it was an open secret among journalists. She patched up her marriage and got together with her husband for some time, but throughout it all, she and Haughey would frequently meet at different Dublin hotels, including the Russell, Hibernian and Sachs, where they often dined or drank together openly. There were numerous stories of tiffs between them; most of these stories were probably apocryphal. If she had thrown as many glasses of champagne in his face as was rumoured, she would have drenched half of Dublin in the process – not to mention all the dinners she supposedly dumped in his lap. She wrote about one night when she had ordered him out of her car in Merrion Street after he had had too much to drink. He telephoned her the next day.

'So you got home,' she said.

'Of course,' he replied. 'I met some citizens who carried me on their shoulders and were thrilled for the opportunity.' This was Haughey's natural arrogance. Within a month of the start of the affair he was already on the road to political recovery.

He tested his popularity within the party by running for a position as national vice-president at the ard-fheis in February 1972. There were five vice-presidents, so he needed only 16.7 per cent of the vote to assure himself of election. This posed little problem, especially when Lynch made no open effort to block him.

Haughey's supporters were ecstatic as he arrived on the platform, where he was greeted by many of the party hierarchy. There were some determined absences from the ranks of the well-wishers, however. Erskine Childers sat silently, reading his newspaper. Dismayed at the prospect of Haughey's return to prominence, he repeatedly urged Lynch not to restore him to the front bench of the parliamentary party.

Childers had already departed the political scene; he was to succeed de Valera as Irish President in 1973. Frank Aiken, one of the founders of Fianna Fáil in 1926, urged Jack Lynch to block Haughey's nomination as a party candidate, but Lynch rejected the idea. Aiken was so annoyed at this that he decided to retire from politics himself.

Aiken initially threatened to give the press his reasons for quitting, but, under pressure from President de Valera and others, he relented and allowed Lynch to announce that he was retiring 'on doctor's orders'. It was a sad end to the long political career of a particularly courageous man, and it was all the sadder that he should leave politics quietly while the truth about his principled stand was distorted.

Lynch and Haughey made only one appearance together during the campaign. This was at a rally arranged in Ballymun for the three north Dublin constituencies – Dublin North, Dublin North-East and Dublin North-Central. Haughey was elected comfortably, with more than half a quota to spare over his nearest challenger, Conor Cruise O'Brien, who had to wait for a later count in order to be elected. Nationally, Fianna Fáil increased its vote from that of 1969, but this time Labour and Fine Gael indicated a willingness to work together, so the Fianna Fáil candidates did not get as many transfers from those parties in the later counts as they had before. It was probably a blessing for Haughey that Fianna Fáil did not get back into government in 1973, because henceforth he was on an equal footing with the bulk of his party in the Dáil. He continued to travel around the country, to wherever he was asked to go by the party.

In February 1975 Lynch's moderate line on the Northern Ireland issue was questioned when Michael O'Kennedy, his spokesman for foreign affairs, called on the British to make a declaration of their intent to withdraw from Northern Ireland in order to 'concentrate the minds' of unionists and cause them to look more favourably on an offer from Dublin to negotiate a solution to the partition question. The Taoiseach, who had been simply calling on the British to express their interest in a united Ireland, was annoyed at the pronouncement, but, rather than confront O'Kennedy, he simply dismissed the difference as a mere change of emphasis. Lynch had clearly backed down rather than confront the hardliners on the issue of the North. This fact became all the more apparent a few days later when he restored Haughey to the front bench as spokesman for health.

The appointment, made in February 1975, was generally believed to have been the result of 'some kind of Republican rebellion inside Fianna Fáil', according to Conor Cruise O'Brien, writing in the *Irish Times.*

This led to an extraordinary outburst from the widow of President Erskine Childers, who had died in office some weeks earlier. Childers's widow had been invited to a Mass that the party had arranged for her late husband and other recently deceased party deputies, but, in a fit of pique over Haughey's restoration, she declined the invitation in an open letter. 'The late President would not benefit from the prayers of such a party,' she wrote. 'Happily for him he is now closer to God and will be able to ask His intercession that his much-loved country will never again be governed by these people.'

Although it had generally been considered a minor position, the post of health spokesman had an added significance at the time because the Minister for Health and Social Welfare, Brendan Corish, was both Tánaiste and leader of the Labour Party. In his new role, therefore, Haughey was given a chance to shine by setting his own performance against that of both his less capable Fianna Fáil colleagues and the lacklustre Corish.

For instance, the vote on the estimates of each department normally allowed the minister to outline his own plans, but Corish made poor use of the opportunity given to him to do this in 1975. His department had been considering a hospital-development plan for the past eighteen months, but he was able to say only that he hoped to announce the new programme soon. 'In the whole speech,' Haughey complained, 'the minister could not announce one single significant new development.' The delay was probably well-advised, because when the proposals were published later in the year they were rejected piecemeal by a succession of different interest groups.

Corish had pledged to bring in a system of free hospitalisation, but he was unable to get the scheme off the ground. He also had difficulties with the Misuse of Drugs Bill, which was first introduced in 1973 but had its second reading after Haughey's return to the front bench. The drugs issue was highly emotive, holding enormous potential for an unscrupulous politician who might wish to whip up public emotions and thereby secure considerable publicity, but Haughey adopted a highly constructive approach. 'This is a situation,' he said, 'which calls for enlightenment, understanding, maturity, judgement and wisdom.' He approved of the 'humane' approach to drugs; this recognised a difference between unfortunate addicts who were coerced into selling drugs in order to feed their own habits and those 'cold, calculating pedlars' who pushed drugs solely for money and were not addicted to them.

Haughey's criticism of the bill was that it did not place enough emphasis on the different categories of drugs. Many uninformed people often became quite vehement in their blanket condemnation of the use of drugs for non-medical purposes, yet these people would be totally oblivious of the fact that drugs include substances present in tea, coffee, tobacco and alcoholic drinks. Haughey was particularly mindful of the fact that tobacco and alcoholic drinks were being advertised in a way that encouraged their misuse.

'Can we regard it as satisfactory that we promulgate these penalty provisions in regard to drugs while at the same time we permit the expenditure of vast amounts of money every year on the promotion of other drugs, which are, in their own way, perhaps just as harmful?' he asked. 'We will have to have a fundamental sorting-out of our priorities in regard to this whole situation.'

As Opposition spokesman, Haughey concentrated his criticism on what he believed was the government's failure to do enough in the area of health because of its unwillingness to allocate sufficient money for such purposes. When Corish introduced a supplementary estimate to cover cost overruns by his department, Haughey was able to say that he had warned him. 'It was obvious to everyone,' he said, 'that the provisions being made were inadequate.'

The Fianna Fáil spokesman was fairly positive in his overall approach to the issue of health. He moved a private member's bill to extend the eligibility for medical cards to a wide range of people, including all those over sixty-five years of age, widows, people with long-term illnesses and those whose earnings were under a certain level, but the government defeated this legislation on financial grounds. Politically, the whole exercise had been a brilliant tactical move. Haughey got the credit for trying to introduce the measures and the government was blamed for killing them. This was not just a cynical political exercise on Haughey's part, however. He obviously believed in what he was doing, and he later proved his sincerity by introducing legislation to give effect to his various suggestions when Fianna Fáil returned to power.

Although Haughey's actions as health spokesman had foreshadowed some of the legislation he would later introduce, there was little indication of any of this in the famous Fianna Fáil election manifesto of 1977. Privately, Haughey was known to have reservations about some of the extravagant promises made in the manifesto, but these reservations had nothing to do with the area of health. Instead, the health clauses consisted largely of platitudes: aspirations with regard to health were voiced, but no specific promises were made in this area.

Fine Gael realised that Cosgrave had made a dreadful mistake in calling the election when he did, because the party's initial poll showed that Fianna Fáil was likely to win by a landslide. Yet the conventional political wisdom was that Jim Tully's reorganisation of the constituency boundaries would hurt Fianna Fáil, which mounted a spirited, well-organised campaign.

Lynch even made an appearance with Haughey in the latter's Artane constituency. The rally was held at Northside Shopping Centre, where the crowd tended to obstruct rather than enhance trading. When one businessman objected that the rally was hurting his business, P. J. Mara suggested he get lost, but the man persisted in complaining.

'Would you ever go and fuck yourself,' Mara snapped.

Indignant, the man went to Haughey.

'I want to complain about the way I was treated by your Director of Elections, Mr Mara,' the businessman protested. 'He told me to "fuck off".'

'And I'm now making it official,' Haughey replied. This was the side of Haughey that some people found so offensive but others found amusing.

The *Irish Times* commissioned a public-opinion poll for just before the election but then refused to believe the poll's findings, which showed that Fianna Fáil was going to win by a landslide. Instead the newspaper predicted, in a banner headline across the front page, that the coalition was likely to win. Lynch was asked by his press secretary, Frank Dunlop, how he thought the election would go. 'I think we might barely make it,' he replied.

The public-opinion polls conducted during the campaign showed that the electorate thought Fianna Fáil would handle various aspects of the economy better than the coalition, but the coalition was preferred in the area of security. As a result, Conor Cruise O'Brien tried desperately to exploit the security issue by raising questions about Haughey's previous behaviour. In an interview with the London *Times* he predicted that a Fianna Fáil government that included the man from Kinsealy would 'turn a blind eye' to the activities of the IRA in Northern Ireland. These remarks promptly generated media interest, and O'Brien was interviewed for news programmes on both the RTÉ and BBC. He also spoke out publicly at a rally in Raheny the same day.

'Can an alternative government which included Mr Haughey be trusted on security?' he asked. 'Can it be trusted in relation to the Provisional IRA? Can it be trusted in relation to Northern Ireland? Can it be trusted – indeed, will it be trusted – in the field of Anglo-Irish relations?' He contended that it was right to bring up such issues because many young people 'simply do not know that when Mr Haughey was Minister for Finance large sums of public money voted for the relief of distress in Northern Ireland were diverted to the purchase of arms and ammunition'. Although he was only a minor member of Lynch's team, Haughey obviously enjoyed enormous influence within his party. In fact, Cruise O'Brien continued, 'many people believe that before very long Mr Lynch will retire from the leadership of Fianna Fáil and that Mr Haughey will succeed him. Are the people of this country prepared to entrust with their security a government which might turn out to be led by a person with the record of Mr Charles J. Haughey?'

Dismissing what he described as 'unfounded allegations', Haughey contended that the electorate had shown its contempt for the charges by giving him the second-highest vote in the country. 'I believe they will treat them [the charges] in the same way on this occasion,' Haughey continued. 'That Dr O'Brien should go to the London *Times* to launch a piece of character assassination against a fellow Irishman is not surprising in view of that newspaper's role in Irish history.'

From Haughey's point of view, there was probably no one from the government benches better than Cruise O'Brien to make such charges against him, as Cruise O'Brien had a highly negative rating with many sections of the electorate. Indeed the *Irish Times* published a poll a couple of days later which showed that he was the member of the cabinet that most people would least like to see as Taoiseach. On the other hand, Haughey was the person that most people would least like to see lead the country if Fianna Fáil were returned to power. Haughey's critics must have found cold comfort in the statistics, however, because the same poll indicated that, although he was not nearly as popular as Lynch, Haughey was clearly the second most popular figure in Fianna Fáil. Moreover, in the event of Lynch deciding to step down, Haughey was a full 12 percentage points ahead of Colley as the choice to succeed him.

In the previous two general elections Haughey and Cruise O'Brien had run against each other in the same constituency, but this time they were separated as a result of the drastic restructuring of the constituencies by the coalition government. Haughey chose to run in Artane, where he stormed home, with more than 11,000 votes from a greatly reduced electorate. With 37 per cent of the first-preference votes, his tally was up by almost 7 per cent. Cruise O'Brien's dropped, on the other hand, and he lost his seat by a narrow margin as Fianna Fáil swept to power with the largest majority in the history of the state.

On the night of the election count Haughey was at the RDS in Ballsbridge, where the Dublin counts were held. When word spread that Fianna Fáil had won the greatest majority ever, Geraldine Kennedy, a political reporter with the *Irish Times*, happened to be standing beside him. This was Lynch's greatest triumph, she reasoned, and he was in an invincible political position. She remarked to Haughey that his chances of securing the leadership of Fianna Fáil were therefore finished.

'Not at all,' he replied, 'they're all mine.' He had been doing the work at the grass roots and had helped a great many of the new deputies in the run-up to the election. He was therefore in a stronger position than before and seemed confident that he would eventually succeed Lynch. Kennedy asked if he would grant her his first interview as Taoiseach, and he agreed. She then asked if that was a promise, and he committed himself.

Little did she realise that barely halfway through the new Dáil, she would be calling on Haughey to fulfill his promise. Jack Lynch, on the other hand, seemed to realise, during a television interview on RTÉ that night, that his big majority could lead to difficulties. Ironically, the seeds of instability had been sown in the midst of the largest majority ever enjoyed by a Taoiseach.

# 9

## 'The worst fucking judge of people'
## Minister for Health and Social Welfare, 1977–1979

Lynch was duly elected Taoiseach when the Dáil reconvened, and he appointed Haughey Minister for Health and Social Welfare. There were apparently some objections to this appointment, but the Taoiseach thought the short fellow from Kinsealy had purged himself of his past indiscretions and had behaved himself since being brought back on to the front bench. 'I felt that I was doing the right thing, the Christian thing and the fair thing in giving him a chance again,' Lynch explained later.

Although Haughey had previously argued that the two departments of health and social welfare were too much for one man, he made no objection when Lynch offered him the dual post. He did not even ask to be assigned a parliamentary secretary. He was obviously intent on demonstrating to the full his own political skills. He had come in from the political cold.

A cabinet committee was appointed to deal with major economic matters. It consisted of the Taoiseach, Martin O'Donoghue, George Colley and Des O'Malley. These people took many of the most important economic decisions. Thus Haughey was a long way from the real centre of power. Nonetheless, the post of Minister for Health and Social Welfare gave him the opportunity to construct a power base, even though the various promises made in the Fianna Fáil manifesto had little to do with either of his departments. There were so many new deputies arriving at Leinster House for the first time as a result of the Fianna Fáil landslide that it took these people a while to settle in. Those who sought Haughey's assistance found him to be highly approachable and helpful, often in marked contrast to other ministers, who were aloof and showed little concern.

Deputies anxious to cut bureaucratic red tape for constituents looking for medical cards or having problems with welfare payments found Haughey very helpful. He was generally concerned, courteous and charming – a far cry from his waspish reputation.

During his two-and-a-half years as Minister for Health and Social Welfare, Haughey generated a considerable amount of publicity to enhance his own political image. He used his administrative and legislative experience to telling effect in securing funding for a wide range of programmes that he had the skill and initiative to get off the ground. He also implemented some legislative measures that received enormous, if not always favourable, publicity. Of course, critics charged that he was just campaigning for Taoiseach: 'Charlie has no plans for health,' one old hand at medical politics contended. 'What he's done is to keep ten balls in the air at the same time and protect his own.'

Haughey worked hard and ensured that he was given credit for both the achievements and the popular measures introduced by his departments. As Minister for Finance before the Arms Crisis, he had received the credit for various concessions to pensioners, and now, as Minister for Social Welfare, he demonstrated his ability to generate publicity to secure credit for the same kinds of concessions in the budgets drawn up by George Colley. Indeed, the Fine Gael spokesman John Boland accused him of 'endeavouring to introduce a budget of his own'.

There were some of the same kind of imaginative give-aways

for which Haughey had earlier been renowned, such as the elderly being given free bottled gas in lieu of their free electricity allowance. In addition, pensioners living alone were given free telephone rental. 'I think,' Haughey explained, 'we must give increasing attention to the problems of loneliness insofar as the old are concerned and see if we can devise, by community action or otherwise, ways of mitigating this feeling of loneliness and isolation.'

The annual cost of all the social welfare improvements combined was estimated at £55 million, while the health budget was up by £45 million, bringing the total estimated expenditure of Haughey's two departments to around £967 million, or about a third of the government's total budget. He proudly declared that more money than ever was being spent on health and social welfare, and he stated that 2,400 new jobs were being created as a result.

'His greatest coup,' according to the *Irish Medical Times,* 'was bought for the modest expenditure of £1 million – the cost of dramatically expanding the role of the new Health Education Bureau,' which had been set up by Corish in 1975. Through the bureau, Haughey launched imaginative publicity campaigns aimed at promoting better standards of fitness and hygiene. He was credited with bombarding the public with exhortations to jog, dance, play games, give up smoking, cut down on alcohol consumption and walk rather than drive.

To many people it seemed as though Haughey had invented health education with these publicity campaigns. He announced that he had given up cigarettes and alcohol – though the latter was not necessarily for life. He thereby presented the public with a reformed image of himself – the new Haughey.

He also introduced legislation giving the Minister for Health 'absolute power at his discretion to deal with this problem of the promotion and advertising of tobacco products'. He then proceeded to ban cigarette companies from sponsoring a wide range of events and made it illegal for competitors in certain events to carry the name of a tobacco company or its products.

The groundwork for a new hospital programme had been done by the previous government, but Haughey implemented the programme by cutting through reams of red tape. He took the design of Cork Regional Hospital and had it used for the new Beaumont Hospital in Dublin, thereby speeding up construction of the new building. He commissioned a new regional hospital in Wilton, Cork, secured funds for a £5 million development at Mullingar General Hospital, authorised an extension to double the size of Sligo General Hospital and had funds provided to start construction of a new general hospital in Tralee.

In July 1978 Haughey announced a new scheme providing for free hospitalisation for all those earning under £5,500 per year. His predecessor had been anxious to introduce free hospitalisation, and the department had drawn up a scheme to achieve this, but consultant doctors refused to implement it. Haughey compromised with them and persuaded the cabinet to approve his scheme. This was another real achievement, because free hospitalisation has not been part of Fianna Fáil's 1977 election manifesto.

In November 1978 hundreds of uniformed nurses descended on Leinster House in a demonstration calling for salary increases. Haughey certainly did not want a repetition of his disastrous refusal to meet the farmers when they marched on his department back in 1966. Some 300 nurses in uniform were therefore invited into Leinster House, where they packed the Dáil chamber, which was turned into a veritable circus by deputies playing to their audience.

Fine Gael proposed 'to set up a commission of inquiry on nurses' pay and conditions,' but, much to the delight of the nurses, Haughey figuratively stole the clothes of the Fine Gael spokesman by introducing an amendment asking the Dáil to 'approve the measures taken by the government to improve the pay, conditions and status of the nursing profession and to welcome the recent decision to establish a commission of inquiry'.

Before the end of the year Haughey had also introduced a controversial family-planning bill, which was drawn up after exhaustive consultations with the Roman Catholic hierarchy and interested parties. The bill immediately came in for strong criticism in liberal circles, where critics took particular exception to provisions restricting the sale of contraceptives to married people and requiring a doctor's prescription for even non-medical contraceptives like condoms. Haughey described the bill as an Irish solution to an Irish problem, but four Fianna Fáil deputies still considered it to be too liberal and defied their party's three-line whip by abstaining in the Dáil vote. Three of them later apologised for this action, while the fourth, Haughey's Arms Trial adversary Jim Gibbons, was recalcitrant. As Minister for Agriculture, Gibbons could easily have arranged to have been away on business during the vote, and his absence would not have been noticed because his vote was not needed. Instead, he stayed around the Dáil until just before the vote was due to take place and then left. Afterwards he announced defiantly that he would not be supporting any stage of the bill.

Gibbons's abstention was the first time since the foundation of the state that any minister had publicly defied the government of which that minister was a member, and his action made a mockery of the constitutional concept of collective cabinet responsibility. Although the abstention was seen as a challenge to Lynch's authority, the Taoiseach took no action on the matter. The first nail had been driven into Lynch's political coffin; the man responsible for this situation was not Haughey but Gibbons, Haughey's implacable critic.

A public-opinion poll conducted during the controversy found that Haughey had the most favourable rating of all the members of the government, including the Taoiseach. Some 75 per cent expressed the opinion that Haughey had done well or very well in his ministry. Only 20 per cent were not favourably impressed with the job he was doing. On the other hand, George Colley had a dismal approval rating, of just 38 per cent, with 53 per cent feeling that he had been doing a poor job as Minister for Finance. Indeed, he had the worst rating of all, with the exception of Pádraig Faulkner, the Minister for Posts and Telegraphs, who was plagued at the time by a protracted postal strike.

Lynch's leadership was being undermined by a variety of factors. The behaviour of Gibbons raised questions about whether he had information dating back to the Arms Crisis that could be used against Lynch and about whether the Taoiseach was therefore afraid to enforce the kind of cabinet discipline envisaged by the expression 'collective responsibility' in Article 28 of the Constitution. The government had also been hit by a series of industrial disputes, farmer unrest over the abortive budget levy and massive uneasiness on the part of taxpayers, who felt that taxes were too high.

Public disillusionment with the government became apparent in June, when Fianna Fáil's vote dropped to 34.6 per cent in the European elections from the 50.6 per cent achieved two years earlier. This was the worst showing in the party's fifty-three-year history. As a result, nervous backbenchers began to look for a change of leadership.

The record twenty-seat majority which Fianna Fáil won in 1977 sowed the seeds of instability in the government, because the party was left holding a large number of marginal seats. Backbench deputies from these marginal constituencies became noticeably uneasy as things began to go wrong for the government.

Five deputies stood out in the movement for change. Dubbed 'the gang of five', they were Jackie Fahey, Tom McEllistrim, Sean Doherty, Mark Killilea and Albert Reynolds. They kept Haughey informed about their plans, but he did not play an active part in the group, which began a slow, relentless campaign to secure Haughey's election as Lynch's successor. They found enthusiastic supporters among deputies like Paddy Power, Síle de Valera, Charlie McCreevy, Sean Calleary and Bill Loughnane. The gang of five and their supporters started sniping openly at Lynch's leadership.

During a speech near Fermoy on 9 September 1979, Síle de Valera delivered a thinly veiled attack on Lynch's policy on Northern Ireland. She essentially accused him of deviating from the core values of Fianna Fáil. This was followed a month later by Tom McEllistrim complaining about the government's decision to allow the British military to overfly Irish territory.

There were rumours that Lynch was going to step down as Taoiseach; Haughey was an obvious contender to replace him. Some people were suggesting that President Patrick Hillery might be a contender for Taoiseach. If Hillery was to be appointed, however, he would have to step down as President and either run in one of the forthcoming by-elections in Cork or have one of Lynch's appointments to the Senate stand down so that the Taoiseach could appoint him to the Senate. No senator had even been elected Taoiseach, though, and it would have been extremely difficult for Hillery to have operated from the Senate. As a result, the idea was never likely to have been much more than a fancy. Nonetheless, some people suggested that supporters of Haughey deliberately spiked the possibility of Hillery seeking to become Taoiseach by spreading rumours that the President was having an affair.

It would have been ironic if these people had suggested that supporters of Haughey adopt such tactics, given that the minister's affair with Terry Keane was well-known in media circles. On 3 October 1979 Hillery called in the editors of the three Dublin national newspapers – Douglas Gageby of the *Irish Times*, Aidan Pender of the *Irish Independent* and Tim Pat Coogan of the *Irish Press* – and Wesley Boyd, the head of news at RTÉ, to ask them how to respond to an unfounded story, which was about to appear in *Hibernia*, suggesting that he was on the verge of resigning.

Hillery told them that he was not having an affair with another woman and that he was not about to resign. Gageby insisted that their conversation was not off-the-record, and the President agreed that it was not. They advised him to talk to their political correspondents, so a further briefing was arranged for that evening. The President read the assembled correspondents a brief statement at this briefing: 'In recent days it has come to my attention that there are rumours circulating as to the possibility of my resigning as President. There is absolutely no foundation for such rumours. I am not resigning.'

The correspondents had already been briefed by the editors, so Hillery was asked about the rumour that he was having an affair. 'I am not involved with another woman,' he said.

He was asked whether there were there any difficulties with his marriage. 'No,' he replied. 'There is not a problem there.'

'Why are you doing this?' Sean Duignan, RTÉ's political correspondent, asked. It seemed amazing to him that the President would deny something that had never been reported.

'Because I'm advised by the government,' the President replied.

It was already getting close to his deadline for the nine o'clock news, so Duignan had to leave early. As he departed, some of the President's people were waiting outside.

'What did he say?' one of them asked.

'He said he wasn't involved with another woman,' Duignan replied.

'Oh, Jesus!' was the last thing Duignan heard as he left the Áras. That probably typified the response around the country when he reported the story on the evening news. Most people were perplexed at why the President would deny a rumour that most people had never heard.

In his book *Garret: the Enigma,* Raymond Smith suggests that the rumour was designed to ensure that Hillery did not enter politics. The people responsible for it were supposedly afraid that he might resign and then successfully contest the leadership of Fianna Fáil. To do this, however, he would not only have had to resign as President but would also have had to persuade one of Lynch's nominees to the Senate to resign and then get the Taoiseach to nominate Hillery to the Senate, because he would have had to be a member of the parliamentary party to run for the leadership. Smith argued that there was a kind of precedent for such a series of events. After losing his seat in the general election of 1957, Sean Moylan had been appointed to the Senate by the Taoiseach, Éamon de Valera, who then appointed him Minister for Lands under a constitutional provision that permitted the appointment of up to two members of the Senate to the cabinet.

In his quest for ministerial talent, Lynch had offered a cabinet post to Senator Eoin Ryan, but the latter declined because to have accepted would have required him to sever his business connections. Lynch also once offered to appoint the Heinz executive and newspaper magnate A. J. F. O'Reilly to the Senate and then appoint him Minister for Agriculture, but O'Reilly declined the offer, probably for the same reason. O'Reilly later explained, however, that he did not believe there was enough room for himself and Haughey in Fianna Fáil. As he so graphically put it, the field was only big enough for one bull.

While appointing somebody to the cabinet from the Senate would have been easy enough, it was absurd to think that a Taoiseach could be elected from the Senate, where he would not even have a vote in the actual leadership contest. Neither could he function in the Dáil. As a result, Raymond Smith's acceptance of the rumour was more a reflection of his own imagination than of political reality. In any event, there was no shortage of absurd theories at the time.

The writer Gordon Thomas outlined a staggering plot that supposedly began in Moscow on the day the planned visit of Pope John Paul II to Ireland was announced in August 1979. Soviet intelligence was supposedly afraid that the Pope's visit could somehow lead to Ireland joining NATO in return for a deal ending partition. 'The KGB were playing for big stakes,' Thomas wrote. 'Their hope was to create the sort of dissension in Irish politics that would forever torpedo any question of unification.'

Were the KGB really so poorly informed that they thought that Ian Paisley and company would be so mesmerised by the presence of the Pope that they would drop all objections to Irish unity? The Soviets supposedly planted among the German press the rumour that Hillery was going to resign for 'personal reasons' as a way of destablising Irish politics and thus preventing a NATO deal. Anyone who believed that fanciful story, which was reproduced in the *Sunday Independent*, probably also suffered from an acute fear of reds under the bed. This theory was just as daft as the scenario under which Hillery would possibly become leader of Fianna Fáil.

In November 1979 Lynch suffered the humiliation of having Fianna Fáil lose two by-elections in his native Cork – including one in Cork city after he had campaigned there personally. His electoral magic seemed to have deserted him. The Cork setbacks were quickly followed by a further political attack by Bill Loughnane, who accused Lynch of having lied to the Dáil about the government's security cooperation with the British. The Taoiseach was in the United States at the time, and he called on Colley to have Loughnane expelled from the party. After a difficult parliamentary-party meeting, however, Colley had to settle for a compromise in which Loughnane merely withdrew his accusation.

'What the fuck are you doing over there? Don't you know Lynch is on the way out?' Haughey said to one of Lynch's entourage. 'Get back, the man is finished.'

The dissidents next began circulating a petition calling for Lynch to step down. Deputies were asked to sign without being allowed to see the other names on the list beforehand. Although more than twenty deputies signed, Lynch's opponents were still well short of a majority.

Had Lynch wished to stay on as Taoiseach, there was little doubt he could have continued, but he intended to go in a few weeks anyway. He no longer had much stomach for the party infighting that was going on, and he was persuaded by Colley and Martin O'Donoghue that then was an opportune time to retire, because Colley would be elected to succeed him.

Colley should, of course, have seen the writing on the wall for his own ambitions when he failed to secure the expulsion of

Loughnane. He would later contend, however, that he had been misled by some deputies, who, he said, had offered him their support while secretly intending to vote for Haughey. Colley was not the most perceptive of politicians.

On 5 December 1979 Lynch announced his impending resignation as Taoiseach. In an effort to prevent Haughey from organising a proper campaign, the meeting to select a successor was called with just two days' notice. From the outset the contest to succeed Lynch was seen as a straight fight between Haughey and Colley. Most members of the cabinet supported Colley, but the backbench deputies were terrified that his low standing in the polls might lead to a repetition of the party's poor showing during both the European elections and the recent Cork by-elections. Haughey, on the other hand, was riding high in the polls. He had been excluded from the government's major economic decisions but, as these had recently turned sour, it was a distinct advantage to him to be seen as an outsider within the cabinet.

Colley's people apparently thought that Haughey would be caught on the hop, but Haughey had been preparing for this opportunity for years. He was supremely confident, as there were few people on the backbenches for whom he had not done favours. Now he expected their backing in return. Sitting in his office on the eve of the vote he totted up his likely support and concluded that he would get fifty-eight votes to Colley's twenty-four.

'Do you know,' Sean Doherty exclaimed, 'you're the worst fucking judge of people I ever met.' It was going to be much tighter than Haughey had calculated.

Des O'Malley, Brian Lenihan and Michael O'Kennedy were mentioned as outsiders who might come into the reckoning in the event that the party could not decide between Haughey and

Colley. O'Malley, who would apparently have been Lynch's first choice, pledged his support for Colley, but Lenihan kept his own counsel. He was asked to nominate Haughey but refused to do so.

'I felt duty-bound to support Mr Haughey during this period,' he later wrote in his book *For the Record*. He realised that the time was not right for himself, so he tried twice to persuade Lynch to hold on for longer. The Taoiseach obviously wanted out, however. Lenihan privately admitted to his family that the choice between Haughey and Colley was a choice between a knave and a fool.

Haughey's people cleverly set his bandwagon rolling with some announcements timed to give him a boost at the right psychological moments. After Vivion de Valera, the former President's eldest son, declined to nominate Haughey, Ray MacSharry, Colley's parliamentary secretary, agreed to do the needful. With reporters waiting outside Leinster House to pick up scraps of news, MacSharry went out and announced rather stiffly, 'I will be proposing Haughey for leader tomorrow.' This apparently caught Colley completely by surprise. On the day of the vote Haughey telephoned Frank Dunlop that the Minister for Foreign Affairs, Michael O'Kennedy, would also be voting for him. 'Michael O'Kennedy is voting for me,' Haughey said, 'spread the word.'

By the time Colley's ministerial colleagues realised that he was in trouble, it was too late. They made frantic efforts to persuade deputies to support him by threatening to cut off funds already allocated for local projects. Garret Fitzgerald later related in his memoirs an extraordinary story about some backbench deputies who said they were being intimidated by Haughey's supporters and wished to know whether Fine Gael could 'do anything to ensure a genuine secret ballot'. He learned, however, that booths were provided so that deputies could vote in private.

One Fianna Fáil deputy later told Fitzgerald that 'despite the polling-booth arrangement some deputies had not felt that the privacy of the ballot had been ensured, because the voting papers, after having been marked at one or other end of the room, had to be deposited in a box near the centre of the room. Some deputies claimed they had been told that, unless they showed their papers to members of the Haughey camp as they walked back to deposit them in the box, they would be assumed to have voted for Colley and would be treated accordingly.'

Colley's supporters controlled the party mechanism at that stage, and if this could have happened without them being forewarned, they were even more out of touch with the rest of the party than anyone could have imagined. Colley had really outmanoeuvred himself by rushing the election.

Colley's supporters would later suggest that Haughey's people had hounded Lynch out of office, but this was grossly unfair. It was Gibbons who had undermined Lynch's authority and Colley and O'Donoghue who had persuaded him to resign early. 'Jack Lynch was a tough man,' Michael Hartnett, one of Haughey's campaign people, noted. 'He might allow you to do a lot of things, but once he had the ball, you could not take it from him. If Jack had wanted to cut us off at the knees, he could have done it with great ease!'

'I wasn't forced out,' Lynch told T. P. O'Mahony. 'I could have held on, and nobody could have forced me out if I didn't want to go.' Once he had decided to go, however, the struggle to succeed him turned into a contest between the government and its backbenchers. 'They were voting to save their jobs and we were voting to save our seats,' was how one backbench member summed up the division. With almost all the ministers behind Colley, backing Haughey gave ambitious backbench deputies the best opportunities of preferment. As a result, Haughey defeated Colley by forty-four votes to thirty-eight.

The ballot papers were immediately burned, and the resulting smoke set off the fire alarm in Leinster House. Some saw this as a portent of things to come, but Haughey's supporters were jubilant. 'Nixon's comeback may have been the greatest since Lazarus,' one of them said. 'But there is only one resurrection that beats Charlie's.'

At the press conference afterwards, members of the cabinet were conspicuously absent as Haughey surrounded himself with backbenchers. Reporters sought to question him on issues on which his silence over the years had been interpreted as a sign of ambivalence. In particular, they were interested in his attitude towards the Provisional IRA. He had not spoken out on this subject before, he said, because he did not have authority from the party to speak on the Northern Ireland question. Now he was unequivocal. 'I condemn the Provisional IRA and all their activities,' he declared.

Another reporter asked about the Arms Crisis, but this was a wound he had no intention of reopening. 'This is very much now a matter for history,' he replied. 'I am leaving it to the historians.'

John Bowman asked whether he would help the historians.

'I will write my own.'

While Fianna Fáil had a comfortable majority in the Dáil, the divisions within the party were so great that Haughey's election as Taoiseach could not be taken for granted. Colley and O'Donoghue had a long discussion with O'Malley as to whether they would vote for Haughey as Taoiseach.

'There were rumours of a split in Fianna Fáil,' Garret Fitzgerald noted in his memoirs. He admitted that it was 'possibly because of the rumours' that he did not begin to write his own Dáil speech on Haughey's nomination until the eleventh hour; at that stage he found the task very difficult. 'Charles Haughey and I had known each other since the autumn of 1943, when we had met while studying several first arts and commerce subjects together in UCD,' Fitzgerald noted. 'Our personal relationship had always been friendly, although not close.'

The Fine Gael leader's speech following Haughey's formal nomination for Taoiseach on 11 December 1979 was really a botched attempt to win the support of disillusioned Fianna Fáil deputies. 'I must speak not only for the Opposition but for many in Fianna Fáil who may not be free to say what they believe or to express their deep fears for the future of this country under the proposed leadership, people who are not free to reveal what they know and what led them to oppose this man with a commitment far beyond the normal,' Fitzgerald said. 'He comes with a flawed pedigree. His motives can be judged ultimately only by God, but we cannot ignore the fact that he differs from all his predecessors in that those motives have been and are widely impugned, most notably but by no means exclusively, by people within his own party, people close to him who have observed his actions for many years and who have made their human, interim judgement on him. They and others, both in and out of public life, have attributed to him an overweening ambition, which they do not see as a simple emanation of a desire to serve but rather as a wish to dominate, even to own, the state.'

Fitzgerald made no specific claims about Haughey's unsuitability for office. Instead, he presented vague, unsupported accusations and then cloaked them with the pretence that he could not be more specific 'for reasons that all in this House understand'. All remarks made in the Dáil are of course privileged, however, so there was no justification whatever for underhand insinuations. If he had reasons for saying what he did, he should have had the gumption to substantiate his assertions. 'It will be for the historians to judge whether placing my views bluntly on the record at that point was counter-productive or whether it may have contributed to my opponent's failure to secure an overall majority at any of the five subsequent general elections,' Fitzgerald argued years later.

Others, like John Kelly and Richie Ryan of Fine Gael, also made caustic comments, as did the long-time maverick Noel Browne, who described Haughey as a dreadful cross between former President Richard Nixon and the late Portuguese dictator Antonio Salazar. 'He has used his position unscrupulously in order to get where he is as a politician,' Browne told the Dáil. 'He has done anything to get power; does anybody believe that he will not do anything to keep power?'

Even back in 1932, when the political climate was still poisoned by the bitterness of the Civil War, Éamon de Valera had not been subjected to such abuse. Every seat in the public gallery and the press gallery were full as Haughey's nomination was being discussed. So were the Opposition seats. Across the floor Haughey sat by himself, with the remainder of the government seats completely empty. He was confronting his tormentors by himself and refusing to allow anyone to reply on his behalf.

Haughey's family, including his seventy-nine-year-old mother, were in the public gallery. She was reported to be 'greatly upset' by the proceedings, and the attacks were resented by the general public. Fitzgerald's own genial image was tarnished, and there was a great deal of sympathy for Haughey, even among people who had serious reservations about him. Some of them might have agreed with the sentiments, but they thought the occasion most inappropriate. He was elected Taoiseach by eighty-two votes to sixty-two.

# 10

## 'QUITE IRRESPONSIBLE IN MONEY MATTERS' TAOISEACH, 1979–1981

Following his election as Taoiseach, Haughey went to great lengths to bind up the wounds within Fianna Fáil by reappointing most of the outgoing cabinet members, even though the overwhelming majority of them had supported Colley. Of 'the gang of five', only Albert Reynolds was given a cabinet post. Nonetheless, Haughey rewarded the loyalty of the other four members of the 'gang' by appointing them Ministers of State.

Four ministers were dropped: Jim Gibbons, Martin O'Donoghue, Denis Gallagher and Bobby Molloy. O'Donoghue's Department for Economic Planning was scrapped, and its permanent secretary and strategic planners moved to the Department of the Taoiseach, which 'changed almost beyond recognition in the few months following Haughey's election as Taoiseach', according to the *Irish Times.* When Haughey took over, the department had only three units – the government secretariat, the Government Information Service and a private office staff – but this was rapidly expanded, with divisions to handle foreign affairs, economic and social policy and cultural and legal affairs and the creation of a personnel division. Within a year the Taoiseach's staff had more than doubled, and it would virtually triple by 1981 as Haughey gathered more of the decision-making functions closer to himself.

Colley was appointed Tánaiste and given a virtual veto over

the appointments of the Ministers for Defence and Justice, but he was far from placated. On 19 December 1979 he told Bruce Arnold of the *Irish Independent* that he and his colleagues believed that Haughey was 'dangerous, should have been blocked from the leadership and should be got out as fast as possible'.

Arnold would later contend that Haughey began subverting the country's Constitution from the moment he took over as Taoiseach, but Arnold's own biography of Haughey would seem to indicate that Colley was guilty of this behaviour. Colley had extracted unprecedented concessions from the Taoiseach for his support, but then, even though he was constitutionally pledged to the concept of collective cabinet responsibility, he essentially began conspiring against the government. This was an intolerable situation.

Earlier that day, the Tánaiste had told a cabinet meeting that Haughey had misrepresented him when he told the press conference after his election that Colley had pledged loyalty and support. In view of the campaign that Haughey's supporters had waged against Lynch, Colley indicated that he no longer felt bound to give loyalty to the Taoiseach.

'Must you?' Haughey asked, according to Bruce Arnold.

'Yes,' Colley replied.

The cabinet papers for this period are still closed, so one must assume that Arnold, a highly reputable journalist, was quoting accurately. Of course, this raises the further question of whether Colley was also guilty of a breach of cabinet confidentiality.

'Since Haughey had been campaigning, or supporting campaigns on his own behalf, for the previous five months,' Arnold argued, 'it was Haughey, not Colley, who had changed the rule about party loyalty within Fianna Fáil.' No evidence has ever been produced that Haughey was actively engaged in the campaign against Lynch. Charlie McCreevy, who later became one of Haughey's most outspoken critics, was adamant that the short fellow was never personally involved in this campaign.

At worst, Haughey would have been guilty of canvassing for the leadership of the party amongst members of the parliamentary party who elected the leader, whereas Colley went outside the party and sought to enlist the help of the press. Colley went public the next day, disavowing what Haughey had said. 'In my speech at the party meeting,' Colley explained, 'I referred to Mr Haughey's ability, capacity and flair and I wished him well in the enormous tasks he was taking on. I did not, however, use the words "loyalty" or "support", which he attributed to me.' Colley fully understood how, 'in the excitement and euphoria' of victory, Haughey had misunderstood him, but now the Tánaiste was setting the record straight. As far as he was concerned the traditional loyalty normally given to the leader of the party had been withheld from Lynch, and it was now legitimate to withhold 'loyalty to, and support for, the elected leader'.

He had made these views clear to Haughey before the cabinet was formed, he said. Since then he had told the Taoiseach that he intended to set the record straight. As far as he was concerned the rule henceforth would be that 'the Taoiseach is entitled to our conscientious and diligent support in all his efforts in the national interest.'

When Geraldine Kennedy of the *Irish Times* asked whether he expected the Taoiseach to seek his resignation, Colley responded rather indifferently. 'I couldn't say what I would expect,' he replied. 'Obviously, if I were asked to resign, it would be a matter for the Taoiseach. It is not for me to say.'

These were extraordinary remarks for any deputy leader to make barely a week into the life of a new government. Naturally they provoked an immediate political crisis. The next day

Haughey summoned Colley into his office. 'Before he agreed to join the government the Tánaiste expressed to me the views which he has now stated publicly,' the Taoiseach explained, in a statement to the press. 'Following our discussion, he has assured me of his full support and loyalty in his office as Tánaiste and as a member of the government.' That was the end of the matter.

As a member of the government since 1977, Haughey was collectively responsible for what had happened to the economy, but he still managed to dissociate himself from the economic difficulties facing the country. On 10 January 1980 he delivered a national address on RTÉ television. 'As a community,' he said, 'we have been living at a rate which is simply not justified by the amount of goods and services we are producing. To make up the difference we have been borrowing enormous amounts of money, borrowing at a rate which just cannot continue.' Yet he made no precise suggestions as to how he intended to tackle the problem.

It was ironic that he should be lecturing people about living beyond their means, because he had himself been spending at a rate that bore little relationship to his income. For the past decade the Allied Irish Bank had been trying to rein in his personal spending. By September 1971, when he was only a backbencher, he personally owed the bank £244,000. He would never be able to pay off the debt on a politician's salary. He agreed to pay off £101,000 by selling £23,000 worth of shares in Tara Mines and Whim Creek, along with £20,000 worth of cattle and his interest in Simmonstown Stud, which was expected to raise £48,000. He would raise the other £10,000 by selling 'other odds and ends,' he said. He told the bank that he was trying to sell the farm he owned in Ashbourne, County Meath, for £100,000.

As he had the assets to cover his bank debts, Haughey viewed his financial difficulties as a mere cash flow problem. The bank fixed his credit limit at £250,000, subject to him halving that debt in three months and clearing it altogether in six months. In June 1972 he obtained a further loan of £100,000 by putting up the Ashbourne farm as security, but this brought his debt down only to £153,000, and by December 1973 he owed £283,000.

'Mr Haughey is quite irresponsible in money matters,' J. J. McAuliffe, the AIB regional manager, wrote the following month. 'He cannot be controlled on a running account. His affairs can only deteriorate further.' He had bought the island of Innishvicillaun off the Kerry coast, where he planned to build a summer home, even though this was an extremely costly venture because most of the material had to be carried to the island by helicopter.

By that September his bank manager, Michael Phelan, was calling on the bank to take action on the account. 'Despite the unattractiveness of the proposition, Mr Phelan recommends sanctions, bearing in mind the likelihood of Mr Haughey being a man of influence in the future,' one internal bank memorandum read. A year later the bank noted that Haughey 'mentioned that the bank did not make use of his influential position and he indicated that he would be more than willing to assist the bank in directing new business, etc.'

In October 1976 the bank asked Haughey to surrender his chequebook, but he refused and 'became quite vicious', according to a bank report. It was the classic case of the bully. The bank had effectively shown that it was afraid to bounce his cheques – as it would do with those of most other customers in his circumstances – so he became aggressive when they asked for his chequebook. Then he had the audacity to request an 'accommodation of up to £350,000' from the bank. This was granted, but by the following April he was being warned, according to bank records, that 'if he failed to honour his undertaking we would be forced to dishonour his cheques.'

Liam St John Devlin, the chief executive of AIB, concluded, however, that it would be impractical to bounce Haughey's cheques because 'he was a popular and powerful leader and a potential Taoiseach'. The most senior people in AIB already had doubts as to whether the bank would ever get its money back. As of 1976 the interest that Haughey owed was being recorded in a suspense account, which meant that the officials suspected it would never be paid.

Once he got back into government in 1977 Haughey's financial situation worsened further. By June 1978 he owed the bank £445,282. The bank was actually charging him penal interest in the hope that he would seek better terms from another bank and clear off his debt with AIB. In July 1979 his bank manager, Michael Phelan, concluded that Haughey obviously 'does not believe the bank will force a confrontation with him because of his position.'

'The account appears to be out of control,' Phelan wrote the following month. Barely three months later, Haughey became Taoiseach, and suddenly the same manager adopted an almost sycophantic approach towards him. 'It gives me great pleasure to convey to you my warmest congratulations on your election to the high offices of leader of Fianna Fáil and Taoiseach and to offer you my sincere good wishes for success in both,' Phelan wrote to him. 'To say the task you have taken on is daunting is an understatement but I have every faith in your ability to succeed in restoring confidence in this little nation.'

AIB had already virtually despaired of Haughey's ability to handle his indebtedness, however. He now owed the bank £1.1

million and his accountant, Des Traynor, who had worked with Harry Boland, set about trying to straighten out the short fellow's finances. Haughey himself turned to Patrick Gallagher for help. Gallagher believed that his father, Matt, who had died in 1974, had deliberately helped make Haughey a rich man by advising him to buy the house and lands in Raheny for £13,000 in the 1950s; Haughey then sold him the property a decade later for over £200,000, enabling him to purchase Abbeville estate in Kinsealy.

The Gallagher deal had been a big election issue in 1969. Planning permission would inevitably be granted for this area once Ireland began to lift itself out of the economic depression it had suffered in the 1950s, prior to the advent of Sean Lemass to power. Dublin was obviously going to spread out and there would have been a demand to build on the land that Haughey bought, regardless of who owned it. Gallagher's advice was not particularly inspired, but Haughey, when he purchased the land, had the advantage of knowing that he had an eventual buyer. By hanging on to the property for a decade, he saw its value appreciate greatly. Some of his opponents tried to suggest that there was something immoral about the profit he made on the whole venture; all profits were immoral to the socialists – except the ones they made themselves, of course.

Matt Gallagher had made a small fortune in wartime Britain. With his brothers he had created a labyrinth of building, mining and plant-hire companies. One of his brothers was deaf and the others used him to avoid conscription. When any of them were called for military service, the deaf brother would report for induction using his brother's name. Being deaf, he was naturally rejected, and nobody outside the family was any the wiser. If the British had known, they would probably have considered such behaviour unpatriotic, but the Gallaghers were Irish. It was barely twenty years since the Black and Tans had been rampaging about Ireland, and most Irish people had had their fill of British patriotism. Nevertheless Matt Gallagher did have a sense of native patriotism.

After the Republic was declared in 1949, he had returned to Ireland and had begun building houses, in both the public and private sectors. In the 1950s there was a great deal of housing deprivation in urban Ireland, with several families often living in a single tenement. He had then branched out into pubs, retailing and banking. He had helped form *Taca* and bring other builders, architects, accountants and business people in general together in a kind of great crusade to build the nation.

'Fianna Fáil was good for builders, and builders were good for Fianna Fáil,' Patrick Gallagher noted. 'There was nothing wrong with that.' In short, Matt Gallagher supported Fianna Fáil because he believed the party was best for the construction industry and thus best for himself and his family. It so happened that he also believed that Haughey was the coming man in Fianna Fáil. He saw himself as part of a great effort to lift Ireland out of its depression so that he, his family and the Irish people as a whole could enjoy a higher quality of life.

'Haughey was financed in order to create the environment which the Anglo-Irish had enjoyed and that we as a people could never aspire to,' according to Patrick Gallagher, who believed that his father saw the construction of a modern Ireland as a great patriotic enterprise. He recalled seeing Donogh O'Malley hugging his father in Cruise's Hotel in Limerick when the bill establishing free secondary education was pushed through the Dáil. 'O'Malley told my father it was a great victory but could sound the death knell for Fianna Fáil, as the younger people would now be educated and their expectations would rise.'

In the aftermath of the Arms Crisis Matt Gallagher, and

later Patrick, supplied the cars which Haughey used on the chicken-and-chip circuit during the 1970s as he rehabilitated himself within Fianna Fáil and laid the groundwork for his successful assault on the leadership. Now that he had achieved his ambition, Haughey turned to Patrick Gallagher for help. On Sunday afternoon, 7 December, he invited Gallagher to come out to Kinsealy to help him out of his financial mess.

'What is the mess?' the twenty-six-year-old Patrick asked.

'£750,000,' replied Haughey.

'Can you get someone to raise half of it?'

Haughey affirmed.

'Say no more, I'll sort it out with Des Traynor,' Gallagher said. He admitted later that his motive in helping Haughey was partly selfish: after all, he was talking to the man who was about to become Taoiseach. 'I was naive enough when I was younger to think I could get a favour. But not a thing. You might be introduced to people who could help, but he was not slow to tell you to go and sort out your own business.'

Anybody who thinks that they could buy favours from Haughey does not know the man, according to Terry Keane. 'They don't understand Charlie's character,' Keane emphasised. Haughey would think the money was his by right. 'It would be like the three wise men putting gold, frankincense and myrrh in front of the Saviour; [he felt] he would have no obligation because [it was] a gift,' she argued.

Even if Haughey had intended to do favours for some of his building and property friends, Colley was determined to frustrate any effort to help those people. John Byrne, a Kerryman who had made his money in construction and Irish dance halls in Britain after the Second World War, returned to Ireland in the Lemass era, like Matt Gallagher, and built a number of prominent buildings, including O'Connell Bridge House, D'Olier House and Parnell House. He leased a great deal of office space to the state, but Colley, as Minister for Finance, blocked any further deals with Byrne, and he enlisted the help of Garret Fitzgerald, the leader of Fine Gael, to get Dublin County Council to block planning permission for any development on what had been Baldoyle Racecourse, which had been bought by Byrne in the 1970s. Certainly in this instance, Byrne's friendship with Haughey was a distinct handicap.

Gallagher's company provided £300,000 as a non-refundable deposit on thirty-five acres of land at the Kinsealy estate, which he would buy for £1.225 million. Two years later Merchant Banking and the Gallagher Group, worth an estimated £70 million, were in liquidation and any claim on the lands at Kinsealy was deemed unrecoverable by the receiver. Even though Haughey was Taoiseach, Gallagher went to jail in Northern Ireland for financial irregularities.

Haughey had talks with his accountant Des Traynor and it was agreed 'that there was only one way to deal with the matter and that was to clear the debt totally'. Traynor made a deal with the bank that Haughey would pay £750,000 by mid-February 1980 and promise to pay £110,000 later, and that the remainder of the debt would be written off. The first figure amounted to all the money he had actually borrowed and a little of the interest, while the £110,000 covered only interest, which was to be cleared as a matter of honour, without any further interest being added.

There were rumours that AIB had written off a large chunk of a loan for Haughey, but nobody was prepared to go on the record with the story, so, in view of the country's stringent libel laws, the media were not in a position to report it. The Opposition attacks on Haughey on the day of his election as Taoiseach had backfired badly and generated a good deal of sympathy for him in the press. For the next two months he enjoyed a virtual honeymoon with the media. While some of Haughey's old enemies were more implacable than ever, he was the 'media's darling'. His victory was clearly welcomed by prestigious editors like Douglas Gageby of the *Irish Times*, Tim Pat Coogan of the *Irish Press* and Michael Hand of the *Sunday Independent*, as well as Vincent Browne of *Magill* magazine.

Geraldine Kennedy of the *Irish Times* went to Frank Dunlop, who had remained on as Government Press Secretary, and told him that on the night of the election count in 1977 Haughey had promised to give her his first interview as Taoiseach. Haughey admitted this to Dunlop but explained that giving her the interview might offend those who had been particularly supportive of him. Haughey therefore decided that he would have to renege on his promise – but that he would tell Kennedy to her face.

Dunlop tried to ensure that Kennedy was let down gently by warning her not to be disappointed – that the Taoiseach felt compelled to go back on his promise but would tell her so personally. When Haughey explained that giving her an exclusive interview would offend other journalists, she thanked him for having the courtesy to tell her to her face and added that she was not really surprised. It was what she had come to expect from what colleagues had been telling her. Haughey asked what they had been saying. 'That you're a liar,' she replied.

Haughey was taken aback. He was not about to confirm what his enemies in the press thought about him, so he agreed to give her his first formal interview after all. For all his combativeness over the years, it would become apparent in the following months and years that he was really a classic bully. When confronted, he frequently backed down, as he demonstrated with both Colley and Kennedy.

The promised interview turned sour when Kennedy asked questions about the Arms Crisis. Haughey threatened to terminate the proceedings if she persisted with her line of questioning. She wrote about this in her report, but her editor excised that material. The seeds of future discord had been sown. She had seen Haughey close up and had not been impressed, while his distrust of journalists was probably strengthened by what he would have seen as the defection of a previous admirer. In the following weeks he repeatedly put off requests for interviews without actually refusing them. As a result, the requests built up to the point where there were over 250 applications from journalists to interview him.

In May 1980, to mark the tenth anniversary of the Arms Crisis, Vincent Browne of *Magill* magazine began a series of articles that reopened the whole affair. Based largely on the reminiscences of Peter Berry, the late Secretary of the Department of Justice, who had died in 1975, they provided an extraordinary insight into the controversial events of the Arms Crisis. A number of people tried to block publication of the articles by threatening to sue the publisher, distributors and sellers of the magazine. Although publication was temporarily delayed by these efforts, the controversy helped generate public curiosity, and the issues of *Magill* carrying the Berry story were in great demand. As a result, Haughey's role in the crisis became the focus of public attention and the Dáil held another debate on the Arms Crisis.

Although the *Magill* articles raised serious questions about Haughey's conduct, Berry had already told the court virtually all he knew about Haughey's involvement in the affair during the two Arms Trials. Berry's startling posthumous disclosures were thus probably more damaging to some of Haughey's critics within Fianna Fáil than they were to the Taoiseach himself.

Browne was actually quite restrained in his own criticism of Haughey's alleged activities. In fact, he concluded that Haughey 'could easily and justifiably defend what he did at the time' but had been so anxious to put the whole affair behind him that he glided over the facts. Thus Browne tended to be more critical of the activities of others. 'While Mr Haughey certainly behaved improperly,' the editor concluded, 'he was and has been innocent of the more colourful charges that have been laid against him concerning the crisis. It can be argued with some force that he was more a victim of the Arms Crisis than anything else.'

Even a vociferous opponent of Haughey like John Kelly of Fine Gael had concluded that the Taoiseach's alleged involvement in gun-running back in 1970 could have been justified when seen in the perspective of the period rather than in the light of the subsequent murderous campaign conducted by the Provisional IRA. It should be remembered that, at the time of the crisis, prominent nationalists were clamouring for guns to defend themselves.

In the course of the *Magill* articles, which appeared in four successive issues of the magazine, Browne wrote that Kevin Boland had tried to persuade Haughey to secure cabinet approval for the planned importation of arms in March 1970. If this conversation took place, there was no way that it could be squared with Haughey's Arms Trial testimony that he believed that the importation was totally proper and that he was unaware that guns were involved. Boland publicly confirmed this. Of course, this would not alter the fact that Haughey's actions prior to his arrest were justifiable. It was his actions following his arrest that were most open to question.

Some of the *Magill* disclosures raised questions about the conduct of others, particularly Jack Lynch and his Minister for Justice, Des O'Malley. The articles demonstrated conclusively that, despite assertions to the contrary, Lynch had been informed of Captain Kelly's activities before 20 April 1970. Moreover, Gibbons now publicly admitted that in 'October–November 1969' he had informed the Taoiseach 'that there were questionable activities on the part of certain members of the government making contact with people they should not make contact with'. Berry's account also gave rise to serious questions about O'Malley's judgment in connection with his private meeting with Haughey less than a fortnight before the Arms Trial was due to begin.

Having initially welcomed Haughey's election as Taoiseach, Browne gradually became quite critical of him because he seemed suddenly to become uncharacteristically indecisive. It was not that the new Taoiseach was confused about the best course to follow but that he lacked the political courage to stand by his convictions when faced with opposition. This vacillation was apparent on the political, economic and diplomatic fronts.

Politically, for instance, Haughey ignored Colley's extraordinary renunciation of loyalty and support. In relation to economics, he identified serious problems confronting the country but then did little about them. He gave no details on the night of his television address of how he hoped to cope with the economic problems, but in the following months his government indicated it would be restricting the free bus service to rural schoolchildren and limiting wage increases in the public sector. The government also announced that a resource tax would be introduced in order to get farmers to bear a fairer share of the tax burden; under political pressure, however, these proposals were quickly abandoned. The most dramatic capitulation was on the public-service pay issue: the government conceded a staggering 34 per cent increase. As a result of this and other extravagant policies, the budget deficit ended up more than 50 per cent over target.

At the Fianna Fáil ard-fheis on 16 February 1980, Haughey again mentioned that the country was living beyond its means, as borrowing was out of control. 'It can be got under control if we follow the old-fashioned, sensible doctrine of living within our means.' Nonetheless, he said that his government's 'first priority' was to end partition. To further this aim, he intended to enlist international help to put diplomatic pressure on the British. As far as he was concerned, Northern Ireland had failed as a political entity and a new beginning was therefore needed. It was noteworthy, however, that he did not call on the British to announce their intention to withdraw from the area. Rather, he asked them to declare 'their interest in encouraging the unity of Ireland by agreement and in peace'. His policy would be to seek the development of 'some new free and open arrangement for which Irishmen and women, on their own, without a British presence but with active British goodwill, will manage the affairs of the whole of Ireland in a constructive partnership with the European community,' he explained.

Haughey went to London to meet Prime Minister Thatcher in May. His chances of advancing his aims in relation to Northern Ireland seemed remote from the outset because, on the eve of their meeting, Thatcher told the House of Commons that the constitutional affairs of Northern Ireland were 'a matter for the people of Northern Ireland, this government and this Parliament and no one else'. In short, she was saying in advance that Northern Ireland was none of Haughey's business. Nevertheless, the two leaders got on quite well together the next day. He brought her a silver Georgian teapot as a present, and she was apparently surprised by his charm. One member of her cabinet later told friends 'he was sure he detected a "sexual" attraction [in Thatcher] for the smallish, rather worse-for-wear Irishman.'

'We had a general and friendly discussion of the scene in Northern Ireland,' Thatcher wrote in her memoirs. 'He kept on drawing the parallel, which seemed to me an unconvincing one, between the solution I had found to the Rhodesian problem and the approach to be pursued in Northern Ireland. Whether this was Irish blarney or calculated flattery I am not sure.'

After their meeting the two leaders issued a joint communiqué emphasising that they had decided to have regular meetings in order to develop 'new and closer political cooperation between our two countries'. The most significant aspect of the communiqué was their agreement that 'any change in the constitutional status of Northern Ireland would only come about with the consent of a majority of the people of Northern Ireland.'

Part of Haughey's overall plan was to wage an international campaign to have diplomatic pressure exerted on the British government to work for a settlement to the Northern question. The Irish-American community had traditionally been the Dublin government's most influential supporter, but Irish-Americans were bitterly divided on the Ulster question, with a large, vocal and well-organised minority supporting the campaign of the Provisional IRA. Ever since his appointment as Irish Ambassador to the United States in 1978, Sean Donlon had sought to isolate these militants, and in the process he fell foul of them and organisations they controlled, like Noraid, the Irish National Caucus and the Ancient Order of Hibernians.

Haughey therefore decided to replace Donlon with someone who could work with all the Irish-American elements so that the Irish-American voice could be consolidated behind his plans for an Irish settlement. He arranged for Donlon to be transferred to the United Nations, but word of the move was leaked and some powerful voices were raised about it in Washington, where Donlon was held in high esteem by influential Irish-American political figures like Thomas 'Tip' O'Neill, the Speaker of the House of Representatives, Senators Edward Kennedy of Massachusetts and Daniel Patrick Moynihan of New York, Governor Hugh Carey of New York and former Governor of California Ronald Reagan, who was then engaged in his successful bid for the presidency. Faced with opposition from such influential people, Haughey backed down and Donlon was allowed to remain in his Washington post.

With his first year as Taoiseach coming to a close, Haughey desperately needed some kind of real achievement. He was obviously indebted for his reinstatement within Fianna Fáil to the so-called green wing of the party, which wanted the government to take a more active part in seeking a solution to the Northern problem. The whole question took on added significance on 26 October 1980, when seven republican prisoners went on hunger strike as part of their H-Block protest for what amounted to political status. Little over a week later, Haughey watched aghast from a by-election platform in Letterkenny, County Donegal, as Síle de Valera revived memories of her Fermoy speech by denouncing 'Mrs Thatcher's lack of compassion' and her 'callous, unfeeling and self-righteous statements'.

Although Haughey made no reference to Síle de Valera's speech during his own address moments later, he was obviously taken aback by it. Immediately after the rally, he and some senior colleagues retired to a local hotel to discuss it. About an hour later Ray MacSharry, as director of elections, issued a statement to the press emphasising that neither the Taoiseach nor any member of the government had seen her script in advance and that her remarks had not reflected the views of the government.

Síle de Valera later expressed surprise at the statement dissociating the party from her remarks. Following her Fermoy speech in 1977, Lynch had banned her from making any public comments on the Northern situation, she said, but Haughey lifted this ban when he became Taoiseach. 'Mr Haughey told me when he assumed office that the ban no longer applied,' she explained. 'I was working under the assumption that there was no ban when I spoke in Letterkenny.'

Privately, Haughey may well have agreed with her sentiments, but he clearly did not like her timing. Since he was beside her on the platform when she made the remarks, it would appear as if he had been openly endorsing what she said unless he issued some kind of repudiation of her comments. He was anxious to dissociate himself from her remarks because he did not want them to impair his relations with the British Prime Minister before their next meeting.

The two leaders' private meeting in Luxembourg during the European summit on 1 December concentrated heavily on the hunger-strike issue. 'He urged me to find some face-saving device which would allow the strikers to end their fast, though he said that he fully accepted that political status was out of the question,' Thatcher noted. 'There was nothing left to give,' she wrote. 'There would be no more concessions under duress.'

They met again in Dublin Castle the following week. Thatcher was accompanied to Dublin by Chancellor of the Exchequer Geoffrey Howe, Foreign Secretary Lord Carrington and Secretary of State for Northern Ireland Humphrey Atkins. The inclusion of Carrington gave rise to speculation, because he had recently played a major role in changing the direction of Britain's Rhodesian policy. Prompted by the Foreign Secretary, Thatcher had agreed to a settlement in Rhodesia which brought Robert Mugabe, one of the guerrilla leaders, to power. Haughey, with his almost messianic belief in his own abilities, seemed to think he had a real chance of persuading the British to settle the Irish question once and for all.

The Taoiseach was accompanied by Brian Lenihan and Michael O'Kennedy, his Ministers for Foreign Affairs and Finance, respectively. The two ministers were included in most of the day-long discussions but not in the private meeting between Haughey and Thatcher, which lasted an hour and a quarter.

Afterwards, the two leaders issued a joint communiqué describing their talks as 'extremely constructive and significant'. In relation to Northern Ireland, they 'accepted the need to bring forward policies and proposals to achieve peace, reconciliation and stability.' In an effort to advance these aims, they agreed to promote 'the further development of the unique relationship between the two countries' by commissioning 'joint studies covering a range of issues, including possible new institutional structures, citizenship rights, security matters, economic cooperation and measures to encourage mutual understanding'. Thatcher complained later that she 'did not involve myself closely enough in the drafting of the communiqué and, as a result, allowed through the statement that Mr Haughey and I would devote our next meeting in London "to special consideration of the totality of relationships within these islands".'

Some hundred reporters from around the world were present at a press conference afterwards, at which Haughey explained that there had been 'an historic breakthrough' – on which he was not, however, prepared to elaborate publicly. Instead, he repeatedly referred the reporters to the text of the communiqué. He was more forthcoming immediately afterwards, however, in an off-the-record briefing for Dublin political correspondents. According to Bruce Arnold, the Taoiseach indicated 'by implication and innuendo' that the British leader had agreed that the joint studies could reconsider Northern Ireland's whole constitutional position; he also anticipated an early end to partition. Moreover,

Lenihan said in an RTÉ interview that the partition question was on the verge of being resolved.

The British Prime Minister promptly denied that there was any intention of altering the constitutional position of Northern Ireland. 'There had of course been no such thing,' she noted in her memoirs. 'But the damage had been done and it was a red rag to the unionist bull.'

Ian Paisley, the Democratic Unionist leader, exploited unionist unease by taking to what he called the 'Carson Trail' in order to demonstrate the intensity of unionist opposition to constitutional change. A series of demonstrations was organised throughout the Six Counties to rail against the joint studies. Paisley vented his spleen particularly against Haughey, a long-standing hate figure among unionists. The DUP leader talked about the ancestors of the unionist people cutting 'civilisation out of the bogs and meadows of this country while Mr Haughey's ancestors were wearing pig skins and living in caves'. At a Newtownards rally he conjured up a picture of the Taoiseach with 'a green baton dripping with blood' in one hand and 'a noose specially prepared for the Protestants of Ulster in the other'.

No doubt the bitterness with which Paisley and his followers reacted to the outcome of the Dublin Castle summit encouraged some optimism in nationalist circles. It was noteworthy that the H-Block hunger strike was called off within ten days. Whether the exaggerated significance attached to the recent summit had encouraged those advising the hunger strikers to engage in some wishful thinking is a matter for speculation, but in time it would become apparent that Haughey and his people had grossly oversold the significance of the summit.

Opposition leaders criticised the Taoiseach for not being more specific about his talks. According to Frank Cluskey, leader of the Labour Party, 'evasiveness' was the single most distinguishing characteristic of the government. 'Everything has come under the heading of confidentiality and secrecy,' he argued. Fitzgerald complained that the government seemed to be trying to bring about Irish unity without the prior consent of the majority of the people of Northern Island; he believed this approach was a recipe for civil war.

Haughey made no apologies for the secrecy surrounding the joint studies. 'To suggest that permanent officials engaged in such studies should try to carry out their task in the full glare of publicity is nonsense,' he later declared. 'We were accused of trying to settle matters over the heads of the people of Northern Ireland when in fact we were seeking to set up a political framework in which they could participate without prejudice to their principles.' At the time, however, he allowed his people to encourage the belief that he was close to a settlement that would end partition, notwithstanding Paisley's ranting.

There was considerable speculation that the joint studies on security matters were aimed at drawing up details of an Anglo-Irish defensive pact which Haughey would sign in return for the ending of partition. This, of course, would undermine the country's avowed neutrality. Joseph Carroll, author of *Ireland in the War Years, 1939-1945*, observed that there was actually 'more heated debate about Ireland's neutrality outside the Dáil during 1981 than during the years of the Second World War'. Although Haughey denied 'unequivocally' that his government was 'discussing or negotiating any kind of secret agreement on defence with Britain or with any other country or group of countries', the speculation continued. This speculation was fuelled by the misgivings voiced by Fitzgerald, together with the Taoiseach's own admission that, if partition were ended, his government 'would of course have to review what would be the most appropriate defence arrangements for the island as a whole'. He also reiterated his own long-standing conviction that the country should align completely with its European partners once the EEC developed 'into a full political union'.

'We could not, and would not wish to, opt out of the obligations and aims inherent in the achievement of the ideal of European unity,' he emphasised. Fitzgerald must have known that Irish neutrality was, despite appearances, never much more than notional: the de Valera government secretly gave the Allies virtually all the help it could. This included allowing Irish diplomats in occupied Europe to be used as American spies. In the circumstances, the country's policy should more appropriately have been described as non-belligerency rather than neutrality. So why did the Fine Gael leader make a fuss about the joint studies on security being a threat to the country's supposed neutrality?

Haughey later contended that Fitzgerald 'was merely pandering to those who do not want the studies to succeed anyway'. The charge was reminiscent of one made in the 1930s by de Valera, who accused the Fine Gael leadership of deliberately trying to frustrate his efforts to negotiate an Anglo-Irish agreement. This charge, of virtually treasonous behaviour, was not without substance. Official documents released in line with Britain's thirty-year secrecy rule contain clear evidence that Fine Gael leaders – no doubt convinced that they were acting in the country's best interest – secretly pleaded with the British not to conclude an agreement with de Valera because it would enhance his reputation and thereby destroy Fine Gael politically. In 1981 Haughey seemed to think that history was repeating itself.

In the aftermath of the Dublin Castle summit the Taoiseach was clearly looking towards an early election, even though the existing Dáil still had eighteen months to run. In January 1981 the government introduced a budget which did not reflect the country's economic plight. Fianna Fáil was due to have its ard-fheis in mid-February, and there was speculation that Haughey would use the occasion to prepare the ground for him to call a general election. On the eve of his planned ard-fheis speech, however, disaster struck, in the form of the Stardust tragedy, in which forty-eight young people were killed in a fire at a discotheque in the Taoiseach's own Artane constituency. In view of the magnitude of the disaster, the remainder of the ard-fheis was postponed. When it was reconvened in April, Haughey referred in his presidential address to 'ending the age-old problem of partition'. 'A year from this ard-fheis, if we persevere faithfully,' he said, 'we may begin to see in a clearer light the end of the road on which we have set out.'

By this time, however, the political climate had already been poisoned by the second H-Block hunger strike, which began on 1 March 1981. This hunger strike, in support of the same demands as the one that had been called off in December, received massive international publicity following the election to Westminster of one of the men involved, Bobby Sands. The hunger strikers vowed to fast to death, and other colleagues pledged to replace them on the fast until their demands were met. Although Sands expected that Haughey would be compelled to support the hunger strikers' demands publicly, the Taoiseach refused to be pressurised, even after Sands and his colleagues began to die. Haughey met with members of the family of a number of the hunger strikers. He tried to get the European Commission for Human Rights involved on behalf of Bobby Sands, but first he needed a formal complaint from a member of the Sands family. He met the hunger striker's mother and his sister Marcella, who signed the document making the formal complaint that the British were violating her brother's right to life and protesting that he was receiving inhuman treatment and was being denied the right of access to his constituents.

Signing the document was a measure of Marcella's desperation, but she had little time for Haughey, whom she had been referring to as '*Amadon*' (a corruption of the Irish for 'fool') in her coded letters. The European Commission for Human Rights sent two representatives to Belfast to investigate the matter, but Sands refused to met them as he did not want to be associated with the complaint.

Privately, Haughey indicated to the families of a couple of other hunger strikers that he would like to be helpful but did not see how he could be of assistance. 'What can I do?' he asked Elizabeth O'Hara, the sister of hunger striker Patsy O'Hara.

She replied that he should ask Thatcher to implement the five demands that had been made by the prisoner, but he said it would do no good to become embroiled in a propaganda battle. She had come with Teresa and Malachy McCreesh, the sister and brother of hunger striker Ray McCreesh. The three of them had a number of meetings with Haughey. When Liz asked point-blank whether he believed in the five demands, he did not answer her question.

Back in 1940, when Éamon de Valera was confronted with a hunger strike involving Jack Plunkett, the brother of one of the executed leaders of the 1916 Easter Rebellion, and Tomás MacCurtain, the son of the Lord Mayor of Cork who had been murdered by the Crown police in 1920, the Taoiseach emphasised that there would be no concessions to hunger strikers, no matter how prominent they were. As a result, he allowed three of the hunger strikers, including Sean McCaughey, the one-time chief of staff of the IRA, to die during the 1940s. De Valera's hard line on hunger strikes had been government policy ever since.

'I can't do anything at this point,' Haughey told Liz O'Hara. She said the Taoiseach did try to reassure them, however.

'Elizabeth, I promise you that Raymond McCreesh and your brother will not die,' Haughey said. During her fourth meeting with the Taoiseach, he asked her 'to ask Patsy to suspend his hunger strike forthwith and to put a formal complaint to the Human Rights Commission.' Liz O'Hara was indignant. She said she had never thought a Taoiseach would ask her to take away her brother's pride, and she told him that the next time she talked to a Taoiseach she hoped it would be somebody else.

On 21 May 1981 Haughey called a general election for exactly three weeks' time, making the campaign the shortest it could be by law. Some of those connected with the hunger strikers believed the date was chosen because, if the hunger strike was still on, the first group would be dead and none of their replacements would yet be nearing death. Although this may well have been the main consideration in choosing the election date, other factors undoubtedly played a greater part in Haughey's decision to call the election while the mandate of the existing Dáil still had a year to run.

Firstly, Fianna Fáil's private polls were indicating that the party was in good standing with the electorate, which tended to be rather volatile at the time. In early March 1981, for instance, Fianna Fáil had enjoyed a comfortable lead over the combined opposition parties. This situation was reversed during April, but on the day after Haughey called the election an IMS poll detected a massive swing back to Fianna Fáil, which enjoyed a 17 per cent lead over Fine Gael, with the Labour Party a further 19 per cent behind. When the 15 per cent who had not made up their minds on how to vote were excluded, the poll estimated that Fianna Fáil would get 52 per cent of the vote – an even greater share than that which gave the party its landslide victory in 1977. Secondly, Haughey's own position had improved dramatically. In the April poll he had trailed the Fine Gael leader by 10 per cent as the preferred choice for Taoiseach, but in the latest poll he led Fitzgerald by 43 to 40 per cent.

An even more important consideration in calling the election at that time were financial pressures. A considerable amount of the money allocated for 1981 had already been spent, and it would be necessary for the government to introduce legislation to secure supplementary funding in the near future. This would almost inevitably lead to increased taxes – which were unlikely to be popular with the electorate.

The government engaged in an orgy of public spending in the run-up to the election. Haughey was handling the country's finances in the same cavalier fashion that he handled his own. 'One senior Fianna Fáil figure contesting a marginal constituency recalls being contacted by the Taoiseach's Department in the early days of the campaign and being told to announce spending programmes of up to £3 million in his constituency,' the journalist Stephen Collins wrote. 'When he queried the request he was ordered to come up with a list of projects and to make announcements pledging government funding. Similar tactics were adopted in other constituencies.'

Tom McEllistrim made so many announcements in his own constituency that he was dubbed 'MacMillions' by *Kerry's Eye*. Another staunch supporter of Haughey, Pádraig Flynn, the Minister of State for Transport, pushed the building of a major airport in a desolate area of his own constituency near Knock, County Mayo. The plan went ahead, with the local airport company being asked to put up only £100 for the multimillion-pound project.

Haughey himself ran a high-profile, presidential-style campaign, in which he used a series of public relations gimmicks, including the unveiling of a plaque to himself in his birthplace, Castlebar. This made 'even his most ardent and closest political colleagues cringe,' according to Vincent Browne. The party adopted 'Charlie's Song', a catchy tune based on an old folk song about Bonnie Prince Charlie. The song, which had been recorded for the election as Fianna Fáil's campaign anthem, was played at all party rallies and exhorted voters to 'rise and follow Charlie'. Haughey toured the country in a whirlwind fashion, travelling by helicopter in order to maximise his exposure.

The names of nine H-Block prisoners, including some of the hunger strikers, were put forward as candidates in an attempt to secure publicity for their cause. It was Haughey's first election campaign as party leader and he had been thrown in at the deep end. Wherever he went during the campaign he was taunted by supporters of the H-Block candidates. In Navan, for instance, he was heckled by Rose Dugdale, who had recently been released from jail. 'Murder, murder,' she shouted repeatedly. 'Who killed Ray McCreesh?' McCreesh was one of the four hunger strikers who had already died.

The Taoiseach received a particularly stormy reception when he went to Ballyshannon, County Donegal, on 28 May. His speech was drowned out by a fire siren and he was jostled by protesters. He also suffered the indignity of being hit on the head with an egg, and when he tried to leave the town his car was blocked by protesters, who kicked and pounded on it while the Gardaí strove to clear the way for him. He was white with anger when he spoke from a platform in Bundoran. 'When my father went out to fight for the freedom of this country he did not do so to have that freedom besmirched by anyone,' Haughey said. Later, in Dun Laoghaire, he narrowly escaped when another protester tried to dump a can of paint on him. Thereafter the Taoiseach's aides watched him very carefully, and he would gather them around him in a kind of human blanket when he wished to escape from the public.

Supporters of the H-Block campaign had targeted Haughey in the blind belief that Fitzgerald could not be less sympathetic to their views than Haughey. They had apparently allowed their emotions to rule their heads, because the Fine Gael leader was even less likely to endorse their demands, given that he had already publicly urged the British government not to accede to them.

Fine Gael ran an effective campaign, with some promised give-aways and tax cuts reminiscent of Fianna Fáil's election manifesto of 1977. In addition, reporters on the campaign trail were much more favourably disposed towards Fitzgerald than they were towards Haughey. Bruce Arnold contended that the media's hostility to the Taoiseach stemmed from Haughey's exaggeration of the significance of the Dublin Castle summit, but the Taoiseach also suffered by being compared with the Fine Gael leader.

Reporters found Haughey the more exciting of the two politicians to cover because he was so unpredictable. 'You don't know when he might lash out and clock someone or suddenly take a flying leap and start biting the furniture,' Gene Kerrigan wrote. They also had the unwanted drama of trying to keep up with him as he was whisked off to the next destination by helicopter, while the reporters scrambled frantically for transport to the next stop, with no hope of getting there on time.

Haughey had a mixed relationship with those covering his campaign. He was very cooperative with photographers and had an inexhaustible appetite for photo calls. He did not feel threatened by the photographers because they did not ask awkward questions. By contrast, although he usually found time to talk to reporters, he gave them very little information and his speeches were 'a series of general banal declarations' without much substance as he trotted out 'well-worn phrases' to provoke applause when desired, according to Olivia O'Leary, who said that Haughey used this refined hustings technique 'with the ease of a veteran performing monkey'.

'He moves and speaks deliberately, looking for the motive behind every question asked,' O'Leary added. 'Attempts at humour are not usually appreciated. Haughey prefers to make his own jokes. One steps warily around him.' Her assessment was essentially endorsed by Vincent Browne, who complained that Haughey uttered 'the same clichés again and again, to the point where reporters on tour with him could anticipate his every utterance'. Almost all those reporters 'developed a deep personal dislike of him, in a manner reminiscent of "The Boys on the Bus" with Richard Nixon in 1968.'

Haughey was touring the country to talk to voters rather than the press. In the circumstances it was normal that he should deliver the same speech in many areas, because the audience – with the exception of the press covering the campaign – was constantly changing. Many of the people who came out to see and hear Haughey were impressed by him. 'He's some fella!' one told Olivia O'Leary. 'I met him in the jacks and he said would I like to come in for a drink. I mean, I never met him in me life before!'

Although Garret Fitzgerald was not as exciting as Haughey, most reporters preferred to cover him because, as a former journalist, he understood and sympathised with their need both to get a story and to file it by a particular deadline. Moreover, as the country's only helicopter-hire service was run by Haughey's son Ciarán, Fitzgerald confined himself to the more conventional modes of travel, and reporters had no problem keeping up with him. Indeed, they often travelled with him on the campaign bus, where he was readily available to answer questions, and he even flattered them by asking their advice on certain issues. As a result, he got on well with them. 'Fitzgerald was the darling of the media,' Bruce Arnold wrote.

The highlight of the campaign was a special television programme in which the leaders of the three main parties, Haughey, Fitzgerald and Frank Cluskey of the Labour Party, were interviewed separately by a panel of journalists. The panel consisted of Bruce Arnold of the *Irish Independent*, Paul Tansey of the *Irish Times*, Michael Mills of the *Irish Press* and Vincent Browne of *Magill* magazine. Most people thought that Haughey came off best, partly because his inquisitors appeared to give him a much rougher time than they gave either Fitzgerald or Cluskey.

'Haughey was fresh and buoyant,' according to Browne. 'He was excellently prepared and in exactly the same frame of mind. He was confident and, above all, cool.' Although he had been particularly favourable towards him in the run-up to his election as Taoiseach, Browne had gradually become quite critical of Haughey's dismal failure to tackle the country's economic problems after identifying this as one of his main aims in both his address to the nation and his ard-fheis speech.

It was not so much that he failed to turn the economy around but that he did not even try to do so. Instead, he made things much worse by contributing to inflation with a massive pay rise for public-service workers. Haughey was vulnerable in the area of economic policy, but the four journalists never cornered him on this issue.

'Straight away Mr Haughey told a whopper, stating that the reason he changed tack on economic priorities in the middle of 1980 was the 80 per cent increase in the price of oil,' Vincent Browne noted afterwards. The increase had actually occurred the previous year, but Browne was not quick enough to react. 'I let him get away with this,' he wrote. 'I could never nail him down on the astonishing about-turn on economic policy he made within six months of taking office.'

'In the break between the Haughey and Fitzgerald interviews

the journalists were very despondent, believing that we had let Haughey off very lightly,' Browne explained. When they viewed the programme afterwards, however, they realised that they 'had been much tougher with him' than they had thought, but by then then it was too late, because they had made the mistake of tacitly agreeing to go easy on Fitzgerald. 'In the event we went too easy,' Browne added. 'Too easy for the good of the programme, too easy in comparison to our toughness with Haughey and too easy for Fitzgerald's own good. Had we been tougher, he would probably have done better.'

After the debate Haughey remarked with delight that he had not lost his temper. There was little doubt that he had been confronted by a biased panel. 'The journalists were agreed about the relative merits of the political leaders,' Arnold noted. 'In respect of Haughey this amounted to a judgement of his considerable ability, flawed by an innate distrust of the media, which was quite absent in both Cluskey's and Fitzgerald's relationships, the latter in particular getting on extremely well with radio and television interviewers and with the press.' The perceived difference in the journalists' approach to the two politicians certainly lent substance to Haughey's charge that the media was biased against him, and it may well have helped whittle away the lead he had enjoyed in the IMS poll at the start of the campaign.

Despite being confronted with some of the ugliest scenes witnessed in Irish politics for decades, the Taoiseach seemed more at ease on the hustings than Fitzgerald. Nonetheless, the Fine Gael leader was the principal political beneficiary of the H-Block campaign, and this probably made the difference that led to Haughey's defeat in his bid for re-election as Taoiseach. As expected, Haughey easily won re-election to the Dáil, with more than a quota to spare, but Fianna Fáil's first-preference votes nationwide, at 45.3 per cent, were down significantly – by 5.1 per cent overall and 8.6 per cent in Munster – from 1977. 'It was Fianna Fáil's poorest showing in twenty years,' Stephen Collins wrote.

'Haughey was defeated by obsession with power,' Arnold concluded in his biography. He had achieved his life's ambition in becoming Taoiseach, but he had inherited his mandate from Jack Lynch and obviously felt that he had to establish his own leadership credentials by leading Fianna Fáil to an election victory. Thus instead of using what power he had to achieve political or economic changes, he used it merely in an attempt to win the next election. 'His timing, which should have directed a measure of concern towards resolving the real problems faced by the economy or bringing about real change in Anglo-Irish relations over the North, was directed exclusively towards electoral advantage,' Arnold continued. 'He exerted no real discipline within his party. He defined nothing for them, in policy terms, and left them puzzled and bewildered. He tolerated indifferent levels of loyalty.'

While there is a good deal of truth in that assessment, it seems that Arnold was conveniently oblivious to the fact that Haughey inherited the financial mess in which the country found itself. Meanwhile, as Anglo-Irish relations had been strained for the best part of 800 years, it was a bit much to blame Haughey for not having resolved these difficulties in the eighteen months he had been in power.

Moreover, Arnold and others in the media were grossly unfair in blaming Haughey for the supposed drop in the Fianna Fáil vote. The party's support, 'at 45 per cent, represented a drop of more than 5 per cent from Lynch's 1977 vote,' Arnold noted. 'He had lost it all.' Using those figures to compare the performances of Lynch and Haughey was a serious distortion.

The party had already lost considerable ground before Haughey took over as Taoiseach, and it would have been more appropriate to compare the latest showing with the party's dismal performance in the 1979 European elections, when it secured only 34.6 per cent of the first-preference vote. Thus it would have been far more accurate to state that the Fianna Fáil vote had gone up 10.7 per cent in two years. Shortly before Haughey became Taoiseach, the party had lost two by-elections in Cork, including one in Jack Lynch's own constituency after he had canvassed there personally. In comparison with those 1979 performances, the latest Fianna Fáil showing under Haughey was in fact little short of phenomenal.

The party had come within half a percentage point of its share of the vote in the 1969 election, when Lynch had led the party to an overall majority of seats in his first general election as party leader. On the other hand, as leader, Haughey secured a higher percentage of the vote for Fianna Fáil in his first general election than either Éamon de Valera or Sean Lemass had before him or Albert Reynolds and Bertie Ahern would after him. The party's tally of seventy-eight seats in 1981 was just two short of the combined total of Fine Gael and Labour. That situation could have been reversed with just 250 extra votes spread over two constituencies in which Fianna Fáil candidates lost the last seats to Fine Gael.

The balance of power was held by one Workers Party deputy, Joe Sherlock, and five independents. One of the independents, John O'Connell, who had recently resigned from the Labour Party, was elected Speaker of the Dáil, so Fitzgerald needed the support of two of the others, whereas Haughey needed the support of four of them. Two of the independents, Noel Browne and Jim Kemmy, were highly critical of Haughey, so the outcome was virtually a foregone conclusion. Browne and Kemmy voted against him, as did Sherlock, with the result that Haughey's nomination to remain as Taoiseach was defeated by eighty-three votes to seventy-nine. Fitzgerald was then elected, and Haughey graciously accepted the verdict, becoming Leader of the Opposition. It was only later that the real cost of his effort to buy the election would become apparent. For the time being he was again out in the cold.

# 11

## 'Against everything and for nothing'
## Leader of the Opposition, 1981–1982

Having confidently anticipated that he would be re-elected as Taoiseach, Haughey was not prepared for his new role of Leader of the Opposition. In the following months he appeared to drift: lacking a positive approach of his own, he reacted negatively to the coalition government's policies.

Although as Taoiseach he had remained fairly quiet about the H-Block campaign, he spoke out following the collapse of the hunger strike after it had claimed the lives of six more hunger strikers, including Kieran Doherty, one of those elected to the Dáil. Despite his supposedly warm relations with British Prime Minister Margaret Thatcher, Haughey now blamed much of the tragedy on her intransigence. He said that she should have conceded to the hunger strikers' demands.

The campaign had focused considerable attention on the Northern question, with the result that it was to remain in the forefront of Irish politics for some time. Fitzgerald wanted to adopt a positive approach towards ending partition by trying to win over the Northern majority with concrete assurances that Northern Protestants would have nothing to fear in a united Ireland. Like Haughey, he accepted that Irish unity should be brought about only with the consent of the Northern majority, but unlike the Fianna Fáil leader, he was prepared to make the Republic more attractive without first waiting for the Northern majority to come to the conference table.

Fitzgerald proposed changing what he believed were sectarian aspects of the Irish Constitution and legal system, which, he said, were 'inbred with the ethos' of the Catholic majority. For years, he argued, Irish nationalists had been blind to their own discriminatory behaviour towards Protestant values while complaining about the manner in which the Protestant majority discriminated against the minority in Northern Ireland. The Republic was therefore a sectarian state, 'though not in the acutely sectarian way that Northern Ireland was,' according to the new Taoiseach. 'Our laws and our Constitution, our practices and our attitude reflect those of the majority ethos and are not acceptable to Protestants in Northern Ireland.'

Before coming to power, Fitzgerald had made no secret of his belief that the confessional approach adopted in Dublin was repugnant to Northern Protestants. 'If I were a Northern Protestant,' he declared in 1978, 'I wouldn't be happy about unification with people who haven't shown themselves to be open-minded. We need to shake people here out of their loyalty to the state to a wider loyalty to the Irish nation. This is so partitionist a state that Northern Protestants would be bloody fools to join it.'

As Taoiseach, therefore, Fitzgerald called for a 'constitutional crusade' to change Southern attitudes in order to break down some of the barriers that had kept the Catholic and Protestant communities divided. Having accepted that the Northern majority could not be coerced into a united Ireland, he suggested that Dublin give formal expression to this view by removing Articles 2 and 3 from the Constitution. Article 2 was the provision which claimed sovereignty over 'the whole island of Ireland', while Article 3 stipulated that the Constitution would apply only to the Twenty-six Counties 'pending the re-integration' of the Six

Counties. These two articles had prompted Northern unionists to adopt 'their siege mentality', according to Fitzgerald. He argued that removal of the articles would placate the unionists 'and open up the possibility of easier dialogue between them and the nationalists in Northern Ireland.'

Haughey dismissed out of hand the need for such a crusade, however. 'The Constitution,' he said in Ennis, at the unveiling of a memorial to the late Éamon de Valera, 'enshrines in Articles 2 and 3 the clear assertion of the belief that this island should be one political unit – a belief stretching far back into history and asserted and reasserted time and again by the vast majority of our people, North and South.'

Over the years, de Valera himself had rejected the kind of approach now being advocated by Fitzgerald, on the grounds that the unionists would look on concessions as a sign of weakness. 'Is there anyone foolish enough to think that if we are going to sacrifice our aspirations they are going to give up their cry of "Not an inch!"?' de Valera asked the Dáil. 'For every step we moved towards them, you know perfectly well they would regard it as a sign that we would move another, and they would not be satisfied, in my opinion, unless we went back and accepted the old United Kingdom – a common parliament for the two countries.'

There was undoubtedly a great deal of validity in what de Valera had said, but in dismissing Fitzgerald's arguments, Haughey had betrayed his snide, invective quality, which many people had found frightening over the years. He did not try to refute the Taoiseach's suggestions with reasoned arguments of his own; instead, he resorted to an emotional appeal that impugned the patriotism of Fitzgerald and those who agreed with him. The Fianna Fáil leader said, for example, that support for deleting Articles 2 and 3 came from 'the remnants of that colonial mentality that still lingers on in Irish life, a mentality that cannot come to terms with the concept of a separate, independent Irish Ireland.'

'Once again,' he continued, 'we are being asked to accept a jaundiced view of ourselves. Once again we are being asked to look only at our faults and to believe that somewhere else things are ordered much better than they are here, and there exists a superior form of society which we must imitate.' There was no reason 'to apologise to anyone for being what we are or for holding the beliefs we do,' he said. 'We angrily reject accusations of either inferiority or sectarianism.'

In decrying the constitutional crusade, Haughey adopted the demagogic technique of endorsing patriotism and then renouncing an unpopular argument that he attributed to his opponent but which, in fact, his opponent had never made. Fitzgerald had not said, nor had he implied, that the Irish people were inferior to anyone. Instead, he had criticised the sectarianism of the Irish system, and Haughey, as Taoiseach, had basically acknowledged a need for change when he indicated his willingness to accept changes if the Northern Protestants would agree to unity. The main difference between the two leaders was a matter of timing – whether the changes should be made first, as part of an effort to win over the Protestants in Northern Ireland, or at the last moment, as a bargaining ploy after the Northern majority had agreed to negotiate an end to partition.

Haughey was opposed to legislating with the aim of currying favour with the unionists. He told a party meeting on 17 October that any changes in the Constitution 'should be undertaken on their merit, not with a view to impressing Northern unionists, the British or anybody else'. Complaining that Fitzgerald's constitutional crusade was 'unnecessary, divisive and unhelpful', he added that now was 'the first time in history that a crusade was started by the infidels'.

Having already impugned the patriotism of those advocating constitutional change, Haughey's use of the word 'infidels' could be taken as a rather underhand way of questioning the religious convictions of the same people. In this case, however, the remark was probably more flippant than sinister. Still, his overall approach to the constitutional issue did little to endear him to people like George Colley, who had served on a constitutional committee which, back in the 1960s, had advocated similar changes to those now being called for by Fitzgerald. Moreover, the committee's findings had been endorsed by Haughey's idol, Sean Lemass.

Anglo-Irish relations had clearly taken a turn for the worse during the H-Block crisis, but things got back on track with a summit between Fitzgerald and Thatcher in London on 6 November 1981. The two leaders afterwards issued a joint communiqué restating the fundamental position of each government. The communiqué reiterated that the goal of successive Irish governments was 'to secure the unity of Ireland by agreement and in peace' and reaffirmed the British view that 'any change in the constitutional status of Northern Ireland would require the consent of a majority of the people of Northern Ireland'. The most significant aspect of the talks was an agreement to establish an Anglo-Irish Inter-governmental Council to give institutional expression to the 'unique character of the relationship between the two countries'. These meetings would first be held at ministerial and official levels, but it was agreed that the respective governments would 'consider at the appropriate time whether there should be an Anglo-Irish body at parliamentary level whose members would be drawn from the British and Irish Parliaments, the European Parliament, and any elected assembly that might be established for Northern Ireland'. This proposal was a product of the joint studies arranged for at the Dublin Castle summit. The purpose of those studies had been so misunderstood that the two leaders now agreed to publish most of them in order to clear up the confusion surrounding them.

Haughey lost no time in denouncing the latest talks. Quoting from the communiqué, he said that Fitzgerald had given what amounted to *de jure* recognition to partition by agreeing 'that the consent of the majority would be required' to change the constitutional status of Northern Ireland. He admitted that he had earlier agreed that change 'would only come about' with the consent of that majority, but he contended that this was only a recognition of the 'practical realities of the situation' and at worst a de facto recognition of partition.

Speaking in the Dáil four days later, Haughey dismissed the joint studies and the latest talks as a betrayal of 'the spirit and letter of the Dublin communiqué' of December 1980. He was arguing that something much more far-reaching had been envisioned at Dublin Castle, but this was not substantiated by the joint studies, which clearly showed that Haughey had been exaggerating the situation. Now he was skating on thin ice in criticising those studies, because he had seen and approved of them before leaving office in July.

While theoreticians and academics might argue for hours about the importance – supposed or real – of a distinction between the *de jure* and de facto positions adopted by Haughey and Fitzgerald, the issue was of little concern to the Irish electorate at large. Such constitutional arguments were a mere side issue to most people, who were much more interested in economic matters.

Haughey was also critical of the government's economic policies. 'Our approach is positive and theirs is negative,' he contended. 'We are development-investment minded, and they are committed to monetarism and deflation.' His economic views were not shared by party colleagues like George Colley, Martin O'Donoghue or Des O'Malley, however. It was Charlie McCreevy, one of his more ardent backbench supporters from 1979, who was the first to speak out publicly on this issue. In an interview with Geraldine Kennedy, the recently appointed political correspondent of the *Sunday Tribune*, McCreevy was particularly critical of Fianna Fáil's performance in opposition. 'We seem to be against everything and for nothing,' he said. When asked if he was disillusioned with the party leader, he pointedly refused to comment, thereby leaving little doubt that he was. On 11 January 1982 McCreevy spoke out again, in a similar vein, complaining that general elections were 'developing into an auction in promises', with scant regard for the national interest. 'We are so hell-bent on assuming power that we are prepared to do anything for it,' he declared.

Bristling under the criticism, which he considered a challenge to his leadership, Haughey asked the parliamentary party to expel McCreevy. The latter allowed the matter to be brought to the brink of a vote before intervening to announce that he would spare the meeting the necessity of a divisive vote by withdrawing from the whip voluntarily, though he nevertheless pledged his continued loyalty to and support for the party.

Fine Gael were by no means immune from McCreevy's criticism. The party had made lavish promises during the June election campaign, but once in government Fitzgerald pleaded an inability to implement the more expensive promises because the country's financial position was much worse than had been believed before the election. This explanation was not entirely candid: Fine Gael had known at the time it made the promises that the country's finances were in bad shape.

Having come to power after promising to reduce taxation,

the more honourable course would have been for Fitzgerald to go back to the country and level with the people that it was not possible to implement his party's promises. As things turned out, this approach would also have been more expedient in political terms, but the Fine Gael leader lacked the political finesse to make the best of his situation, especially when Fianna Fáil were so obviously divided. Instead, his Minister for Finance, John Bruton, introduced a particularly harsh budget on 27 January 1982. It was always going to be a close-run thing. Dick Spring, a Minister of State in the government, had been seriously injured in a car accident in early December: he had crushed some vertebrae in his back. He was recovering at his home in Tralee, but Haughey gave orders that nobody was to pair with him. He therefore had to fly to Leinster House by helicopter and was carried into the Dáil on a stretcher.

Bruton's budget was controversial from the outset. He not only reneged on his party's promise to introduce certain tax reforms but violated a further promise by trying to put VAT on clothing and footwear. As a result, the government, which was dependent on the support of two independent deputies, was defeated when one of them, Sean Dublin Bay Loftus, voted with the Opposition. The Taoiseach was therefore compelled to seek a dissolution and ask for a general election under circumstances which were less favourable than they would have been if he had had the courage and integrity to seek a mandate for abandoning his party's campaign promises.

The Taoiseach was strangely buoyant from the moment the defeat of his government was announced. 'I experienced a moment of total exhilaration,' he later wrote. 'This was it. We were going into battle on a budget that we could defend with conviction and enthusiasm, both on social and financial grounds. We would be able to contrast our vigorous tackling of the financial crisis and the honesty with which we had prepared the budget against Fianna Fáil's appalling four-year record of extravagance and the dishonest budget they had produced a year earlier, in which spending figures had been arbitrarily slashed without any policy decision being taken to implement these nominal cuts.'

After Fitzgerald's announcement that he was going to seek a dissolution and ask the President to call a general election, Haughey made several efforts to contact President Hillery in an attempt to persuade him to exercise his constitutional right not to dissolve the Dáil. Article 13 of the Constitution specifically stated that 'the President may in his absolute discretion refuse to dissolve Dáil Éireann on the advice of a Taoiseach who has ceased to retain the support of a majority.'

Fitzgerald had lost a vote on what amounted to a matter of confidence, so the President did not have to accede to his request for a dissolution. Neil Blaney apprised Haughey of the situation and suggested that the latter notify the President of Fianna Fáil's readiness to form a government. This was a real chance for the President to exercise one of his few discretionary powers because of the numerical situation in the Dáil. If the deputies who had voted against the budget were prepared to support Fianna Fáil, Haughey would be able to form a government. Even if this government did not last very long, the party would then at least have the advantage of fighting the next election as the party of government, with all that that entailed. It was therefore worth a try.

Of course it was highly insulting to think that Hillery would not be aware of what was one of his main constitutional prerogatives. Moreover, he had scant regard for the short fellow, especially as he thought Haughey's supporters had been responsible for spreading rumours about him supposedly having an extramarital affair.

Although there were precedents for a head of state refusing to dissolve parliament – in Canada in the 1920s and Australia in 1975 – such a situation had never occurred before in Ireland. The big question was whether the President would use his discretionary power. Brian Lenihan, who had sat next to Paddy Hillery at the cabinet table for eight years, was asked for his opinion. 'We wouldn't get anywhere with Hillery,' he replied

The Fianna Fáil front bench decided, nevertheless, that a statement be issued highlighting the availability of the Fianna Fáil leader. 'It is a matter for the President to consider the situation which has arisen now that the Taoiseach has ceased to retain the support of the majority in Dáil Éireann,' Haughey declared. 'I am available for consultation by the President should he so wish.'

Haughey suggested someone telephone the President to apprise him of this statement. 'He nodded at me,' Lenihan recalled. 'He has a habit of making requests by nodding his head instead of actually saying anything. I shook my head.'

'I am not the man for the job,' Lenihan said. It was not that he saw anything wrong with calling; he simply felt that it would be a waste of time.

Haughey then nodded to Sylvester Barrett, who, as a fellow Clare man, was on particularly good terms with the President. Barrett left the room to telephone, but the duty officer manning the telephone switchboard at the Áras told him that the President was not available.

If this was just a courtesy call to inform the President of Haughey's statement, Barrett could have accomplished his task by merely leaving a message. Instead, Barrett tried again later, as did another Fianna Fáil deputy, Brian Hillery, a cousin of the President. None of them got through, however. Independent deputies Neil Blaney and Sean Dublin Bay Loftus also tried.

Haughey called himself, in apparent exasperation, and became quite abusive when the duty officer, Captain Barbour, refused to put him through.

Garret Fitzgerald had in fact not gone straight to the President but had given a press conference and had then been delayed for a while. It was not until around ten o'clock – about an hour and three-quarters after the vote – that he reached Áras an Uachtaráin. 'I was ushered into a disturbed and indeed quite angry President Hillery,' he later wrote. 'The Áras had apparently been besieged with phone calls.' The President 'was so upset by what had happened,' according to Fitzgerald, 'that he kept me there for three-quarters of an hour, thus leading many back in Leinster House to speculate that he might in fact be exercising his prerogative, the inappropriateness of which in current circumstances he was so vigorously propounding to me.'

The next day, the President, in his capacity as Commander-in-Chief of the Army, ordered that the Chief of Staff, Lieutenant General Hogan, ensure that Captain Barbour's military record was in no way compromised by his failure to facilitate Haughey on the telephone the previous evening. The captain had simply been following instructions, the President explained.

It would later be suggested that the Fianna Fáil leader had told the officer that his career might be affected by his decision, but Haughey vehemently denied this. There were distinct signs of emotion in his voice when he spoke on the matter. 'My father was a distinguished army officer until he left the defence forces through ill-health,' he said. 'I myself have been an officer in the defence forces. I was brought up to believe in the integrity of our defence forces and the army and I have the highest respect for them. I would never have insulted an army officer of our defence forces in any way, and I never will.'

The whole affair was really a storm in a teacup. The fact that phone calls were made was leaked to the press, but the calls did not become an election issue until nearly nine years later, when they almost brought down Haughey's fourth government and played a key role in undermining Brian Lenihan's bid to succeed Hillery in 1990.

Despite his failure to talk with the President, Haughey was in an upbeat mood when he met the media the next morning. He wanted to make the rejected budget the central issue of the election campaign. He said that he placed a very high priority on the need to dispose of 'most of the provisions of yesterday's budget', but he was deliberately vague about his own plans. He then became irritated when journalists continuously pressed him for details of how he would handle the economy.

Faced with apparent contradictions in what Haughey was saying, reporters asked him to reconcile these differences. Haughey said, for instance, that he was opposed to creating employment simply by adding people to the public payroll, while on the other hand he blamed government policies for having allowed 5,000 vacancies to develop in this sector. He said that, if elected, his government would have to decide whether to fill the vacancies or leave people on the dole. The implications of this statement were unmistakable: he was intimating that he would fill the vacancies but was not actually committing himself to doing so. He also indicated that he would retain food subsidies, which the coalition government planned to remove.

Previously, Haughey had opposed food subsidies because they subsidised the wealthy as well as the poor. By abolishing them, he contended, the state would have more money to help the needy by increasing welfare payments. Now, however, he seemed to engage in some political gymnastics in order to exploit the unpopularity of the government's effort to abolish the subsidies. He intimated that it would be possible to retain them in a 'self-financing' manner by using them to keep down inflation and thus restrict wage claims. In that way, he argued, it might be possible to save more than the subsidies cost, but he emphasised that this was only a theory put forward by some economists and that he had 'a basic and inherent distrust of theoreticians'.

Reporters pressed him to be more definite. They were not about to allow his vagueness to go unchallenged. 'I'm not here to be cross-examined!' he exclaimed angrily, at one point.

'Mr Haughey, this is a press conference,' John Bowman of RTÉ reminded him. 'You *are* here to be cross-examined.'

'I've answered that question already!' he declared.

'You didn't answer it,' a reporter replied. But Haughey had answered it in as much detail as he was prepared to, and that was that.

Vincent Browne was insistent that politicians on all sides should 'be forced to state precisely' the cost of any scheme they propose and to outline how they were going to pay for it. 'Already Fianna Fáil is ducking this one,' he wrote. 'Any politician who refused to state precisely how any of his or her proposals is going to be paid for is either attempting to fool the electorate or is an idiot. Either way, they shouldn't be elected.'

Journalists were not the only people critical of Haughey's initial performance. Fianna Fáil's newly appointed spokesman on finance, Martin O'Donoghue, was privately very critical of it. Before the introduction of the rejected budget, the party's front bench had decided on a policy of accepting both the government's proposed spending and its projected deficit but arguing about the details of both.

Haughey obviously departed from this agreed course at his press conference. As a result, it was intimated strongly to him afterwards that if he continued to campaign as he had begun,

O'Donoghue, Colley and O'Malley would repudiate his policies. He therefore agreed to adopt the economic approach advocated by O'Donoghue, who was invited to prepare a speech for him. In this speech, Haughey accepted the government's targeted deficit. 'We would stick to the same levels of borrowing and the current budget deficit,' he told a party rally, 'because it would not be sensible, wise or prudent to depart [from these levels] too much.' He contended that some of the harsher aspects of the defeated budget could easily be eliminated, however.

If Haughey hoped that taking this line would unite the dissidents behind him, he must have been sorely disappointed. In an interview on RTÉ radio's *This Week* programme the next day, for instance, O'Donoghue beat around the bush rather than say whether he thought Haughey was fit to be Taoiseach. The interviewer asked the question four times, and each time O'Donoghue pointedly avoided answering it. In another RTÉ interview ten days later, Colley similarly refused to say that he hoped Haughey would be the next Taoiseach.

When Haughey tried to explain how the government's budget targets could be met without adopting the harsher measures proposed, he and his economic advisers were accused of 'creative accounting' because their figures simply did not add up. The shortfall was referred to as 'Fianna Fáil's funny money'. His credibility on such matters was further questioned at the height of the campaign when *Magill* magazine published a leaked Department of Finance document showing that his government had deliberately underestimated expenditure in the run-up to the 1981 general election.

The Fianna Fáil leader's image had clearly become an electoral liability: he trailed Fitzgerald by more than twenty points in the public-opinion polls. In the last such survey before election day, Haughey was the choice for Taoiseach of only 33 per cent of the electorate, compared with 56 per cent for Fitzgerald. Albert Reynolds, Fianna Fáil's National Director of Elections, accused Fine Gael of conducting a smear campaign. That Haughey was being treated unfairly was acknowledged by some of his most outspoken critics. 'There was a lot of personal sniping against Charlie Haughey, which was unfair,' Geraldine Kennedy admitted. 'It could just as equally have been done on Garret Fitzgerald, and it wasn't.'

Fianna Fáil dissidents had been hinting that their leader was an unsuitable person to lead the country, and the media reflected this, even though no specific evidence was cited to justify the unstated reservations about him. 'Because they were unstated and therefore unsubstantiated, they were unfair,' conceded Sean Duignan, RTÉ's political correspondent.

On election day there was a sensational development: Haughey's election agent and solicitor, Pat O'Connor, was arrested on a charge of double-voting. He and his family had inadvertently been registered to vote at two different polling stations. O'Connor and his daughter had requested ballot papers at both places, but to secure a conviction it was necessary to prove not only that they had deposited two ballot papers each but also that they had voted correctly each time. If they had deliberately or inadvertently spoiled their voting papers, they would be deemed, under the existing law, not to have voted. As there was no way of identifying the ballot papers to prove that either of them had voted properly once, much less twice, the court found them both not guilty.

Haughey was not personally involved in any of this, but his name was immediately dragged into the affair because O'Connor, as well as being his election agent and solicitor, was also a close personal friend. Haughey's opponents predictably used the affair against him. Jim Gibbons, who had just been re-elected after a seven-month absence from the Dáil, lost no time in raising the spectre of an impending challenge to Haughey. 'I expect the question of the leadership will be raised at the first meeting of the parliamentary party,' he told reporters after his victory.

This was promptly interpreted as the first move in a bid to get rid of Haughey. As the count continued, the *Evening Herald* went on sale with a bold front-page headline: 'Leadership Fight Facing Haughey'. Some hours later it became apparent that Fianna Fáil were going to be three seats short of an overall majority in the Dáil. Disgruntled members of the party openly contended that Haughey had been an electoral liability.

One of those who had just lost his seat, William Kenneally, the outgoing chairman of the parliamentary party, told Geraldine Kennedy that the party would have fared much better under a more popular leader. Kenneally stated therefore that he 'would not be surprised' if the leadership became an issue in the very near future. She reported that 'a movement seemed to be brewing' within Fianna Fáil to overthrow the 'leader as he struggles to form the next government without an overall majority'. Stung by the story, Haughey described the report as 'rubbish' during an interview that afternoon on RTÉ's lunchtime news programme. 'If I were in the *Sunday Tribune*,' he said, 'I would be inclined to look after my own future.'

Speculation about the leadership was certainly not helping Haughey's chances of regaining power. He needed the active support of at least two deputies from outside his own party and the abstention of another in order to replace Fitzgerald. The odds of getting the necessary votes were in Haughey's favour, because he needed only the support of either the three Workers Party deputies or three independents. Both Neil Blaney and Tony Gregory, the newly elected Dublin independent, shared Haughey's nationalist outlook. John O'Connell, the sitting

Speaker, could be neutralised by being reappointed, and Haughey could virtually take Blaney's support for granted. As a result, all Haughey needed was the support of Tony Gregory. 'I have seventy-eight seats, plus Blaney, and O'Connell will be *Ceann Comhairle*,' Haughey told Gregory on 23 February. 'I need your vote to become Taoiseach. What do you want?' he asked the deputy.

Of course, securing the necessary support was likely to prove more difficult amidst the uncertainty about Haughey's hold on the leadership of Fianna Fáil. He therefore had a meeting of the new parliamentary party called for 25 February, with a view to selecting the party's nominee for Taoiseach. His desire to have the issue resolved speedily was understandable, if only as an effort to remove the uncertainty that surrounded it. Of course, his opponents felt he was simply trying to deny them time to organise properly. They went into action, holding a series of back-room meetings at which Colley threw his support behind O'Malley, who then became the front-runner among the potential challengers.

O'Malley began canvassing for support with the help of Colley, Seamus Brennan, Martin O'Donoghue and others. Although many deputies had reservations about the timing of a challenge, given that there was a real chance of Fianna Fáil getting into power, O'Malley's people were encouraged by the response. At one point they were convinced that they had the support of a majority of deputies, and their optimistic predictions were reflected by the media.

Vincent Browne published a list in *Magill* of thirty Fianna Fáil deputies who he believed would probably vote against Haughey, while he could count only seventeen probable supporters of the leader. On the eve of the party meeting, the *Irish Independent* had a front-page article by Bruce Arnold with a headline running right across the top of the page that read: 'My score so far: Haughey 20, O'Malley 46, Unknowns 15'.

The headline was an example of sloppy sub-editing: Arnold had referred to only thirty-six deputies as being prepared to support O'Malley. The newspaper made no effort, however, to correct the mistake, which was particularly significant because the figure cited would have been a clear majority of Fianna Fáil deputies, while Arnold's list was five short of the vital number. Suddenly O'Malley became a money-on favourite with bookmakers, and a rumour spread that Haughey was about to announce his retirement as leader of Fianna Fáil on the eve of the challenge.

Stephen Collins, a young reporter with the *Irish Press*, was sent to Leinster House to find out if there was any truth in the rumour. With the help of photographer Pat Cashman, he met Haughey, who was always very cooperative with photographers. Cashman had approached a newly elected Fianna Fáil deputy and asked to get a picture of him with the Boss. The deputy promptly brought Cashman and Collins to Haughey's office, where, after the photographs had been taken, Stephen seized the opportunity to ask about the rumour.

'I approached him and asked bluntly if he was going to resign that day,' Collins wrote. 'The reaction was one of instantaneous and overwhelming anger.'

'Would you fuck off,' Haughey shouted, as he made a run at the young reporter, backing him up against the wall. 'That's "F" "U" "C" "K" "O" "F" "F",' he shouted in Collins's face.

Cashman interceded to say that Collins had been sent to ask the question and was only doing his job. Haughey promptly cooled down. 'What was your question again?' he asked.

This time Collins repeated the question with a little more care, saying that the news desk at the *Irish Press* had been informed that Haughey would resign that day. 'That's complete nonsense,' Haughey replied, calmly. 'I have no intention of resigning.' With that he walked away. The encounter was an example of the short fellow's quick temper. Collins later had many encounters with Haughey, who thereafter 'always acted with courtesy and generally with good humour,' the reporter stated.

When the incident occurred, however, Haughey was clearly under pressure and his people were running scared, despite the fact that Albert Reynolds, whom the dissidents thought was in their camp, told Collins that Haughey would beat off the challenge easily. 'Who else will be able to deal with Gregory and the Workers Party?' Reynolds said.

Throughout that day and into the early hours of the next, Haughey's supporters bombarded dissident and wavering deputies with telephone calls urging them to support their man. At around midnight, O'Malley formally announced that he would be challenging for the party's nomination the next morning.

Bruce Arnold's list actually hurt O'Malley's chances, because it had the dual effect of shocking Haughey's people into action and providing them with the names of deputies on whom to concentrate their pressure. Nonetheless, Haughey could feel justifiably aggrieved about the way in which the *Irish Independent* was covering the story; he had particular reason to be aggrieved about the reports emanating from dissident sources. What those people had to say was newsworthy, even when it was inaccurate, but inaccurate charges should have been identified as such. On the morning of the parliamentary-party meeting, for instance, the *Irish Independent* ran a front-page article in which Raymond Smith not only repeated a dissident prediction that O'Malley had 'sufficient votes to oust Mr Haughey' but also quoted one of the dissidents as saying that 'what's happening now is an exact carbon copy of how Mr Lynch was forced out of the Fianna Fáil leadership through a sequence of events.'

The implications were unmistakable – Haughey and his supporters had brought down Lynch and were now getting some of their own medicine. Lynch had retired voluntarily, however. Although there had been sniping against him in 1979, it had been Gibbons, one of Haughey's bitterest critics and the man who set the ball rolling in this latest challenge, who was the first to break party discipline, by refusing to support the government's contraception bill that April. Moreover, it was one of O'Malley's strongest backers, O'Donoghue, who had persuaded Lynch to retire early, in the belief that the time was opportune for Colley to win the leadership. Consequently it was unfair of the press not to question the scenario then being painted by the dissidents.

Aspects of the *Irish Independent*'s coverage were undoubtedly biased against Haughey, but the *Irish Times* and *Irish Press* leaned heavily towards him in their editorial comments. The *Cork Examiner* was more detached, but it nevertheless predicted that he would win. The *Irish Independent* was the only national daily which carried an editorial leaning towards O'Malley.

There was a great air of expectation around Leinster House that morning. Photographers and a television camera were allowed into the meeting room beforehand. The dissidents were sitting with a shoebox on an empty chair, to evoke memories of Jack Lynch's election, in which an empty shoebox had been used to collect the vote. Haughey stage-managed his own entrance for the television camera. He was ceremoniously announced so that his supporters could greet him with a 'spontaneous' burst of applause. The press were then ushered out.

Pádraig Faulkner was one of the first deputies to speak. He had opposed Haughey in the past, but he said was supporting him this time, and he urged O'Malley not to go through with the challenge because such a contest would be too divisive and would rip the party asunder. Jim Tunney, Rory O'Hanlon and Liam Lawlor – all of whom had been listed as anti-Haughey deputies by both Vincent Browne and Bruce Arnold – spoke in a similar vein, but it was Martin O'Donoghue who delivered the most devastating blow of all, when he urged that there should be no contest.

Suddenly it seemed that O'Malley's support had evaporated. He announced that he would not allow his name to go forward, and Haughey was chosen by acclamation. The whole meeting was over in a little less than an hour.

Afterwards Haughey was triumphant. 'You got it wrong!' he crowed to a reporter on his way into a press conference. He was particularly annoyed at the *Irish Independent*. When Raymond Smith asked a question without first identifying himself, Haughey acted as if he did not recognise him.

'Who is this man?' he asked.

'You can call me Mr Smith, or Raymond, or Ray, but you don't have to ask who I am.'

'To me,' Haughey said contemptuously, 'you are just a face in the crowd. Now what is your question?'

It was a bad start to the press conference, at which Haughey's annoyance at the *Irish Independent* would surface repeatedly. He interrupted in the middle of one question as Smith was saying that 'certain names have been mentioned in the papers as to who might vote against you . . . '

'I am delighted you mentioned that,' Charlie interjected, 'because your particular newspaper published perhaps the falsest list of names in Irish journalism.' He emphasised ad nauseam that he had been selected unanimously, and he complained repeatedly that media speculation about the O'Malley challenge had turned out to be just 'so much rubbish'.

Haughey would seem to have had a justifiable grievance over the unprofessional way in which the *Irish Independent* had so credulously reported the things it had been fed by the dissidents. For instance, O'Malley was quoted the next day as complaining that the parliamentary-party meeting had been called at short notice in order to frustrate his challenge. O'Malley was reported as having denounced the hurried way in which the meeting was called as 'a three-day squeeze-job', despite the fact that neither he nor his dissident colleagues had objected in December 1979 when Jack Lynch had called the party to select his successor with just two days' notice.

It was understandable that the press listened to the views of dissidents; the impending challenge was a major news story. Charges like the accusation that Haughey had overthrown Lynch, however, should have been identified as inaccurate. Instead, Raymond Smith reported the claim, and the *Irish Independent* essentially endorsed it, with an editorial charging that Haughey 'himself overthrew Mr Lynch'. This was, strictly speaking, not correct: the Fianna Fáil dissidents had in fact been responsible for pushing Lynch early. All the same, many of the dissidents may have become victims of their own propaganda about the supposed desire for Haughey's removal after this was so unquestioningly reported, especially in the *Irish Independent,* which accused Haughey of having an 'apparent persecution complex'. That newspaper betrayed an editorial bias not only in its uncritical reporting of accusations made by dissidents but also in the prominence it gave to stories that were critical of the Fianna Fáil leader. On the morning after O'Malley's challenge had fizzled out so pathetically, for instance, the newspaper had a lead story with the following headline running across the top of the front page: 'Lynch Endorses O'Malley and Predicts He Will Lead FF'. The former Taoiseach had issued a statement in an apparent effort to console O'Malley. Jack Lynch was clearly partisan, as was his right, but the *Irish Independent* made no effort to conceal its bias in giving the statement such prominence.

After O'Malley's challenge was out of the way, Haughey could return in earnest to the negotiations with Tony Gregory. Although he had never tired of expressing his admiration for his father-in-law's political acumen, Haughey seemed curiously oblivious to the example set by Sean Lemass under similar circumstances back in 1961. Fianna Fáil had lacked a majority at that time, but Lemass refused to deal with anyone. Before the Dáil voted on his renomination as Taoiseach, he proudly proclaimed that he had not, and would not, ask for support from outside Fianna Fáil. He had made no deals, but he was re-elected anyway.

Haughey showed weakness from the start in that he went to Gregory's headquarters. Gregory produced a long list of specific demands on matters relating to employment, housing, health and education in Dublin, especially in the inner-city area. Throughout the discussions, Haughey seemed to have a stock response to Gregory's demands: 'You're pushing an open door,' he repeatedly said.

This was not the only thing Haughey was working on. He also had approaches made to the Fine Gael deputy, Richard Burke, to see whether he would be interested in being appointed Irish Commissioner to the EEC. This would necessitate his resignation from the Dáil and would mean that Fianna Fáil would need one fewer vote in order to gain power. Burke killed the speculation on this issue, however, with a statement emphasising that there was 'no possibility' that he would fail to vote for Garret Fitzgerald for Taoiseach when the Dáil reconvened on 9 March 1982. 'It was clear he wasn't interested in the other independents,' Gregory said afterwards. 'He believed I could accommodate him.'

Fitzgerald also tried to win over Gregory with lavish promises, but the Fine Gael leader was in a weaker position because, in addition to Gregory, he needed the support of the Workers Party and at least one other independent and so could not offer as much to Gregory. Haughey won out in this auction for power by agreeing to have £4 million allocated to employ 500 extra men in the inner city, have 3,746 new jobs created in the same area within the next three years, have IDA grants raised to attract new industries to the city, acquire a twenty-seven-acre port and docks site, provide government money to build 440 new houses in the inner city and another 1,600 in the rest of Dublin, have free medical cards provided for all pensioners, have the supplementary welfare system overhauled, increase the number of remedial teachers in the inner city and nationalise Clondalkin Paper Mills if no other option for the mills could be agreed upon within three months. These were only some of the policies outlined in the agreement, which both Haughey and Gregory signed as principals. The document was then witnessed by Michael Mullen, the General Secretary of the Irish Transport and General Workers Union.

'As the Mafia say,' Charlie proclaimed, as he shook hands with Gregory following the signing, 'it is a pleasure to do business with you.'

# 12

## 'Go dance on somebody else's grave'
## Taoiseach Again, 1982

Once the deal with Gregory was done, Haughey was assured of victory in the contest for Taoiseach. In fact he would probably have been elected even without Gregory's support because the three Workers Party deputies voted for him. His first task after receiving his seal of office as Taoiseach was to appoint a cabinet. Colley had rejected his overtures for support during the run-up to the abortive O'Malley challenge, so Haughey decided not to appoint him Tánaiste or give him a veto over who should be appointed Minister for Justice or Minister for Defence. Although Haughey offered Colley a cabinet post, the latter declined it and returned to the party's backbenches for the first time in almost twenty years.

The cabinet still consisted of a cross-section of the factions that existed within Fianna Fáil. O'Malley and O'Donoghue were included from the dissident wing. Ray MacSharry was appointed Tánaiste, and both Sean Doherty and Albert Reynolds, two of the three members of the gang of five that were still in the Dáil, were given cabinet posts. The other, Tom McEllistrim, was appointed a Minister of State. Patrick Connolly, who had been a counsel on Haughey's defence team during the Arms Trial, was appointed Attorney-General.

The appointment of Doherty as Minister for Justice raised most eyebrows. While serving as a member of the Gardaí's

Special Branch, he had forged close ties with Haughey prior to the Arms Crisis. He had served as Minister of State for Justice in the new Taoiseach's first government, and his appointment was viewed with uneasiness within the Department of Justice. He was the only former Garda ever to be appointed to the portfolio.

Haughey again announced that his first priority was to settle the partition problem, and he set out for the United States, where he hoped to use the St Patrick's Day celebrations to enlist support for his efforts to block an impending British effort to forge an internal settlement within Northern Ireland by establishing an elected assembly that would gradually be given devolutionary powers. As far as the new Taoiseach was concerned, Northern Ireland was a failed political entity, so any attempt to achieve an internal settlement of the Northern question was doomed to failure.

Even before the publication of the plan for 'rolling devolution', as it was called, the Taoiseach and John Hume, the leader of the SDLP, issued a joint statement denouncing the initiative of James Prior, the Northern Secretary. The Secretary went ahead and published his plans anyway. 'The Prior initiative,' Haughey complained on 23 May 1982, 'will be regarded in history as one of the most disastrous things that has ever happened in Anglo-Irish relations.' For one thing, the establishment of the proposed assembly would greatly weaken any chance the Taoiseach may have had of persuading Thatcher to move boldly on the partition question.

Haughey's relations with Thatcher were already strained as a result of his exaggeration of the level of agreement reached at the Dublin Castle summit of 1980, coupled with what the British believed were Haughey's efforts to exploit the partition issue in order to paper over his serious political difficulties at home. On the other hand, the Haughey government was annoyed at the extortionist tactics being employed by the British in vetoing new farm prices within the EEC in order to have Britain's budgetary contribution to the community lowered. The situation was further complicated as relations reached a new low during the international crisis over the Falkland Islands.

When Argentina invaded the Falklands – or Las Malvinas, as the Argentinians call them – on 1 April 1982, most Irish people did not even know where the islands were. Britain had seized the Falklands from Argentina in 1833, but now the overwhelming majority of the islands' inhabitants wished to remain British. As a result, Britain protested against the seizure to the United Nations Security Council, prompting that body to pass Resolution 502, which called for an immediate withdrawal by Argentina from the islands. Ireland was a member of the Security Council at the time, and the Irish representative supported the resolution. Nonetheless, Haughey's government indicated that it was reluctant to support a British request for an EEC embargo on trade with Argentina. He was personally 'very cool' towards the proposed sanctions, but his government eventually went along with the other EEC countries in unanimously implementing an embargo.

Irish trade with Argentina was fairly small, in any case. In fact, the total value of trade between the two countries in 1981 amounted to little over £15 million. While the trade balance between the two nations was in Ireland's favour, the Irish Meat Marketing Board predicted that the embargo would favour Ireland to an even greater extent because Irish beef could replace Argentinian imports to the British market.

For almost three weeks, there was little hint of any real dissatisfaction with the position taken by Haughey's government. Then, however, Síle de Valera issued a statement to the press on 22 April criticising the government's handling of the crisis on the grounds that it eroded the country's supposed traditional policy of neutrality. As she had lost her seat in the Dáil, her intervention was not all that significant, but Haughey had to take notice a couple of days later when Neil Blaney spoke out.

'We should support Argentina,' Blaney declared, 'for both political and economic reasons: politically, because of the continued British occupation of the Six Counties of Northern Ireland, and economically, because Argentina is one of the few countries with which we have a credit trade balance.' As Blaney was one of the independent deputies on whose support the Taoiseach was dependent, it was later argued that the Donegal deputy's remarks prompted Haughey to reverse his government's policy on the Falklands dispute. By this time, however, Haughey had already got some room for manoeuvre by appointing Dick Burke of Fine Gael as Irish Commissioner to the EEC.

It will be remembered that Haughey had approached Burke with the offer of this post around the time of Haughey's negotiations with Tony Gregory but that Burke had insisted that he would have to vote for Fitzgerald for Taoiseach first. Following his election as Taoiseach, Haughey renewed the offer to Burke, who, after some dithering, agreed to take the appointment. This required his resignation from the Dáil, leaving a vacancy in the Dublin West constituency.

The *Irish Times* and *Irish Press* praised Burke's appointment to the EEC, but the *Cork Examiner*, which generally adopted a rather bland, non-partisan editorial line, came out with a blistering condemnation of Haughey's assertion that the appointment was made purely in the national interest. 'The Taoiseach must be entirely contemptuous of the intelligence of the Irish people to insult them with this sort of hypocrisy,' the editorial exclaimed.

With Burke's appointment to his new post, Fine Gael had temporarily lost a seat in the Dáil. Moreover, the Taoiseach confidently expected that Fianna Fáil would win the by-election because his wife's sister-in-law had only very narrowly missed winning the seat in the general election.

Haughey's policy change in relation to the Falklands dispute probably had more to do with his own philosophy than with political necessity; after all, he had been reluctant to implement sanctions against Argentina. He reversed his policy following the sinking of the Argentinian battleship the *General Belgrano*, which went down with the loss of several hundred lives, marking the real beginning of the Falklands War.

The Haughey government announced that it would be calling on the UN Security Council to bring about an immediate end to hostilities and would also be seeking the withdrawal of the EEC's economic sanctions against Argentina, on the grounds that they were no longer appropriate. 'We were never very enthusiastic about the imposition of sanctions,' the Taoiseach told a press conference on 6 May, 'but the argument was persuasive that they could be instrumental in applying pressure to achieve the implementation of Resolution 502 and so lead to a diplomatic solution.' While Ireland could agree to sanctions supporting the UN resolution, he said that 'sanctions complementing military action are not acceptable to a neutral country.'

The Irish announcement was bitterly resented in Britain, where Haughey's attitude was seen as a blatant attempt to undermine British support within the Security Council and the EEC. 'It appeared that he was going out of his way to make Britain's position difficult,' said Northern Secretary Jim Prior.

The Taoiseach had already denounced Britain's devolution proposals for Northern Ireland as 'an unworkable mistake', much to Thatcher's irritation. 'But what angered me most,' she wrote, 'was the thoroughly unhelpful stance taken by the Irish government during the Falklands War.' Both Ireland and Italy called for the removal of sanctions against Argentina. The rest of the EEC compromised: they retained their sanctions while allowing the Irish and Italians to go their own way.

From the Irish standpoint, the whole affair was largely symbolic. As most Irish imports from Argentina were trans-shipped through Britain, the decision was unlikely to have any practical effect in terms of trade. It was Ireland's moves in the Security Council which the British resented most because no reference was made to implementing Resolution 502. If the Irish proposal was accepted, Argentinian forces would be able to remain on the Falkland Islands pending a diplomatic settlement. As a result of the invasion, which was in contravention of the UN Charter, Argentina would therefore undoubtedly enjoy an advantage that would not otherwise have existed.

Haughey was making no apologies for his government's behaviour. As an elected member of the Security Council, Ireland had a particular responsibility to do what the country could to secure a peaceful settlement. 'It would be easier to stay quiet and do nothing but that would be an abnegation of responsibility in this appalling situation,' he contended. 'Undoubtedly, when there is an emotional situation over the Falklands in Britain and elsewhere, there will be misunderstanding. What we must do is keep our heads, act responsibly, act as a peace-loving nation.'

The Taoiseach deplored the escalation in the South Atlantic. 'In-built into any war is escalation of this sort,' he said. 'We went along with sanctions when they were in support of diplomatic political pressure. Once it became clear that they could be seen to support military activity, we had, as a neutral state, no alternative but to withdraw from the sanctions position and hope that our stand will be understood by the British government.'

What was not generally known at the time was that the British had sunk the *General Belgrano* even though it had been well outside the exclusion zone proclaimed by Britain and had been moving further away from this zone for some hours. The sinking was obviously a deliberate attempt to provoke a full-scale war. Although the Irish media were generally supportive of the Dublin government's stance, it reported some strong criticism of this stance from abroad. The British Prime Minister was reported to be furious with Haughey. 'If he was to turn up tomorrow with a silver coffee pot,' one British government source was quoted as saying, 'she'd likely crown him with it.'

Also in London, Gerry Fitt was more forthright in his condemnation of Haughey's government. 'The bellicose and belligerent statements emanating from the extremely anti-British government are not representative of the Irish people,' he said. As British forces were gaining the upper hand in the Falklands at the same time as the Irish representative was calling for a ceasefire at the Security Council, the British viewed this call as being favourable to Argentina. 'It is not seen as humanitarian,' Fitt continued, 'but as an attempt to help the Argentinians and stop the British now they are on the islands. Ireland is not seen as neutral but as having come down in favour of the Argentinians.'

In the midst of the chauvinistic fervour that swept Britain, there was a considerable wave of anti-Irish sentiment and some virulent anti-Irish propaganda. 'It is tempting to yearn for a return of the Vikings to plunder Ireland's coastal area and rape her nuns so that we, too, can have an opportunity to declare high-minded neutrality and demand a diplomatic solution,' Auberon Waugh wrote in the *Sunday Telegraph*.

Irish goods suffered a decline in sales; orders from Irish factories were cancelled, and a large number of British tourists planning to visit Ireland during the summer made alternative arrangements. What had promised to be a good Irish tourist season turned into a disaster, as British travel agents cancelled bookings. For some Irish people the ideological stand in pursuing peace justified the economic losses, whereas others were more critical.

The Argentinian regime – a military dictatorship that had seized power from a democratically elected government in the mid-1970s – had been particularly tyrannical and had shown scant regard for human rights. As a result, it had little international support. Garret Fitzgerald claimed that Haughey was exploiting the international crisis in order to win the radical nationalist vote in an impending by-election in Dublin West to fill the seat vacated by Dick Burke.

The subsequent by-election was held at the height of the Falklands War; at this time Haughey was being accused of playing the green card for all it was worth. Nonetheless, the Fine Gael candidate retained the seat with a couple of thousand votes to spare. Suddenly what had been called 'one of the most extraordinary political strokes' of Haughey's career had turned sour; he had given a plum job to someone outside his party and received nothing in return.

'Strokes and deals have surely had their day,' Vincent Jennings, the editor of the *Sunday Press,* declared, before concluding that perhaps 'some of Mr Haughey's advisers have studied too well at the John Healy College of Convolution and mistake razzmatazz for substance and action.' This signed editorial, coming in a newspaper that had traditionally been seen as a Fianna Fáil organ, was almost like *Osservatore Romano* criticising the Pope. It raised many eyebrows and may well have provided the impetus for Colley to launch another thinly veiled attack on Haughey the following weekend.

Denouncing 'a new style of politics and politicians', Colley contended that 'the idea seems to be spreading that in politics success is all important no matter how achieved, that any deal or "stroke" or promise is justified if it results in the achievement or the retention of power. This is, of course, not so, and I think it is time the whole idea was challenged.' His outburst was reminiscent of his remarks about 'low standards in high places' a decade and a half earlier, and, just as he did on that occasion, he rather disingenuously denied that he was referring to Haughey or to members of the existing government but insisted that he was talking about the whole political system.

'I am not as naive as to think that there have not always been people in politics who have believed that any price is worth paying to stay in office or to get into office,' he told Geraldine Kennedy. 'The big difference now is that, while these people always existed in politics and always will, in the last three years there has been a tendency for this to be accepted at the top in politics rather than just among certain individuals who were not at the top.' By referring to the last three years and specifically mentioning Burke's appointment, it was obvious that Colley had indeed been referring to Haughey in his remarks.

Even Kennedy, whom the dissidents had been feeding with inside information for several months, had to acknowledge the inconsistency of Colley and other dissidents who had been criticising what was going on while at the same time propping up the government they were denouncing. Nonetheless, Kennedy held Haughey responsible even for the inconsistencies of the dissidents.

'They have become compromised by Mr Haughey's politics of power,' she wrote. 'Their party comes before the country.' She blamed Haughey for the erratic behaviour of the dissidents because, she contended, he had polluted Irish politics. According to her, his opponents both inside Fianna Fáil and on the Opposition benches had been compromising themselves in a futile attempt to beat him at his own game. 'In playing politics the Machiavellian way,' she concluded, 'Charlie is the Prince.'

Haughey was soon faced with another – and much more crucial – by-election, following the death of Fianna Fáil's John Callanan. With victory in the Galway East by-election crucial to the government's survival, Fine Gael pulled out all the stops. On 22 June former Minister for Justice Jim Mitchell caused a sensation by disclosing that telephones which Haughey had installed in his office shortly after his election as Taoiseach in December 1979 could be used to listen in, undetected, on all telephone conversations in Leinster House and the adjoining Government Buildings. The implication of his charge was that the previous government had tapped the telephones of all members of the government, the Dáil and the Senate.

Within a week of becoming Taoiseach, Haughey had personally requested to have the Private Automatic Branch Exchange (PABX) system, which he had used as Minister for Health and Social Welfare, installed in his new office. This contained a telephone console with a loudspeaker and an executive override button that could be used either by a secretary to listen in to a call or by the minister to issue instructions to a secretary over the telephone without terminating a call. While the override was being used, there was supposed to be a bleep on the line every six seconds, but the consoles installed in Haughey's office and later in other offices were programmed in such a way that a user could listen in to a conversation undetected. Using the consoles, someone could dial the number of any telephone served by the Leinster House exchange and, if the number was engaged, listen in to the conversation, undetected, by turning on the loudspeaker, replacing the telephone in its cradle and then pressing the override button.

The telephones had been reprogrammed since the previous year to eliminate the extraordinary override capabilities, so the media realised that Mitchell's timing was dictated by political considerations. Almost all the national newspapers offhandedly dismissed the idea that Haughey knew about the override capabilities. Even the *Irish Independent*, the one newspaper that tended to take Fine Gael's allegations seriously, warned that those had 'to be kept in perspective if we are not to get bogged down in a Watergate-style scenario'.

Some facetious allusions were made to the Nixon White House. When Haughey invited the press into his office to explain the affair, an extractor fan on the ceiling suddenly started working. 'The tape recorder is running!' a reporter exclaimed.

'No,' cried the Taoiseach defensively, 'they are for the smell.' There were two extractor fans in white casings on the ceiling to deal with odours from the kitchen underneath the room. The *Irish Times* published a cartoon of Haughey that showed his console with a massive tape apparatus overhead and a depiction of Nixon in the background.

There were in fact similarities between the phone systems used by Haughey and Nixon. The American President had had 'hotlines' installed in the offices of state governors so that they could contact the White House directly in the event of an emergency. One governor who had his hotline checked found that it remained live to the White House even when the telephone was in its cradle. As a result, the hotline could be used as an electronic bug capable of overhearing all conversations in the governor's office. When the telephones of other governors were checked, some thirty were found to have the same 'fault', which was attributed to the telephone company.

Although Geraldine Kennedy stopped short of accusing

Haughey of wittingly having the override facility, with its extraordinary capabilities, installed, she nevertheless wrote that a majority of Dáil deputies thought he 'would at least be capable of such an act'. Haughey dismissed the idea as 'absolutely ludicrous'. 'I never asked for an override facility and I didn't even know the facility was there,' he explained. He had only learnt this in late 1981, when Fitzgerald had informed him of it, he said. 'I handed over those telephone consoles to the incoming Taoiseach, Dr Fitzgerald, and I think that speaks for itself.' If there had been anything sinister, he would not have been so foolish as to have left the evidence behind him.

Fine Gael were not in a strong position to exploit Haughey's expressed ignorance about the capabilities of the override button because two consoles, which had been ordered while Fianna Fáil were still in power, had been installed with Fitzgerald's approval after he took over as Taoiseach in July 1981. Like Haughey, the Fine Gael leader stated that he was totally unaware of the significance of the equipment at the time. No one doubted for a moment that Fitzgerald was telling the truth, but some media people seemed to question Haughey's statement.

During August, while Doherty was out of the country on holiday, Haughey took over temporarily as Minister for Justice and soon found himself in the midst of one of the most sensational scandals in the country's history. The scandal involved a man who was being sought by the police in connection with two recent murders and was arrested in the apartment of the Attorney-General, Patrick Connolly, on 13 August 1982.

Malcolm MacArthur had been staying with the Attorney-General for the previous nine days, during which time he had travelled in Connolly's state car and accompanied the Attorney-General to a hurling match. At this match, he had been introduced to Garda Commissioner Patrick McLoughlin and had asked him about the investigation of 'that dreadful murder' – which MacArthur had committed himself. The story could have come straight out of some far-fetched murder movie.

The Taoiseach came in for intense criticism as a result of some ham-fisted efforts by the authorities to conceal MacArthur's connection with the Attorney-General. The Garda Press Office and the Government Information Service initially refused to confirm that MacArthur had been arrested in Connolly's apartment. As a result, the press reported only that the arrest had taken place in the complex in which Connolly was living rather than that it had happened in his apartment. Nevertheless, wild rumours about the affair began circulating almost immediately. The *Evening Herald* reported that MacArthur was being investigated for the murder of Charles Self, an RTÉ producer who had been bludgeoned to death earlier in the year. That murder had received extensive publicity over the months because of protests of police harassment from the gay community. It was widely believed that Self, who had been active in gay circles, had been killed by another homosexual.

The rumours were fuelled when the *Sunday Tribune* broke the news the next day that MacArthur had in fact been arrested in the Attorney-General's apartment. This gave rise to unfounded speculation about a possible homosexual relationship between Connolly and MacArthur. Suddenly Dublin was awash with 'an endless stream of rumours, innuendoes, and lurid tales,' according to a report in the *Guardian*.

The media had to be very careful, of course, about reporting such rumours because of the danger of a libel action, but an official denial could easily have been used as the basis for a story about the rumours. There was no homosexual connection between Connolly and MacArthur; the rumours were without foundation. MacArthur was not involved in the murder of Self, and Connolly was not a homosexual, but one can easily imagine the public reaction to a headline such as 'Government Spokesman Denies the Attorney-General is Gay'.

'We were dealing with a situation where an innocent man was being made the victim of some scurrilous rumours, and we felt any denials should come from him,' explained Ken Ryan, the deputy director of the Government Information Service. 'We knew that any denials from us would be taken as giving greater weight to the rumours. But this did not excuse the evasiveness about MacArthur's arrest in Connolly's apartment.

'Surely,' the *Irish Times* declared, 'nearly two days did not elapse before the Taoiseach or some other cabinet member woke up to the fact that rumour thrives when news concerning prominent people can be construed by the public as seeming to be played down.' Haughey excused his own initial dithering in relation to the affair on the grounds that it was, as he put it, 'grotesque', 'unbelievable', 'bizarre' and 'unprecedented'. Those words prompted Conor Cruise O'Brien to coin the acronym 'GUBU'.

The Attorney-General was already on his way to New York when the story of his connection with the scandal broke, so Haughey requested that he return to Dublin immediately. The Taoiseach accepted Connolly's resignation upon his return. Connolly then issued a statement explaining that he had been a long-time friend of MacArthur's girlfriend and had invited MacArthur to stay in his apartment during a visit to Dublin without any idea that he was wanted for questioning in connection with a crime. There was little else he could say on the matter, as the case was sub judice.

The spotlight was then turned on Haughey himself. He gave a press conference at which he had to face some particularly thorny questions. When he was asked whether there was anything untoward in the relationship between MacArthur and Connolly, it was obvious what the journalist was hinting at, but the Taoiseach refused to accept the question. He was under intense pressure, and the strain showed as he slipped up when he was asked why nobody had complimented the Gardaí on their handling of the investigation.

It was known that the police had set up a surveillance unit outside Connolly's apartment some days before the arrest. They might therefore have saved the Attorney-General and the government considerable embarrassment if they had arrested MacArthur outside the apartment. 'It was a very good piece of police work,' Haughey replied, praising the Gardaí for their painstaking efforts in 'putting the whole thing together and eventually finding the right man'.

Haughey had personally had the benefit of a briefing from Garda Commissioner McLoughlin and John Courtney, the head of the Murder Squad. MacArthur made a full statement admitting his guilt and wrote a note to Haughey stressing that Connolly 'had no knowledge whatever of any wrongdoings of mine and must be considered utterly blameless'. Courtney explained the situation to Haughey, with the result that he was aware that there was no doubt about MacArthur's guilt before the press conference. But, of course, the case had not yet been disposed of by the courts, so the Taoiseach's allusion to MacArthur as the 'right man' was clearly prejudging his guilt before the formal trial. Faced with television lights, cameras and an army of reporters, he did not appreciate the implications of what he had said until told about it afterwards by an aide. Reporters were then asked to withhold the remark, as it had been inadvertent.

Some sections of the British media, relishing the Taoiseach's embarrassment following what was seen as his unhelpful attitude during the Falklands War, seemed to take a keen delight in highlighting the gaffe. Irish reporters had to be more circumspect, however, because of the fact that the case was sub judice. Although they could not report what Haughey had said, they highlighted the fact that the Taoiseach had made a prejudicial comment. The *Sunday Tribune* described the remark as 'a gaffe for which the greenest junior reporter would be sacked out of hand'.

This was unfair on two counts. First of all, it made the unspecified comment seem much worse than it had in fact been. Secondly, it should be noted that reporters have a chance of reading over their stories to correct them, while a politician answering questions at a press conference has no such opportunity. In delicate circumstances, politicians usually confine themselves to written statements. On this occasion the Taoiseach facilitated the journalists by answering their questions personally, and he could feel understandably aggrieved at the way in which his gaffe was highlighted.

Much of the affair could be put down to bad luck on Haughey's part. There was no question of any misconduct by the Attorney-General. He was 'entirely innocent', Garret Fitzgerald later wrote in his memoirs, yet Connolly and the Taoiseach found themselves in the eye of a political storm of an unprecedented nature. 'If Charlie had ducks, they'd drown on him,' John Healy concluded, in his *Irish Times* column.

Of course, Haughey did have ducks, on his Kinsealy estate. One day in the Dáil restaurant, Martin O'Donoghue ordered duck from the menu, only to be told that the last of the duck had been served. Overhearing the conversation from an adjoining table, Haughey remarked that he had plenty of duck at Kinsealy. The following weekend a brace of ducks was delivered to O'Donoghue's home with a note to the effect that they had been shot at dawn on Haughey's estate.

The Taoiseach's personal popularity and that of his government had been sliding steadily, and the MacArthur affair exacerbated this trend. In an MRBI poll published on 18 September, only 36 per cent of respondents expressed satisfaction with the way in which he was doing his job, while 59 per cent expressed dissatisfaction; the public's dissatisfaction with his government was even greater.

The MacArthur affair was so extraordinary that credence was easily given to sensational rumours surrounding two other events which occurred within days of the publication of that poll. The first of those incidents occurred when the authorities sought to cover up the crash on 22 September near Ballyduff, County Kerry, of a state-owned escort car that had been assigned to protect the Minister for Justice. It seemed as if nothing had been learned from the Connolly affair. Had a proper statement been issued promptly after the accident, the whole matter would probably have been cleared up without any of the wild rumours that ensued, but the authorities pretended for the next four weeks that nothing had happened.

Tom McEllistrim, who had been with Doherty that night, told the press he had driven the minister back to the hotel at around two o'clock in the morning and had seen him to his bedroom door. The ministerial party had been seen entering the hotel around 4.30 am, however. People asked why, if there was nothing to hide, McEllistrim was not telling the truth about the time of his arrival at the hotel that night.

Despite the fact that the crashed car had remained at the scene for some hours, the Garda Press Office initially denied that there had been an accident at all. The *Irish Times* located the car, which was being repaired in a Dublin garage, and the paper published a photograph of the garage-owner frantically trying to pull across the garage door in a vain effort to conceal the car. It was only then, some four weeks after the crash, that the Gardaí finally admitted that there had been an accident. Due to this deceit by officials, the whole affair was blown out of all proportion, and credence was given to unfounded rumours about Doherty driving the car and having a woman passenger. In fact, however, the Special Branch driver was the only person in the vehicle at the time of the accident.

McEllistrim later admitted that he had not been candid about the time of the group's return to the hotel because he had felt that he should not admit having been in a pub after hours. 'You mustn't say to the press that you were inside a pub until four o'clock in the morning,' he explained, with a laugh.

Meanwhile, Doherty's name was dragged into another scandal when his brother-in-law, Garda Thomas Nangle, was acquitted of a charge of assault on a County Fermanagh man after the latter had failed to turn up to court in Dowra, County Cavan, on 27 September. The man had been detained for the day by the RUC for no apparent reason. At his request, the Gardaí were informed of his detention, but the Dowra court was told only that he would not be attending, and no reason was given for his absence; the judge therefore dismissed the case.

'OK, some fucking guard had some contact with a guy in the RUC or something like that,' one of Doherty's colleagues told Geraldine Kennedy. 'We all know that something happened along the line.' But attempts by the media to investigate the matter further came up against a stone wall.

Although Haughey was not involved in the Ballyduff or Dowra incidents, the two affairs contributed towards further straining his already bad relations with the media. In both cases, and in the Connolly affair which preceded them, the media had a duty to investigate and report what had happened, but they were clearly frustrated by the authorities. At no stage was there any indication that the Taoiseach tried to discipline those who had deliberately sought to mislead the press in at least two of the affairs. By his inaction he effectively endorsed such behaviour. As a result, the time seemed ripe for another push to get rid of him.

Late in the afternoon of Friday 1 October 1982, Charlie McCreevy dropped a political bombshell by placing a motion of no confidence in Haughey's leadership on the agenda of the Fianna Fáil parliamentary-party meeting to be held the following Wednesday. Haughey had tried to dismiss the challenge to his leadership in February by pretending that the whole thing had been dreamt up by the media, but this time he met the challenge head-on. Interviewed on RTÉ's *This Week* programme at lunchtime on Sunday, Haughey indicated that he was going to demand a roll-call vote on the issue so that the dissidents could be identified, because the party was fed up with 'the small section of deputies' who were continually sniping at him.

'The Fianna Fáil organisation wants to get back to a situation where we have the strength that derives from discipline,' Haughey said, 'and I will ensure that discipline will be enforced.' He added that he was going to begin by insisting that all members of his government should pledge their loyalty to him as the elected leader of Fianna Fáil. 'I will insist,' he declared, 'that the cabinet stand four-square behind me, with no shilly-shallying.' He had no doubt he would be victorious. 'I am,' he said, 'absolutely confident of the outcome. As Sean MacEntee said: "Go dance on somebody else's grave".'

Haughey argued that the McCreevy motion was a creation of the media. He would later cite the fact that Geraldine Kennedy had been consulted in advance by the dissidents as conclusive proof that the media had been involved in a conspiracy against him. She had been tipped off by Peter Prendergast, the general secretary of Fine Gael, that something was brewing within Fianna Fáil, and she had learned of McCreevy's intentions after making enquiries among the dissidents. The dissidents, in turn, asked for her advice on media matters like deadlines because they wanted to arrange things so that the whole affair would receive maximum publicity on the Sunday before the parliamentary-party meeting. A case can therefore be made for saying that Kennedy was involved in the attempt to remove Haughey, but there is no evidence to substantiate his charge that the media itself was implicated in this attempt. She was the only reporter who knew beforehand what was going to happen; her colleagues were deliberately kept in the dark.

As of that Sunday, when Haughey first made his charge about the supposed media conspiracy, none of the national newspapers had time to formulate an editorial stand on the McCreevy motion, with the exception of the *Sunday Tribune,* which of course had been forewarned about the motion by Kennedy. When the four national daily newspapers took editorial stands, the *Irish Times* and *Irish Press* were clearly opposed to the motion, the *Cork Examiner* was again largely dismissive of it, confidently predicting Haughey's survival, while the *Irish Independent* merely implied that it was time for a change.

Three of the four political commentators who wrote about the motion in those newspapers were obviously critical of Haughey, but these people split evenly on the question of his removal. This was because Conor Cruise O'Brien opposed the McCreevy motion in the hope that Haughey's survival would help destroy Fianna Fáil at the next general election. John Healy, writing in the *Irish Times,* predicted that the dissidents would be routed. They had shown themselves incapable of organising a proper attempt to remove Haughey in the past, and he saw no reason to believe they could do better this time. He concluded that Haughey was as 'blessed with his enemies as he is cursed with his friends'.

There was a certain amount of manoeuvring by both sides prior to the parliamentary-party meeting. The Taoiseach secured the support of the party's National Executive, while Colley announced that O'Malley and O'Donoghue would be resigning from the cabinet rather than support Haughey. The two men then waited until the morning of the meeting to submit their letters of resignation, thereby ensuring that the dissidents received positive publicity right up to the start of the meeting.

It was clear from an early stage that there would be a vital test of strength between the two sides on whether the vote should be taken openly or in secret. Rule 83 of the Fianna Fáil *Corú* ('Constitution') specifically stated that 'every ballot throughout the organisation should be held by secret ballot'. The dissidents' position was not all that strong, however, because the parliamentary party was traditionally free to make its own decisions without being dictated to by the party itself. Moreover, during the Arms Crisis Jack Lynch had demanded and secured an open vote of confidence. Now some of his supporters were demanding that his successor should agree to a secret vote, and they were being undermined by the precedent they themselves had set.

The parliamentary party meeting began at 11 am on 6 October, with eighty of the eighty-one Fianna Fáil TDs present, as well as twenty-seven senators and five members of the European Parliament. Though the atmosphere was tense, the proceedings were conducted in an orderly manner. It was decided to discuss McCreevy's motion and the method of voting simultaneously. McCreevy explained that he was objecting to Haughey's leadership because there had been a lowering of political standards, the economy had been mishandled and the party had failed to secure a majority in two successive general elections. He said that people wanted to be governed, not bought, and emphasised that it was time 'to get decency back into the party'.

Haughey was obviously nervous when he spoke. He paused frequently to choose the right words or rummage through notes. He defended himself and his government on the grounds that they had been facing unprecedented difficulties in the deepest recession since the 1930s. He said that, having worked hard to prepare a new plan to tackle the economic situation, they should be given a chance to let it work. Under the circumstances, he felt that the motion was not only divisive but badly timed.

This time the dissidents were determined that there would be no repetition of the debacle surrounding the abortive challenge in February. They had arranged for people to speak in favour of the motion in order to prevent a precipitate collapse of their challenge, as had happened earlier. Thus the meeting dragged on throughout the day and into the night, with adjournments for lunch and tea. During the latter break, the dissidents seemed very pleased with themselves.

Some senior deputies, including Pádraig Faulkner and Michael O'Kennedy, had called for a secret ballot, and the dissidents were hopeful of winning this crucial test of strength. They had again overestimated their support, however. When a roll-call vote was taken on whether the vote on the actual motion should be by secret ballot, the voting was twenty-seven in favour, with fifty-three preferring an open vote. The subsequent vote on the McCreevy motion was then defeated by fifty-eight votes to twenty-two.

Haughey had won, and some of his supporters were anything but magnanimous in victory. 'These people have been flushed out now, once, finally and for all,' was how one supporter put it. 'The situation after tonight is that they had better be ready to kiss Haughey's ass or get out of the party,' he added.

The mood was so ugly that Gardaí tried to persuade McCreevy to leave Leinster House by a side entrance, but he refused to do so. As he emerged by the front door, surrounded by six Gardaí, he was met by a jeering group of Haughey supporters, many of whom had been drinking throughout the day as they waited for the outcome of the meeting. When Gibbons left the building shortly afterwards, he was not only jeered loudly but jostled by the unruly crowd. It was one of the ugliest scenes witnessed in Irish politics for many years. One of the hecklers tried to attack Gibbons and in fact landed a glancing blow on him. These incidents, which were captured on television, were probably more damaging to the government than anything else that had happened that day.

The next IMS poll, published on 23 October 1982, showed that Haughey's popularity had slumped even further and the standing of his party had dropped to its lowest level since the polls began, in 1974. Only 23 per cent of those sampled were satisfied with the way his government was running the country, and his personal popularity had dropped another 4 per cent, to 32 per cent.

Aside from this, Haughey's government was already in trouble as a result of the death on 18 October of Bill Loughnane and the hospitalisation the next day of Jim Gibbons following a heart attack. Its prospects for survival were practically wiped out by the publication of Fianna Fáil's new economic program, *The Way Forward*, which called for stringent financial policies to tackle the country's economic difficulties. Tony Gregory and the three Workers Party deputies announced that they would be voting against the government's new economic policies. When they did, the government was defeated and Haughey was obliged to resign and ask the President to call a general election. The Taoiseach and his cabinet would stay in power until after the new Dáil convened following the election, but their political prospects were bleak, if the polls were anything to go by.

Initially the campaign was a rather dull affair. This was the third general election in eighteen months, with the result that there was little public enthusiasm for it, especially as there was scant difference between the policies of the two main parties on substantive issues. The leaders of both Fianna Fáil and Fine Gael had, for instance, each endorsed the recently published wording for a constitutional amendment to prohibit abortion. Haughey tried to exploit the issue by contending that Fitzgerald was not sincere in his support for the proposed amendment. The Fine Gael leader denied this claim and, to strengthen his denial, promised to ensure that the referendum on the issue would be held before the end of March 1983.

In the circumstances, the media accepted Fitzgerald's denial, but Haughey had in fact been right. Before endorsing the wording publicly, Fitzgerald had told Dick Spring, the newly elected leader of the Labour Party, that he was personally opposed to the published wording but, at the insistence of his party, felt compelled to endorse it. Thus Haughey was robbed of an election issue.

Haughey next accused Fitzgerald of stealing official documents, in particular the financial document from which Fitzgerald had quoted during the two politicians' television debate in February. The Fine Gael leader had been Taoiseach at the time, however, and had therefore been entitled to have the document. Consequently, few people took much notice of this charge. Haughey was much more successful in the next few days, when he and his colleagues began playing 'the green card'.

Gerry Collins cited an address in the House of Lords in

which the Duke of Norfolk had said that the Fine Gael leader had told him over lunch some months earlier that Britain's devolution plans for Northern Ireland were acceptable. This charge might well have died, like the others, but for a rather distorted report about remarks supposedly made by Jim Prior, the Northern Ireland Secretary, during a visit to the United States.

Fitzgerald had planned to make one policy statement on the Northern Ireland question, and Prior had been asked what policy he would like to see the Fine Gael leader adopt. While normal political prudence should have dictated that a government minister would not comment on policy matters in a foreign election campaign, the Northern Secretary had replied that he would welcome a policy calling for an all-Ireland police force. Fitzgerald had suggested the establishment of such a force in May, during a televised lecture, and had gone on to advocate the establishment of an all-Ireland court structure. Prior emphasised that he did not know what policy Fitzgerald was going to put forward. 'We will have to wait and see,' Prior had said. Prior was somehow mistakenly reported to have said that Fitzgerald was going to advocate the establishment of an all-Ireland court and police force. This, of course, gave the impression that the Fine Gael leader had consulted with or confided in the Northern Secretary beforehand.

Haughey immediately denounced the proposal and pounced on the mistaken report of Prior's remarks, claiming that there was 'collaboration' or 'collusion' between Fitzgerald and the British, whom he accused of interfering in the Irish electoral process. The Fianna Fáil leader contended that the British had been trying to help Fitzgerald 'in return for the support he had given British policy'.

These charges obviously struck a nerve, because Fitzgerald responded with what the *Irish Independent* described as 'the most bitter personal attack of the election campaign'. He accused Haughey of adopting an attitude towards his proposals that was 'indistinguishable from [that of] Paisley'. The Fine Gael leader was obviously rattled, and Haughey exploited the issue by suggesting that the proposal would undermine Irish independence because it would mean that the RUC would begin operating in the Twenty-six Counties and that unarmed Gardaí would be sent to the North.

'What these foolish men are proposing to us,' Haughey told a campaign gathering in Carlow, 'represents an insidious and dangerous threat to our future security because, up until now, we were able to administer our own security polices as an independent and sovereign nation.' If those proposals were implemented, he added, 'violence and bloodshed will be extended to our country as a whole, without any benefit to anybody.' One Fianna Fáil speaker on the same platform accused Fitzgerald of acting as a 'quisling'.

At a press conference on the last Saturday of the campaign, Haughey charged that Fitzgerald, in talking with the Duke of Norfolk, who had been head of intelligence at the British Ministry of Defence before retiring fifteen years earlier, had, either wittingly or unwittingly, had 'discussions with what in fact is a trained British spy'. Of course, the Fine Gael leader rejected this claim: he said that he had met Norfolk simply in the latter's capacity as the senior Catholic peer and thus the leader of Britain's Catholic lay population. Nonetheless, Fitzgerald had left himself open to the charge of overstepping his responsibilities. 'Dr Fitzgerald, with no official standing, was over in London taking some action over the Prior initiative, which was seen as promoting the proposal,' Haughey contended. 'That sort of initiative should be left to the Irish government of the day, rightly or wrong.'

The Taoiseach was right. Fitzgerald left himself wide open to misrepresentation by engaging in discussions with a member of the British parliament – even if that person was only an obscure member of the House of Lords. Of course, Haughey's criticism would have sounded more sincere if he had not, under comparatively similar circumstances as leader of the Opposition, met privately with Prior for over an hour in the latter's London apartment on 13 December 1981.

Fitzgerald complained that Fianna Fáil were conducting a campaign of personal vilification. Haughey dismissed this charge as laughable, given the 'cold, calculating and vilifying character assassination' of himself by members of Fine Gael in collusion with various journalists. At one point during a press conference on the last Saturday of the campaign, Haughey looked pointedly at Bruce Arnold and reached for a file as if he were going to produce evidence in support of this accusation. Although he then seemed to change his mind, the incident left a lasting impression on some of the journalists present.

On that day, the *Irish Independent* carried an article in which Arnold criticised the Fianna Fáil leader for saying there was a campaign of vilification against him when there was no evidence that such a campaign was taking place. On the other hand, Arnold continued, 'it would be hard to find a more textbook set of examples of vilification' than Haughey's own charges against Fitzgerald of being untrustworthy on the pro-life amendment, of stealing secret documents, of colluding [with the British] over the Northern Assembly and of collaborating with the British government.'

Arnold had previously sided with the dissidents in denouncing what he called 'the democratic travesty of a roll-call vote'; this stance not only ignored the fact that all votes in the Dáil are taken openly but also conveniently allowed the dissidents to forget that they had supported Lynch when he set a precedent by demanding a roll-call vote of the parliamentary party during the Arms Crisis. 'On sensitive issues like the confidence ballot provoked by Mr Charles McCreevy,' Arnold contended, the Taoiseach's 'behaviour has been so erratic, contradictory and perverse as to represent a serious assault by Mr Haughey on himself'. It was not Haughey's behaviour but that of the dissidents which had been erratic on that occasion, however.

Arnold demonstrated his bias against Haughey in the way in which he summarily dismissed all Haughey's charges against him as examples of vilification without analysing the bases for those charges. In some instances, there was a case for Fitzgerald to answer. He had not been completely honest on the pro-life issue, and his motives in discussing the Northern Assembly with the Duke of Norfolk were left open to question, especially when Norfolk was later quoted as saying that the Fine Gael leader approved of the Prior initiative while the Dublin government was opposed to it.

The media demonstrated impartiality in reporting the full details of Haughey's criticism of Fitzgerald, even though none of the editors of the four national daily newspapers took his charge of sinister collusion seriously. The *Irish Press* roundly denounced the Fine Gael leader's security proposals and accused him of starting the vilification with the 'flawed-pedigree' speech back in 1979 but still dismissed Haughey's accusation that Fitzgerald had colluded with the British. 'No one seriously believes that he is in active collusion with the British government in the North, any more than anyone sees the Duke of Norfolk as a British spymaster,' the *Irish Press* declared. In fact, in a rare demonstration of unanimity, all four newspapers carried editorials rejecting the collusion charge, with its quisling undertones. Both the *Irish Independent* and the *Cork Examiner* categorised the collusion charge as 'a red herring', while the *Irish Times* dismissed it as 'much ado about nothing'.

At one time or another, each of the national newspapers was critical of Haughey. Some of the criticism was valid, and some was unfair. Writers like Geraldine Kennedy and Bruce Arnold were unfair to blame him for the questionable behaviour of his opponents or contend that his unjust treatment at the hands of the media amounted to self-inflicted abuse. On the other hand, Haughey must share blame for ignoring the disgraceful behaviour of his supporters. In all probability, their intimidation only strengthened the convictions of the two writers. As courageous journalists, these two people were not about to soften their views because of physical threats or menacing telephone calls in the middle of the night, not to mention taps placed on their telephones.

It should also be remembered that some political commentators, including John Healy and Proinsias Mac Aonghusa, were very sympathetic towards Haughey. Since the early 1960s Healy had complained with monotonous regularity about Fine Gael engaging in campaigns of vilification against Haughey. Healy was also probably the first senior journalist to question the motives behind the sacking of Haughey and Blaney during the Arms Crisis. 'The gutting of Charlie Haughey and Neil Blaney was something of a minor classic in the art of gut politics,' Healy wrote before that week was out. In the aftermath of the Arms Trial, Mac Aonghusa was particularly bitter in his column in *Hibernia*. At one point he outrageously contended that Lynch was 'urgently in need of psychiatric treatment'. He also argued that the British were behind an effort to destroy Haughey because they could not control him and that, in contrast, they regarded Lynch 'as a puppet to be manipulated at will'. Although *Hibernia* drowned in a flood of costly libel suits before the decade was out, Mac Aonghusa continued to write in the *Sunday Press* under the pseudonym Gulliver.

There was certainly very little evidence to support Haughey's charge that the media conspired against him during the two challenges that were waged against his leadership of Fianna Fáil in 1982. Those challenges were mounted with so little notice that there had been practically no way in which any of the journals or even the Sunday newspapers could have influenced proceedings. Thus media influence over the contest was largely confined to the national newspapers and current-affairs programmes on radio and television. In both contests, Haughey gave lengthy radio interviews to present his own case. On the other hand, the dissidents, mindful of McCreevy's temporary expulsion from the parliamentary party in January, had to be very careful about what they said publicly. Hence it fell to journalists to explain the dissident point of view, and this naturally lent credence to the suggestion that the media was involved in a conspiracy against Haughey.

For such a conspiracy to have existed would undoubtedly have required the collusion of the editors of at least some of the national newspapers. Yet on the two occasions that Haughey was challenged by the dissidents in 1982, the *Irish Times* and the *Irish Press* supported him editorially, while the *Cork Examiner* remained aloof. Only the *Irish Independent* leaned towards the dissidents. Thus the bulk of available evidence supports the conclusion that, while some elements of the media were probably unfair to Haughey, the media as a whole was not – and it was certainly not involved in a conspiracy to oust him.

On RTÉ's *This Week* programme on the last Sunday of the campaign, the Taoiseach repeated his accusation that Fitzgerald had met with a British spy by having lunch with the Duke of Norfolk. 'Now you can go from there and draw any conclusion you like,' he said. 'I have drawn my conclusions that he was, in fact, cooperating or collaborating, or whatever word you like to use, with the British government,' he added.

With Haughey again impugning Fitzgerald's patriotism, relations between the two leaders became even more strained. When they met for a televised debate towards the end of the campaign, the normally cooperative Fitzgerald refused to shake hands with Haughey or even allow his photograph to be taken with him before the debate. This seemed like a calculated ploy to throw Haughey off balance, and it apparently worked.

Whether playing the green card made a difference to the outcome of the election may be open to question, because there was a significant divergence in the findings of independent polls conducted by MRBI and Research Surveys of Ireland. The latter detected a massive 10 per cent swing in favour of Fianna Fáil over Fine Gael following the introduction of the nationalist issue into the campaign. On the other hand, the MRBI polls conducted at around the same time showed little movement in the parties' standing. In fact, these had Fianna Fáil remaining static, with Fine Gael and Labour gaining a percentage point each.

The election returns showed that the last MRBI poll slightly underestimated Fianna Fáil's strength and overestimated that of Fine Gael, while the final RSI poll did the opposite in each case. All of the figures in both of those polls were within the stated 3 per cent margin of error, but the RSI poll was out by only 1 per cent, while the MRBI poll was out by 2 per cent. Thus if the previous RSI poll had been accurate, it would appear that the green card had come up trumps for Fianna Fáil.

Haughey again won re-election comfortably, easily heading the poll in his constituency, but his personal tally was down by around 1,500 votes, which was representative of a nationwide swing to Fine Gael and Labour. These two parties won enough seats to combine to form a majority government.

When the new Dáil convened on 14 December 1982, Haughey's name was put forward for Taoiseach. His nomination was defeated by eighty-eight votes to seventy-seven, and Fitzgerald was then elected in his place.

# 13

## 'Desperately worried about the Kennedy woman' The Telephone-Tapping Scandal, 1982–1983

The new government had been in office for barely a week when the public received the first indication that Haughey was about to become embroiled in the biggest political storm since the Arms Crisis. Peter Murtagh, the security correspondent of the *Irish Times*, reported that the telephones of Bruce Arnold and Geraldine Kennedy had been tapped 'officially', that is with the full knowledge and approval of the last Minister for Justice.

Haughey quickly denied any involvement in this scandal. 'I wouldn't countenance such action,' he declared during an RTÉ interview the next day. He called for a judicial inquiry so that the charges could be investigated fully. 'The capacity to listen in to phone conversations is one which must be kept under the very closest, rigid scrutiny,' he said.

Back in 1964 he had assured the Dáil that there were safeguards to ensure that telephone-tapping could not be abused for political purposes. The request for a tap had to come from the Garda Commissioner or a deputy commissioner, who had to be satisfied that the person to be tapped was involved with a subversive organisation or engaged in organised criminal activities. Moreover, an officer of the Justice Department had then to advise the minister on the application. 'The Minister for Justice cannot initiate the procedure,' Haughey said. 'He can act only when a written request comes to him from a responsible authority and when he and his departmental advisers are satisfied that the information concerned can be obtained in no other way.' Thus, he reasoned, 'the connivance of a whole group of people would have to be available before there could be the slightest possible abuse of power.'

'I don't think any politician himself should ever initiate because that would be an abuse,' Haughey explained, when asked about the reported taps on the telephones of Arnold and Kennedy. 'There's a very limited number of reasons which justify the issue of warrants, and it's to combat crime or subversion. Now I don't think either of the two journalists whose names have been mentioned would come within that category.'

Although he expressed concern about the allegations, he took his time in questioning Doherty about them: he did not broach the subject with them until 21 December. He then said that Doherty had assured him that there was nothing to worry about, and so he did not bother to pursue the matter further.

Doherty had asked Deputy Garda Commissioner Joe Ainsworth to have a tap placed on Arnold's telephone. Commissioner Patrick McLoughlin duly authorised this request, on Ainsworth's recommendation. When the Department of Justice official charged with vetting the application asked for the reason for the desired tap, Ainsworth explained that Arnold was 'anti-national in outlook' and 'might be obtaining information from sources of a similar disposition'. There was no question of Arnold being involved with criminal or paramilitary organisations, so the official recommended that the tap should not be authorised, but Doherty ignored the advice and signed the necessary warrant. As was mentioned previously, Bruce Arnold quoted from an exchange between Haughey and Colley at the cabinet meeting of 19 December 1979 in his biography of the short fellow. There are further indications that Colley was probably his source. Colley was not in the cabinet, however, when the tap was put on Arnold's phone on 10 May 1982. When the tap produced nothing of value in the following weeks, it was discontinued on 12 July, in the immediate aftermath of the override controversy. By then, Geraldine Kennedy had replaced Arnold as the greatest thorn in the Taoiseach's side.

Kennedy seemed to have the confidence of someone who was privy to what was happening in the cabinet. On 11 July 1982, for instance, she quoted some cabinet exchanges and disclosed that the government had decided to reverse its economic policies and adopt an approach of fiscal rectitude. In another article, she reported that Haughey had held secret talks in an effort to come to a political arrangement with the Labour Party; any hope of this was killed, however, when she broke the news of the discussions.

Haughey complained to Hugh McLoughlin, the publisher of the *Sunday Tribune*, about Kennedy's articles. McLoughlin in turn told Conor Brady, the newspaper's editor, to keep a tighter control on Kennedy and go easy on Haughey. He explained that the Taoiseach was 'desperately worried about the Kennedy woman' and wondered who in Fianna Fáil was talking to her. Brady, of course, refused to divulge Kennedy's sources.

A few days later Doherty asked for, and then formally authorised, a tap to be placed on Kennedy's telephone for reasons of 'national security'. In the past, 'security' grounds had been cited, but never 'national security', and as a result the Department of Justice opposed the tap. The tap was introduced anyway, on 28 July 1982, and remained on the telephone until 16 November.

Haughey stated afterwards that he knew nothing about the tap. In fact, even the Garda Commissioner, who had formally requested it, was not aware that it applied to Kennedy's telephone because this phone was in the name of a previous tenant of the apartment in which she was living.

The tap on Kennedy's telephone provided interesting information. Among the calls intercepted was a conversation in which she forewarned Peter Prendergast of the plan by Fianna Fáil dissidents to challenge Haughey with the McCreevy motion at the start of October. It was noteworthy that Doherty requested extra copies of these intercepts on the eve of the parliamentary-party meeting which was due to discuss the McCreevy motion. Immediately after this meeting, there was a curious incident, in which the Taoiseach's son, Ciarán, walked up to Kennedy.

'I want to tell you one thing,' Ciarán Haughey said to her. 'You'll be hearing from us.' Kennedy asked him whether this was a threat. 'You can take it as such,' he replied.

Kennedy thought at the time that Ciarán Haughey was annoyed at some remarks she had made on television the previous night. Of course, she did not know then that there was a tap on her telephone. But did Ciarán Haughey know? For whom did Doherty want the extra transcripts of the conversation? Although he did not admit it at the time, almost a decade later Doherty indicated that he had informed the Taoiseach about the taps and said he had given him one of the transcripts.

On 20 January 1983 Michael Noonan, the new Minister for Justice, confirmed that Arnold and Kennedy's telephones had indeed been tapped and that the procedures outlined by various Ministers for Justice had not been followed in either case. He also disclosed that Ray MacSharry had borrowed sophisticated Garda equipment and had secretly recorded a conversation with Martin O'Donoghue on 21 October 1982. The tape was then transcribed by the Gardaí. In addition to these disclosures, Noonan announced that Commissioner McLoughlin and Deputy Commissioner Ainsworth would be retiring from the Gardaí in the immediate future.

When interviewed on RTÉ's lunchtime news that day, Haughey accepted responsibility for what had happened but at the same time tried to distance himself from the abuses. 'Any head of government must take responsibility for anything that happens during his administration,' he said, 'but I want to make it crystal-clear that the government as such and I, as Taoiseach, knew absolutely nothing about any activities of this sort and would not countenance any such abuse.' He was particularly dismissive of the suggestion that the taps were connected with his own leadership problems within Fianna Fáil.

'I wouldn't need any such secret information from any such sources,' he contended. 'I know as a politician and leader of the party exactly what is going on in the party and who is saying what. The idea of resorting to telephone-tapping or any other devices to get that sort of information is ludicrous.'

But if it was ludicrous, why had he been so interested in learning Geraldine Kennedy's sources only days before the tap had been placed on her telephone? In a front-page article in the *Sunday Press*, where she had taken over as political correspondent following the collapse of the *Sunday Tribune*, she disclosed that Haughey had asked her publisher about her sources back in July. This story, which raised some serious questions, undoubtedly hurt Haughey politically.

Haughey appointed a four-man committee within Fianna Fáil to investigate the whole affair. It was headed by Jim Tunney, the new chairman of the parliamentary party. From the very outset Tunney discounted any suggestion that Haughey might have been responsible for any misconduct. 'All the evidence shows that Mr Haughey knew absolutely nothing about it,' he declared on the day the committee was set up. Those remarks did not inspire any confidence in the determination of the investigative committee to find out what had really happened.

In the following days the controversy escalated, with both Doherty and MacSharry making ham-fisted efforts to defend their own actions. MacSharry had not really used the Garda equipment for 'bugging' purposes. The term 'bugging' generally refers to eavesdropping electronically on the conversations of others. He simply recorded a conversation to which he was a party himself. Of course, if this was only 'a personal matter', as he declared, then he should not have borrowed Garda equipment and should not have wasted the time of the Gardaí in transcribing a private conversation.

This was only a trivial matter, for which he should not have been pilloried in the press, but he allowed the matter to be blown out of all proportion by giving the impression that O'Donoghue had offered him money at this meeting to turn against Haughey. This impression was heightened on 22 January when Tony Fitzpatrick, the Fianna Fáil press officer, indicated to reporters that Doherty was about to issue a statement which would not only confirm that O'Donoghue had offered £100,000 to MacSharry to withdraw his support for Haughey back in October but would also authoritatively show that previous governments had tapped the telephones of journalist Vincent Browne, the headquarters of the Workers Party and even a foreign embassy in Dublin. These revelations had the makings of an even bigger story than the Kennedy-Arnold tapes. Reporters were kept waiting for the story for eight hours, and then Fitzpatrick denied that there had ever been any question of issuing such a statement.

The whole thing was apparently an effort to exploit the early deadline for the Sunday newspapers in order to stampede the press into publishing rumours without taking responsibility for them. When this blatant news management was discussed at a meeting of the Fianna Fáil parliamentary party meeting the next day, Haughey contended that the reported manipulation was just a Fine Gael propaganda ploy, notwithstanding the fact that the story had originated with the Fianna Fáil press officer.

Haughey was clearly on the defensive. Although he had already stated publicly that there was no justification for the taps, he now sought to justify Doherty's actions on the grounds that 'national security' had been endangered by 'cabinet leaks'.

'What leaks?' Pearse Wyse asked.

'The Fianna Fáil farm plan had appeared for instance in the *Farmers' Journal*,' replied Haughey, to a chorus of incredulous laughter.

'Isn't it strange then that you would tap the telephones of journalists working in the *Tribune* and the *Independent*?' rejoined Wyse.

Both Kennedy and Arnold had indeed been privy to some cabinet discussions, though in Arnold's case the material had not yet been published. If the cabinet leaks were the real justification for the taps, it seems very strange that neither journalist was ever cited for any specific leak by Doherty. Moreover, Noonan explained that what the men transcribing the tapes 'were expected to look out for was material of a political interest. Apart from the fact that some of them have said so explicitly, the proof is in the fact that the excerpts that were transcribed by them were for all practical purposes exclusively concerned with party-political matters.'

Some fair-minded Garda thought that this was so wrong that he warned a leading member of Fine Gael that the government was using telephone taps for political purposes. Peter Prendergast then warned various member of the party's front bench and leading members of the Labour Party about the taps. Garret Fitzgerald was so afraid of that his telephone was tapped that he would not hold any sensitive conversations in a room that contained a telephone; he would unplug the phone first and move it to another room. Dick Spring told a number of people during October not to mention anything confidential on the telephone because he was afraid that it was tapped. There was a palpable sense of fear in political circles during the final days of Haughey's GUBU government.

The government's argument that the taps were justified for reasons of 'national security' was exactly the same as that used by Richard Nixon to defend the misdeeds of his people during the Watergate scandal in the United States almost a decade earlier. The latest Irish scandal was rapidly beginning to look like a repetition of Watergate. 'The parallels to the Nixon White House are uncomfortably close and to the point,' thundered Vincent Jennings in a signed editorial in the *Sunday Press*. 'Wall-to-wall distrust and paranoia; anyone who disagrees with the leadership is an enemy – or, worse, an "anti-national". Get them, the expletive deleted.'

There was a number of other remarkable similarities between the Nixon presidency and what had happened to Haughey in recent months. For instance, the override affair resembled the White House's use of hotlines to the offices of the state governors. There was also a parallel with Haughey's prejudicial allusions to Malcolm MacArthur before his trial: during the murder trial of Charles Manson, Nixon had complained that the press were glamourising 'a man who was guilty, directly or indirectly, of eight murders'. Moreover, Haughey and Nixon each contended that they were victims of a media conspiracy. Both Watergate and what some called the Liffeygate scandal began as a result of tampering with telephones, but there was no evidence at the time that either leader was personally involved in the wrongdoings which initially led to those two political crises. Nevertheless, both leaders tried to defend the actions of their people on the grounds that 'national security' had been endangered.

There was one enormous difference between the two scandals, however. Watergate was the subject of a thorough, exhaustive investigation in which congressional leaders were careful to avoid any suggestion that they had engaged in a political vendetta. The Democratic Party leadership went to great pains to ensure that their Republican counterparts in Congress were satisfied that the investigation was being conducted in an impartial manner. In the end, Nixon was brought down not because of his involvement in the initial crimes but because he impeded the investigation of these crimes by engaging in a cover-up.

On the other hand, there was only a superficial investigation into the so-called Liffeygate scandal. Some of the things that had happened while Haughey was Taoiseach could well have been more serious than any aspect of Watergate. For instance, the implications of the Dowra affair were enormous. There were claims that the police had engaged in the most blatant form of obstructionism and that they were behind a virtual kidnapping designed to frustrate the judicial process. Were the Gardaí involved, and if so, why, and at whose behest? Surely the investigation of the affair should not have been left to the Gardaí themselves.

Serious questions were also left unanswered about the possible use of the override facility. In late 1980, after a couple of telephone conversations with John Bruton at Leinster House, Peter Prendergast picked up his telephone to hear some people discussing the two conversations, apparently with a view to making a report about what had been said. Who were those people? For whom were they preparing the report? How did they bug the conversations? Was the override used in this instance, and if so, was it used again during the seven months that Fianna Fáil remained in power?

Was it just a coincidence that Haughey was asking questions about Geraldine Kennedy's sources just before Doherty asked for the tap to be placed on her telephone? Was there any justification for basing the request for the tap on grounds of national security? Why did Doherty ask for copies of the transcripts of the tap intercepts on the eve of the crucial parliamentary-party meeting in October? Did he show this material to anyone? Why did Ciarán Haughey single out Kennedy after that meeting? Did he know the dissidents had taken her into their confidence? If so, how did he know? These questions had enormous potential ramifications. The answers might possibly have cleared the people involved of all suspicions of wrongdoing.

Doherty contended that there was a sinister plot to bribe politicians. 'We had information,' he later stated, 'that large sums of money were on offer to sway politicians, that a foreign intelligence service was operating in the country and that information from within the cabinet was being made available in an unauthorised manner.

'That was the security background to the 1982 situation,' he explained. In the aftermath of the Falklands War, it was not beyond the bounds of possibility that Britain's MI6 would be prepared to pay a few hundred thousand pounds to oust Haughey, especially in the light of efforts already made by that organisation to oust Britain's own Prime Minister, Harold Wilson, in the 1970s. The sum involved would have been only a drop in the ocean when compared with the money spent - not to mention the lives lost - in the Falklands or Northern Ireland.

'I myself was offered £50,000 in cash to help oust C. J. Haughey as Taoiseach,' Doherty continued. Even people within Fianna Fáil who were quite critical of Doherty and convinced that he was the victim of his own overactive imagination have nevertheless accepted that he genuinely believed there was a sinister plot against the government. If one were to accept that foreign money was being used as he has suggested, it would throw a new light on events. The matter should therefore have been investigated. Haughey called for a judicial inquiry into the affair; in light of all the unanswered questions relating to the affair, such an inquiry was certainly warranted.

Haughey's opponents automatically assumed that he was guilty and expected everybody else to think the same. The coalition government was so intent on securing his removal that it decided against holding an inquiry, supposedly for fear that the delay involved in setting up a tribunal might afford him an opportunity of regrouping his forces and holding on to the leadership of Fianna Fáil. But there was also another reason.

The government was pillorying Haughey and his people for tapping journalists, which was depicted as an unacceptable way to behave in a democracy. Nonetheless, the previous Fine Gael-Labour coalition had tapped the phones of both Tim Pat Coogan and Vincent Browne. The government left further investigation of the affair to the media, which were not equipped for the task.

The issues involved were much too serious to leave any room for the view that they were being used to skewer a few politicians and roast them on the fire of public opinion. In comparison with the Watergate investigation, Haughey was being railroaded. The taxpayer, meanwhile, would be screwed, as Kennedy, Arnold and Browne all successfully sued the state for invasion of privacy.

Haughey was indeed responsible for having appointed Doherty, who left himself wide open to the charge of having abused his official powers by becoming involved in local police matters in his own constituency. It should be emphasised, however, that Doherty broke no law by initially suggesting a tap be placed on a telephone. He merely ignored guidelines set by his predecessors. If they had the power to set such guidelines, then he had the power to change them. If the next government really believed his actions were so terrible in this regard, why was no attempt made to change the law? Doherty's contention that his actions were warranted left the two journalists in an invidious position. He should have been made to substantiate his charge, but he could not be expected to do so without a judicial inquiry because the matter was covered by the Official Secrets Act. Kennedy and Arnold later testified that they were led to believe there would be such an inquiry, which they wanted in order to clear their own names. Faced with the government's subsequent inaction, however, they had to sue the state as their only way of demonstrating that Doherty's actions represented an unjustifiable invasion of their privacy.

Surely, after Noonan had highlighted the whole affair by forcing the early retirement of the two senior Gardaí, the media should have insisted that more information be divulged. As it was, the only public accusation leveled against McLoughlin or Ainsworth was of having carried out the instructions of the Minister for Justice. It could hardly have been in the public interest that servants of the state should appear to be so badly treated, yet there was no outcry from the media. In addition, Ray MacSharry was unfairly pilloried.

In the midst of the rash of unfounded rumours, MacSharry had been mistakenly led to suspect that he was going to be offered a bribe, so he took the natural precaution of taping his own conversation. To have done otherwise would have been foolish in the extreme, because if the situation had been as he mistakenly suspected it was, he could have left himself open to the charge of seeking a bribe. The tape was his form of insurance. The media, stampeded by Noonan, simply ignored such matters, however, and became preoccupied with Haughey's political fate.

Haughey certainly seemed to be in a precarious position, with his party dispirited and leaking badly. Within a week, Michael O'Kennedy had begun canvassing openly for the party leadership, and he was quickly followed by O'Malley and Gerard Collins, who was encouraged to throw his hat into the ring by the small fellow himself. There were rumours that Haughey had written a letter of resignation and would formally announce his decision to step down at a meeting of the parliamentary party on 27 January, by which time all four national daily newspapers had carried editorials depicting his position as party leader as untenable.

There was general agreement in the media that morning, as the parliamentary party gathered for its weekly meeting, that Haughey was all but finished politically. This view was reflected in the papers' editorials and opinion columns as well as on the news pages. Those predictions were made on the basis of incomplete calculations, however. Each of the newspapers published lists of deputies who were supposed to be opposed to Haughey, but when the names in all of those lists were compiled in one master list, they still did not add up to a majority of Fianna Fáil deputies. Most deputies were apparently keeping their views to themselves. The reporters simply jumped to the wrong conclusion. The *Irish Press* took the extraordinary step of publishing what amounted to a political obituary – over two pages reviewing Haughey's career. The media were clearly writing him off, but he refused to be pushed out.

At the party meeting, Ben Briscoe proposed that the standing orders be suspended so that the leadership issue could be discussed. Although he objected to this, Haughey was not able to prevent a debate, but he was adamant that he was not going to be driven out of office by a 'vindictive press'. 'I will take my own decision in my own time,' he declared.

This was generally understood by those present to mean that

he intended to step down within a few days. Even Mark Killilea, one of the original gang of five who had spearheaded Haughey's drive for the leadership, admitted to the press that he believed the leader was indicating his intentions of resigning. Eileen Lemass was reported as saying that Haughey was finished and should recognise the fact.

Some people believed that he would have been forced out at this meeting if the issue had been put to a vote. There was widespread agreement within the party that the press had been unfair to him, however, so there was no desire on their part to force the issue when he seemed prepared to step down. A number of deputies at the meeting were close to tears.

'I love you, Charlie Haughey,' Ben Briscoe blurted out at one point.

'I love you, too, Ben,' Haughey replied.

'I hope the papers don't hear about this,' groaned David Andrews, at the back of the room.

The confidentiality of the meeting was a shambles, however, as reporters were given verbatim details of what had been said, including Haughey's charge that the media were conducting a campaign of vilification against him. It all seemed so reminiscent of Nixon's final hours in the White House that one columnist for the *Irish Times* contacted Carl Bernstein, the famous Watergate reporter, for his views on the Irish situation.

While the *Irish Press* admitted that Haughey 'had certainly been targeted in some sections of the media', the newspaper refuted as 'simply untrue' his implied charge that the media had created the current crisis. The national press as a whole agreed. 'The media did not tap telephones nor bug conversations,' the *Cork Examiner* declared. 'The media is entitled to question why this was done. The media did not mount a campaign against Mr Haughey; that came from within his own party, and the media is fully entitled to report it. The media did not initiate moves for his removal from the leadership. Again these came from within Fianna Fáil – his own party and his own colleagues.'

Of course, Haughey still had some admirers in the press. Proinsias Mac Aonghusa contended in his *Sunday Press* column that 'no other Irish public figure has ever undergone such a sustained media campaign of vilification as Charles J. Haughey.' In the same newspaper, Desmond Fennell criticised journalists in general for conducting a trial by the media. 'With the *Times*-RTÉ-*Independent* axis in the forefront,' he wrote, 'virtually all of them decided to become prosecutors and hostile interrogators, magnifying forensically the charges against the accused.' Just because one of Haughey's appointees had 'been publicly embarrassed and another has been shown to have abused his power is no grounds for Mr Haughey to resign as leader of Fianna Fáil,' Fennell contended.

Brian Lenihan fancied himself for the leadership and went so far as to draft a statement of his candidacy. As he was not taken seriously as a prospective leadership candidate, however, he threw his support back behind Haughey, who was apparently encouraging people to run in order to confuse the contest before he began his fightback over the weekend.

A massive campaign was undertaken on his behalf at grassroots level; a large demonstration by his supporters was held outside Fianna Fáil's general headquarters in Dublin. He and his people frantically sought middle-ground support to allow him to stay on for a few weeks until the ard-fheis, at which he could enlist his greatest support within the party. Those wishing to get rid of him, however, began to react to his survival efforts on Monday 31 January. They made preparations to draw up a petition of deputies calling on him to stand down at the next parliamentary-party meeting, which was due to be held on

Wednesday 2 February. Suddenly fate seemed to come to the leader's rescue.

Clem Coughlan, one of the deputies who had already called publicly for Haughey's resignation, was killed in a car accident on Tuesday morning. It was deemed inappropriate for the parliamentary party to discuss the leadership issue the next day, given that it was normal for party meetings to be adjourned as a mark of respect for a deputy's death. Nonetheless, the party's dissidents were determined that another meeting should be called for Friday, the day after Coughlan's funeral.

At the outset of the Wednesday meeting Haughey delivered a short tribute to the deceased deputy. Next, the chairman, Jim Tunney, spoke of Coughlan's tragic death and called for a minute's silence. Immediately afterwards, with Mary Harney on her feet calling to be recognised, Tunney announced in Irish that the meeting was adjourned until the following week. He then bolted out the door. 'Dammit!' exclaimed one disgruntled deputy. 'He just ran out of the room.'

There was considerable resentment at Tunney's action. Forty-one deputies and seven senators signed a petition calling for a parliamentary-party meeting to be held on Friday 4 February. They seemed determined that the leadership issue should be settled before the following Wednesday, when the coalition government was due to bring in its first budget. This would be a golden opportunity for Fianna Fáil to score political points, especially as a harsh budget was expected. The chance would be lost, however, if the party was still embroiled in a leadership wrangle, because this would undoubtedly divert media attention away from the budget. As a compromise, it was agreed to hold the meeting on Monday, which would allow the leadership issue to be resolved before the budget and also give the Tunney Committee time to complete its report.

Some of the forty-one deputies who had signed the petition were supporters of Haughey who had signed in order to learn what the dissidents were planning, but the media mistakenly assumed that all forty-one were likely to call for the leader's resignation. The press therefore concluded that as only thirty-seven deputies were needed for an overall majority, Haughey would definitely be toppled. He seemed to increase the tension himself late on Thursday afternoon when he issued a controversial statement.

He said that, 'despite everything that a largely hostile media and political opponents at home and abroad could do to damage not only me but the great party and traditions of Fianna Fáil,' a large number of members and supporters had called on him to stay on as leader. Consequently, he continued, 'having calmly and objectively considered the situation in all its aspects, I have decided that it is my duty in the best interest of the party to which I have devoted all my political life to stay and lead it forward out of these present difficulties. I am now, therefore, calling on all members of the party to rally behind me as their democratically elected leader and give me that total support that I need to restore unity and stability, to reorganise the party, to give it a new sense of purpose, to restate our policies, to re-establish and implement the traditional code of party discipline and to make it clear that those who bring the party into disrepute, cause dissension or refuse to accept decisions democratically arrived at can no longer remain in the party.'

On the two previous occasions when Haughey's leadership had been challenged, his supporters contended that the dissidents did not have the right to remove him, even with the support of a majority of the parliamentary party. Back in February 1982, when O'Malley was challenging for the leadership, the circumstances had been somewhat different, but the arguments used on each occasion were similar. On the eve of O'Malley's abortive challenge, Brian Lenihan had emphasised on a *Today Tonight* programme that the challenge was not for the leadership, because Haughey was already the leader, but only for the party's nomination for Taoiseach. Haughey would remain as party leader regardless of the outcome, because even though he had initially been elected leader by the parliamentary party, his selection had subsequently been confirmed by the party's ard-fheis, which was the supreme body within the organisation. Thus, from a *de jure* standpoint, he could be removed only by an ard-fheis or through his own resignation.

Likewise, in October, after McCreevy had introduced his motion of no confidence, it was noted that Haughey would remain as Taoiseach regardless of the outcome of the vote. He had been elected to the office by the Dáil, so by law – irrespective of whether he had the majority support of his own party – he would remain as Taoiseach until replaced by the Dáil. Consequently, many people believed that Haughey's statement in February implied that the parliamentary party did not have the authority to remove him; he had not specifically put forward this argument, however.

Briscoe was particularly critical of the statement. 'It was a most dreadful statement from a party leader,' he declared during an RTÉ interview. 'If you examine it line by line you could only come to the conclusion that Mr Haughey no longer recognises the right of the parliamentary party which elected him to remove him from office.' Briscoe therefore decided to force the issue by formally tabling a motion for Monday's meeting calling for 'the resignation of Mr Charles J. Haughey as party leader now'.

The press lost little time in denouncing Haughey's statement, with editorials in three of the four national newspapers. The *Cork Examiner* took the unusual step of carrying an editorial condemnation of the Taoiseach on its front page. If recent events 'had happened in any other allegedly civilised country,' the editorial declared, 'the leader of the day would have been long since gone.' Only the *Irish Press* did not condemn Haughey in an editorial, but it noted afterwards that so much damage had been done by the controversial statement that Haughey had to issue a further statement stressing his willingness to 'accept the democratic will of the parliamentary party'.

Amid all the furore, Haughey issued his clarifying statement on Saturday 4 February, emphasising that he would accept the decision of the party meeting. 'I want it stated publicly and clearly,' he declared, 'that any decision of the parliamentary party will be fully accepted by me.'

Interviewed on RTÉ lunchtime news the next day, he stressed that his statement on Thursday had been misinterpreted. He would, he emphasised, 'with honour and dignity accept any decision of the parliamentary party'. He said that, although he was confident of victory, if somebody else were elected to succeed him the next day, this person would be accepted as president of the whole Fianna Fáil organisation. 'That's the way it's been done in the past,' he added; 'that's the way it will be done in the future.'

The overwhelming majority of political commentators had already written Haughey off, and very few dared to predict his survival. The idea that he might not be beaten was treated virtually as a joke. 'We're going to miss Charlie all the same!' John Healy wrote the previous week, but by the morning of the crucial meeting he concluded that Haughey had a fighting chance of survival. He therefore included a spoof request in his column for someone who might have 'a job for a troupe of coffin-dancers who are free, due to a last-minute cancellation'.

The odds seemed very much against Haughey retaining the

leadership. After initially excluding the possibility of his survival, the bookmakers listed him in only joint fourth place with Michael O'Kennedy, behind Gerard Collins, Des O'Malley and John Wilson. Collins was being quoted as odds-on favourite, with Haughey back at 4 to 1 to retain the pary leadership and at a staggering 20 to 1 against being Taoiseach after the next general election. 'Even paying exaggerated respect to Mr Haughey's recuperative power and ability to survive,' the *Cork Examiner* declared, 'today should see the end of the Haughey era.'

The meeting, which lasted throughout the day and late into the night, began with skirmishes over whether to discuss the leadership issue first or the report of the Tunney committee, which had been set up to investigate the tapping controversy. O'Malley's supporters wanted to discuss the leadership, but this was beaten on a vote. All of those present, including senators and members of the European Parliament, were able to vote on this issue, so the outcome was not necessarily indicative of the feelings of Dáil deputies. Still, Haughey had clearly won the first round. He also won the next round by having his own proposal for the expulsion of Doherty and O'Donoghue from the parliamentary party deferred until the next meeting. While the two of them were therefore entitled to remain with their voting privileges intact, the move clearly favoured Haughey. Doherty had already indicated his intention of supporting Haughey, but O'Donoghue, who had lost his Dáil seat in the recent election, was only at the meeting in his capacity as a member of the Senate, so he had no vote in the leadership contest. Haughey then got a further boost when the Tunney committee reported that there was no evidence to link the leader directly to the telephone-tapping.

Following a four-and-a-half-hour discussion on matters relating to the Tunney report, Briscoe formally proposed his motion calling for Haughey's resignation. He had apparently done little to secure support for this motion, however, because he did not even have a seconder lined up. For a moment it looked as though the motion would fail for lack of a seconder, but McCreevy filled the void. Deputies then spoke for and against the motion.

Haughey's supporters portrayed their man as having been crucified by a hostile media, which, they said, should not be allowed to dictate how Fianna Fáil ran its affairs. They stressed the leader's willingness to expel Doherty and O'Donoghue, thereby distancing himself from their deeds. His backers also exploited the idea that certain moneyed interests wanted to get rid of him; they contended that forcing him out of office would be tantamount to admitting that Fianna Fáil was for sale.

Haughey's opponents, on the other hand, accused him of presiding over a succession of scandals which had done enormous damage to the party. He was depicted as a distinct electoral liability: it was emphasised that he had failed to secure a majority in three consecutive elections. These people, and the media in general, conveniently forgot that Éamon de Valera had also failed to secure such a majority in his first three general elections as party leader and that Sean Lemass had never won an overall majority.

Most of those at the parliamentary party meeting on 7 February 1983 felt that the media had been unfair to Haughey. His critics both inside and outside the party had never been seen to give his leadership a real chance, and in recent days they had been trying to get rid of him with almost indecent haste. Indeed, at this meeting they did not even want to wait for the Tunney report. All this enabled Haughey to retain the support of many middle-ground deputies at this critical point. People like a fighter who battles against the odds, and Haughey had seemed to be battling against enormous odds for the past several days.

Even individuals who despised him were heard to express a begrudging admiration for his tenacity.

This time Haughey agreed to a secret vote. In all probability this was to his advantage, because opponents who had had their own ambitions for the leadership thwarted for the present could now back him, as he was likely to be more vulnerable than a new leader. In addition, there were those who, according to one reporter, had been 'kissing Charlie on all four cheeks in October' but had recently found it necessary to express public reservations about him. Under the cloak of secrecy they were quietly able to return to the Haughey fold.

When the votes were counted, Haughey survived, gaining a majority of seven. Reporters who heard the news outside were stunned. 'I saw at least two of my colleagues in the media turn visibly pale, total disbelief showing on their countenances,' Raymond Smith wrote. 'We did not believe our ears.'

'The scenes that night inside and outside Leinster House were as extraordinary and as frightening as they had been the previous autumn,' Bruce Arnold wrote. He walked through Leinster House with two colleagues, who were clearly uneasy in his presence when they entered the crowded hallway. 'Angry supporters there included Haughey's brother Jock, who launched himself towards me but was intercepted by two ministerial police drivers and held back by them,' Arnold continued. He and some other journalists were advised to leave by the less-used door at the Leinster Lawn side of the building.

# 14

## 'Uno Duce, Una Voce'
## Leader of the Opposition, 1982–1987

After Fitzgerald's election as Taoiseach on 14 December 1982, Haughey graciously accepted his successor's victory. 'We wish him well in this difficult assignment,' the Fianna Fáil leader said. 'For our party, we will go into Opposition with, I hope, dignity and honour. We will endeavour in Opposition to discharge our responsibilities as constructively as we can and with as great a sense of reponsibility as we can, conscious of the fact that it will require not only the arduous efforts of the government but the full and constructive cooperation of the Opposition in the Dáil to help the country meet the serious difficulties which confront us.'

With Haughey's third successive failure to lead Fianna Fáil to an overall majority in a general election, it was obvious that there would be another move to oust him from the party leadership, but the dissidents bided their time. They were in no great haste for the moment. He, on the other hand, was intent on strengthening his own base within the party. When O'Malley announced his own candidacy for one of the five vice-presidential positions in Fianna Fáil, Haughey asked him to withdraw because the move would be interpreted as a challenge to the leadership. 'That job is for old fuddy-duddies,' Haughey told him on 13 January.

O'Malley was unmoved. He noted that the description did

not fit a decade earlier, when Haughey had begun his political comeback following the Arms Crisis by successfully running for the office.

The telephone-tapping scandal broke the following week, and preparations for the party's ard-fheis faded into the background. The dissidents decided that this was their chance to get a new leader. Haughey renewed his call for a judicial inquiry but despite the fact that he had initially requested such an inquiry the previous month, his call was seen by some observers as a desperate play for time in order to hold on to the leadership until the ard-fheis.

From the outset, O'Malley dismissed the idea of a judicial inquiry. 'The record of these inquiries is not very satisfactory,' he declared on a *Today Tonight* interview on the night that Noonan formally confirmed the existence of the taps. O'Malley was obviously in sympathy with those who wished to oust Haughey, but their efforts failed.

In the aftermath of the crisis, Haughey's position as party leader was more solidly based than at any time since he was first elected. After all, he had increased the margin of his initial victory over Colley in 1979. Back then, he had six votes to spare out of seventy-eight, and in February 1983 he increased that to seven out of seventy-three. His position was further strengthened at the party's ard-fheis later in the month, when his supporters were in almost total control. The extent of this control became evident when O'Malley failed in his bid to win one of the vice-presidential positions. Of course, this virtual takeover of the party would still meet with some resistance.

It was not only party members but the general public who were growing tired of all the leadership challenges and changes. Since 1977, when Liam Cosgrave had stood down as leader of Fine Gael and Brendan Corish had done the same as leader of the Labour Party, the political scene had been in near-chaos.

Lynch had been pushed in 1979, and Frank Cluskey had to step down as leader of the Labour Party after he lost his Dáil seat in 1981. Michael O'Leary, Clusky's replacement, then resigned in a huff the following year after his policies were repudiated by the Labour Party. On top of all those changes, there were the three unsuccessful heaves against Haughey's leadership.

In March 1983 there was a brief controversy when Paul W. Mackay, a former financial auditor of the party's books in Haughey's own Dublin North-Central constituency, circulated a letter to all Fianna Fáil deputies stating that the party was 'financially bankrupt'. He complained of being dropped as auditor in June 1982 because he had persistently demanded full information about election expenditures during the two most recent general-election campaigns. 'Traditionally,' he admitted, 'the financial affairs of the party have been shrouded in secrecy, with the full financial facts only available to a handful of people. This situation may have been appropriate in the past but, in my view, is not [appropriate] at the present time.'

Mackay's letter epitomised the weakness of the dissident position. Haughey's opponents posed as men of principle who were appalled at the way things were being done, yet when they were in a position to do things differently themselves, they behaved in the same way. It was not a matter of principle; it was a question of power.

Haughey essentially adopted a two-prong approach in his quest to regain the reins of government. He sought to consolidate his position within Fianna Fáil while at the same time trying to improve the party's position vis-à-vis the government. His approach towards the government was largely negative. Instead of bringing forward positive policies, he merely reacted on an ad hoc basis to whatever the government was doing.

The Taoiseach, Garret Fitzgerald, operated with one eye constantly trained on Haughey. This was particularly apparent on the question of setting up the New Ireland Forum, the brainchild of John Hume. Fitzgerald supported the idea of formulating a united nationalist position on the partition issue, but he was initially unable to persuade his cabinet colleagues to back this proposal. The cabinet voted by twelve to three against establishing a forum, but, fearing that Haughey would endorse Hume's idea at the February ard-fheis, Fitzgerald privately persuaded a majority of his colleagues to go along with the idea. Just two days before Haughey's presidential address to the ard-fheis, Fitzgerald issued a statement calling for the establishment of the New Ireland Forum. In so doing, he took much of the wind out of Haughey's sails because, as anticipated, the Fianna Fáil leader duly endorsed Hume's proposal two days later.

Of course this was not the first time that Fitzgerald had outmanoeuvred Haughey. The previous November the short fellow had tried to embarrass the Fine Gael leader just before the general election by publishing the wording for a pro-life amendment to the Constitution. Fitzgerald responded by enthusiastically endorsing the proposal, despite his own better judgement. Before publicly endorsing the wording he telephoned Dick Spring, the newly elected leader of the Labour Party, to say that he was personally opposed to the referendum but his colleagues were insisting he support the wording rather than risk the danger of being depicted as pro-abortion.

He later found himself in an extremely embarrassing position as Taoiseach when the Protestant churches came out against the proposed amendment. He tried to introduce a new wording that was acceptable to Protestant leaders, but Haughey insisted that the promised referendum should go ahead on the published wording. When some dissident members of the governing parties indicated that they were prepared to stand with Fianna Fáil on the issue, Fitzgerald was forced into a corner, and his political ineptitude was mercilessly exposed. His government eventually brought in the necessary legislation for a referendum on an amendment which he urged the electorate to reject. Its ultimate passage, against the wishes of the state's small Protestant minority, left the constitutional crusade in tatters.

Even before the voting, Fitzgerald admitted that it was necessary to put the constitutional crusade in cold storage until after the New Ireland Forum had completed its work. At its first session, which was held on 30 May 1983, Haughey emphasised that Northern Ireland was ' a political anachronism'; he urged the Forum to develop a nationalist position so that Northern unionists could be invited to a conference at which a new constitution could be drawn up for the whole island.

Notwithstanding his genuine desire for harmony with the unionists, Haughey was viewed with deep suspicion on the other side of the border. He and his family were subjected to considerable pressure following the publication, in late 1983, of the book *The Boss,* written by journalists Joe Joyce and Peter Murtagh. A blistering indictment of Haughey's short-lived government of 1982, it was probably the most interesting and provocative book ever published on contemporary Irish politics.

Despite its subtitle, 'Charles J. Haughey in Government', the book was not so much about Haughey in government as it was about the events which occurred while he was in power during 1982. In some cases he had no connection with the events under discussion and the authors might have taken a more dispassionate look at the role he played in the events with which he was involved.

Although readers were undoubtedly familiar with much of

the material in the book because of the media's extensive coverage of the relevant issues, the authors brought out new information on virtually every facet of the story. They had the advantage of being able to provide a broader picture than the media had been able to give in the midst of the events. There was detailed coverage of the dismissed charge of double-voting against Haughey's election agent and a thorough account of events leading to the O'Malley heave, the Gregory deal, and Burke's appointment to the European Commission. There was also fresh material on the MacArthur affair and on the Dowra case, in which Sean Doherty's brother-in-law Garda Thomas Nangle had the charges against him for assault dismissed after his victim, James McGovern failed to turn up in court after being 'lifted' by the police in Northern Ireland in an obvious attempt to prevent him from testifying. McGovern later won civil suits against both the police who detained him and the man who assaulted him.

*The Boss* was particularly good on the politicisation of the police and the wire-tapping of journalists. It conveyed effectively the fear that permeated opposition circles in 1982. Frequently, the authors did not give their own conclusions but instead led the reader to a point where certain conclusions seemed inescapable. When they made judgements, however, they seemed to judge Haughey by one set of standards and his critics by a different one.

Haughey was depicted in a most unfavourable light over the Gregory deal, while Fitzgerald came off lightly even though he had also tried to make a deal with Gregory. Dick Burke's appointment to the European Commission was portrayed as a piece of cynical opportunism, even though the reaction of Fine Gael was even more cynical, because, with the experience he had already gained in the post, Burke was obviously better qualified for the position when Haughey appointed him than he had been when he was first appointed by the coalition government in 1976. Short-term party considerations were paramount within Fine Gael, so it was unfair to argue that Haughey was the only one who had put his own or his party's considerations first.

The authors went even further in relation to Haughey's slip of the tongue in referring to Malcolm MacArthur as 'the right man' at the press conference following the resignation of the Attorney-General. Haughey was 'clearly in contempt of court', Joyce and Murtagh wrote. 'His aides pleaded with reporters not to publish or broadcast this remark,' the authors added. 'Those working for the Irish media were unable to, in any event, because if they did, they would have been as guilty as Haughey.' This implied – very unfairly – that Haughey's remark had been premeditated.

When MacArthur's lawyers tried to have Haughey cited for contempt of court, the judge accepted that he had made a genuine mistake, but the authors seem to question the judge's decision. 'It did not stop some people thinking that the remark was part of a huge conspiracy to keep the case out of the courts and thus protect certain unnamed people, politicians and lawyers,' they wrote. 'Haughey, acting Justice Minister at the time and indeed himself a former Justice Minister, knew exactly what he was doing,' they claimed. Of course, some foolish people will believe anything. It was wrong, however, to give credence to such distorted views by repeating them without identifying them as nonsense.

Haughey was already aware that MacArthur had made a full statement admitting his guilt, so the state effectively had an open-and-shut case. Only the legal formalities had to be completed. In the circumstances, Haughey's slip in complimenting the Gardaí for their handling of the case and coming up with 'the right man' was understandable. Still, as Taoiseach he could not escape responsibility for the activities of his Minister for Justice. Haughey had, after all, selected him. The book documented some outrageous behaviour on the part of a number of individuals, but Malcolm MacArthur was the only person convicted of wrongdoing. Whose fault was that? The various accusations certainly warranted a thorough investigation, but the authors never tried to analyse why Haughey's call for a judicial inquiry had been ignored. No doubt his opponents suspected he was just playing for time, but were they also afraid that a proper investigation would show that they too were guilty of some of the more colourful charges?

The pressure on Haughey at the time showed at a meeting of the New Ireland Forum when Dick Spring, the Tánaiste and leader of the Labour Party, accused him of having leaked some information to the press.

Haughey indignantly refuted the suggestion. 'No one has suffered more than I have from journalists,' he emphasised. He asked whether Spring realised what the media had done to him, and at that point he broke down and wept openly, to the amazement of the various delegations. Ray MacSharry then led him, still weeping, from the room.

That afternoon the four leaders – Fitzgerald, Spring, Haughey and Hume – had a leadership meeting at the Forum. Fitzgerald and Hume paired off, leaving Spring with Haughey, who explained that he and his family were very upset over the contents of *The Boss.* He said that his children had been victimised throughout their lives as a result of his involvement in politics. On one occasion he mentioned that his daughter Emer had come home in tears after leaving a gymkhana in Northern Ireland early because she could not put up with the abuse she had received as a result of the fact that he was her father. Having grown up as the son of a Dáil deputy, Spring was easily able to empathise with the Haugheys in this matter, even though he had good reasons not to sympathise with the short fellow himself.

Back in January 1982, when Spring was recovering from serious back injuries sustained in a car accident, Haughey had refused to allow anyone to pair with him on the forthcoming vote on the budget. As a result, Spring had had to make the arduous journey from his home in Tralee in considerable pain. He had been flown by helicopter and then taken into the Dáil chamber on a stretcher for the vital vote. To make things worse, it was a wasted journey because the government was defeated on the budget anyway. Yet now, possibly for the first time, Spring had genuine sympathy for Haughey, who had shown himself in a very human light that day.

'Immediately after the afternoon session,' Fitzgerald noted in his autobiography, 'Dick and I were discussing Haughey's breakdown together when we both suddenly realised that, in response to queries from the *Sunday Tribune* about our likely Christmas reading, we had each mentioned *The Boss* as a book that we would would want to read during the break.' Both felt so sorry for Haughey that Garret asked Vincent Browne, the editor of the *Sunday Tribune,* to replace *The Boss* with other works in the lists supplied by Dick and himself. Browne, who felt that *The Boss* was unfair to Haughey in many respects, readily agreed. Having had a tap of his own telephone authorised by ministers in both Jack Lynch's last government and two different Fine Gael governments, Browne had more reason than most to know that many of the insinuations being made against Haughey could just as easily have been directed against his opponents.

Easons, the country's main book distributor, refused to handle *The Boss,* for fear of becoming involved in costly libel suits, but the work was still a runaway bestseller. There was some further embarrassment early in the new year with the publication of a briefing document circulated within Fianna Fáil circles by the party's acting press officer, Ken Ryan, who had called on the party's local public-relations officers to inform party headquarters without delay of any stories that 'might be incriminating to opposition deputies or councillors'. Coming so soon after the sensational material in *The Boss,* the affair proved particularly embarrassing. Sean Doherty also began making embarrassing noises as he became restless for the restoration of the Fianna Fáil whip. At the time of its removal, he had thought that Haughey had had no choice. A scapegoat was needed and he willingly allowed himself to be used as one. 'I was a very willing recipient,' he said. 'I carried the can for the party. I no longer feel that obligation.'

Notwithstanding the numerous questions raised in *The Boss* about his conduct, Doherty maintained that he had done nothing wrong and that he had been the victim of a conspiracy. But he landed himself back in controversy in April 1984 when the *Tuam Herald* published an interview in which he advised Raymond Smith to 'keep in close touch with his doctor and not be alone in his own house because he might not be able to take care of himself.' Smith considered the remarks a threat.

Doherty had again become an embarrassment to Fianna Fáil, so, with the European elections coming up in June, he had to forget about rejoining the parliamentary party. The question of his readmission was quickly forgotten about, anyway, when a controversy arose following the publication of the report of the Forum for a New Ireland on 2 May 1984.

In outlining the nationalist desire for an end to partition, the report emphasised that 'the particular structure of political unity which the Forum would wish to see established is a unitary state, achieved by agreement and consent, embracing the whole island of Ireland and providing irrevocable guarantees for the protection and preservation of both the unionist and nationalist identities.' The Report then went on to note that consideration was also given 'in some detail' to other structural arrangements. In particular, the 'federal/confederate state and joint authority' were examined and outlined separately.

Following publication of the report, Fitzgerald, Spring and Hume gave the impression of being open-minded and willing to consider all of the structures outlined or any other proposals which might resolve the Northern problem. The report specifically stated, for instance, that the Forum parties 'remain open to discuss other views which may contribute to political development'. But Haughey promptly contended that only a unitary state would be acceptable because none of the other models he had outlined 'would bring peace or stability to the North'. He was obviously dismissing federation, confederation or joint Anglo-Irish authority as possible solutions.

Suddenly the report itself was overshadowed by this apparent dispute between the nationalist leaders. Haughey went on RTÉ's *Day by Day* programme the next morning to accuse the media of having distorted his views in a way that was 'most unfortunate and totally uncalled-for'.

'I did not dismiss anything in the report at all,' he contended. 'I said it spoke for itself. What any one of us might or might not have preferred doesn't matter.' Instead of highlighting the slight differences that remained between himself and the other nationalist leaders, everyone should 'concentrate on the fantastic amount of agreement' that existed between the various participants, he argued. It briefly looked as though he was backing down somewhat when he said it was unfortunate that politicians and journalists had been catapulated into instant comment. 'It would have been better,' he added, 'if we had all been able to sit back for two or three days, read the report and then give our reaction.' But it soon became apparent that he had not changed his views about limiting a possible solution to a unitary state. On 11 May he stated that it was 'dangerous and foolish to be putting a whole range of alternatives to the British government'.

Some in Fianna Fáil were upset at the way in which Haughey was committing the party to a policy without the parliamentary party so much as discussing the report. Senator Eoin Ryan, who had been privately clamouring for a party meeting to consider the report, publicly took issue with Haughey over the matter. The senator warned that the emphasis on the unitary-state model would frighten the British off discussions.

It was two weeks after the publication of the report before Haughey's critics had a chance to voice their concern within the parliamentary party because, as far as Haughey was concerned, any such discussion was going to have to wait on electoral considerations. The regular weekly meeting due to be held on 9 May was postponed so that Haughey could be in Cork when the party's candidates for the upcoming European elections submitted their nomination papers.

By the time the parliamentary party finally sat down to discuss the report, Haughey's colleagues were confronted with a *fait accompli,* because he had firmly established a party line and any backtracking would undoubtedly have led to speculation about his leadership – this time in the midst of the European election campaign. He was ready to meet any possible challenge head-on.

He moved a motion congratulating himself and Fianna Fáil's twelve other Forum delegates 'on their splendid contribution to the purpose of the Forum both in its work and the subsequent presentation of the report'.

Senator Ryan proposed an amendment stipulating that the

leader should enunciate policy only 'after discussion with the parliamentary party', but this was rejected and the motion was then carried unanimously. By implication the rejection of Ryan's amendment amounted to a formal acknowledgement that, henceforth, the party leader would be entitled to announce policy without consulting his colleagues.

Following the three-hour meeting, Des O'Malley was openly critical of the way in which party debate on the Forum had effectively been stifled. With the campaign for the European elections already under way, his remarks were widely resented in party circles. Seizing the opportunity, Haughey called for O'Malley's expulsion from the parliamentary party. The haste with which a meeting was held – with little more than twenty-four hours' notice – was in stark contrast to the two weeks taken before a meeting was convened to discuss the Forum report.

Haughey personally proposed the removal of the party whip, and his motion was carried by a sizeable majority of fifty-six to sixteen. Henceforth, there could be little doubt about the extent of his control of the party.

'*Uno duce, una voce*!' P. J. Mara, Fianna Fáil's new press officer, joked with journalists afterwards as he goose-stepped around the press briefing room in Leinster House with an index finger over his upper lip as a mock moustache. 'We are having no more nibbling at my leader's bum.'

This extraordinary comment was made facetiously and was never intended for publication, but Geraldine Kennedy did not think it was off the record, so she mentioned it in her column in the *Sunday Press*. This was then taken up by Conor Cruise O'Brien, who exploited the incident during the election campaign. The Italian phrase, meaning 'One leader, one voice', was a slogan used by fascists under Benito Mussolini. Haughey was furious.

'You go into that room where they all hate me, and you give

them this,' he snapped, after reading the report.

'It was just a throwaway line,' Mara replied. 'Geraldine has no sense of humour; she is deadly serious.'

'Yeah, yeah, yeah,' Haughey said. 'But for fuck's sake, Mara, be careful in future, you must resist your baser instincts. Put a button on your lip.'

In early 1984 Mara had been appointed Fianna Fáil press officer after the position had been turned down by both Frank Dunlop and Sean Duignan. Mara, a brilliant raconteur with an inexhaustible font of witty remarks, epigrams and inside stories about happenings within Fianna Fáil, was a great mimic. He could be outrageously irreverent about Haughey.

After the furore over Kennedy's disclosure that he had referred to Haughey as 'Duce', Mara began describing him as the Caudillo, the title given to Franco, the Spanish dictator. Despite his playful scarcasm, Mara was intensely loyal to Haughey. After all, he had supported him throughout the Arms Crisis and had driven him on the rubber-chicken circuit during his darkest days. Many of Mara's stories were unprintable because they were either ribald or potentially libellous, but the journalists felt that he was giving them an invaluable inside glimpse of Haughey. He talked to them, and with them, but not down to them. His off-the-cuff remarks and humorous asides cut through official pomposity or political blather. He never allowed the job to turn his head but always conveyed the impression that he considered himself one of the lads. 'He manages to keep reporters on side by wit, impudence and telling them to fuck off – something they love,' Liam Collins of the *Sunday Independent* wrote.

Opponents tried to depict Fianna Fáil candidates in the European election as representatives of a neo-fascist party, while the candidates, for their part, attempted to turn the election into a referendum on the performance of the government at home. Although the combined vote of Fine Gael and Labour was marginally ahead of that of Fianna Fáil, the latter won eight of the fifteen seats, to give the party its first overall majority in any election since Haughey had taken over as leader. This result was a 60 per cent improvement over the five seats the party had won in 1979. It was the first and only time that Fianna Fáil won a majority of the seats in a European election, but Bruce Arnold still concluded that 'it really represented a fourth electoral defeat for Haughey'. With some people, Haughey simply could not win.

This was especially true among an influential group of journalists which included Arnold, Michael Mills of the *Irish Press* and Dick Walsh of the *Irish Times*. They had all been admirers of Jack Lynch and blamed Haughey for undermining him. 'I happen to like those journalists,' P. J. Mara explained, 'but I think that in relation to CJH they suspended all sense of fairness, so much of their output concerned this demon Haughey who could do no right.'

Before the end of the year Haughey felt secure enough to permit Doherty's return to the party fold. Doherty had formally applied for readmission in January, but this application was not considered at a party meeting until eleven months later, on 5 December 1984, when it was brought up under correspondence at the start of a regular meeting. At the time, there were only twenty-six deputies in attendance and the application was passed unanimously. There were nine deputies present who were believed to have voted against Haughey's leadership in February 1983, but none of them objected to Doherty's readmission. By this time Haughey's position vis-à-vis the government had been enhanced following Fitzgerald's disastrous summit with Thatcher in November.

Thatcher was not only privately unreceptive to the ideas put forward in the Forum Report, but at a press conference afterwards she seemed to go out of her way to be dismissive of the various structures outlined in the document. 'That is out . . . That is out . . . That is out,' she declared, referring in turn to a possible unitary state, federation or confederation, and joint authority. When Fitzgerald gave a televised press conference immediately afterwards, he was not aware of her comments, which had already been televised live in Ireland. As a result, his demeanour – he behaved with diplomatic decorum, in blissful ignorance of what he later described as Thatcher's 'gratuitously offensive' display – left him looking particularly weak and ineffective. From a public-relations standpoint, the summit and its pathetic aftermath were disastrous.

The Taoiseach subsequently tried to blame Haughey for the government's difficulties with Thatcher. She obviously had little sympathy for the aspirations of Irish nationalists. This was hardly surprising: only weeks earlier she had narrowly escaped being killed when a bomb went off in the Brighton hotel at which she was staying during the Conservative Party Conference. Nevertheless Fitzgerald attributed her attitude to suspicions created by Haughey's conduct following the Dublin Castle summit of 1980.

'We witnessed a disastrous process when an Irish leader, for his own short-term political advantage, in anticipation of an early election, exaggerated beyond any reality a so-called "historic breakthrough" with Mrs Thatcher,' the Taoiseach stated during the adjournment debate winding up the autumn session of the Dáil on 14 December 1984. 'The boasts of that occasion created some ephemeral approval on the part of his own party,' he continued. 'But, tragically, the very process of exaggeration immediately destroyed any prospect of developing a real dialogue with the British about doing something for the people of

Northern Ireland,' he said. Fitzgerald went on to accuse the Fianna Fáil leader of having exploited 'the misery of the people of Northern Ireland' for short-term electoral gain.

Haughey was indignant. He promptly protested and accused Fitzgerald of having lied in alleging that he had exploited the misery of the Northern people. The Fianna Fáil leader was ordered to withdraw this unparliamentary charge of lying or leave the chamber. In the circumstances he chose to walk out in protest.

Early in the new year the government was confronted with an internal crisis over its attempts to amend Haughey's family-planning act to permit the sale of non-medical contraceptives like condoms without a doctor's prescription. Some members of the Catholic hierarchy vociferously opposed the new bill, and a number of Fine Gael and Labour deputies threatened to vote against the measure. In the circumstances, there was a real chance that the government would be defeated, but Fianna Fáil's hopes in this regard suffered a serious setback when O'Malley spoke out strongly in support of the bill.

O'Malley recognised that the Catholic Church had exerted an undue influence on political life in the Republic. Ever since the Mother and Child controversy of 1951, no political party had dared to defy the hierarchy. That controversy had centred on Noel Browne's determination to introduce free health care for all mothers and children, regardless of means, because the country had one of the highest infant-morality rates in Europe. But the Archbishop of Dublin, John Charles McQuaid, the son of a medical doctor, was opposed to socialised medicine, which he somehow equated with godless communism.

With the backing of the hierarchy, McQuaid said that only those who could not afford to pay for such health care should be covered by the scheme. He demanded a means test, and the government backed him. Browne baulked and resigned from the government; he then published his correspondence on the matter, thereby sparking a controversy that ultimately brought down the government.

O'Malley read through the Dáil debate on the Mother and Child controversy and was appalled by its contents. 'It is incredible that a member of this House and of the government of the day could be as craven and supine as they were, as we look back on them now,' he told the Dáil. But he had to ask himself, 'Has the atmosphere changed?' The hierarchy was now opposing the bill to legalise the sale of condoms without a doctor's perscription, and the whole thing was threatening to bring down the government.

The idea that the Catholic Church – or any church – would be accorded an effective veto over the lives of citizens challenged the very core of republicanism. In O'Malley's view the real issue had nothing to do with contraception. It was a question of freedom and private conscience. 'I do not believe that the interests of this state, of our Constitution and of this republic would be served by putting politics before conscience in regard to this,' he told the Dáil. 'There is a choice of a kind that can only be answered by saying that I stand by the republic, and accordingly I will not oppose this bill.' It was a stirring speech. Barry Desmond, the Minister for Health and deputy leader of the Labour Party, described it as 'the finest I have heard in thirteen years in the Dáil'.

Although no longer in the Fianna Fáil parliamentary party, O'Malley was still a member of the organisation. In view of that membership, he did not take the logical step of voting for the bill. Instead he absented himself from the Dáil while the vote was being taken. Nevertheless, some people believed that his comments had weakened the resolve of dissidents within Fine

Gael and Labour and had thus helped save the government considerable embarrassment.

'The feeling was that we would have won, had he decided to support us and bring a few others with him,' was the verdict of one Fianna Fáil deputy. O'Malley suddenly became the scapegoat for the Opposition's failure to bring down the government. Worse still, he had shown up the party's much-vaunted republicanism as highly pretentious. What did the party really stand for – the whims of its leader?

A special meeting of the Fianna Fáil National Executive was convened to discuss a motion calling for O'Malley's expulsion from the organisation 'for conduct unbecoming a member'. Haughey left nobody in any doubt that he was in favour of expulsion. In the run-up to the meeting he told a number of people who tried to intercede on O'Malley's behalf, 'It's him or me.'

O'Malley, who was permitted to address the meeting, requested that the vote on his expulsion be by secret ballot. Haughey, on the other hand, asked for a unanimous decision. 'I want it to be unanimous, for the good of the party and the organisation,' he declared on three different occasions. When it became apparent that this was out of the question, he demanded a roll-call vote. Whatever about the parliamentary party being free to establish its own procedure, the National Executive was bound by the party's *Corú,* which stipulated that all votes should be secret. Yet none of the eighty-two members present, even those determined to support O'Malley, dared challenge Haughey's ruling. A roll-call vote was taken, and the motion to expel O'Malley was approved, by seventy-three votes to nine.

Interviewed on RTÉ radio the following morning, O'Malley admitted that his difficulties with Haughey went back to the time of the Arms Crisis. 'I came to know in some detail about those events and all the details surrounding them, and I inevitably began to form certain opinions then, and quite honestly those opinions have never left me,' the Limerick deputy explained. The implication of this was that, as a result of his special access to information while serving as Minister for Justice, O'Malley had come to know something about Haughey which was even more damning that anything that had yet been revealed. This seemed like another variant of the 'flawed pedigree' approach, in which a sweeping accusation was made against the Fianna Fáil leader with no attempt to substantiate it. The interviewer did not pursue the matter at the time, but many months afterwards, on *The Late Late Show,* Gay Byrne challenged O'Malley to 'put up or shut up – stop saying these things, or else say what you mean.' But O'Malley refused to clarify the matter.

Two of the three members of the party's National Committee of Fifteen who voted against O'Malley's expulsion were defeated when they stood for re-election at the next ard-fheis. One of them admitted to this writer that Haughey had probably not orchestrated their defeat; he had not had to do so. They had not voted as he had wished, so, in the spirit prevailing within the party, they were considered disloyal and were politically eliminated. One of their replacements was Captain James J. Kelly of Arms Crisis fame; Kelly had joined the Fianna Fáil fold after a spell in Kevin Boland's abortive Aontacht Éireann.

Haughey's critics within the parliamentary party had effectively been silenced, and he had the satisfaction of seeing the party improve its standing in the country. In the local elections of June 1985 the party received more than 11 per cent more first-preference votes than the two governing parties combined. By October Fianna Fáil had stretched its lead to a staggering 19 per cent, in a public-opinion poll conducted by RSI. Haughey was 14 percentage points ahead of Fitzgerald.

The Taoiseach desperately needed something to boost both his own flagging leadership and his government's weakening position. For some time he and a number of his cabinet colleagues had been preoccupied with secret talks with the British concerning Northern Ireland, and his best hope seemed to be in gaining some kind of significant concessions from the British. With the government obviously making preparations for a propaganda campaign to secure popular support for an impending agreement with Britain, Haughey voiced grave misgivings about such an approach and warned of the danger of 'a sell-out'. On 5 October he complained about 'a well-orchestrated media campaign which is under way at present, not just here but among Ireland's friends abroad, to condition public opinion and prepare the ground for some as-yet-unspecified development'.

'This is a time for great vigilance,' he continued. 'There is a great deal at stake. The Irish people must not again have a treaty imposed or be asked to accept some dubious settlement entered into in response to the short-term political needs of those involved.' Ignoring his own complaints about Fitzgerald's contacts with Prior and Norfolk in 1982, he now sent his deputy leader, Brian Lenihan, to the United States in an effort to ensure that prominent Americans would not be stampeded into supporting the forthcoming Anglo-Irish agreement, which was signed at Hillsborough Castle near Belfast on 15 November 1985.

Lenihan tried to persuade Haughey not to take a stand against the Anglo-Irish Agreement. Nonetheless, he persuaded himself that, in going to the United States to push Haughey's line, he was just doing 'another job for the party', even though Lenihan knew this was nonsense, according to his biographer, James Downey. Tip O'Neill, the Speaker of the House of

Representatives, gave Lenihan a frosty reception and then dismissed him without paying him much attention.

One senior member of the British government described the agreement as 'very modest', according to *Time* magazine. 'If it were any more modest,' he added, 'we could scarcely call it an agreement.' Indeed in tangible terms there was not much in the agreement other than a decision to establish an Intergovernmental Conference, which would consist of representatives of the Dublin and London governments and would consider a wide range of matters relating to the administration of Northern Ireland. Fitzgerald described this as 'almost joint authority'. The conference was to have its own secretariat based in Belfast, but there was no derogation of Britain's actual sovereignty over Northern Ireland. On any matter on which the representatives of the two governments could not agree at the Intergovernmental Conference, the British would have the final say. Even so, the whole arrangement amounted to a recognition by the British that the Dublin government had a right to be consulted on matters relating to the internal affairs of Northern Ireland.

Haughey dismissed this aspect of the agreement as insignificant because, he contended, the Irish government had always had a right to make its views known. 'This arrangement gives them nothing more on that score,' he added. 'Perhaps it gives them a formal way of doing so, but it doesn't change the right or the status of the government in doing it,' he argued.

In the past, however, Irish leaders who had tried to intercede with the British on behalf of Northern nationalists were often told, in effect, to mind their own business. It should be remembered, for instance, that as late as the eve of Haughey's first formal meeting with Thatcher, the British prime minister had told the House of Commons that the affairs of Northern Ireland were a matter for the people of Northern Ireland, her government, the Westminster Parliament 'and no one else'. Thus the establishment of the Intergovernmental Conference was at least a symbolic step away from the old entrenched position adopted by Thatcher and her precedessors.

Another important aspect of the agreement was a formal declaration by the two governments 'that if, in the future, a majority of the people of Northern Ireland clearly wish for and formally consent to the establishment of a united Ireland, they will introduce and support in the respective parliaments legislation to give effect to that wish'. Again, Haughey tried to dismiss the significance of this aspect of the agreement by contending that it contained 'nothing new'. He argued that this had always been the position because it was 'unthinkable' that the British government would stand in the way of Irish unity if the majority wished it. 'The alternative would be nonsense,' he contended, 'so "Thanks for nothing" is what I say to that.'

In trying to belittle this aspect of the agreement, Haughey screamed in the face of history. If the British had been willing to accept the wishes of the majority back in 1920 or 1921 there would have been no partition in the first place. Moreover, the British state papers for the late 1940s contain numerous references to Britain's need to retain a physical presence in Northern Ireland for strategic purposes. Indeed, one of Haughey's staunch admirers had already pointed out that a 1949 cabinet memorandum emphasised that Britain could not allow the area to withdraw from the United Kingdom 'even if the people of Northern Ireland desired it'.

Haughey voiced his strongest objections against what he contended were the constitutional implications of the agreement. He vehemently denounced the first article of the accord, which stated 'that any change in the status of Northern Ireland would only come about with the consent of a majority of the people of Northern Ireland'. The Fianna Fáil leader complained that this provision was 'in total conflict with the Constitution, and in particular Article 2 of the Constitution', which claimed sovereignty over the whole island. 'For the first time ever,' he continued, 'the legitimacy of partition, which is contrary to unification, has been recognised by an Irish government in an international agreement.' He added that the agreement was also 'totally against the principles enshrined in the New Ireland Forum Report.'

'From our point of view it gives everything away,' he said. 'It confirmed the status of Northern Ireland as an integral part of the United Kingdom and it confirmed that there would be no change in the status without the consent of the Northern unionists.'

Haughey's constitutional arguements ignored Article 2(b) of the agreement, which clearly stated that 'there is no derogation from the sovereignty of either the Irish government or the United Kingdom government.' Although it may well have been inserted as a sop for Northern unionists, that clause also guaranteed the Republic's constitutional position because it meant that there was no derogation of the Republic's *de jure* claim to sovereignty over the Six Counties.

Admittedly, the agreement contained a recognition of the fact that the area was under alien rule, but Article 3 of the Republic's constitution already recognised that fact. Fitzgerald had astutely anticipated Haughey's criticism regarding the constitutionality of the agreement and had carefully prepared a trap. The clause to which the Fianna Fáil leader took such extreme exception was taken practically verbatim from the communiqué which Haughey and Thatcher had issued following their first summit meeting back in May 1980. When the Taoiseach disclosed this, Haughey suddenly found himself at pains to explain why the very words he had used five-and-a-half years earlier should now mean something different. If agreeing to those words constitutued a sell-out, then it was he who had been guilty of the sell-out, in May 1980.

In an effort to have the Hillsborough agreement viewed in the best possible light, the government orchestrated a very successful public-relations campaign to ensure that international support was lined up and then publicised almost simultaneously at home. The SDLP came out strongly in favour of the agreement. The party's deputy leader, Seamus Mallon, who had previously been seen as an admirer of Haughey, was particularly enthusiastic about it. On top of this, the hysterical reaction to the agreement by Ian Paisley and his supporters undoubtedly made the deal seem more attractive to nationalists on both sides of the border. The authorities in Dublin did not claim an end to partition was in sight, as Haughey had intimated and Lenihan had indicated in December 1980, but Paisley might just as well have said as much in his demagogic rantings. He described the agreement as the 'process of rolling Irish unification'.

Haughey was not impressed. 'The agreement,' he said, 'is either worthy of support or it is not, and no snow job or public-relations job can change that.' He had clearly been outmanoeuvred in the short term, at any rate, because the agreement was greeted with considerable approval throughout the Republic.

The next IMS poll detected a dramatic drop in Fianna Fáil support and, for the first time in sixteen months, Fitzgerald moved just ahead of Haughey as the popular choice for Taoiseach. O'Malley seized this opportunity on 21 December 1985 to launch, along with Mary Harney, who was still a member of the Fianna Fáil organisation at the time, a new party, the Progressive Democrats. The new party flourished initially, drawing considerable support from disillusioned voters who had supported Fine

Gael in November 1982. But there was little comfort for Haughey because satisfaction with his performance dropped to its lowest point since the black days of 1983, and he trailed both Fitzgerald and O'Malley as the people's choice for Taoiseach in an RSI poll published on 18 January 1986.

There were two further defections from Fianna Fáil the following week, when Pearse Wyse and Bobby Molloy joined the Progressive Democrats. Of the twenty-two deputies who had voted against Haughey's leadership in October 1982, only nine were still in the Fianna Fáil parliamentary party a little over three years later. All but one of the most vocal of these critics were outside the party; the exception was Charlie McCreevy, whose vulnerability was dramatically exposed in the run-up to the local elections in 1985, when he was denied the party's nomination to run for Kildare County Council. Any vague doubts which may have remained about Haughey's grip on the party leadership were thus well and truly laid to rest.

The Progressive Democrats had their strongest support in the Limerick East constituency, where elements of the Fianna Fáil organisation defected en bloc. Haughey sent Brian Lenihan to Limerick to conduct what James Downey described as 'a weird inquisition into the loyalties of those who had stayed in Fianna Fáil'. Lenihan seemed to take a vicarious delight in putting the boot into those who had been perceived as supporters of Des O'Malley. He described the Progressive Democrats as having 'fascist tendencies'. In time he would pay dearly for that attack.

Meanwhile, Fine Gael was threatened with a massive defection of liberal voters, who had been attracted by Fitzgerald's promise of a new Ireland that would be pluralist and non-sectarian. The Taoiseach introduced legislation for a referendum to end the constitutional proscription against divorce.

Fianna Fáil officially remained aloof during the ensuing

referendum campaign. Nevertheless, Haughey later admitted that most members of the parliamentary party had privately campaigned against the proposed amendment. He had consistently predicted that the amendment would be rejected by the electorate, but he admitted that he had been surprised by the magnitude of its defeat. Fitzgerald's constitutional crusade, already mortally wounded by the success of the Pro-Life amendment, was effectively buried by the rejection of his divorce amendment. In the wake of this rejection, the government was noticeably divided.

Probably the strongest factor keeping its various elements together was the desire to keep Haughey out of office. The Taoiseach and his people therefore exploited the 'Haughey Factor', as it was called, attacking him at every opportunity. They blamed him for the country's economic ills, and there were howls of indignation from Fine Gael after he told a Bodenstown gathering on 12 October 1986 that the position of Northern nationalists had 'serious worsened' in the eleven months since the signing of the Hillsborough agreement. Haughey was accused of pandering to Republican sympathisers in order to gain their political support.

Haughey's opponents seemed to scrape the bottom of the barrel when they raised a furore after the Libyan leader, Colonel Gaddafi, described Haughey as his 'very dear friend' during an RTÉ television interview. Minister for Industry and Commerce Michael Noonan disingenuously contended that Gaddafi's comments would damage IDA efforts to attract American industry to Ireland. He conveniently ignored the fact that his own complaints and those of his colleagues did more than anything else to publicise the Libyan leader's remarks. The coalition government was trying to hold on to power by exploiting doubts that had been raised about Haughey's suitability for office.

In the run-up to the 1987 general election Haughey built up teams of advisers. Frank Wall, the general secretary of Fianna Fáil, did most of the work in organising the party, with help from Mara, Sean Fleming, Paul Kavanagh, Peter Finnegan, Roy Donovan, Denis McCarthy, Conor Crowley, Gerry McCarthy and Haughey's daughter, Eimear. Martin Mansergh was in charge of research, but others, like Brendan O'Kelly, Gerry Wrixon, Paul McNulty and Noel Mulcahy, worked on the policy side of the preparations to regain power. They drew up policy documents that included a proposal for the Financial Services Centre – an idea suggested by Dermot Desmond.

Of course, this was preparation for when Fianna Fáil got back into power. The first task was to get elected, and the publicity and campaign side of things were initially the most important. Haughey's team of public-relations advisers included Martin Larkin of Saatchi & Saatchi, Frank O'Hare of The Creative Department, Des Byrne of Behaviour and Attitudes, James Morris of Windmill Lane and Tom Savage and his wife, Terry Prone, of Carr Communications. The team developed a broad, integrated advertising strategy. They came up with a couple of powerful campaign slogans: 'Health cuts hurt the old, the sick and the handicapped' and 'There Is a Better Way'.

Haughey had been carefully cultivating his image for some time. In December 1984 he sought to extend his appeal to young people by giving an exclusive interview to John Waters of *Hot Press.* At the outset Waters explained that he wished to talk about various issues, such as crime and vandalism. 'I don't think I could say that I approve of youngsters knocking off BMWs and so on,' Haughey stated. 'Although, I must admit, I always had a hidden desire to do something like that! But in my day, if a guard said to you, "Fuck off", you fucked off as quick as you could.'

The war was on in Europe during his teenage years and there was little work to be found in Ireland, so friends of Haughey's often threatened to join the British Army. '"Fuck you!" they would say,' he recalled, '"I'll go off and join the British Army if you don't appreciate me or treat me properly!"'

When asked what aspect of Irish society angered him most, Haughey looked Waters directly in the eye. 'I could instance a load of fuckers whose throats I'd cut and push over the nearest cliff, but there's no percentage in that!' he replied with a laugh. 'I hate smug people. People who think they know it all. I know from my own experiences that nobody knows it all. Some of these commentators who purport to a smug know-allness, who pontificate . . . I suppose if anything annoys me, that annoys me.'

He talked about his upbringing, life in Dublin, holidays in Derry and later on Innisvicillaun, and television programmes, such as the popular soap opera *Dallas*, which was watched by some members of his family. 'Sometimes I might sit through it,' he said. 'I think it's shit. I think it's terrible shit. But then I know that that's a minority view.'

The interview came to an abrupt end when Waters asked if there was a particular day that Haughey would always remember as the happiest. 'Oh, fuck off!' he replied with an exasperated laugh. 'No! You're turning into a fuckin' woman's diary columnist now!' Haughey liked young people and he was really showing off with young John Waters, demonstrating that he could relate to the young, but he was not as 'with it' as he thought, because he obviously did not realise that *Hot Press* would relish the idea of printing the interview, complete with expletives. When the magazine came out, much of the interview was repeated in the *Irish Times,* and its extracts were then prominently discussed on the RTÉ morning news, much to Haughey's horror.

When Mara went into Haughey's office that morning the

Boss was sitting with his head in his hands. He didn't look up. 'Mara,' he snapped, 'you've finally blown it! I'm ruined! Get out of my sight!'

He was in a foul mood for some hours. 'He's eating children in the raw state!' Pádraig Ó hAnracháin warned another aide.

But as the morning went on friends called to congratulate Haughey on what they thought was an excellent interview, because it showed him as he was, rather than putting forward a cultivated, stodgy political image. People knew that Haughey's politically correct image was cultivated for the media, but the Waters interview got behind the mask and provided a glimpse of the real man – the person who admitted that he considered the media 'a load of fuckers'. The proper Haughey was a bore, whereas the real one was a much more exciting individual, who admitted that he robbed orchards as a boy and intimated that he had missed out on the thrill of joyriding as a young man because there were so few cars on the roads back then. He had also expressed regret at not having been a bit younger when the sexual revolution of the 1960s took place.

The joyriding remarks were clearly over the top and an embarrassment, but the real Charlie was the one that those who loved him preferred – not the prim and proper reformed character that he tried to project in public. By midday he had recovered his buoyancy and invited Mara out to lunch as his way of apologising to him.

Garret Fitzgerald's advisers and image men were described as the 'national handlers', whereas Mara ridiculed the depiction of himself as a 'handler' by describing himself as a 'national fondler'. 'When I want to know what the Irish people are thinking, I ask P. J. Mara,' Haughey once said, obviously parodying de Valera's famous remark about looking into his own heart. 'And do you know what he says to me?' Haughey continued. 'He says, "Would you ever cop yourself on?"'

A further aspect of the makeover of Haughey's image was his cooperation with RTÉ in the making of a programme about his holiday island. In this he portrayed himself as the all-Ireland man – the Dubliner who was born in Mayo, had his roots in Derry and spent his holidays in Kerry.

A mammoth volume of his speeches was collected and edited by Martin Mansergh and published in 1986 under the title *The Spirit of the Nation* by Mercier Press. Mercier had earlier published *Operation Brogue,* which suggested that British intelligence had been behind the train of events that led to the telephone-tapping controversy. The British intelligence community had sought to undermine Prime Minister Harold Wilson, and it would be surprising if they had not also engaged in some dirty tricks against Haughey. Rather than provide any real insight into the events of the time, however, *Operation Brogue* drew heavily on the imagination and emotions of its author, John M. Feehan.

Feehan, who had been a captain in the army during the Emergency period of the World War II, had a penchant for conspiracy theories. After leaving the army he established Mercier Press, which was the leading book publisher outside Dublin. He was personally convinced that much of Haughey's troubles were caused by British intelligence deliberately undermining the Fianna Fáil leader because of his views on Northern Ireland. Feehan also wrote a short biography, entitled *Haughey: the Statesman,* that was supportive of the short fellow. This book is a model of how a biography should not be written because it was more forecast than record.

In Feehan's view, the government of the country was in the hands of the civil servants, who had become so cautious and lethargic that the system was virtually stagnating. 'Haughey will have to face the fact that the present civil-service system is just not satisfactory,' Feehan wrote. 'There is every reason to believe that Mr Haughey has that incisive political sensitivity which enables him to judge the inner patriotic spirit of the Irish people . . . Haughey shares with great statesmen past and present the proven ability to learn from his own mistakes.' Haughey had clearly been ineffective as Taoiseach on his two previous spells in that office, but he had been highly efficient in his other ministries, and Feehan confidently predicted he would be highly efficient again, next time as Taoiseach, notwithstanding the hostility of the press.

'I am always intrigued by the fact that whenever anything bad can be said about Haughey it will be said loudly and openly, without any attempt being made to examine in depth the prevailing circumstances. Such one-sided treatment is not, however, meted out to others. No matter how many major blunders they make, certain elements in the media will either find or invent excuses for them,' Feehan wrote.

He predicted that upon his return to power Haughey would take on the civil service and reverse what the author believed was the Anglophile bias of the coalition government. He forecast that Haughey would end extradition to Britain and would respond effectively to what he believed were the disastrous implications of the Anglo-Irish Agreement. 'Haughey has promised that he will repudiate it in its present state when he gets into power,' Feehan concluded. 'In doing so he will redeem the honour, integrity and safety of the Irish people.'

Of course, Feehan realised that the personal attacks on Haughey would continue. 'This time the campaign to vilify Haughey is likely to take on a more subtle form. The crude personal attacks that failed so dismally in the past will hardly be repeated. There will, of course, be veiled suggestions that the source of his personal wealth is somewhat suspect. Needless to say, not a shred of evidence will be produced to back this up. Indeed, if the evidence were properly researched it would probably show that his possessions were acquired by hard work and business acumen. This aspect of his career will be carefully concealed in case the public might jump to the conclusion that his financial and business acumen might be of benefit to the country.'

Initially it was not envisaged that *The Spirit of the Nation* would be a big book, but it soon began to grow out of all proportions as Martin Mansergh produced voluminous material and kept adding the texts of more speeches to it. It was never the kind of book that was likely to be in great public demand, and it soon grew so long that it threatened to become a financial disaster for Mercier Press unless Fianna Fáil guaranteed to buy the bulk of the copies. A meeting arranged between Haughey and the publishers quickly degenerated into an acrimonious affair. Haughey was unwilling to commit party funds to the project there and then. Feehan rose to leave in indignation but was prevailed upon by one of his directors to remain, as Haughey explained that the problems would be sorted out. The bulk of the print run was subsequently purchased by Fianna Fáil on its publication.

It was during this period that Haughey finally gained control of Fianna Fáil's finances. A struggle had been raging behind the scenes since he first took over the leadership of the party, in December 1979. At that time Des Hanafin was secretary of the Fianna Fáil General Election Fund-Raising Committee, which had replaced Taca as the party's main organisation for generating finance. Hanafin had been responsible for doing away with Taca in 1969, and under his guidance the affairs of the committee remained highly confidential. It operated from behind closed doors in Room 547 of the Burlington Hotel, and no accounts of its income or expenditure were published or even disclosed to the party leader.

Lynch was happy with this arrangement, but Haughey had different ideas. He insisted on a proper report about control of the party's finances. This was drawn up by Daniel M. McGing, a senior partner in Kean and Company and one of its major associate, Coopers and Lybrand. The report was delivered to Haughey personally on 11 March 1980. In the report, which was marked 'Private and confidential', McGing suggested certain changes in relation to the fund-raising committee functioning from the Burlington Hotel, because party headquarters were being effectively excluded from fund-raising.

'It might be considered that this situation is a less than desirable one from the point of view of Fianna Fáil because, although the Burlington Hotel fund is operating under the Fianna Fáil name, it would appear that the trustees have no control over its activities or the disposal of its monies,' McGing argued. Hanafin was a strong supporter of Colley and had aligned himself with Haughey's opponents. For the next fifteen months he refused to give up what was known as the Black Book, which contained a secret record of hundreds of party subscribers. The fund-raising committee was given a target of £600,000 for the general election of June 1981. Although it reached this goal, the campaign cost the party £1.2 million, and it became necessary to take out loans from AIB and the Bank of Ireland.

The general election of February 1982 cost the party a further £750,000. It was believed that much more money could have been raised for that election campaign had it not been for the in-fighting within Fianna Fáil. A few days before the election was called, Haughey's friend and election agent, Pat O'Connor, got hold of a list of party subscribers. When Hanafin's committee went to the people listed in the Black Book during the campaign, they were frequently told that O'Connor had already been in touch with them on behalf of the party.

On 26 February 1982, the day after O'Malley's abortive heave, Haughey dismissed Hanafin, but the latter argued that the leader had no right to fire him because he was independent of the leader. Haughey therefore invited all members of the party's fund-raising committee – with the exception of Hanafin – to his Kinsealy home. In his private bar Haughey got all but one of the members present to sign a document instructing Hanafin to hand over the complete fund-raising accounts to Fianna Fáil headquarters in Upper Mount Street. The only person who refused to sign was Gerry Creedon of Gypsum Industries.

Haughey was back in government during much of 1982, and it was during this period that rumours spread that he was in deep financial trouble. Des Traynor had taken over his finances and there is still considerable confusion about the sources of Haughey's money.

Traynor opened a series of accounts on Haughey's behalf at Guinness & Mahon bank. In Haughey's principal resident account, a total of £1,245,530.91 was deposited between February 1979 and May 1987, when the account closed. In all there were twenty-six lodgements made; these lodgements varied in size from £326.23 to £285,000 – the amount of a cheque drawn on Dunnes Stores at the time the account was being wound down. A second resident current account opened in May 1983 was closed the following January after a total of £211,344.50 had been lodged in it. In 1981 £74,996.83 was credited to a loan account in Haughey's name. There was also a further loan account taken out in the joint names of Haughey and his former business partner Harry Boland. This account, which was opened in November 1981, had a total of £229,756.82 deposited in it before it was closed, in September 1984.

Harry Boland denied any knowledge of this account. He said he had only learned about it when the bank contacted him almost a decade and a half after the account had been closed. He noted that he always used the Irish form of his name for banking purposes. Moreover, he denied any knowledge of a £50,000 draft made payable to 'H. Boland' that had been drawn on the account on 29 January 1982. He was emphatic that he had never received that cheque, even though it was apparently drawn in his name. It is unclear what the purpose of the account was. In September 1984, when the account in the joint names of Haughey and Boland was closed down, Haughey obtained a £90,000 loan from the Agricultural Credit Corporation for the purpose of purchasing brood mares and cattle. When the time came for him to repay the loan the following August, Haughey called John Hickey, the chief executive of the ACC.

'We discussed the repayment of the loan,' Hickey noted. 'We came to an agreement that I would roll over on the principal providing he paid the total interest due, which he duly did.' Haughey paid £12,544 in interest and the loan was secured by a chattel mortgage. By August 1986 the interest rate had gone up and Haughey was late with the payment. He finally paid off the interest in November, which by then amounted to £15,901.

It is not possible to determine the total amount of money deposited in the various accounts because there were instances in which money was moved from one account to another, which led to duplication. It is even more difficult to determine who provided the money for the lodgements. Guinness & Mahon should have had microfiche records of its transactions, but these mysteriously disappeared. Records at the Bank of Ireland – from where much of the money was transferred, through the account of Amiens Securities Ltd – were kept only for the statutory period and were then destroyed. Various tribunals have since unearthed some of the sources of Haughey's finance during this period. In May 1983 P. V. Doyle authorised the transfer of

£40,000 to Haughey from one of his accounts. The following month he authorised a further £50,000. Doyle actually took out a loan for Haughey at Guinness & Mahon bank in 1983 and another one in 1985. In effect he was guaranteeing loans which amounted to £170,000 in total. The credit committee of Guinness & Mahon also authorised a personal, unsecured credit facility of £200,000 for Haughey on 3 April 1985, but, unsurprisingly, the Fianna Fáil leader exceeded even that.

On 20 January 1987, when Garret Fitzgerald resigned and called a general election, Haughey owed Guinness & Mahon £280,000. On the eve of the general election, therefore, his finances were again in terrible shape. He had made no effort to pay off the £110,000 debt of honour at AIB and he owed the ACC over £90,000 and a further £170,000 on the loans secured by Doyle. As the general-election campaign got under way, six cheques from Dunnes Stores, totalling £32,000, were lodged at Guinness & Mahon for Haughey's benefit.

He would later claim that Des Traynor had looked after all his accounts during these years. Nonetheless, various leading business people – Joe Malone, former chief executive of Bord Fáilte, Seamus Purcell, Cruse Moss, Xavier McAuliffe and former Ceann Comhairle John O'Connell – testified that he had asked them for money for his son Ciarán's helicopter business. 'Haughey told me he was asking a few friends to make a contribution of £5,000 each,' O'Connell explained. The former Ceann Comhairle had joined Fianna Fáil only a couple of months earlier, in January 1985. 'I presumed that a lot of members of the party had been asked to contribute,' O'Connell said. 'If ever you want a lift in a helicopter, don't hesitate to ask,' Haughey told him.

There was a further curious incident that year when O'Connell was approached at a social function in London and asked by the wealthy Arab Kemal Fustok to convey £50,000 to Haughey. No explanation was given for this request at the time, but Fustok – who made regular trips to Ireland to attend the Goff bloodstock sales – later stated that the money was payment for a horse. The cash was transferred to one of Haughey's accounts via an account in the name of Amiens Securities. Seamus Purcell said that Haughey invited him to Berkeley Court Hotel, Dublin, for a 'general discussion on the meat industry' in 1985. As Purcell was about to leave, Haughey mentioned that Ciarán 'needed a bit of capital' for his helicopter business, and Haughey asked Purcell for £12,000. Purcell agreed and Haughey said that Traynor 'would be in touch'.

It was obviously improper of Traynor to be involved with Celtic Helicopters. He was not only a director of Aer Lingus but also chairman of one of its subcommittees; this subcommittee oversaw the performance of the Aer Lingus subsidiary Irish Helicopters. At the same time Traynor was involved in raising £80,000 from investors for the rival company Celtic Helicopters, which was jointly owned by Ciarán Haughey and John Barnacle, who put up a mere £60 each for the firm. This obvious conflict of interest may explain why Haughey was not as insulated by Traynor in his financial dealings in relation to Celtic Helicopters as he was in relation to other transactions.

There could be little doubt that Traynor was handling most of the money, but was this just so that Haughey could plausibly deny that he was involved in the matter if questions were asked about it later? This issue was one that a tribunal investigating Haughey's affairs would have to examine. What can be stated here with confidence is that Haughey had essentially gained control of Fianna Fáil's finances before the general election of 1987, even though his own personal finances were in very bad shape.

It was therefore ironic that he had the gall to pillory the

government over its mismanagement of the country's economy. The budget deficit of 1986 was £1.39 billion, the highest ever recorded, while unemployment at the end of the year was also at record level, of 250,178, even though some 40,000 people had emigrated during the year. The *Economist* reported in January that things in Ireland were so bad that the International Monetary Fund was threatening to intervene. Haughey therefore berated Fitzgerald and his colleagues. 'The failure of this government has been significantly contributed to by an invasion of the corridors of government by a coterie of professional economists, preaching defeatist, monetarist doctrines and peddling unrealistic and unacceptable policies,' Haughey contended. 'No previous government has given so much patronage and influence to a whole troupe of economists, who seem determined to re-establish economics as a dismal science.'

He promised that Fianna Fáil would, if elected, aid ailing companies. 'We adopted a deliberate policy of intervening and providing state aid to keep firms going,' he argued. 'We were constantly pilloried for doing so and accused of extravagance and mismanagement. The obsession with budgetary arithmetic to the exclusion of everything else is preventing positive thinking. It is an intellectual straitjacket,' he said. 'We intend to implement a major programme of economic recovery, especially in the tourist, horticultural and entertainment areas.' Fianna Fáil also campaigned hard against the government's health cutbacks, with poster boards proclaiming that 'Health cuts hurt the old, the poor and the handicapped.'

'It doesn't take guts to confront the old, the sick and the poor,' Haughey declared during the campaign, but he emphasised that he was not promising any panacea because things were in a perilous condition. 'There are no easy times ahead,' he warned. 'The situation is extremely critical. We are literally in a state of economic collapse.'

As usual, his opponents sought to exploit the Haughey factor. Mary Harney of the Progressive Democrats suggested that her party might support Fianna Fáil, but only if the party got rid of Haughey first. 'I will never vote for Haughey for Taoiseach and will leave the PDs if they ever do,' Harney had warned. 'Mr Haughey in office might throw a brief and reckless party,' Garret Fitzgerald warned, 'but the hangover in the years that followed would be worse than anything we have ever experienced.' Haughey responded by promising to keep spending 'at 1986 levels in real terms'.

In February 1987 Haughey became the first leader of the party to fail to gain an overall majority in four consecutive general elections. Just three seats short of a majority, Fianna Fáil were very unlucky. With a total of less than 500 extra votes spread over eight specific constituencies, the party would have won eighty-nine seats, which would have given them a very comfortable majority. Haughey was again blamed for the failure; this time with real justification, because he had driven Des O'Malley out of Fianna Fáil and was thus indirectly responsible for the formation of the Progressive Democrats, who won fourteen seats, the best first-time showing by any party since the first time Fianna Fáil contested a general election, in 1927. Four of the Progressive Democrats were former Fianna Fáil deputies and at least a further half-dozen of them were former members of the party. Although staffed mainly by former Fianna Fáil activists, the Progressive Democrats had their greatest appeal among floating voters who had drifted to Fine Gael at the last election. A great many of these voters would probably have voted for Fianna Fáil otherwise, so the arrival of the Progressive Democrats probably denied Fianna Fáil an overall majority.

As Haughey sought to form a government, the media again concluded that he was fighting for his political survival. If he failed to cobble together a government, it was generally believed that he would be toppled as party leader.

Realistically, Fianna Fáil was the only party that could form a government. This time Haughey made it clear that he would not deal with anyone. He offered to support the re-election of the Speaker, Tom Fitzpatrick of Fine Gael, but the offer was denounced as stroke politics, which he indignantly refuted. 'It would enhance the standing and the prestige of the office,' Haughey said. 'It was the tradition in previous years that the outgoing Ceann Comhairle was re-elected by the incoming Dáil.'

Fitzpatrick would have been willing to stay on, but he was instructed by Fine Gael to decline the offer. Fianna Fáil therefore approached Sean Tracy, an independent deputy, who jumped at the chance to become Speaker. Haughey felt that he could depend on the support of Neil Blaney in the vote for Taoiseach, which meant that all eyes turned to Tony Gregory again. Gregory was ready to come to an agreement, but Haughey insisted that there would be no deal this time. As a result, Gregory announced that he would not support the Fianna Fáil leader; this raised the unprecedented spectre of a hung Dáil.

John Kelly, the former Fine Gael minister, suggested a power-sharing arrangement between Fianna Fáil and Fine Gael, but Haughey ruled that out. 'Fianna Fáil is not interested now – nor will it be in the future – in arrangements of that kind,' he said. 'If need be,' he added, 'there will have to be another general election.'

On the eve of the Dáil meeting, the main story in the *Irish Times* was a report that Fine Gael sources were contending that, if the Dáil failed to elect anyone, Garret Fitzgerald 'would not necessarily have to report to the President'. He could postpone his resignation for a couple of days in order to allow further consultations to find a candidate who would win a majority vote in the Dáil, these sources asserted. John Murray, the Attorney-General in Haughey's last government, argued, however, that the Taoiseach would have to resign immediately under Article 28.10 of the Constitution.

At the time, the whole affair looked like an attempt to flush out an alternative candidate from within Fianna Fáil. Back in 1948 Richard Mulcahy, the leader of Fine Gael, had been unacceptable to some of his party's potential allies in the Dáil. Fine Gael therefore put forward John A. Costello for Taoiseach, and he was elected with the blessing of Mulcahy, who remained party leader. Thus there was a precedent for having a deputy who was not a party leader as Taoiseach. Although four men – Fitzgerald, Haughey, O'Malley, and Spring – were nominated for Taoiseach, only Haughey had any chance of winning. Everything seemed to depend on Gregory, with the result that there was a distinct air of tension when he rose to speak in the Dáil.

He had waited in vain, he said, for the right-wing parties to act responsibly in getting together to form a government. 'They are motivated by petty party self-interest and personality differences and have sought to divert attention from their irresponsibility by isolating me, as if the burden of responsibility rested with me alone,' he continued. He stated that, rather than precipitate another election, he would abstain from voting. This was greeted with some applause and an audible sigh of relief from all sides of the house.

Haughey had successfully called Gregory's bluff. The voting ended in a tie – eighty-two for and eighty-two against Haughey's nomination – and he became the first Taoiseach to be elected on the casting vote of the Speaker in 1927. Fitzgerald promptly congratulated Haughey and went on to say that Fine Gael would not attempt to bring down the government, as long as it sought to introduce the necessary corrective measures for the economy. Although Fitzgerald resigned as leader of Fine Gael the next day, his successor, Alan Dukes, pursued this policy as part of what became known as the Tallaght Strategy.

# 15

## 'The short and the tall of it'
## Taoiseach, 1987–1989

Haughey appointed Brian Lenihan Tánaiste and Minister for Foreign Affairs. The other ministers were Ray MacSharry, Finance and Public Service; Gerard Collins, Justice; Michael O'Kennedy, Agriculture; Michael Woods, Social Welfare; Albert Reynolds, Industry and Commerce; Ray Burke, Energy; Brendan Daly, Tourism, Fisheries and Forestry; Pádraig Flynn, Environment; Bertie Ahern, Labour; Rory O'Hanlon, Health; Michael J. Noonan, Defence; Mary O'Rourke, Education; John Wilson, Communications; and John Murray, Attorney-General.

The new government's first task was to tackle the economic crisis. The Ministries for Finance and Public Service were merged into the new Ministry for Finance, with some twenty-five civil servants being redeployed as a task force to help the Revenue Commissioners collect taxes, while the Ministry for Tourism was raised to a cabinet-level department as part of Haughey's promise to promote tourism. Ireland had essentially been going backwards in recent years in the midst of great international growth. Its position then was a throwback to the 1950s, when the country had stagnated during an international economic boom.

When Haughey first became Taoiseach the country was, like himself, living beyond its means, but this time things were even worse, because it had been doing so for so long. The national debt was over £25 billion, more than four times greater than it had been in 1979. This debt had in fact doubled during the four years of apparent economic stringency of Fitzgerald's government, and the cost of servicing the debt had grown by 20 per cent each year since 1980. By 1986 Ireland was internationally recognised as one of the worst-managed economies in the Western world. The ratio of the country's public debt to its gross domestic product was 140 per cent, the highest in the world.

The previous Fine Gael–Labour coalition, which had awarded politicians a 19 per cent increase at the outset of their term, undermined the moral position from which they called on everybody else to hold the line. Haughey's government now provided leadership by blocking a 15 per cent pay rise for members of the Dáil and public servants. His government was then in a stronger position to call for pay restraint from everybody else.

Ray MacSharry, the new Minister for Finance, was determined to tackle the problem. Labour had walked out of the last coalition because they could not agree with the stringent budget being advocated by Fine Gael, but MacSharry introduced an even tougher budget on 31 March 1987. 'There can be no concessions to interest groups, and all sections of the community will have to bear some of the burden,' he warned. Borrowing would be reduced below what had been proposed by Fine Gael and taxes would be increased. He also announced that three separate housing-grant schemes were being terminated immediately. These included an energy-saving measure in which grants were given to people to insulate their houses. 'The purpose of this budget is to initiate economic recovery,' Haughey told the Dáil. 'We had to face the stark reality that the rate of Exchequer borrowing could not be sustained.'

The next day there were some heated words at the Fianna

Fáil parliamentary-party meeting, which lasted over four hours. Pádraig Flynn, the new Minister for the Environment, insisted that the government was legally obliged to provide finance for as many as 10,000 grants because people had already spent money on the projects. He was backed by Albert Reynolds. The housing grants were initially projected to cost around £100 million, but they had already cost over £189 million, and MacSharry was adamant that no further money would be borrowed for them. If the extra money that Flynn was calling for had to be found, it would have to be cut from somewhere else in the current year's expenditure. As it was, the government was also cutting £30 million in rates support to local councils. This would mean that local governments would probably have to reintroduce water and refuse charges – something that Fianna Fáil had strongly opposed while in opposition. Haughey led from the front on this occasion. 'Cut the codology,' he told the parliamentary party. 'If you cannot take the heat, get out of the kitchen.'

This was only the beginning of the process. Many more cuts would have to be introduced in the following months. On 13 May Haughey sent a letter to each of his ministers. 'All options should be considered, including the elimination or reduction of particular schemes and programmes, rooting out overlaps and duplications between organisations, the closure of institutions which may have outlived their usefulness, the scaling down of the operations of organisations and institutions and the disposal of physical assets which are no longer productively used,' he wrote. 'A radical approach should be adopted and no expenditure should be regarded as sacrosanct and immune to elimination or reduction.'

This approach was naturally portrayed as a political U-turn. Haughey had vigorously opposed every effort of the previous government to cut public expenditure, but now his government was implementing even more stringent cuts, and he had the audacity to insist that he was following a consistent policy. 'Let me remind commentators that as far back as 1982 the basic strategy that we proposed in *The Way Forward* was to take firm action by rejections in public expenditure to eliminate the deficit combined with developmental measures,' he explained. 'That is still our basic philosophy.'

Fine Gael and Labour had brought down his government because of the stringency of *The Way Forward,* and when they then tried to implement the policies outlined in that document, he played their game and opposed them. Now he was essentially going back to the policy he had advocated in 1982, but this time the new Fine Gael leader, Alan Dukes, announced that his party would support the government in introducing the necessary economic policies. Thus the government had no difficulty implementing the budget provisions. It was an incongruous sight: the diminutive Haughey and the lanky Dukes walking up the steps of the Dáil to the same voting lobby. 'The short and the tall of it,' the Taoiseach joked, to the general laughter of the House one day.

While Haughey was trying to straighten out the country's economy, his own finances were again in a dreadful state. In 1986 Des Traynor had left as managing director of Guinness & Mahon Bank to take up the position of chairman of Cement Roadstone Holdings, and the bank was taken over by Japanese investors. These investors did not care whether Haughey was Taoiseach or not – they insisted that his overdraft be cleared. Although Traynor moved Haughey's account to a subsidiary, Ansbacher Cayman, the new owners still wanted order to be restored to the account. Traynor therefore decided to raise around £700,000 by tapping six business contacts. One of those he approached was the auditor of Dunnes Stores, Noel Fox, who talked to Ben Dunne, the family member who was then controlling the company.

'I think Haughey is making a huge mistake trying to get six or seven people together,' Dunne argued. 'Christ picked twelve apostles and one of them crucified him.' Dunne offered to pay all the money himself, which he believed to be around £700,000, but he intended to source it abroad, which was going to take some time. Before the end of the year, Dunne had provided two sterling cheques. One, for £182,630, was given to Traynor by Noel Fox, while the other, for £205,000, was made payable to John Furze, a director of the Ansbacher Cayman Bank. Of that, £105,000 was used to pay off Haughey's overdraft with the ACC. The following July Dunne was again approached through Fox, and he provided a cheque for £471,000 and another £150,000 in April 1989. Thus in two years Haughey received over £1.1 million from Dunne, but none of this became generally known until almost a decade later.

Jim Mitchell, the chairman of the Dáil's Public Accounts Committee, subsequently contended that the Ansbacher Cayman Bank was used to 'launder money' for either illegal tax-evasion or legitimate tax-avoidance purposes. At the time tax evasion was rampant. In 1988, for instance, the government introduced a tax amnesty allowing people to pay off tax that had previously been evaded without incurring either penalties or interest. It was estimated that about £30 million in evaded taxes would be collected in this way, but over £500 million was actually collected that year.

Of course, even before the tax amnesty dramatised the extent of tax evasion, ordinary workers whose tax was deducted at source felt that they were paying an unfair share of the tax burden. This explains their uneasiness over pay restraints that existed in semi-state bodies like RTÉ, CIE, Bórd na Móna and the ESB; the government sought to tackle this problem by negotiating a Programme for National Recovery with the social partners. There was a brief power strike, but in the face of government determination the ESB workers settled for a 3.5 per cent wage increase.

The main union leaders – Billy Attley, John Carroll and Peter Cassells – had tried to interest the previous government in negotiating a national plan with the labour unions. 'If the government and employers are willing to negotiate a national plan covering jobs, tax reform, social welfare and public finances,' Attley had declared in Galway the previous October, 'trade unions are willing, as part of the plan, to agree policies on income determination.'

The new government seized on this opportunity, and talks were held throughout the summer of 1987. The report of the National Economic and Social Council, *A Strategy for Development 1986–1990,* published in November 1986, was used as the basis for negotiations. It advocated first stabilising and then reducing the national debt while at the same time reforming the tax system, introducing measures to promote economic growth and taking steps to reduce social inequality. Much of the negotiation on the government side was done by Pádraig Ó hUiginn, the Secretary of the Department of the Taoiseach, and Kevin Murphy, the Secretary of the Department of Finance. Ó hUiginn played the role of the diplomat, mediating between the Irish Congress of Trade Unions and the Federated Union of Employers, while Murphy played the role of the technocrat.

The plan envisaged that wage increases, which had been running at 5 per cent in the industrial sector, would not exceed 2.5 per cent for the next three years. This was less than inflation, which was projected to run at 3.5 per cent. With the clawback in taxes, the plan was expected to cost the government less than £200 million. The plan – which included escape clauses for those in the private sector who could not afford to pay increases – had built-in job targets for the beef industry, the computer-manufacturing sector and the new International Financial Services Centre, which was projected to employ 7,500 people in three to four years. The government expected to more than recoup the cost of the pay increase in taxes collected as a result of the extra employment, and the sweetener for the workers was that this would be passed on in the form of tax relief.

'Haughey may not have been dealt the perfect hand in that election, but he can rarely have played his cards so skilfully,' Gerald Barry of the *Sunday Tribune* concluded. During the summer the Taoiseach made the best of a unique sporting occasion as the nation watched the final days of what was arguably the greatest single Irish sporting triumph of the century, Stephen Roche's victory in the Tour de France cycle race. Haughey went to Paris for the final stage. Garret Fitzgerald had never shown any interest in sport, but Haughey was able to tap the mood of the country. Even people who knew very little about cycling rejoiced at the victory of the Dubliner, who received a hero's welcome on his return home. He had earlier won what was generally considered the second-greatest multi-stage race, the Giro d'Italia, and he capped this with the triple crown of cycling by winning the World Championship. Roche's successes were followed later by Ireland's qualification for the finals of the European soccer championship in Germany. These were the first of a series of unprecedented Irish sporting accomplishments on the international stage. Haughey recognised that Ireland's sporting success had the capacity to lift the spirit of the nation at a time when this spirit was particularly low.

The Tánaiste, Brian Lenihan, raised many eyebrows that autumn when he argued that people should not be worried about the high rate of emigration, which was running at around 40,000 young people annually. 'They should do what they have to do,' he said. 'The world is now one world and they can always return to Ireland with the skills they have developed. We regard them as part of a global generation of Irish people. We shouldn't be defeatist or pessimistic. We should be proud of it. After all, we can't all live on a small island.' Countries like Belgium and Holland, however, were much smaller than Ireland but were nonetheless able to support much larger populations without their people being compelled to emigrate. It was an admission of a gross failure on the part of the government that the Tánaiste should accept that people had to emigrate to make a living.

The Labour Party and the Progressive Democrats provided the main opposition as Fine Gael essentially propped up the government in the national interest. Opponents sought to highlight Haughey's other political U-turns with the help of critics in the media. Only the previous October he had promised that 'Fianna Fáil will attempt to renegotiate the Anglo-Irish Agreement when returned to power because the pact has worsened the situation for the nationalist community.' Yet now that Fianna Fáil was back in government, he treated the agreement as a binding international treaty that had to be implemented. He adopted essentially the same attitude towards the ratification to the Single European Act, about which he had expressed grave reservations while in opposition. His opponents were in a weak position to oppose him because they had previously endorsed both the Anglo-Irish Agreement and the Single European Act.

In return for the say in the affairs of Northern Ireland that the Irish government had been given by the Anglo-Irish

Agreement – a situation which the unionists found highly objectionable – Dublin had promised to increase security cooperation with Britain. 'It will lead the government into an impossible political situation, in which they will find themselves assuming responsibility for actions and being involved in situations, particularly in the security field, over which they can have no control,' Haughey had warned two years earlier. He was particularly opposed to the idea of extraditing suspected terrorists to the United Kingdom. The extradition issue came to a head in the autumn of 1987 following an upsurge in militant republican activity. This activity included the kidnapping for ransom and brutal treatment of dentist John O'Grady and the interception by the French authorities of the *Exund,* heavily laden with armaments for the IRA. There was also one of the worst outrages of the whole Northern troubles – the Remembrance Day bombing in Enniskillen. Haughey promptly expressed his 'anger and revulsion' at the 'depths of savagery' to which the country had sunk. 'Those responsible must be repudiated utterly,' he insisted, 'and no effort must be spared to ensure they are brought to justice.'

If Haughey had intended to take a hard line on extradition, the ground had been cut from under him. 'The recent combination of events – the seizure of a massive shipment of arms by the French authorities, the kidnapping of John O'Grady and the slaughter at Enniskillen – bring the whole question of subversive threats to the security of this state into a new and urgent focus,' he told the Dáil. 'We are not soft on terrorism, domestic or international, and we must give a clear and unequivocal signal to that effect.'

Refusing extradition at this point would have had drastic implications not only for the Anglo-Irish Agreement but also for Anglo-Irish relations. Although Haughey really had no choice over extradition, he still met with strong reservations on this issue within Fianna Fáil. He told the party's National Executive that the Extradition Act would be given a three- to six-month trial period. 'If I feel that an Irish citizen is getting a raw deal under this act,' he assured the parliamentary party, 'I will not hesitate to annul it.' He got a standing ovation for this promise, but when he invited contributions, Hugh Byrne, Síle de Valera, David Andrews and Charlie McCreevy all opposed extradition. Most of the fifty-seven members present expressed misgivings about the Extradition Act during the meeting, which lasted over four hours.

With so many reservations among party members, it seemed inevitable that there would have been reservations within the cabinet too, but Haughey was so firmly in control of that body that none of his ministers expressed the slightest dissent publicly. In addition to the government's strong line on extradition, the Gardaí began a nationwide search for arms in the aftermath of the Enniskillen outrage. They uncovered a major IRA arsenal, containing ninety Kalashnikov rifles, five machine-guns and ninety pounds of Semtex explosives, near Malin Head in Donegal. Among the places searched was the home of Neil Blaney, who accused Haughey of going back on a promise to him the previous March to 'let the Extradition Act wither away'. Haughey denied this. 'Deputy Blaney was not entitled to and did not get any commitments or assurances from me about anything,' the Taoiseach insisted.

When Blaney and Tony Gregory both affirmed their determination to vote against the government over extradition, the Opposition inflicted a couple of defeats on the government in relation to some demands by the Irish National Teachers Organisation as well as over the abolition of the National Social Service Board, whose functions were being transferred to the

Combat Poverty Agency. Since Fine Gael had indicated its willingness to back the government on major issues like the economy and extradition, Haughey swallowed the defeats on minor issues. He also accepted a private members bill on Judicial Separation and Family Law Reform, proposed by Alan Shatter of Fine Gael.

The Extradition Act was passed with Fine Gael support, but not before Haughey had insisted that the Attorney-General had to be satisfied that the person being extradited would get a fair trial. Although this looked like merely a perfunctory stipulation at the time, it took on real significance before very long.

For his part Haughey said that relations with Britain were good and that too much attention was being paid to personalities. He was probably right. It was generally assumed that his relations with Margaret Thatcher had been seriously strained ever since the Falklands War. The media wrongly assumed that she got on better with Fitzgerald; in reality she preferred Haughey. 'I found him easy to get on with, less talkative and more realistic than Garret Fitzgerald,' she wrote in her memoirs. 'Charles Haughey was tough, able and politically astute, with few illusions, and, I am sure, not much affection for the British.'

'Fitzgerald prided himself on being a cosmopolitan intellectual,' she wrote. 'Unfortunately, like many modern liberals he overestimated his own powers of persuasion over his colleagues and countrymen. He was a man of as many words as Charles Haughey was few. He was also, beneath the skin of sophistication, even more sensitive to imagined snubs and more inclined to exaggerate the importance of essentially trivial issues than Mr Haughey.'

Haughey was aware that there had been some secret talks in an effort to get Sinn Féin and the Provisional IRA to adopt a constitutional approach. The Belfast-based priest Alex Reid, a native of Tipperary, had approached him in 1986 to meet Sinn

Féin President Gerry Adams, but Haughey was afraid of the consequences of such a meeting in view of his own role in the Arms Crisis. 'It came as no surprise when he didn't meet me,' Adams later remarked.

Nonetheless, Haughey had his adviser Martin Mansergh keep in touch with Fr Reid, and the Taoiseach remained in contact with Cardinal Tomás Ó Fiaich, who was personally in touch with Adams. The Cardinal briefed Haughey at Kinsealy about his contacts, as did John Hume, who began secret meetings with Adams in 1987. In March of the following year Haughey asked the future Taoiseach, Bertie Ahern, to join Martin Mansergh in meeting Adams and some colleagues. 'He explained that because of the sensitivities of it, if it ever came out that meetings were going on, then, in effect, I would be on my own,' Ahern said.

'Surely if anything comes out people will say Haughey must have known what was happening because Martin Mansergh was party to it,' Ahern argued.

'We'll be able to get over that one,' Haughey replied.

Ahern and Mansergh met Adams, Mitchel McLoughlin and Pat Doherty in a Dundalk monastery. Most of the talking during the two-hour meeting was done by Mansergh and Adams. Ahern later explained that they had tried to impress on the three Sinn Féin leaders that attitudes in the Republic were changing and that they now believed that the unionists 'had to be accommodated' and 'their views had to be taken into account'.

The three Sinn Féin representatives had another meeting with Ahern and Mansergh in June 1988. 'All during the discussions it was quite obvious to me that Adams, Doherty and McLoughlin were people on a hook and wanted to get off the hook while at the same time not giving up on the core principles they felt strongly about,' Ahern noted. Haughey was not prepared to meet the Sinn Féin leaders unless they gave up violence, so a meeting that might have speeded up the process leading to an IRA ceasefire never materialised.

While others acted as go-betweens with Sinn Féin, the Taoiseach was content to allow the spotlight to remain on economic matters. Anglo-Irish relations returned to the foreground in January 1988, however, when the British Attorney-General, Sir Patrick Mayhew, told the House of Commons that there was evidence of RUC attempts to pervert the course of justice in relation to the Stalker Inquiry.

In May 1984 John Stalker, the Deputy Chief Constable of the Greater Manchester Police Force, had been appointed to lead an inquiry into the killings of six unarmed men by the RUC in 1982. In May 1986 Stalker was removed from the inquiry and put under investigation as a result of his friendship with a supposedly corrupt businessman, who, it turned out later, was actually being set up by the police in an obvious effort to discredit Stalker. This was the kind of scandal that should have rocked the police force to its foundations, but while admitting that there had been police involvement in the perversion of the course of justice in relation to the six killings, the Secretary of State Tom King added that there would be no prosecutions in the public interest.

This was a frightening admission that was tantamount to admitting that the police had been involved in murder but the government was going to do nothing about it because it would be too embarrassing. Haughey complained that the episode would do 'the gravest damage' to public 'confidence in the ability and intention of the authorities to uphold the rule of law and administer justice fairly'. A planned meeting between the Chief Constable of the RUC and the Garda Commissioner was promptly cancelled.

Writing in the *Sunday Independent*, which enjoyed the largest circulation of any Irish newspaper, the eminent historian Professor Ronan Fanning compared Mayhew's decision with the suppression of General Strickland's Report into the burning of Cork city by the Black and Tans in December 1920. 'What is at issue is no more and no less than the moral authority of the police force,' he noted.

Shortly after this, Anglo-Irish relations received another jolt when an appeal by the Birmingham Six against their conviction for the 1974 Birmingham pub bombings was turned down. The six denied involvement in the bombings and said that they had been going home to Northern Ireland for a funeral at the time of their arrest. Forensic tests had indicated that they had been handling nitroglycerin, but experts on a television programme had demonstrated that the tests carried out by the forensic scientist had been very suspect: the experts showed that the tests would have been positive if the men had been playing cards on the train, as they claimed they had been. The men also said that they had been beaten up in the police station to force confessions from them. A woman police cadet testified at the appeal that she had been in the station and had seen no indication that the men had been assaulted, but she then changed her evidence and admitted perjury. Nonetheless, the appeal judges discounted her evidence because she had perjured herself in the first place. Chief Justice Lord Denning had remarked that accepting the appeal would 'mean that the police were guilty of perjury, that they were guilty of violence and threats, that the confessions were involuntary and were improperly admitted in evidence and that the convictions were erroneous'. This he described as such 'an appalling vista' that it could not be contemplated. The evidence that this had already happened in relation to the Stalker Affair in Northern Ireland was already being covered up. Following another appeal in 1992, the convictions were thrown out as unsafe, but a great many people in Ireland had believed at the time of the previous appeal that this was the case.

Anglo-Irish relations were portrayed as being at their lowest ebb since Thatcher's infamous dismissal of the suggestions of the Report of the Forum for a New Ireland. Haughey came under pressure to suspend the Extradition Act and there was talk about the Anglo-Irish Agreement being in tatters. This was the Taoiseach's chance to scrap the agreement that he had opposed when he was in the Opposition, but he insisted 'that the Anglo-Irish Agreement must remain'. His U-turn on the agreement was now complete.

In February Haughey's government suffered another political defeat over plans to close Barrington's Hospital in Limerick. This was the constituency of Des O'Malley, the leader of the Progressive Democrats, who had managed to elect a running mate as well. The Progressive Democrats tabled a Dáil motion calling for the hospital to be kept open, and Willie O'Dea, the local Fianna Fáil deputy, came under intense pressure over the issue. It was clear when Fine Gael decided to support the motion that the vote was going to be very tight.

'It's going to be 79-79 and it's up to you, Willie,' O'Malley told O'Dea, when the voting strength of the two sides became apparent. The Speaker invariably broke ties in favour of the government, so O'Dea voted with the Opposition and the government was dealt its third parliamentary defeat just a couple of days before the Fianna Fáil ard-fheis was due to begin. As a result there was strong speculation that Haughey would announce a general election. Several key cabinet members, including Albert Reynolds, Ray MacSharry, Pádraig Flynn, Gerry Collins and Health Minister Rory O'Hanlon, reportedly advocated that the Taoiseach call an election. 'I'll go home and sleep on it,' Haughey is said to have told his cabinet.

The latest public-opinion poll indicated that support for Fianna Fáil was at 47 per cent, which was up 3 per cent on the general election, while Haughey's own popularity had climbed back up to 40 per cent; both figures were appreciably lower than when Garret Fitzgerald had called the last general election, however. If support for Fianna Fáil slipped during the general election campaign, as it usually did, Haughey would again fail to secure an overall majority, so he held firm. He could have allowed speculation to build up interest for his televised address at the ard-fheis, but instead he announced his decision the following morning rather than allow any momentum for an election to build up.

The Northern question and Anglo-Irish relations inevitably figured prominently in Haughey's televised speech. 'It would be naive to expect that public sentiment in Ireland towards extradition would not be affected by the distressing cases of the Birmingham Six, who are widely believed in this country and elsewhere to be innocent,' he declared. But he evoked 'the horror of Enniskillen' to temper his remarks. 'The graveyards are full of monuments,' he added. 'Is it now time for a new kind of monument – a monument to the common sense and willingness of both traditions in Ireland to come together in mutual respect and a shared sense of responsibility for our common future?' In view of the uneasiness over the Stalker Affair and the rejection of the appeal of the Birmingham Six, Haughey's speech was particularly moderate. He appealed for 'an opportunity to hear at first hand from the representatives of the unionist tradition how they would see these things come about.'

In the following days there was a distinct thaw in the unionist attitude towards Haughey; this coolness went back to the Arms Crisis, almost twenty years earlier. James Molyneux, the leader of the Ulster Unionist Party, said that he had been encouraged by the Taoiseach's attitude, especially his willingness to reconsider the Hillsborough Agreement. Molyneux indicated that there was a possibility of a breakthrough based on the original Haughey formula of the 'totality of relationships' between Britain and Ireland. He added that he did not share the 'blind, unreasoned hatred' of others towards the Taoiseach, who was not, he asserted, 'the villain of the piece'. Molyneux was paying Haughey a compliment when he described the Taoiseach as tough, ruthless, and efficient. Some unionists were now even expressing a preference for Haughey over Fitzgerald. Secret meetings were arranged in England between Martin Mansergh and Enoch Powell, the former unionist member of parliament, in the hope of arranging a meeting between Haughey and Molyneux, but nothing came of the whole thing.

Anglo-Irish relations received another jolt in March 1988 when three IRA members were shot dead in Gibraltar. Despite claims to the contrary, the three were gunned down in cold blood in the streets there. Although they were apparently planning to plant a bomb, all were unarmed when they were confronted and no effort was made to take them alive. The whole thing smacked of another aspect of the shoot-to-kill policy. Tension mounted in Belfast after the funerals of the IRA members at Milltown Cemetery, when a loyalist gunman launched a gun and hand-grenade attack on mourners, killing three people and wounding many others. The situation was complicated even further during one of the ensuing funerals, when a couple of undercover British officers drove into the funeral cortège by mistake. They were dragged from their car, beaten, stripped and killed. These incidents were recorded on video and televised on news programmes. Neil Blaney claimed that the Anglo-Irish Agreement was virtually valueless, but Haughey continued to disagree with this view.

On the domestic front Haughey continued to promote his stringent economic policy, which was demonstrably bearing fruit. The official figures published in March 1988 indicated that inflation had dropped to below 2 per cent for the first time in a quarter of a century. The government was maintaining its tough stance on the rod-licence dispute, which was symbolically important, even though the policy itself was a disaster because it resulted in the state losing much more in tourist revenue than it would have collected in rod-licence fees. In May 1988 Haughey thought he had worked out a settlement with Archbishop Joseph Cassidy of Tuam, but this broke down within hours when the fishermen repudiated the virtual capitulation agreed by the archbishop. Even though the government lost money on this dispute, its strong stand undoubtedly strengthened its position in other areas by convincing people of its determination and thus staving off other potential confrontations. It was all part of the process of firm, determined government.

An IMS poll published at the end of April 1988 indicated that Haughey was the most admired person in Ireland, while an MRBI poll around the same time found that 55 per cent of those surveyed were satisfied with his performance as Taoiseach. For the first time since coming to power, he was being perceived as a strong leader, but he ran into difficulties in the summer with the Ombudsman, Michael Mills, over cuts to Mills's office, of which the staff had already been almost halved. Mills, who had been a political correspondent with the *Irish Press* for almost twenty years, had been close to both Lemass and Lynch. He had also been favourable to Fitzgerald but had never been very supportive of Haughey, with the result that there was little love lost between the two men. Faced with the demise of his new office, Mills fought back by going on air and giving details of his difficulties. He accused the government of a lack of commitment to the office of Ombudsman.

Dukes was initially supportive of Mills, and Garret Fitzgerald, who had retired to the backbenches following his resignation as leader of Fine Gael, backed him particularly strongly during a radio interview on 6 June 1988. He demanded that the Taoiseach agree to staff redeployment to defuse the situation. Dick Spring told Haughey that Labour would support a compromise of redeployment of extra staff from other departments to the Ombudsman's office, but this offer was rejected. Dukes agreed instead to a government amendment to review the situation in three months. This did not actually commit the government to anything after the review was completed.

The Fine Gael compromise was reminiscent of its capitulation on health cuts twelve months earlier. Dukes had then pulled the party out of a confrontation with the government after the Taoiseach promised to consider setting up a Dáil committee to examine health spending. No such committee was ever established and the issue was simply dropped. Many believed that the Opposition would have won on the redeployment of staff to the Ombudsman's office, and some Fine Gael deputies looked on with horror as Labour accused Dukes of 'craven capitulation'.

As well as being Taoiseach, Haughey functioned as Minister for Foreign Affairs during the summer of 1988 in place of Brian Lenihan, who was seriously ill with a liver complaint. In June Haughey went to the United Nations for a meeting of the General Assembly, where he delivered a forceful address on disarmament. Unfortunately the proceedings received little coverage in the United States, even though there were twenty-seven heads of government present.

That year Haughey again seized on the opportunity of exploiting a sporting achievement. The Irish soccer team began its campaign in the European championships in Germany by defeating England and followed this with a draw against the Soviet Union in a match that the Irish were unlucky not to win. The team needed only a draw to qualify for the semi-final but went out to a late, freak goal to Holland, who went on to beat the Soviet Union in the final. Haughey went to Dublin Airport to greet the members of the team upon their return. An estimated quarter of a million people turned out to welcome the players home. Although there was some resentment that he was cashing in on something in which the government had absolutely no involvement, the enthusiasm of the massive crowd for the team and its English manager, Jack Charlton, was so great that the voices of dissent were drowned out. The occasion was contributing to what was being called 'a national feel-good factor'.

In July Haughey visited Australia, where he travelled from Perth to Sydney. He had been due to attend the Australian bicentennial celebrations in January but could not go due to the political situation at home. He got on extremely well with Prime Minister Bob Hawke, who had the same kind of reputation as Haughey as a bon viveur. The Australian leader had been enjoying high ratings in the polls even though these had slipped by more than 20 points to around 53 per cent in recent months. He joked that the Australian people were still waving at him, but with fewer fingers than before.

The Taoiseach presented Hawke with a valuable collection of microfilm records of Irish people sentenced to transportation to Australia in the nineteenth century. The gift was, of course, for the Australian people and received a good deal of publicity, because as many as a quarter of Australians claimed ancestry from Irish people transported to the continent. The gift captured the imagination of a great many people and Haughey was very well received and clearly enjoyed being the focus of so much attention. 'It is altogether a tremendous and rewarding experience,' he said.

On 7 July 1988, just before leaving Dublin, however, the *Evening Press* broke the story that a month earlier Abdullah Bin Abdulaziz Al Saud, the Crown Prince and brother of King Khaled of Saudi Arabia, had given expensive gifts to the Haugheys, who kept them. Unlike many other countries, which stipulated that gifts over a certain value received from visiting dignitaries had to go to the state, there was no such policy in Ireland. Margaret Thatcher later regretted, for instance, that she had to leave in Downing Street the famous Georgian teapot that Haughey had given her.

The Saudi Crown Prince, who spent little more than twenty-four hours in Ireland, had given Maureen Haughey a diamond necklace and a matching set of earrings. Initial reports suggested that the gift was worth around a quarter of a million pounds, but the *Irish Times* subsequently suggested that its real worth was nearer to £25,000. The actual value of the necklace – if it was ever valued – was not made public on the grounds that this would be gauche and insulting to the Prince, who had also presented gold ceremonial daggers to Haughey and some of his ministerial colleagues.

Haughey, for his part, presented the Crown Prince with a Waterford crystal globe that he had reportedly paid for himself. It was not until the Dáil reconvened in October that the Opposition were able to ask about the jewels, but at the time Haughey was ill in hospital, having suffered an acute bout of coughing and bronchial spasms. He apparently suffered a respiratory arrest, but this was mistakenly reported as a cardiac arrest. His heart had not stopped, but he had stopped breathing. This appeared to be another of his great escapes, and the questions about the jewels were fielded and dismissed by the

Tánaiste, Brian Lenihan, who insisted that Haughey had done nothing improper.

During the Dáil recess the extradition issue had come to the fore again when Gerard Harte had been extradited to Northern Ireland on 23 August 1988. Shortly afterwards, Robert Russell, a Maze Prison escapee, was also handed over to the RUC. The Supreme Court had ruled in the Russell case that IRA members, acting to 'reintegrate the national territory by force of arms', were not entitled to have their actions regarded as political offences because the Constitution gives the Dáil and the government the sole authority to make such decisions.

John M. Feehan had predicted that Haughey would stand up to the British in 1985 when he wrote *The Statesman*, but now he suggested that the book ought to have been consigned 'to the dustbin, where it really belonged.' He wrote a follow-up book entitled *An Apology to the Irish People.* 'I am flabbergasted that I could have been so naive,' he explained. 'How wrong I was. How terribly wrong. And now I am wondering if, even in this book, I can purge my stupidity.'

Although the extradition question seemed to have been settled by the transfer of Robert Russell in September, a further problem arose over a British demand for the extradition of Fr Patrick Ryan, a priest wanted for questioning by the British in connection with terrorist offences. At the time he was being held in Belgium, but the Belgian premier, Wilfried Martens, and his cabinet ignored their legal advice and sent Fr Ryan back to Dublin on a Belgian military aircraft.

Haughey and Thatcher had a tense meeting in Rhodes on the fringes of the European summit. 'There was a frank exchange of views on what happened and where the case now stood,' Haughey told the press afterwards. The Attorney-General, John Murray, objected to the extradition of Fr Ryan on the grounds of prejudicial pre-trial publicity, but it was made clear that the priest could be tried in the Republic.

On discussing the 1987 Extradition (Amendment) Bill on 27 November 1987 Haughey had explained that 'the major source of concern here is that an extradited person should get a fair trial in the receiving country.' The 1965 Extradition Act had, he argued, provided 'specifically that extradition should not be granted for any ordinary criminal offence if there are substantial grounds for believing that a person's position may be prejudiced on account of his race, religion, nationality or political opinion.' The courts had full jurisdiction to refuse extradition in any case where they suspected that the rights of the person whose extradition was requested might be prejudiced on such grounds. While there was no specific mention of a role for the Attorney-General in the act, this would have been covered under the duties of his office.

When the issue of Fr Ryan's possible deportation first arose, it was discussed by Haughey, Lenihan and Gerry Collins. The Attorney-General's advice was sought, and he was supplied with a dossier containing not only the prejudicial coverage of the case by the British tabloid press but also transcripts of relevant radio and television interviews and copies of extracts from British parliamentary debates on the matter.

In his quasi-judicial role, Sir Patrick Mayhew, the British Attorney-General, had decided to suppress the Stalker-Sampson Report on the shoot-to-kill policy in Northern Ireland and not to pursue policemen who had been involved in obstruction of justice. As a result the British were not in a position to make much out of John Murray's decision to block the extradition of Fr Ryan. They were free to test the case in the Irish courts, and the priest could also be prosecuted under the Criminal Law Jurisdiction Act, which permitted a British prosecution to be made in an Irish court, or vice versa. But the Dublin government was embarrassed by the triumphalist bragging of some of Fr Ryan's supporters, especially that of the priest's brother, who declared, 'We took the knickers off Maggie Thatcher.'

Haughey 'never appeared politically so secure in the leadership of his party or in the high office he occupies,' Stephen Collins of the *Sunday Press* noted at the beginning of 1989. 'His government's dazzling performance on the economy has seen five-year targets achieved in just two, with the national debt finally stabilised.'

'A lot of people, including some in the government, who talk about snap elections don't understand the man at all,' one former minister told Collins. Ireland had never had the European presidency while Haughey was Taoiseach, so he had never presided over a European Community summit, which was a task that he would have relished. 'He is not going to put that at even the slightest risk by calling an election,' a Fianna Fáil deputy said. It would be Ireland's turn for the European presidency again in the first half of 1990.

The forthcoming European elections of June 1989 were portrayed as the first real opportunity for Fianna Fáil to test the party's electoral popularity since Haughey's return to power. Therein lay a real difficulty, however. Although critics had given Haughey little credit four years earlier, the party won an overall majority of the Republic's seats in that election, for the first and only time in the history of direct elections to the European Parliament. The party was really on a hiding to nothing in the forthcoming election. They were unlikely to get any more credit for holding their own next time, even though that would have been a magnificent achievement. If Fianna Fáil lost seats, on the other hand, this would probably be portrayed as a rejection of Haughey.

In the following weeks there was a series of minor controversies following the closure of the Irish Sugar Company in Tuam. Liam Lawlor of Fianna Fáil was accused of having a conflict of interest because of his position on the Dáil committee in charge of state-sponsored bodies. He had access to an Irish Sugar Company report even though at the time he was a non-executive director of one of the companies owned by Larry Goodman, who was interested in buying the Irish Sugar Company. Despite Opposition demands that he quit the committee, Lawlor refused to do so. He insisted that he was just a victim of 'personality politics'. Dick Spring was suspended from the Dáil when he tried, rather too persistently, to question Haughey on Lawlor's potential conflict of interest.

Haughey then moved to nip the Lawlor affair in the bud by essentially forcing Lawlor to step down. 'I explained to him that there was a danger that the committee would not be in a position to carry out its functions independently, objectively and in a non-political way if he remained a member, and he said he would resign from the committee,' Haughey explained. Immediately afterwards Lawlor announced that he was resigning, though he was adamant that he had always followed proper procedures in his dealings.

The government would provide full cooperation to determine the facts behind the Lawlor affair, Haughey promised. Either a joint committee or the Committee on Procedures and Privileges could investigate the matter. He even suggested the establishment of a tribunal of inquiry, if necessary, but the Opposition insisted on a full Dáil debate on the issue of Lawlor's replacement on the State-Sponsored Bodies Committee. The government tried to stave off such a debate. The Opposition was warned that, if the government were defeated on the matter, a general election might ensue. Fianna Fáil duly suffered its fifth Dáil defeat, by sixty-nine votes to sixty-seven. This result was the party's own fault, however, as two Fianna Fáil deputies missed the vote due to a misunderstanding.

'The two lads who didn't turn up were the lucky ones,' one party deputy said afterwards. 'The Boss was so annoyed, he savaged the ones who were there.' As it was, Dick Spring should have been most embarrassed because he missed the vote due to his suspension. If the two missing Fianna Fáil deputies had voted, Spring's absence would undoubtedly have cost his side the vote; this must have made the foul-up all the more unpalatable to Haughey. As with the defeat the previous year, it was just days before the Fianna Fáil ard-fheis was due to begin in Dublin.

In his televised address at the ard-fheis, Haughey again concentrated on economic matters. He warned that the semi-state companies could no longer rely on huge subsidies from the hard-pressed taxpayer. 'They must all understand that they now have to perform in an economic environment radically different from that in which most of them were established,' he said. 'Their future depends on their ability to perform efficiently and, where appropriate, profitably.'

The government had appeared to be biting the bullet on this matter. This was particularly evident in the recent closure of the Sugar Company in Thurles, the constituency of the Minister for Agriculture, Michael O'Kennedy, who had the unenviable task of assuming ministerial responsibility for the closure. But then, in March, Barry Desmond, the deputy leader of the Labour Party, raised some issues about questionable incidents involving one of the businesses of the beef baron, Larry Goodman.

In 1986 the authorities had discovered evidence of a scheme to defraud the EC by claiming export credit on meat being sent to Egypt. Austin Deasy of Fine Gael had helped negotiate an £80 million deal to supply meat to the Egyptians while he was Minister for Agriculture in Fitzgerald's government. But the documentation to secure EC export credit was falsified, both by exaggerating the weight of the meat and including trimmings that were not eligible for export credit.

The authorities realised that this was an obvious case of fraud, but for some reason the fraud squad was not called in to investigate for almost two years, by which time there had been a change of government. The company involved was penalised by the Department of Agriculture, which withheld £1 million of EC money and threatened to withhold as much as £10 million.

The government had essentially inherited the mess and was trying to clean it up quietly. Haughey accused Barry Desmond of 'trying to sabotage the entire beef industry in this country' by raising the issue in the Dáil. In the light of what had happened, there were many questions that needed to be answered, but the government was not prepared to set up a judicial inquiry. When the Labour Party and the Progressive Democrats persisted with questions, Haughey sought to distance himself from the affair. He accused opponents of trying 'to involve me in a matter about which I had no official knowledge and for which I had not official responsibility.' This was patently disingenuous.

On 23 January 1988 Goodman visited Haughey's home and informed him that his company might have to pay as much £10 million as a penalty for fraudulent activities. Two days later Donal Creedon, the Secretary of the Department of Agriculture, apprised Haughey of the same thing. Creedon later explained that he had told the Taoiseach this 'in passing' as he was being ushered out of the office. 'He didn't register any reply, good, bad or indifferent,' Creedon explained. 'My view is that he wanted to get rid of me as quickly as possible.' Haughey admitted that Creedon 'did mention' the matter to him. 'I think it's equally clear that he was only mentioning it peripherally,' he added. 'Certainly, at that time, it didn't impact on my mind at all.'

That fraud had nothing to do with Fianna Fáil. It occurred before Haughey's return to power; he went along with the low-key approach adopted by the previous government in order not to damage the image of the beef industry. Of course, he would have been anxious to help the beef industry because of its national importance. The fact that beef-industry players had also been particularly generous contributors to Fianna Fáil may have been purely coincidental, but it was a convenient coincidence. Goodman International had given the party £50,000 towards the 1987 general-election campaign, while Pascal Phelan's Master Meats had contributed £30,000 and Hibernia had given £25,000.

Ever since his time as Minster for Agriculture, Haughey had believed that the beef industry was not realising its true potential because most of the cattle were being exported on the hoof. In 1964 he noted, for example, that 'more money can be earned by processing and selling primary goods than by producing them.' Larry Goodman had been very successful in establishing food-processing plants, and Haughey saw him as the kind of self-made man who could revolutionise the beef industry in Ireland. Born into a County Louth cattle-dealing family in 1940, Goodman had left school at the height of the Irish recession in the mid-1950s at the age of sixteen. He began dealing in sheep and cattle and after ten years bought the heavily mortgaged Anglo-Irish Meat Company in Ravensdale. He became arguably the greatest personal Irish business success as he built up a phenomenally successful food business that was turning over £60 million worth of beef annually in the 1970s. The EC was producing more beef that it consumed, so the excess was initially bought and stored in 'intervention' in order to keep prices up. Later, export refunds were given to those who exported the surplus beef outside the EC.

Garret Fitzgerald's coalition government encouraged those

exports when he came to power in December 1982. His government initially provided £20 million worth of insurance cover for exports from Goodman's Anglo-Irish Beef Processors. Over the next three years the ceiling for this cover was raised to £55 million. In May 1986, however, the Minister for Industry and Commerce, Michael Noonan, announced that the government would provide no further insurance cover as the other EC countries considered 'that Iraq was too high a risk'. According to the Department of Industry and Commerce, 'the Iraqis were so desperate that they would take anything from anybody who is prepared to supply it and if the supplier was not worried about getting paid.'

The government had been providing the insurance cover for the Goodman organisation even though the Department of Agriculture was aware that some of Goodman's companies had been adopting fast-and-loose practices. In October 1983 bogus documents were handed in to the Department of Agriculture to claim refunds. The department reported the matter to the Garda Fraud Squad in May 1984. Following Fianna Fáil's return to power in 1987 Michael O'Kennedy, the new Minister for Agriculture, learned about the investigation into Goodman's companies but said that he did not tell Haughey about it. Haughey explained that it would not have mattered anyway because he did not consider the fraud 'all that significant'.

Haughey was prepared to put a great deal of trust in Larry Goodman's plans to boost the food-processing industry with a £260 million investment to create a high-tech, high-added-value food industry which would get Irish beef out of its rut of dependence on EC intervention sales. Goodman personally explained this to the Taoiseach on 9 April 1987. Haughey was accompanied on that occasion by Albert Reynolds, Ray MacSharry, Michael O'Kennedy and Joe Walsh, the Minister of State for Food. Goodman was calling on the government and the EC to provide

75 per cent of the entire £260 million cost of his development plan, which aimed to create 1,150 new jobs in the industry.

Goodman was demanding £90 million from the Industrial Development Authority, while the IDA was prepared to offer only £13 million initially. On 18 May Goodman met Haughey at Kinsealy and complained about the impossibility of the IDA's negotiating stance. Afterwards Reynolds and Walsh were told by Haughey to use 'their good offices as honest brokers to get the negotiations back on the rails'.

Following 'encouragement' from Reynolds, the IDA agreed to increase its offer from £13 million to £20 million. Privately, the IDA had decided to go as high as £25 million. Under pressure from Reynolds, they eventually offered Goodman £30 million. A press conference was held at the Department of Agriculture on 18 June 1987 to announce the £260 million plan publicly, but it promptly ran into difficulties when the IDA insisted on a performance clause in relation to job creation before offering the £30 million.

On 3 March 1988 the IDA informed Goodman that the performance clause could not be deleted, so Goodman lobbied for Haughey's support 'to get the IDA to see the wisdom' of the closure. Five days later the government directed the IDA to remove the performance clause from the contract, even though the 1986 Industrial Development Authority Act specifically stated that the IDA was not answerable to the government in such matters. Haughey had gone to extraordinary lengths to support Goodman in relation to the plan, which in any event never really got off the ground. Before long, difficulties arose over insurance cover for Goodman's beef exports to Iraq.

As Minister for Industry and Commerce, Reynolds quickly moved to reintroduce the insurance coverage that had been terminated by the coalition government in 1986. Reynolds was a self-made man with a disregard for bureaucratic caution. His political strength was in getting things done rather than talking about them. A man of few words, he liked to characterise himself as a pragmatist. 'I don't make any bones about it that I operate a department on the basis of no long files, no long reports,' Reynolds later testified. 'Put it on a single sheet, and if I need more information I know where to get it.'

He liked Goodman's ideas and was determined to provide government help for them, despite strong opposition to this approach from his civil servants. He was convinced that 'there was no way that the Western states or indeed many of the Arab states were going to allow Iraq to lose the war.' Moreover, Haughey, who was favourably disposed towards Iraq, wished 'to be as helpful as possible to Iraq during the course of the war, so that when the war was over, we would be well placed to develop that market'.

As Minister for Health in the late 1970s, Haughey had visited the Ibn-al-Bitar hospital, which was run by PARC, a subsidiary of Aer Lingus. 'During my memorable visits to your country,' he wrote to Saddam Hussein afterwards, 'I saw at first hand what was being achieved and decided that Ireland should seek a closer relationship with Iraq and develop mutually beneficial economic ties. The establishment of a resident embassy in Baghdad in 1986 was an expression of this desire.' Haughey added that he was pleased 'that some Irish economic interests have been able to contribute to what Iraq has achieved in the economic and social fields under your leadership and guidance'.

Reynolds reintroduced insurance cover on exports to Iraq to a ceiling of £35 million. 'I knew there was a window of opportunity appearing,' he explained. 'I made what I regarded as a right decision for the Irish people, for the Irish farmers and for the Irish beef industry.' Haughey was never slow to jump into the spotlight when it came to claiming credit for successful policies, but when the reintroduction of the insurance coverage turned sour, he essentially disowned any part in the policy and blamed Reynolds for the whole thing. He said that 'the question of guiding the government on whether or not to reintroduce export credit insurance was the primary responsibility of the Minister for Industry and Commerce, who took into account the relevant factors.'

'So far as I can recollect,' Haughey said, the decision was not 'conveyed or made known' to him. He also denied knowing about the scale of contracts which Goodman had negotiated with Iraq until the matter came before the government in September 1987. On 2 July Goodman had signed a $134.5 million contract in Baghdad, even though the Insurance Corporation of Ireland had warned Reynolds's department against providing insurance: 'We strongly recommend that no further credit be offered to Iraq under the export-credit scheme by the Minister for Industry and Commerce.' Reynolds had already been warned that 'we ought not be offering cover because Iraq, on the foregoing experience, is a bad risk.'

Haughey claimed that he had 'no recollection of Goodman telling [me] about the Iraqi contract signed in July'. He could not remember being informed about the whole thing by anybody. His professed ignorance was incredible, as a memorandum for government on 8 September 1987 explained that the ceiling for the insurance cover was being raised because of Goodman's $134.5 million contract. The Department of Finance was vehemently opposed to increasing the credit ceiling for Iraq. MacSharry did not agree with his officials but put their arguments to the cabinet anyway. The cabinet duly authorised the whole thing.

The potential benefit to the Irish exchequer was minimal, while the risk was phenomenal. More than four-fifths of the beef that Goodman exported to Iraq was taken from intervention, even though the terms of the contract stipulated that cattle were to have been slaughtered by the halal method not more than a hundred days before the expected date of arrival in Iraq. The intervention beef would not have been slaughtered by the halal method and it would have been butchered years rather than days before export. Goodman contended that the Iraqis knew this, and there was some evidence to support his contention, but by not fulfilling the terms of the contract he provided the Iraqis with a perfect excuse to renege on payment.

Iraqi payments to Goodman for 1987 began to fall due on 5 September 1988. ICI wrote to the Department of Industry and Commerce urging that no further credit be extended. On 21 October one of Goodman's organisations met the department and asked for £325 million more cover. At this point Reynolds indicated that he had been given virtual carte blanche to extend insurance cover up to £500 million at a cabinet meeting on 8 July 1988. The memo for government contained a proposal to increase the insurance ceiling to £500 million, but there was no record that the cabinet had approved this. It seems that the cabinet decided that MacSharry and Reynolds could agree a new limit between themselves, but the Supreme Court ruled that nobody had a right to investigate the matter because it was covered by cabinet confidentiality. MacSharry agreed to raise the limit to £250 million shortly before Reynolds took over as Minister for Finance, in December 1988.

By Christmas £51 million was 'seriously overdue' from Iraq. As it became apparent that things were going seriously wrong, Haughey began to distance himself further from the beef deal. 'I am not going to speak to every dog in the street,' he said. 'Albert Reynolds can meet them.' Nevertheless Haughey met Goodman a couple more times, on 25 January and again on 11 February 1989. Each time the Taoiseach said words to the effect of, 'For God's sake, what was happening and why was no action taken?'

By the end of January 1989 £61.2 million was overdue. The state was probably not liable for the insurance coverage because the Goodman organisation did not provide the beef in accordance with the contract, but at this point the state guaranteed the banks the loans.

The Opposition and the public were not aware of most of these details at the time. The whole thing might have been quietly resolved, like other scandals, had the government not begun to unravel in the following weeks after suffering another Dáil defeat over the issue of haemophiliacs infected with HIV due to tainted blood products. The government planned to offer £250,000 as a one-off payment to be shared by all those haemophiliacs who had been infected, but the Labour Party introduced an amendment raising the payment to £400,000.

Haughey was out of the country at the time on an official visit to Japan. He flew back in the middle of the controversy on 26 April 1989. He was not even supposed to be in the Dáil that day as he had been paired with Alan Dukes, who went to a soccer international at Lansdowne Road. On learning that the government was facing its sixth defeat, Haughey stormed into the Dáil.

'He was hopping mad and just fit to be tied,' one deputy told Stephen Collins. 'In front of the Opposition whip he heaped abuse on his own ministers and chief whip for having allowed the crisis to develop.' Jim Higgins, the Fine Gael whip, witnessed the scene and quietly backed out of the door during the tirade. He noted that ministers there were obviously stunned by Haughey's outburst, in which the Taioseach said he could not tolerate another defeat and would call a general election if the government was beaten. The threat of an election spread around Leinster House like wildfire. Haughey led virtually his entire cabinet into the Dáil chamber to listen to Labour's health spokesman,

Brendan Howlin, wind up the debate on funding for haemophiliacs.' Reynolds sat down beside Haughey and reportedly pleaded with him not to call an election without at least sleeping on the matter.

Dukes was contacted about the crisis and returned to Leinster House, so his pairing arrangement with the Taoiseach was cancelled by mutual agreement. Haughey was enjoying his highest level of popularity, with 67 per cent of voters expressing satisfaction with his performance as Taoiseach, compared with only 38 per cent in May 1987, just after he had assumed office. Some 54 per cent of those polled indicated a voting preference for Fianna Fáil, which would give the party a massive landslide victory if people voted the same way in a general election. When Fianna Fáil duly lost the vote in the Dáil, there was little doubt that Haughey intended to call a general election; this time he had allowed his pique to get the better of his judgement.

The Constitution stipulates that a general election must be held not less than twenty-one days and not more than thirty days after the dissolution of the Dáil. As a result, the election would have had to be held before the end of May. As the European elections were already scheduled for 15 June, this would have necessitated two national elections within a month. If the haemophiliac question had been made an issue of confidence beforehand, Haughey would have had no choice in the matter, but, having failed to declare it as a confidence issue, he would now have difficulty justifying the unnecessary expense of two national elections so close together. Haughey therefore waited until 25 May, to call the general election in conjunction with the European elections.

Fine Gael made desperate efforts to avoid the election, going so far as to offer to negotiate a formal economic accord with the government to provide backing on agreed legislation. During the legislative year beginning in October 1988, Fine Gael had voted with the government on forty-two occasions, abstained eight times and voted against only twelve times. Such cooperation between the two major parties was unprecedented, with the result that there was a strong public perception that the general election was unnecessary.

Fianna Fáil gave two reasons for calling the election. First, there was a danger the government would be defeated on the health budget, which would necessitate a general election anyway. Second, it was argued that there was a need for political stability as Ireland was due to take over the presidency of the European Community at the start of the new year. Neither argument was convincing. Most people suspected that the election was just an attempt by Haughey to shake off the Opposition shackles that were forcing him to pursue responsible policies. The factor that may well have weighed heaviest on Haughey was the possible impending scandal over Iraq not meeting its beef payments. Before the European elections, Iraq was likely to be in default by more than £160 million. This had the makings of the greatest financial scandal in the history of the state, and it would be virtually impossible for a minority government to contain the whole thing. Therefore Haughey made a desperate gamble for an overall majority.

The so-called Haughey factor reappeared as an election issue. Although its influence had possibly been exaggerated in earlier elections, this phenomenon undoubtedly had an impact in tight races, where a comparatively small number of votes could mean the difference between victory and defeat. Ever since the Taca controversy of the 1960s, Fianna Fáil had been vulnerable to the suspicion that it was prepared to do improper favours for businessmen in return for contributions to party funds. People may argue over whether this was unfair, but there was little doubt that the public tended to look with deep suspicion on any kind of cosy relationship between a Fianna Fáil government and the business community.

Haughey became particularly vulnerable when it was disclosed that Larry Goodman had been allowed the unprecedented privilege of keeping his private jet at the Army Air Corps base in Baldonnel. This uneasiness over the beef dealings, coupled with the perception that the election was unnecessary, tended to have a corrosive effect on Fianna Fáil support among floating voters. The party's support declined steadily in the three weeks before polling day: Fianna Fáil's support dropped to 47 per cent in the first opinion poll published after the election was called, to 45 per cent the following week and to 41.1 per cent in the actual vote on election day.

Party workers found a great deal of resentment on the doorsteps. Having campaigned strongly against health cuts in 1987, they found themselves having to explain why Fianna Fáil had instituted even more severe cuts, curtailing programmes that Haughey had introduced while Minister for Health in Jack Lynch's last government. 'It gives me not the slightest bit of pleasure to have to cut back the very programmes I put in myself,' Haughey explained during the campaign. He made a particularly damaging admission on the health situation during a phone-in programme on RTÉ radio, when he said that he 'wasn't aware of the full extent of the problems and difficulties and hardship it was causing'.

This was an extraordinary admission: it was tantamount to acknowledging that he did not know what his government was doing. Some people saw it as an indication that his political judgement was slipping, and that impression was compounded by the election results, which were little short of disastrous from his standpoint. In the outgoing Dáil, Fianna Fáil had eighty-one seats, but it returned with only seventy-seven, seven short of an overall majority. The only party to lose more heavily than Fianna Fáil was the Progressive Democratic Party, which lost eight of its fourteen seats.

Fianna Fáil's dramatic reversal had the impact of making what had once been unthinkable now look attractive. As Sean Tracy could be reappointed Speaker, the six seats won by the Progressive Democrats just happened to be the number that Haughey needed to form a government. On his past record he had been ready to pay dearly for the support he required, and Mary Harney realised that there was an opportunity for her and her colleagues – all of whom were former members of Fianna Fáil – to salvage something from the election disaster.

'However we may dislike certain people or parties,' she said, 'we have to play our part in giving this country a government for the foreseeable future.' She was clearly signalling the possibility of an arrangement between the two parties, but her colleague Pearse Wyse seemed to throw a wet blanket over the idea of any cooperation while Haughey remained as Fianna Fáil leader. 'I believe that no man, including Mr Haughey, has the right to stand in the way of stable government,' Wyse said. 'In no circumstances could I bring myself to vote for him as Taoiseach.'

The Progressive Democrats had pledged to vote for the Fine Gael leader, and they decided to keep their commitment when the Dáil met to select a Taoiseach on 28 June 1989. But in the interim Dessie O'Malley and Pat Cox, who had just been elected to the European Parliament, held exploratory talks with Haughey. They insisted that the price of Progressive Democratic support would be a coalition. When Haughey said he could 'never sell' that to Fianna Fáil, O'Malley smiled. He said that Haughey should not 'make a mistake in underestimating his ability to sell anything to his party'.

As expected, Haughey's nomination as Taoiseach was defeated

by eighty-six votes to seventy-eight, but so also were the nominations of Alan Dukes and Dick Spring to the position. Under the Constitution, Haughey would remain as Taoiseach until a successor was elected, but there was some confusion as to the correct constitutional procedure, as this had never happened before.

Haughey proposed that the Dáil adjourn until 3 July to give him a chance to form a government. He said he would not be advising the president to dissolve the Dáil at this stage, as it would not be in 'the best interests of the country to precipitate another general election' so soon after the last one, if this could be avoided. He and his cabinet colleagues would continue in office and the 'day-to-day business of the government will be carried on uninterrupted,' he said.

Alan Dukes raised no objection. Prior to the first meeting of the last Dáil in 1987, Fine Gael sources had been claiming that the Taoiseach could have up to forty-eight hours before resigning. But Dick Spring insisted that Haughey was constitutionally obliged to go to the President to resign his office formally. Haughey said he had had advice from the Attorney-General that 'time was not of the essence' and that he had 'up to a week' before having to resign.

Article 28.10 of the Constitution stipulates that 'The Taoiseach shall resign from office upon his ceasing to retain the support of a majority in Dáil Éireann unless on his advice the President dissolves Dáil Éireann and on the reassembly of Dáil Éireann after the dissolution the Taoiseach secures the support of a majority in Dáil Éireann.' The Taoiseach was obviously obliged to resign unless he called for another general election. Much of the argument on this issue was really only academic, because the following paragraph of the Constitution states that 'the Taoiseach and the other members of the government shall continue to carry on their duties until their successors shall have been appointed.' It was just a question of procedure, but in such matters procedure is important.

Haughey was leaving himself open to the charge of refusing to resign, in defiance of the Constitution. He and Neil Blaney had been the first ministers in the history of the state to refuse to resign when called upon to do so by the Taoiseach, during the Arms Crisis. Now Haughey would be setting another constitutional precedent.

During a two-hour recess he was convinced by colleagues that, regardless of the advice he had received from the Attorney-General, it was politically imperative that he resign as soon as possible. Immediately after the recess he announced his intention of tendering his resignation to the President. He added that he would not ask for a dissolution but would continue to try to form a government. The Dáil then adjourned for four days, until the following Monday, 3 July 1989.

The Progressive Democrats made it clear that they would not prop up a minority Fianna Fáil government, no matter what inducements were offered to them; they were interested only in a coalition. Fianna Fáil, however, had a long-standing policy of not going into coalition with anybody. The Fianna Fáil National Executive voted unanimously against coalition and Haughey went on RTÉ's *This Week* programme on 2 July 1989 to say that he was totally opposed to the idea.

This, of course, raised the spectre of another election; such a prospect would now be strictly a matter for the President, who had the authority to refuse to dissolve the Dáil, as the Taoiseach had ceased to retain majority support. Haughey contended, however, that the 'accepted wisdom' had always been that the President would never exercise this power.

When the Dáil reconvened the next day, Haughey asked for a further adjournment until the afternoon of 6 July. Dukes agreed to this, but not before making a hard-hitting speech in which he criticised Haughey's attempt 'to prejudge the response that the President might make to advise on a dissolution of the Dáil'. Was it ironic that he, of all people, should adopt such an attitude? Haughey's remarks were in sharp contrast 'with his actions in January 1982', when he had tried to get the President to reject Garret Fitzgerald's request for a dissolution of the Dáil, O'Malley observed.

When the cabinet met the next day, it was evenly split on the issue of coalition, with senior members like Albert Reynolds, Pádraig Flynn, John Wilson, and Michael O'Kennedy firmly opposed to the proposal. Brian Lenihan, on the other hand, felt they had no choice. He argued that, under the circumstances, they would be able to sell the idea of coalition to the party.

Flynn stunned his colleagues with a vicious attack on Haughey, whose lust for power had put them in the invidious position in which they found themselves, he said. Later that afternoon he went on RTÉ's *Today at Five* to say that a coalition was out of the question. 'All the members of the cabinet are unanimous for no coalition,' he said. 'The National Executive, the parliamentary party and the grass roots have indicated this is a core value which we must preserve.'

When Haughey met the Progressive Democrats shortly afterwards, he formally agreed to form a coalition, subject to an agreement on a joint programme for government. On being asked about remarks concerning opposition to this strategy within the party, he was dismissive. 'I haven't told them yet,' Haughey replied.

The next day, Thursday 6 July, the Dáil reconvened and Haughey asked for a further adjournment, until 12 July. Dukes again agreed, but he warned that this was the last time. 'One thing is perfectly clear,' he said. 'The issue before us must be resolved before this House meets next Wednesday.'

Details of policy matters relating to the programme for government were negotiated by Albert Reynolds and Bertie Ahern for Fianna Fáil and Bobby Molloy and Pat Cox for the Progressive Democrats. Issues on which they were unable to agree and matters relating to the composition of the government were then left to the two leaders. Fianna Fáil were insistent that the Progressive Democrats were entitled to only one seat in the cabinet due to the number of their TDs in relation to the number of those of Fianna Fáil, but O'Malley insisted on two. He realised that Haughey was under strong pressure from within the cabinet and he expressed sympathy for the Taoiseach at one point.

The parliamentary party allowed Haughey freedom to negotiate a coalition, but not before Máire Geoghegan-Quinn had made some bitter comments. 'Don't ask me to accept that what is being done is in the national interest,' she said. It was simply being done to satisfy the leader's desire for power, she argued. Most of the backbenchers, however, were so anxious to avoid a further election that they favoured coalition. 'They're more enlightened than some of my cabinet,' Haughey remarked caustically.

By the eve of the Dáil meeting the only outstanding issue was the question of whether the Progressive Democrats would be offered one or two seats in cabinet. Albert Reynolds told RTÉ that the party had authorised Haughey to give the Progressive Democrats only one seat, but Haughey gave in to O'Malley's demands and agreed to appoint him and Molloy to the cabinet and Mary Harney as a Minister of State. In addition, the Progressive Democrats were promised three seats in the Senate out of the eleven to be appointed by the Taoiseach.

'Never in the history of Irish politics,' one disgruntled Fianna Fáiler declared, 'has so much been given by so many to so few.'

# 16

## 'He did more than his critics ever did'
## Taoiseach, 1989–1992

After he was again elected Taoiseach on 12 July 1989, Haughey's first task was to appoint his cabinet. This time he was going to have to find places for the two Progressive Democrats. By prior agreement, Des O'Malley was to be appointed Minister for Industry and Commerce and Bobby Molloy Minister for Energy.

In all previous coalitions the leader of the second party was appointed Tánaiste, but Brian Lenihan was to retain that post within the government, though now, after his successful liver transplant, he was moved from Foreign Affairs to the less strenuous portfolio of Defence. Yet the political reality was that Des O'Malley, who became Minister for Industry and Commerce, was effectively the man with the real clout. 'I am nominally Tánaiste in this government but the reality of the situation is that O'Malley is the real Tánaiste,' Lenihan noted. 'He is the actual number two in the government.'

Haughey reappointed half the outgoing cabinet to the same positions: Reynolds at Finance, Ahern at Labour, Flynn at Environment, O'Hanlon at Health, Woods at Social Welfare, O'Rourke at Education and O'Kennedy at Agriculture; John Murray was reappointed Attorney-General. Gerard Collins was seen as the big gainer, as he was moved from Justice to Foreign Affairs and replaced at Justice by Ray Burke, who had to make way for O'Malley at Industry and Commerce, while John Wilson was moved from Communications to the Marine. The only new Fianna Fáil face in the cabinet was the surprise choice of Seamus Brennan, who was given Transport and Tourism. Three ministers were dropped: Michael Smith made way for Molloy and Michael Noonan lost out at Defence. Brendan Daly was seen as the most unlucky person to have lost his post because he had loyally borne the brunt of the hostility during the rod-licence dispute as Minister for the Marine.

There was enormous resentment within Fianna Fáil over the coalition arrangement with the Progressive Democrats. Reynolds and Ahern were annoyed at the way in which they had been undermined and then belittled as negotiators by Haughey, who had arrogantly proclaimed that he had not yet told his colleagues the party's policy on the issue.

Máire Geoghegan-Quinn was particularly disappointed. She was not only passed over for a cabinet position again, she had the added indignity of watching her constituency rival, Bobby Molloy, being elevated to the cabinet. When Haughey first became Taoiseach, in 1979, he had dropped Molloy and appointed Geoghegan-Quinn, who became the first female minister since Independence in 1921. This time she was given the junior European Affairs ministry; this was a particularly significant position because Ireland was due to take over the presidency of the European Community in January 1990.

Jackie Fahey, one of the original 'gang of five' who had helped organise the push that brought Haughey to power in 1979, got nothing. Fahey was so annoyed by this that he resigned from the Fianna Fáil parliamentary party in a fit of pique. 'I agree with Des O'Malley,' he said, 'Fianna Fáil is run in a very undemocratic fashion.'

The three Progressive Democrats that the Taoiseach was to appoint to the Senate could not be named until after the Senate elections, so Fianna Fáil's annoyance at that aspect of the coalition arrangement festered through the summer and into the autumn. Jackie Fahey reportedly warned that he would resign his Dáil seat if Haughey appointed Fahey's constituency rival Martin Cullen, but it was O'Malley who was going to suggest the names of the three Progressive Democrats to the Taoiseach. Martin Cullen was duly appointed, along with John Dardis and Helen Keogh, but Fahey did not carry out his threat. Instead he sulked for a couple of months more and then requested readmission to the parliamentary party.

There was further controversy over the Senate's election of a Cathaoirleach ('chairman'). There was a contest for the Fianna Fáil nomination between Sean Doherty, another member of the original gang of five, and Haughey's long-time critic Des Hanafin. The Taoiseach did not take an open stand on the race, but his supporters would have had no doubt that he favoured Doherty over Hanafin. If he had not wanted the former Minister for Justice, he would only have had to mention this to some of his own loyalists. As it was, Doherty won by the narrowest margin possible. The vote was actually tied at sixteen each, but Doherty won when his name was drawn from a hat. The three Progressive Democrat appointees, who had been instructed by their party not to vote for Doherty, supported his Fine Gael opponent in the contest for Cathaoirleach, but Fianna Fáil had an overall majority of their own in the House and Doherty's election was essentially assured.

There were no other difficulties between Fianna Fáil and the Progressive Democrats until the end of the year, when Haughey was essentially compelled to reappoint Michael Mills as Ombudsman. The latter's term was due to terminate on 3 January 1990, during the Dáil recess. Dick Spring therefore brought up the issue just before the holiday. Haughey contended that there were legal difficulties in reappointing Mills as the law stipulated that the Ombudsman's term was for six years and he had to retire at the age of sixty-seven. Mills was already sixty-two years old and would not be eligible to serve a full term. Under pressure from O'Malley, the Taoiseach duly found an easy way out of the dilemma. Mills was reappointed but would step down after four-and-a-half years, when he reached the mandatory retirement age.

This was the first time in government that Haughey had been openly forced to give in to the Progressive Democrats, but it would not be the last. Each time the Progressive Democrats compelled him to make a concession, this rankled with members of the Fianna Fáil parliamentary party, even though the whole idea of abandoning the party's 'core values' in joining a coalition had not weighed very heavily with Fianna Fáil supporters. A public-opinion poll found that 85 per cent of those who had voted for Fianna Fáil approved of the compromise on coalition. Haughey had clearly overcome that hurdle and again seemed firmly in control as party leader. With his penchant for hyperbole, Brian Lenihan, the Tánaiste, pronounced that 'Charlie would lead Fianna Fáil into a united Ireland, a united Europe, a united world and then,' he added, 'into the next century.'

Lenihan was campaigning quietly for the presidency, as Paddy Hillery was constitutionally obliged to step down in November 1990 at the end of his second term. In December 1989 Haughey seemed to encourage the rumours of Lenihan's interest in the office at an annual Fianna Fáil dinner. 'He will still be one of us, whatever high office he is called to during the next decade,' the Taoiseach said, to tremendous applause. Lenihan further encouraged the speculation by declaring publicly, 'I would be honoured, as any Irishman would be honoured, to run for the presidency.'

At the beginning of 1990 it was Ireland's turn to assume the EC presidency, which rotated among the member states every six months. This was the fourth time that Ireland had had the presidency since joining the then EEC, but it was only the second time that Fianna Fáil had been in power during an Irish presidency of the organisation. Ominously, the previous time had been during the second half of 1979, when Jack Lynch was coming to the end of his political reign. Now, ten years later, Haughey seemed almost as vulnerable as Lynch had been.

Yet the presidency afforded Haughey a broad international stage, especially as there was so much happening in Europe. The Berlin Wall had come down in 1989 and the two Germanies were moving precipitously towards unification. Normally a summit meeting of all EC heads of government was held every six months in the country holding the presidency, but there was so much happening in early 1990 that Haughey enjoyed the privilege of hosting two summits in Dublin. The first, on 28 April, was to discuss the transformation of the European Community into the European Union and the implications of German reunification, which could have posed a serious problem if countries like Britain and France had exhibited their traditional fear of a greater Germany.

In preparation for what became known as Dublin One, Haughey travelled to each of the European capitals for talks with the various heads of government. 'In the old days, that would have been inconceivable,' he explained. That work would previously have been done by the diplomatic service, but Haughey preferred the more direct contact of personal meetings. 'I was concerned to make sure that the affairs of the Community were managed effectively to take all these dramatic happenings on board,' he said. 'It was a period of great excitement and great satisfaction, in the knowledge that one was participating in the events of an important period of history.' He realised that this was a truly momentous time in European history and he was anxious to be at the centre of things.

'I would very much like to see the Community having a much more coordinated approach to foreign policy,' he explained. 'The Community does now have a united voice on many issues and the general view is that this could be developed further.' He was also anxious that there should be closer ties between the EC and the United States. In late February he went to Washington for discussions with President George Bush and suggested afterwards that the EU should also have twice-yearly meetings with the American President. Traditionally after a meeting such as that between the Irish and American leaders, there would be some kind of perfunctory remarks about discussing the partition question, but not this time. Bush and Haughey were talking about Europe and America's role there, and Haughey was not about to sully these talks by dragging in more provincial considerations for his own domestic political purposes.

The following week in the Dáil Haughey suggested that Ireland join the Conference on Security and Cooperation in Europe in order to 'take part in any security and confidence-building arrangements embracing Europe as a whole'. Back in 1967, when he had travelled to the various European capitals with Jack Lynch in order to hold negotiations to get into the EEC, both of them had made it clear that a common security arrangement would pose no problems for Ireland. 'There was general agreement that if, in the fullness of time, the Community ever brought forward some arrangement for its own security, we in Ireland would have to consider participating in such a Community arrangement, and that is still the position,' Haughey told the *Irish Times*. 'Slowly but surely I think the Community has been working towards a common international position.'

Before this would happen, however, he believed that the single market and economic and monetary union would be in operation.

Through his shuttle diplomacy he helped secure an agreement on how to handle German unification and develop a two-year programme of EC institutional reform with the aim of securing eventual political, economic and political union. Afterwards, in a speech to the European Parliament, the German Chancellor, Helmut Kohl, gave Haughey considerable praise for the role he had played in the negotiations.

Early in Ireland's presidency of the EC, the French newspaper *Le Monde* had carried an intriguing profile of Haughey as a man who 'thirsts for respectability and international recognition'. Describing him as 'one of the richest men in Ireland' as well as 'an enthusiast of good living and good wines', the article, written by Dominique Dhombres, the newspaper's London correspondent, noted that Haughey's three great passions were 'politics, women and horses'. But the Taoiseach could hardly have been flattered that the one international figure with whom he was compared was the disgraced American President Richard Nixon, because Haughey, like Nixon, was 'a survival artist', the paper reported. As in Nixon's case, there were also questions about how Haughey had secured his wealth. Although the Taoiseach was 'discreet' about the source of this wealth, Dhombres alluded to rezoning land, which 'it seems that he bought at the right time'. The journalist further suggested that Haughey's career had been helped by the fact that he had married the daughter of Sean Lemass.

Characterised as 'a visceral nationalist' who had 'an unfathomable hatred of the English, which he shares with a good number of his compatriots', the Taoiseach was depicted as a person who had grown 'wiser' with experience. Whereas Éamon de Valera had rather shamelessly exploited the international stage to highlight the partition issue, Haughey was expected to be more circumspect. Although the issue of German unification might have afforded him a God-given opportunity for exploiting the partition issue at home, Haughey adopted the role of the cautious statesman. Despite the fact that he had been 'the implacable enemy of all compromise with London', he had 'transformed himself into a faithful, even fastidious observer of the Anglo-Irish Agreement', according to Dhombres.

On 15 March Dick Spring confronted Haughey with details from the liquidator's report following the collapse of Merchant Bank, which was owned by Patrick Gallagher. There was a reference to a 'gift of loans' to Haughey of around £20,000 on which no effort had been made to pay any interest or repay the money. The money had been given to Larchfield Securities, the official owner of Haughey's property, which was owned by Haughey's daughter and three sons. Spring wished formally to confront the Taoiseach with the information, so he put it in a letter and delivered it personally. 'He could not have been more courteous,' Spring recalled. 'He glanced at my letter and thanked me for having the courtesy to give it to him personally.' The next day he sent a messenger with a reply to the Labour leader. 'I read your letter yesterday with disbelief,' he wrote. 'I categorically reject your outrageous suggestions and find it deeply offensive that you would write to me in this tone.'

RTÉ's current-affairs department prepared a programme on the collapse of Merchant Bank. 'I gave an interview on the subject to an RTÉ reporter,' Spring noted. 'I also gave the correspondence to him and to his producer,' he said. This material was woven into the story, but then, at the eleventh hour, the programme was completely re-edited and Spring's material was dropped. 'When I raised the matter with management people in RTÉ, they assured me the programme would be shown in full in due course, when "certain legal difficulties" were overcome,' Spring wrote. 'I'm still waiting!'

April would be a particularly busy month for Haughey. He had the Dublin One summit at the end of the month, but first there was the annual Fianna Fáil ard-fheis in Dublin, where he emphasised that the sweeping changes in Europe offered the prospect of Irish unity. 'The modern world offers all who live on this small island countless examples of ways in which divisions can be overcome and new, fruitful relationships devised,' he argued. He wanted people to realise that, in helping to build a united Europe, they would be developing a unified Ireland. 'There is no doubt that the development in the Community is going to bring the North and South much closer together economically, financially and socially,' he explained in an interview with the *Irish Times*. 'I think it's not too romantic to think in terms of a united Ireland as part of a united Europe.'

In his ard-fheis address Haughey played down the difficulties in the North, for a change. He merely hinted at progress behind the scenes in the ongoing secret negotiations. 'Is it possible at least to discern some indications of a change of mind emerging among those who have supported or tolerated the use of violence?' he asked the ard-fheis. 'It is only when violence has been laid aside that the way will be open to the widest possible dialogue involving all strands of opinion and belief.'

This ard-fheis should have been a triumph for Haughey, especially in his role as titular President of the EC, but instead it looked more like his last hurrah. The ard-fheis was poorly attended and the enthusiasm that his supporters had exhibited in earlier years was clearly missing. The vote for the Committee of Fifteen on the National Executive, which was always keenly contested, was down by one-third on the previous ard-fheis. Those most notable by their absence were the people who had been Haughey's backers. The big talk among delegates who turned up was not about various proposals but about who would succeed Haughey. Bill Loughnane, who headed the vote for the Committee of Fifteen, represented the new generation of the party. His father had been a strong Haughey supporter who had done a great deal to destabilise Jack Lynch in his final months, but now young Bill said that Haughey should step down after the European presidency.

The Taoiseach had again been hurt by the antics of Sean Doherty in the Senate. Even though he had been given legal advice not to preside at a hearing to suspend Senator David Norris for having wrongly assused him of misconduct, Doherty not only presided over the suspenion of Norris but withheld from his colleagues the legal advice he had been given. Norris resorted to the courts and, although the judiciary was naturally reluctant to interfere with the legislature, it took a stand in this instance because Doherty's behaviour was an affront to natural justice.

There followed an intense debate within Fianna Fáil before the party eventually decided to support him against a no-confidence motion introduced by the Opposition. But there was so much opposition to Doherty within Fianna Fáil itself that it was obvious that he had lost the confidence of a majority of the Senate.

Looking back on the press coverage of the period with the benefit of hindsight, the analysis of Stephen Collins, the political correspondent of the *Sunday Press*, stands out as particularly perceptive. He noted that the two main contenders in the succession stakes were Albert Reynolds and Gerard Collins, with Reynolds clearly in front, partly because he seemed to enjoy the support of Bertie Ahern. The latter and Reynolds were still smarting at the way they had been treated by Haughey during the coalition negotiations. Reynolds had openly ridiculed the coalition in a highly publicised speech in Kanturk, County Cork, on 18 February 1990. 'I hope,' he said, 'that the temporary little arrangement which we have with our junior partners won't be there all that long and that we'll be back to where we were at the start.'

The apparent cooperation between Reynolds and Ahern was forcing Gerard Collins closer to Haughey for the moment, but Stephen Collins suggested that the lack of opportunities to promote people might militate against Haughey, who had been too cautious. 'On past experience he will make the minimum changes but that course will now carry very real dangers,' Collins said.

The week after the ard-fheis, Haughey made his first visit to Belfast in thirty years, to speak at the Institute of Directors Conference at the Europa Hotel. Ian Paisley tried to mount his usual protest, but he got comparatively little support. Haughey was not there to rail against partition. Instead he talked about the economic benefits of cooperation; both parts of the island should have been each other's best customers, but neither's trade with the other amounted to more than 5 per cent of their exports.

With all the travelling and high-powered negotiations, Haughey was in his element. To say that he was as happy as a pig in shit would be to convey altogether the wrong image, because he was doing things in real style. Almost £12 million was spent on organising the two Dublin summits.

Dublin Two, the main semi-annual summit, passed off almost unnoticed in Ireland – at least outside Dublin – because it clashed with Ireland's first appearance in the soccer World Cup. The final summit meeting coincided with a forgettable game between Ireland and Romania that had an unforgettable finish. The Irish won on penalties to qualify to meet Italy in the quarter-finals of the competition. Most Irish people who were old enough can probably tell you where they were during that penalty shoot-out, but very few knew that there was a summit meeting in Dublin that day. After the game RTÉ went over to the press area at Dublin Castle, where the journalists had been watching the game too. The camera captured the hard-bitten John Healy, who had been hired to look after the international press, reduced to tears of joy at the outcome of the game.

The following week Haughey flew out to the Italian match and invited Alan Dukes and Dick Spring to accompany his ministerial party on the executive jet. 'I considered it my duty as head of the government to attend in Rome,' the Taoiseach explained, 'to demonstrate the total support of the Irish people for all the team.'

After the game, which Ireland lost by one goal to nil, Haughey went down on the field and waved to the Irish crowd, which was estimated at over 10,000. He was roundly booed. He had never shown any real interest in Irish soccer before the team became successful. In fact, when he was Taoiseach he had bragged that he had never attended a soccer game at Lansdowne Road. Before the crowd could turn too ugly, however, Jack Charlton came to the rescue. His appearance was greeted with loud cheering and applause that obliterated the hostility towards the short fellow.

An estimated half-a-million people turned out in Dublin to welcome home the team, but this time Haughey entertained them in his office, while his son Sean was welcomed to the civil reception as Lord Mayor of Dublin. He was abused by sections of the crowd, but Charlton came to his rescue too.

With the presidential election due in November 1990, there was a good deal of speculation that Haughey might run for the office. He was expected by many to step down as Taoiseach at the end of Ireland's presidency of the European Community in July 1990, and it seemed natural enough that he would move on to Phoenix Park at this stage of his political career, especially when questions had been raised about his health.

Notwithstanding his public benediction of Lenihan's candidacy the previous December, Haughey had misgivings about this candidacy because Lenihan's election would undermine the coalition's majority in the Dáil. The government would have to win the ensuing by-election in the Dublin West constituency, which, of course, was where Haughey had unhappy memories of the by-election defeat eight years earlier, when Liam Skally of Fine Gael had won the seat following Dick Burke's second appointment to the European Commission. A number of cabinet ministers were uneasy about the invitation, and Haughey did nothing to allay their disquiet. In fact, he quietly encouraged an alternative to Lenihan by sending out feelers to Fine Gael to run an agreed candidate for President such as the distinguished civil servant T. K. Whitaker. Jack Lynch might have been prepared to stand if invited, but Haughey would not give him the itch.

Lenihan played down his own uneasiness about Haughey's support. In April he told the press that Haughey was 'a tremendously loyal person to his friends, generous in spirit and a very kind and considerate person in all his personal relationships and dealings'. One cannot say whether he was trying to reassure himself or merely put pressure on the Taoiseach. In the coming weeks John Wilson, the Minister for the Marine, indicated that he was interested in running for the presidency. If he won, Fianna Fáil would have little difficulty winning a by-election in his Cavan-Monaghan constituency. 'The more suspicious of my supporters felt that Mr Haughey was behind the Wilson gambit,' Lenihan wrote. By then, however, Lenihan's campaign for the nomination had gained an unstoppable momentum, and Wilson's challenge was easily brushed aside, by fifty-four votes to nineteen.

At the start of the presidential campaign Lenihan was odds-on favourite to win. Over the years he had enjoyed a high profile, especially in recent months after his successful liver transplant. He was well liked by politicians on all sides of the Dáil and also by the press. Lenihan was the kind of man who facilitated journalists and, unlike Haughey, he never took offence at their criticism. He was also liked by the public, as was evident from the extent of his support, which was more than double that of his nearest rival, Mary Robinson.

During the campaign Robinson began to eat into his lead, as expected, but her liberal views on matters like divorce and contraception were seen as a distinct liability among conservative voters. The various public-opinion surveys were indicating that if Lenihan did not win on the first count, he would win easily on transfers from the Fine Gael candidate, Austin Currie, who had been reluctant to run and got into the campaign much too late. Fine Gael was floundering in its efforts to boost his candidacy.

Currie tried to depict Lenihan as unsuitable for the office on the grounds that he was too close to Haughey and could not therefore be trusted to act independently. 'It is difficult to see how the habits of loyalty to Mr Haughey for half a lifetime will be abandoned by Mr Lenihan if elected President,' Currie said at the launch of his campaign. Fine Gael charged, for instance, that Lenihan had not demurred when Haughey had initially refused to resign following his defeat in 1989. This, Lenihan contended, was untrue, because he had been among the first to advise Haughey that he should resign. The second issue raised in relation to Lenihan's judgment was that he had sought, at Haughey's behest, to interfere with the President's 'absolute discretion' on the question of granting Garret Fitzgerald a dissolution of Parliament following the defeat of his government's budget in January 1982.

Fitzgerald and Lenihan appeared on RTÉ's *Questions and Answers* on 22 October 1990, when the issue of the President's discretionary powers was raised by the former Taoiseach. Lenihan was fairly dismissive of the matter because the option had never been used by any President.

'Why the phone calls to try to force him to exercise it?' Fitzgerald asked, alluding to what had happened in 1982.

'That's fictional, Garret,' Lenihan replied.

'It is not fictional, excuse me. I was in Áras an Uachtaráin when those phone calls came through and I know how many there were.'

Somebody in the audience asked Lenihan directly if he had made any phone calls to the Áras that night. 'No, I didn't at all,' he insisted. 'That never happened. I want to assure you that never happened.'

Lenihan had forgotten, however, that he had told a student during a taped interview in May that he had called President Hillery that night and had spoken to him. 'I got through to him,' Lenihan had said. In hindsight, he said the whole thing was a mistake because the President was not the type of man who would break new ground. 'But of course,' Lenihan added, 'Charlie was gung-ho.'

In an article in the *Irish Times* on 27 September, the student, Jim Duffy, wrote that Haughey, Lenihan and Sylvester Barrett had made phone calls to the President on the night of the budget fiasco. Dick Walsh, the political editor of the newspaper, was anxious to run a follow-up story, but Duffy was reluctant to give Walsh further information on the matter. He allowed Walsh to hear the taped interview and agreed to the *Irish Times* running a low-key story on 24 October to the effect that it had corroborative evidence. By this stage the whole thing was gathering a momentum of its own. Gay Byrne challenged the *Irish Times* on his radio programme to publish the evidence, if it had any. Lenihan reaffirmed his denial on RTÉ radio's *News at One* and on *Today at Five*, on which his campaign manager, Bertie Ahern, mentioned Jim Duffy and suggested that his tape had been stolen.

With the political temperature rising, Duffy decided to release the pertinent segment of the controversial tape after he had been named on RTÉ by Bertie Ahern. The *Irish Times* then did the most extraordinary thing in convening an afternoon press conference. Rather than running the story as an exclusive on its own pages, it gave the story to the world, setting off a political firestorm.

Lenihan was caught completely by surprise. He rushed over to appear on RTÉ's early-evening news to explain his side of the story without even hearing the tape: he heard it for the first time on the programme. Rather than candidly admit that he had no recollection of the interview, he tried to bluff his way out of the situation by looking straight into the camera. 'My mature recollection at this stage is that I did not ring President Hillery. I want to put my reputation on the line in that respect,' he said.

The interviewer, Sean Duignan, realised that Lenihan could not have it both ways. Either he wasn't telling the truth now, or else he hadn't told the truth to the student. 'I must have been mistaken in what I said to Duffy on that occasion,' Lenihan replied. 'It was a casual discussion with a research student and I was obviously mistaken in what I said.' Yet it could not have been just a casual slip; it was not just one mistake. Duignan quoted from the transcript of the conversation.

'But you made a phone call?' Duffy asked.

'Oh, I did,' Lenihan replied.

'Sylvester Barrett made one?'

'That is right.'

'And Mr Haughey?'

'That is right.'

'Well,' Lenihan said, interrupting Duignan, 'in fact, that is wrong, and I want to emphasise it here. From my mature recollection and discussion with other people, at no stage did I ring President Hillery on that occasion or any other time.'

'They are all going to come after you demanding that you pull out of the race,' Duignan suggested. 'Do you not think that in all the circumstances you should?'

'I will not pull out of the race. I am not going to do so on the basis of a remark made to a university student, to whom I was doing a very great service in providing background for material he was gathering on the presidency.'

It was a pathetic performance, made all the worse by Lenihan's ridiculous efforts to project sincerity by looking straight into the camera and using the phrase 'mature recollection' on four different occasions. Either he was lying now or he had spun a cock-and-bull story to Duffy. If the latter was true, it was certainly ludicrous to describe the interview as 'a very great service'. What he said to Duffy was a 'casual oversight', he explained minutes later during an interview on radio news. 'I am telling you the honest truth. And I like to be honest. I have been honest all my life in politics,' he asserted.

'What state of mind could you have been in to be so very wrong over such a very wide area?' Olivia O'Leary asked him some hours later on *Today Tonight*. 'One knows that you've been sick recently. But were you on some drugs or something?'

'Not at all,' Lenihan replied, breaking into a broad smile. 'That's an outrageous suggestion.' Much later in his book, *For the Record*, Lenihan provided a plausible explanation for his behaviour when he admitted that at the time of the Duffy interview he was on strong drugs to ward off rejection of his new liver. A common side effect of those drugs is a partial loss of memory, but he admitted this only long after the campaign had ended.

During the campaign itself, Lenihan's behaviour seemed inexplicable. He had obviously been lying to somebody and, by protesting his honesty, he seemed to be lying to everybody. In the circumstances, many people felt he was insulting the intelligence of the electorate. There was uproar in the Dáil the next day when the Opposition tried to raise the issue of the Lenihan tape and the telephone calls to the Áras. 'Brian Lenihan should be hauled in here and hung, drawn and quartered,' Jim Mitchell of Fine Gael declared.

Haughey was incensed. 'The leader of the Opposition is hurling false accusations around the House,' he said. 'Before he makes any more accusations about telling lies or untruths, he should look behind him at Deputy Garret Fitzgerald, who has been completely exposed as telling lies.' Haughey had to withdraw that accusation, but of course the damage had been done.

Haughey had gone over the top in accusing Fitzgerald of lying. Fitzgerald had said on *Questions and Answers* that if the various Fianna Fáil people had not called the Áras on the night in question, somebody had done a good job of imitating them. This was taken by some people as an insinuation that he had overheard the calls, but Fitzgerald had already made it clear that he was simply told at the Áras that the various people had telephoned.

The Progressive Democrats decided to demand Lenihan's resignation from the government. On Monday Haughey had Ahern explain the situation to Lenihan, but the latter said that he would not resign, as such a move would destroy his campaign.

Haughey therefore called an impromptu session of the Fianna Fáil members of his cabinet at his home to discuss the situation. Neither Lenihan nor his sister, Mary O'Rourke, were invited. With the Progressive Democrats insisting on Lenihan's resignation, many of those present felt he had to go, and there was little doubt that the Taoiseach favoured this course.

The next morning Lenihan broke off campaigning in the south to fly to Dublin to meet Haughey at his home. They had a twenty-minute meeting, at which Haughey explained that the government would collapse if Lenihan did not resign. 'The Taoiseach advocated that the best option open to me was my resignation,' Lenihan recalled. He said my resignation would help rather than damage my campaign for the Presidency. He said most people would respect me for standing down in the national interest in order to avoid a general election. Pressing the point further, Mr Haughey said that if I resigned, Dessie O'Malley would issue a statement congratulating me on my decision.

'I listened to all this patiently,' he continued. 'I then countered that my resignation would be tantamount to an admission that I had done something wrong as Tánaiste and Minister for Defence which rendered me unfit to serve as a member of the cabinet.' Lenihan protested his honesty. 'I put it to the Taoiseach that he and Mr O'Malley knew that I was telling the truth because both of them were on the Fianna Fáil front bench on the night the phone calls were made.' But that was only part of the problem.

O'Malley had succinctly summarised the situation during an RTÉ radio interview over the weekend. 'Mr Lenihan has given two diametrically opposed accounts of what happened, and they can't both be true,' he said. For some reason Lenihan seemed curiously unable to see that protesting his honesty in the circumstances seemed to be compounding the lie. Haughey explained that the Progressive Democrats were insistent 'and the only acceptable solution' was his resignation.

The meeting between Haughey and Lenihan had to be cut short as the Taoiseach was due to meet Queen Beatrix of the Netherlands, who was arriving in Dublin Airport on a state visit. Ahern told Lenihan that the Progressive Democrats were going to pull out of the government if Lenihan had not resigned by five o'clock that afternoon.

Haughey was asked at Dublin Airport by waiting reporters about rumours that Lenihan was about to resign. 'Brian Lenihan did not offer his resignation nor did I seek it,' he replied. 'Anything like that would be a matter for my old friend Brian Lenihan personally. I would not exert pressure on him in that regard, nor would my colleagues,' he continued. He apparently thought Lenihan would resign voluntarily.

The two men met again after lunch. 'This time Mr Haughey was pushing resignation harder than before,' Lenihan noted. 'He handed me a three-page prepared resignation statement.' Lenihan promised to give Haughey his answer before five o'clock. When he did, it was another refusal. 'If I resigned, my credibility and reputation would be destroyed,' Lenihan said.

That evening Pádraig Flynn was sent to persuade Lenihan to resign, but Mary O'Rourke intercepted Flynn and told him where to go in no uncertain language, which left him muttering to himself. At that stage Haughey had apparently resigned himself to the idea that the government would fall because he did not believe that he could weather the storm within the party if he sacked Lenihan, but then came word of a poll to be published in the *Irish Independent* the next day. The survey found that Lenihan was trailing very badly in the presidential race, with just 31 per cent support against 51 per cent for Mary

Robinson. With those kind of figures, it was obvious that fighting a general election so that Lenihan could retain his job would be extremely risky, and there is nothing more likely to concentrate the minds of politicians than the possibility of losing their seats. Next morning the Fianna Fáil parliamentary party met and expressed confidence in the Taoiseach to do as he thought fit. Word was passed to the Progressive Democrats that Lenihan would be given the choice of either resigning or being dismissed.

This drama was being played out behind the scenes as the Dáil debate on the no-confidence motion began. Haughey took the offensive. 'I would rather any day have Brian Lenihan, who would, for whatever reason, give an impulsive, inaccurate version of something that happened eight years ago, than a group of Fine Gael conspirators who, with a cold, ruthless determination, planned to trap and destroy a decent man,' he said. 'There is not the slightest doubt that Brian Lenihan did not speak to President Hillery on the telephone on that night of January 27, 1982. In fact, President Hillery did not speak on the telephone to anyone in Fianna Fáil that night. The Tánaiste was carefully set up by Fine Gael, with the willing collaboration of a Fine Gael activist, in a way that breached the ethics of research,' Haughey continued.

Haughey was personally stung by the recent accusations that he had actually threatened the army officer at the Áras over the telephone that night. This was something which only came out during the latest controversy. The Opposition was charging that this was a criminal offence and should be investigated.

'I reject that allegation with contempt and I ask why it is being brought up now after eight years. Why is it being raised now and being cast at me in this way?' Haughey declared. 'The people opposite, who are making this allegation, have been in government themselves,' he continued. 'They had all the records at their disposal. They knew all about the gossip and chat going on since 1982. Why did they not investigate it? They did not because they knew it was a tissue of lies and a fabrication and that is what I brand it here in this House.'

Dick Spring responded with a particularly virulent speech, which many people found offensive. 'This debate is not about Brian Lenihan when it is all boiled down,' he said. 'This debate, essentially, is about the evil spirit that controls one political party in the Republic. And it is about the way in which that spirit has begun to corrupt the entire political system in our country. This is a debate about greed for office, about disregard for truth and about contempt for political standards. It is a debate about the way in which a once-great party has been brought to its knees by the grasping acquisitiveness of its leader. It is ultimately a debate about the cancer that is eating away at our body politic – and the virus which has caused that cancer, An Taoiseach Charles J. Haughey.'

Shortly after six o'clock Lenihan telephoned Haughey. The call lasted a little over a minute. At the outset Haughey asked Lenihan whether he intended to resign.

'No,' Lenihan replied.

'It would have helped your campaign, you know,' Haughey asserted.

'We'll agree to differ on that,' Lenihan retorted.

'Brian Lenihan has been a friend, a loyal and trusted colleague with whom I have served in the Dáil for well over a quarter of a century,' Haughey told the Dáil minutes later. 'Most people in this House will understand that what I have to do I do with great sadness and great sorrow.' Lenihan had failed to comply with the request for his resignation, the Taoiseach stated. 'Accordingly,' Haughey added, 'I propose to exercise my constitutional prerogative and advise the President to terminate his appointment as a member of the government.'

'Charlie won't be able to live with this,' Chris Glennon of the *Irish Independent* was subsequently told by a seasoned backbencher, who predicted that the Boss would 'probably stand down in a few months'. Haughey was castigated for having abandoned his old friend, but in this instance he really had little choice. He made mistakes in the affair, but his biggest mistake was not that he had not given Lenihan enough support but that he had overstepped the bounds of propriety in the way in which he supported him – both by his attack on Garret Fitzgerald and his statement to the press at Dublin Airport.

Lenihan had put his own personal considerations before the government and the party. It was he who had got into the mess. He really had only himself to blame, but he tried to blame a whole range of people, from Haughey to Fitzgerald, Duffy and the *Irish Times*. His subsequent explanation about being on strong drugs and not remembering the Duffy interview was both plausible and believable, but his real problem was in denying that calls had been made to the Áras in the first place. There would have been no controversy had he told the truth on *Questions and Answers*. There was nothing wrong about informing the President that Fianna Fáil was ready to form a government. If Fine Gael were contending that Paddy Hillery was incapable of making an independent decision after talking to anyone, that would have been even more insulting than trying to contact him.

Lenihan's dismissal provoked a strong reaction from the grass roots of the party and a great wave of sympathy for him. He began to regain lost ground by leaps and bounds and might even have turned the election around had it not been for some unfortunate remarks by Pádraig Flynn on the radio programme *Saturday View* on the final weekend of the campaign. On this programme he seemed to question Mary Robinson's suitability as a wife and mother, referring rather dismissively to her 'new interest in family and being a mother and all that sort of thing. But none of us, you know, none of us who knew Mary Robinson very well in previous incarnations ever heard her claiming to be a great wife and mother.'

Flynn was promptly upbraided by an indignant Michael McDowell, the chairman of the Progressive Democrats. Flynn's remarks offended women voters in particular. That afternoon Ahern was campaigning with Lenihan when he was accosted by a woman who grabbed him by the lapels. 'It's bastards like Pádraig Flynn,' she said, 'that are ruining the party my father loves. Why do you let him on the media.' Ahern had no idea what she was talking about as he had not heard the programme. Flynn's gaffe, compounded by McDowell's tongue-lashing, put paid to Lenihan's chances in the election.

Although Haughey turned up for the final Fianna Fáil rally of the election campaign, Lenihan's family tried to keep the Taoiseach and the candidate apart. But Haughey bided his time and eventually seized the moment to raise Lenihan's hand aloft as if they had resolved their differences.

In spite of all this, Lenihan comfortably headed the poll, with 44.1 per cent of the vote against Mary Robinson's 38.9 per cent. Nonetheless, Robinson then got 76.7 per cent of Austin Currie's transfers, to win by over 86,500 votes.

Tension ran high within the party afterwards because there was intense resentment that the Taoiseach had again surrendered to the demands of the Progressive Democrats. At the last parliamentary-party meeting before the election, Sean Power of Kildare asked the Taoiseach what he would do if the Progressive Democrats came looking for his own head.

There was a degree of soul-searching at the next parliamentary-party meeting, which lasted some five hours. Haughey was obviously expecting trouble. His popularity had dropped precipitously. In the next public-opinion poll his favourable rating dropped to 41 per cent, down 16 per cent since the beginning of October. There again seemed to be a kind of consensus that he could not survive very long because the grass roots of the party seemed to have turned on him. Although many people thought that he should have stepped down at the end of the European presidency, nobody moved against him. Those who had ambitions to succeed him were waiting for somebody else to launch a challenge, apparently fearing the old adage that he who wields the dagger never wears the crown. Liam Lawlor was the only person to raise the issue of Haughey's leadership during the meeting. He read from a prepared script that dealt with the need for a thorough reorganisation of the party and a 'review of the leadership' which overshadowed all considerations. He got no support for this proposal, as it was generally felt that his timing was poor.

After the meeting Haughey went to the Dáil chamber. He was obviously in elated mood as he skipped down the steps of the chamber. At the end of the steps he clasped his hands together and raised them over his head like a winning boxer. Ivan Yates of Fine Gael was speaking at the time. 'I see you have survived yet again, Taoiseach,' Yates remarked. Haughey smiled broadly and went to sit in his seat.

In the following days there were reports of individual councillors and some ten different Fianna Fáil cumainn passing resolutions of no confidence in the party leadership. Haughey accused the media of having whipped up the whole thing. 'Stop trawling around the country and trying to get a cumann here or a councillor there to say negative things,' he complained in an RTÉ interview. 'Please, RTÉ, get on with your proper business of reporting reality and not fiction.'

There were reports that Lenihan would run for the presidency of Fianna Fáil at the party's forthcoming ard-fheis in March. He obviously felt a deep sense of betrayal, especially due to the fact that he had been ousted at the behest of the Progressive Democrats. Having been particularly active, even enthusiastic, in purging O'Malley's supporters from Fianna Fáil after the Progressive Democrats were established, Lenihan was the author of his own problems. He had told his family that Haughey was a knave in 1979, but he supported him during every subsequent heave. He was then surprised and aggrieved that the so-called knave would turn on him. If he really believed that Haughey was a knave, then by enthusiastically supporting him through thick and thin Lenihan essentially betrayed everyone – the membership of Fianna Fáil, the decent people who helped to elect him, the electorate as a whole and ultimately even himself.

'Brian Lenihan should never have been our candidate,' Haughey complained to Liam Lawlor amidst rumours that the former Tánaiste planned to run for the presidency of Fianna Fáil at the next ard-fheis. 'I knew something would go wrong. What's he up to now saying he will stand for the presidency of the party? That would create a two-headed monster.'

On 11 December Lenihan announced that he had no intention of running for the presidency of Fianna Fáil, because that position had always been combined with the leadership of the parliamentary party. 'Of course,' he pointedly stated, 'in the event of a vacancy arising on some future occasion in the leadership of Fianna Fáil I intend to contest that vacancy.'

In early 1991 the political spotlight turned to the Gulf War. There was some controversy when Haughey's government decided that it would provide refuelling facilities at Shannon Airport for Allied forces on their way to the Gulf. The Labour Party and Democratic Left objected that this was a violation of the country's avowed neutrality. 'Under international law, in any military conflict there are only two kinds of states – belligerent ones and neutral ones,' Dick Spring contended. 'If we are refueling the aircraft of a belligerent state we forfeit the right to call ourselves neutral.'

Iraq, a member of the UN, had violated the UN Charter by invading Kuwait, another member state. The issues involved were quite clear, in Haughey's view. 'In face of a challenge as great as this the UN Charter must be upheld,' he told the Dáil. 'If the UN should crumble, as did the League of Nations, and if the charter should lose its relevance as the rule of law, then the underlying anarchy of relations between states would quickly reassert itself so that each would again have good reason to fear every other. To adapt what Éamon de Valera said in different circumstances to the League of Nations in 1932 – we must show unmistakably that the charter "is a solemn pact, the obligations of which no state, great or small, will find it possible to ignore".'

Haughey's statesmanlike approach, which had the backing of Fine Gael, was in contrast to the more parochial approach of the younger Spring. A subsequent public-opinion poll indicated that even though 70 per cent of the electorate believed that the country should remain neutral, 54 per cent agreed with providing refuelling facilities to Allied forces.

Haughey had not replaced Brian Lenihan as Minister for Defence, and the Taoiseach apparently intended to use the occasion of the new appointment for a cabinet reshuffle, which would have seen the transfer of Mary O'Rourke from Education to Labour, Bertie Ahern from Labour to Environment and Pádraig Flynn from Environment. Flynn baulked at this, however. Due to the impact of his remarks about Robinson in the final days of the presidential campaign, he feared that if he was moved it would look like he was being demoted. He told colleagues that he would resist any move. 'I'm not going,' he said defiantly.

Faced with Flynn's open defiance, Haughey merely appointed Brendan Daly as Minister for Defence and dismissed all talk of a reshuffle. Regardless of whether the Taoiseach ever had any intention of making other cabinet changes, his authority was undoubtedly weakened by the perception that he was not only unwilling to stand up to the Progressive Democrats but also afraid even of members of his own party within the cabinet. It was just one more indication of his weakened grip on the leadership. He had allowed people to think that his procrastination for three months in the appointment of Lenihan's successor was to facilitate a major cabinet reshuffle, but then, in the face of apparent opposition, he had funked it. Some of his own backbenchers openly began asking whether 'he has the bottle for the job any more'.

During March Haughey felt that he was upstaged by President Robinson, who was invited by Bord Fáilte to deliver a taped television address to the United States. The Taoiseach learned of this only on hearing favourable reports about the address, which went down particularly well. Haughey, possibly annoyed that he had not been invited to give the address himself, was very agitated. He summoned Martin Dully, the chairman and chief executive of Bord Fáilte, to his office.

'The Boss is in terrible form,' P. J. Mara warned Dully. 'You're going to get bawled out.'

'I wasn't very graciously received,' Dully noted. 'I was told there was a protocol for accessing the Park – through the Taoiseach's office – and that Bord Fáilte, a state agency, had no right to approach the Park directly for anything. What could I do but try not to apologise for what all the evidence showed had been a successful campaign?'

'A lot of his language was unparliamentary, but then that was no different from his language in certain other crises,' Dully explained. 'That was his style.' During the rod-licence dispute, for instance, which did enormous damage to tourism in the west, Dully had asked Haughey to back down, only to be met with a torrent of abuse. He left the office that time vowing never to bring up the subject with him again.

Haughey clearly resented sharing the spotlight with President Robinson. He wanted to limit her press interviews. She contended that the government had no power to limit her interviews or other speeches. When the Dalai Lama was visiting Dublin in March, she wanted to invite him to Áras an Uachtaráin, but the government objected as this would cause complications with the Chinese. She therefore made arrangements to meet him at the Chester Beatty Museum in Ballsbridge, but she got two letters warning her that this 'would be considered very unhelpful by the government'. She believed this was 'Haughey's doing'. Even though it could have led to a constitutional crisis, she was determined to go ahead.

'If there is a price to be paid for this meeting, then I have got to pay it, whatever it is,' she explained. Shortly before leaving for the meeting, she was informed that Haughey had completely backed down: she was free to meet the Dalai Lama without any objections from the government. In fact, two cabinet members, Bertie Ahern and Mary O'Rourke, also met the Dalai.

The Fianna Fáil ard-fheis in March 1991 afforded Haughey the usual opportunity for media coverage at home. In the past, Brian Lenihan had always acted as the warm-up speaker, to rouse the crowd before introducing Haughey. This time it would have been inappropriate for Lenihan to have done this, so Máire Geoghegan-Quinn was chosen to do it. 'We could have lived in easier times,' she told the gathering. 'We could all pick moments we wouldn't want to live through again. But I can say with absolute certainty to all of you, and for all of you, there will never be a time like it again. Never such excitement, never such achievement, never such heartache, never such happiness as the time they will talk of as the Haughey era.'

At the beginning of March Haughey gave some interviews about the end of the Gulf War. In one with Caroline Erskine, the political correspondent of Century Radio, he was asked about a recent circuit-court decision upholding the conviction of Virgin Records for selling condoms. He explained that his government would certainly be bringing in new legislation as the law was 'outdated and unsatisfactory'.

The big talking point of Haughey's presidential address at the ard-fheis was his call for new legislation on the sale of contraceptives. 'Family-planning legislation must keep abreast of changing conditions in society such as the emergence of the deadly threat of AIDS,' he said. 'To protect the health of the community and to remove anomalies and outdated restrictions, it is the government's intention to make family planning generally available.' AIDS was spreading in Ireland. In the past three months the number of AIDS cases had increased from 174 to 190. There were already 1,090 people infected with HIV, and the figure was doubling every eighteen months.

In the circumstances, maybe Haughey's proposals should be characterised as more necessary than brave, but they certainly represented a departure from his more timid approach to such matters in the past. He was suggesting that condoms should be sold at outlets like Virgin Records and that the age limit for purchase of condoms be lowered to sixteen, which was the age at which people could legally marry. Even though it made no legislative sense to suggest that the more than 1,000 people who were currently married under the age of eighteen were not old enough to purchase contraceptives, this did not deter the

Catholic hierarchy from maintaining its tough stance on the issue.

Haughey's speech was greeted with outbursts from Cardinal-designate Cathal Daly, Archbishop Desmond Connell of Dublin and Bishops Jeremiah Newman of Limerick and Brendan Comiskey of Wexford. 'Do we want to project to young people the message that condoms have to be freely available as part of their entertainment, as part of their enjoyment, as a normal part of a night's dancing, a normal sequel to a few drinks?' Cathal Daly asked. Bishop Comiskey accused the government of creating 'a morally and spiritually bankrupt country which can only offer condoms to its young people in place of jobs.' It was a nakedly political speech, but things had changed since the days when all the parties vied with each other in their protestations of subservience to the hierarchy. 'It is extraordinary that no political party is prepared to defend what so many people regard as fundamental values of family life,' Archbishop Connell complained.

Some people felt that Haughey was trying to win over younger voters by adopting a liberal agenda in response to Robinson's victory. As a young senator in 1971 Robinson had introduced a bill to reform the 1935 act banning the import, manufacture, advertising and sale of contraceptives. Her bill had received no support after John Charles McQuaid, then Archbishop of Dublin, denounced condoms as 'a curse upon our country'.

Legislation on contraception had proved extremely divisive over the years. By defying the party whip and refusing to back the contraceptive bill proposed by Haughey back in 1979, Jim Gibbons had arguably put the first nail in Jack Lynch's political coffin. Sean Tracy had been expelled from the Labour Party for voting against a contraceptive bill in 1985. Des O'Malley, the leader of the Progressive Democrats, and Mary Harney, his eventual successor, had both been expelled from Fianna Fáil that year at the behest of Haughey for not voting against the same bill. That was when Haughey's opposition to such legislation had essentially caused the split within Fianna Fáil that ultimately led to the formation of the Progressive Democrats.

'It is irresponsible to throw the national community into the kind of acrimonious, divisive debate which is bound to follow the introduction of this legislation,' Haughey complained in 1985. Now some of his cabinet colleagues would adopt the same line, as he ran into strong opposition to his proposal to lower the age limit to sixteen.

So many of the politicians had taken such strong stands on this issue in the past that it was difficult for them to change now without appearing hypocritical. 'I would rather be wrong with the bishops than be right with those who are attacking them,' Jim Tunney, the chairman of the Fianna Fáil parliamentary party, had declared in 1974. This was still the attitude of many of his colleagues, and in the face of their opposition Haughey dithered. He went to the Vatican for the consecration of Cathal Daly as a cardinal and held a reception for him at the Irish embassy.

'The modern Irish church takes the view that her role and function is to advise and counsel and to leave matters of state to the government and to the Oireachtas,' Haughey said at a reception. That was the way he would have liked it to be, but in the following days he essentially capitulated on the contraception legislation.

By then everything seemed to be going wrong for the government. On 13 May 1991 ITV's *World in Action* programme highlighted abuses of the beef-intervention system by Larry Goodman's companies. The opposition parties promptly demanded a Dáil debate, but Haughey tried to block this – which was a tactical blunder. Even though he was riding high in the polls, enjoying a favourable rating of 56 per cent at the time, the Progressive Democrats, who had called for a judicial inquiry while in opposition, forced him to concede both a judicial inquiry and a prompt debate.

When the Dáil held a special session on 24 May to debate the charges made on the *World in Action* programme, Haughey gave a commanding performance, tearing into his critics, who were describing Goodman as his personal friend. He quoted from the official files indicating that, as Taoiseach, Garret Fitzgerald had met Larry Goodman 'on a regular basis'. The Fine Gael–Labour coalition was the first to introduce export credit insurance on beef exports to Iraq, and they had facilitated Goodman in every way they could. On 27 May 1985, for instance, John Bruton, as Minister for Industry and Commerce, had urged the Minister for Finance to help develop exports to Iraq. 'I believe we have developed a particular relationship with Iraq and that they have been consciously putting business our way,' Bruton wrote. 'I believe also that this accounts for their excellent payment record.'

Haughey could have added that the bulk of the wrongdoing exposed on the television programme happened while Fine Gael and Labour were in power, but he did not wish to go down that avenue because this would hurt Irish business by damaging the beef industry. 'I am not criticising the government of that time for doing what they did in acting for the benefit of a single company belonging to Mr Goodman,' the Taoiseach stated. 'What I wish to do, however, is point up the double standards being employed by the people who have been making allegations now for some time.

'In the light of the Fine Gael–Labour record it is nothing

less than blatant duplicity to attempt to attribute blame to Fianna Fáil for a policy which they initiated and steadily pursued,' Haughey explained, much to the irritation of both Bruton and Spring. Haughey had adopted 'a small-minded and cowardly approach' by quoting selectively from the files, according to Bruton, who accused the Taoiseach of having engaged in 'a hypersensitive, partisan and mean-minded exercise'. Spring denounced what he called the 'vileness' of the Taoiseach's tactics.

Some of the Fianna Fáil deputies seemed to derive pleasure from the squealing of Bruton and Spring. 'Charlie never ceases to amaze me,' a deputy remarked afterwards. 'It is only when his back is to the wall and he looks cornered that he really shows his political ability. From now on the pressure is on Labour and the Workers Party to put up or shut up.' Had Haughey acceded to the demand for that debate immediately, he might have been able to forestall the full-scale inquiry that followed.

In the next few days he also stood up to President Robinson, at least temporarily. She had been defying him by giving public interviews despite his objections. She actually gave ninety-two interviews during her first year in office. The following was a typical piece of advice given to her by Haughey's office: 'The Taoiseach remains of the view and advises that the President should decline to be interviewed, because it would be difficult to see how the President could avoid being embroiled in matters of government policy in discussing the subjects listed by the reporter.' She replied that she would avoid encroaching on politics and then proceeded to ignore his advice. But the Taoiseach blocked her from delivering the annual Dimbleby lecture on British television by using the government's power to stop her from travelling abroad. When she asked for a reason for this action, she was merely informed that it was 'not appropriate' for her to go, even though President Hillery had delivered a similar lecture in Italy. 'At the time,' Robinson later explained, 'I felt that Haughey was quite determined that I'd already had enough outings. That I'd been pushing out the frontiers. It wasn't just that it would be inappropriate for me to do it, but also that he didn't want me to have the profile of doing it.'

Haughey felt that the government had a constitutional right to limit the President's public interviews and he decided to confront her in person, armed with senior counsel's opinion. But she was an eminent constitutional lawyer in her own right. 'It was a case of taking on someone in her own area of strength, and he almost immediately regretted it,' she recalled with a laugh. 'We had quite a discussion and I really enjoyed myself. This was my territory.'

She was not impressed with his senior counsel's advice. 'That's one lawyer's opinion,' she told him.

'I suppose you can get any opinion you like out of a lawyer if you pay them,' an exasperated Haughey conceded, with a smile.

'When we began to debate and discuss, it didn't work very well,' Robinson noted. 'He said at one stage, "We'll come back to the Constitution", and I said, "Any time, Taoiseach. I would be delighted." But we never did, and I think that was the end of an overt attempt to rein me in.'

Things were going particularly badly for the government. Its favourable rating dropped to just 39 per cent in June, but even more ominous was the rise in the number of those who were dissatisfied with the government's performance; this figure increased from 34 per cent to 52 per cent in the same period. Haughey's personal rating was down only slightly, to 48 per cent, which meant that he was running well ahead of his government, but he was still blamed when Fianna Fáil did dismally in the local elections at the end of June 1991. The party's vote dropped to 37 per cent, which was down by 8 per cent on the previous occasion and even lower than the 38 per cent showing that had undermined Jack Lynch in 1979. It was the party's worst-ever performance. Fianna Fáil had gone into the election with a majority in eleven of the thirty-four county and borough councils and effective control of seventeen councils but ended up with just three councils after the election. Haughey was not pleased when he was asked to comment on the result while attending an EC summit in Luxembourg. 'As Ronald Reagan said when asked about the Kelley lady's book,' he replied, 'I wouldn't be able to reply to that in polite language.'

During the summer Haughey essentially washed his hands of the contraceptive issue by handing the whole question of the sale and distribution of condoms to the regional health boards. There had been little real pressure on him to take up the cause in the first place, and there had been no real political demand to lower the age limit to sixteen. Yet by taking a stand on the issue and then backing off without a fight, he further undermined his own leadership.

'The decision of the government to pass the buck on the issue of the availability of condoms to the health boards is an eloquent witness to the degeneration of political leadership in this country,' the *Sunday Tribune* proclaimed in an editorial. 'On what is certainly one of the most critical issues, at least symbolically, in our public life our political leaders want to evade, shuffle, cop out.' At this point Haughey seemed to run out of luck. For the next six months virtually everything seemed to go wrong: a series of financial controversies erupted, beginning with the Greencore scandal.

In 1987 the Irish Sugar Company – or Greencore, as it would become known following privatisation in 1991 – gave an interest-free loan of £1 million to four of its executives to enable them to purchase a shareholding in Sugar Distributors. Eleven months later Irish Sugar bought the executives' shareholding for over £8 million – a profit of over £7 million in just eleven months for a personal outlay of just £10,000 each.

When the transactions came to light at the beginning of September 1991, Chris Comerford, the company's chief executive, was persuaded to retire from Greencore, but not before negotiating a golden handshake worth about £1.5 million for himself. News of this exacerbated public outrage over the affair. Subsequently, a series of business scandals gradually came to the fore.

Questions were quickly raised about transactions relating to both the acquisition of a new headquarters site for Telecom Éireann and the purchase of the old teacher-training college at Carysfort as a graduate business school for University College Dublin. There were also controversies over a sewer pipe laid through Haughey's estate in Kinsealy, the spending of over £166,000 by the Electricity Supply Board on wind experiments on his island off the Kerry coast and the leaking of sensitive information to Celtic Helicopters, owned by Haughey's son Ciarán.

The Telecom Éireann controversy arose following reports that Michael Smurfit, the chairman of the board of the company, had a financial stake in United Property Holdings, which had once owned the building purchased for a new headquarters for Telecom Éireann. Smurfit had a 10 per cent share in UPH, a property-development company mainly owned by Dermot Desmond, the founder and chief executive of National City Brokers, which had handled the privatisation of Greencore and had recently been retained to advise on the privatisation of Telecom Éireann. UPH had purchased the controversial site for £4.4 million and had then sold it shortly afterwards for £6.4

million. Dermot Desmond helped Hoddle Investments acquire the building, which was then sold to Telecom for £9.4 million. It had more than doubled in price at a time when property values were dropping.

Examining the various business controversies is beyond the scope of this study, except inasmuch as Haughey was dragged into the story. He was known to have been friendly with people like Goodman, Desmond, Smurfit and Bernie Cahill, who was the chairman of the boards of Greencore, Aer Lingus and Feltrim, a mining company largely owned by Haughey's son Conor. These people were part of what was being called 'the golden circle' – a group of top businessmen to whom the government seemed particularly helpful.

As top businessmen with proven track records in having made their companies successful, these men were probably the country's best hope of providing extra employment. Hence it was natural that the Taoiseach should have extensive contacts with them. Nevertheless he appeared to try to distance himself from them when the affair broke.

Desmond, who had formulated the idea for the Financial Services Centre, was just a 'business friend' as opposed to a 'personal friend', Haughey contended. He proceeded to call on him, Smurfit and Séamus Páircéir, the chief executive of UPH and chairman of the Custom House Docks Authority, 'to stand aside' while the various controversies were being investigated. In each instance he was careful to stress that he was not implying that any of them had done anything wrong. 'I say all that without any implication, the slightest scintilla or suggestion that there is anything wrong,' he emphasised. Nine years earlier he had been roundly denounced for not having asked the Attorney-General to step aside when the MacArthur affair broke. Now that he was asking these people to stand aside, he was castigated because he did not forewarn them of his intention. No matter what he did, his opponents were going to criticise him for doing the wrong thing.

The next day he was drawn further into the growing list of controversies when Nora Owen of Fine Gael raised questions about a sewer pipe that had recently been laid through his Kinsealy estate by Dublin County Council, reportedly to service some nearby cottages. As the work, which cost £78,000, had been deemed unnecessary by the council in 1985, there were some legitimate questions that needed to be answered. But Owen proceeded to raise the stakes in the affair in the Dáil by charging that this was not the first time that Haughey had been involved in this kind of controversy. 'After all, hasn't he experienced this before on his landholding on the outskirts of Dublin in the Donaghmede area in the late 1960s?' she asked. 'In that instance, rumours and stories abound of undue pressure put on Corporation engineers to extend pipes onto his land. Whether or not these rumours or allegation are true, the facts speak for themselves. The Taoiseach's former land was rezoned, thereby greatly inflating the value of the land, and many hundreds of houses are now built on that land. One can be forgiven for sensing a touch of déjà vu!'

The controversy over Haughey's land, which had been an election issue in 1969, had initially been prompted by charges that he had benefited from recent tax legislation introduced by himself, but that charge was convincingly discredited at the time. There were also intimations that there was something immoral about the way in which the value of the property had appreciated from £50,000 to a little over £200,000 in just ten years, but while that kind of jump in value seemed extreme in relation to previous decades, it was actually quite modest when compared to either of the next two decades.

The controversy surrounding the land had nothing to do with extending pipes in 1969. It seemed that rumours were growing with time. Yet nobody in the media challenged Owen's extravagant insinuations, which were reproduced verbatim in the *Sunday Tribune*, even though she did not cite a shred of evidence to support them.

A further controversy emerged after the disclosure that NCB had fouled up after being commissioned in 1986 to do some work for Irish Helicopters, a subsidiary of Aer Lingus. A report containing confidential information supplied to NCB by Irish Helicopters was sent to a rival firm, Celtic Helicopters. Due to a postal error, however, the material was delivered to Irish Helicopters. The issue had been resolved quietly between the various companies some time ago, but suddenly it became the subject of public controversy, no doubt because Celtic Helicopters was partly owned by Haughey's son Ciarán.

'The Taoiseach must say if he had any hand in inducing Mr Desmond of NCB to attempt to pass on this information to his son's company,' John Bruton demanded, under the protection of Dáil privilege. As a result the media were able to highlight the affair in a way that suggested that the whole thing may have been the result of Desmond's friendship with the Haugheys. It was ironic that NCB had been hired while the Fitzgerald government was in power. There was no evidence that Desmond had been personally involved in the affair, but this did not deter Bruton or the media. Some of them asked light-heartedly whether Haughey, having redefined his friendship with Desmond, was about to redefine his relationship with own son, Ciarán.

When controversy erupted over the purchase of Carysfort, Haughey insisted that the place had been bought at the instigation of the UCD authorities. 'UCD proposed to us that they acquire Carysfort,' he asserted during a radio interview on 22 September.

'UCD carried out an examination of Carysfort through their own mechanism and decided that the asking price for it was great value,' he continued.

'Was the UCD approach perhaps made at the prompting of the government?' he was asked.

'No,' Haughey replied. 'Certainly not.'

The government was criticised for not having bought Carysfort when it was offered for sale in August 1989. The asking price then was £8.5 million. The chance was passed up at the time, but the government provided the money for UCD to buy the college twelve months later for £8 million.

In the process, £500,000 was saved on the asking price. In other walks of life, those responsible for such an outcome might be complimented, but not in politics. Even when the government gets something right, the Opposition will inevitably complain, on some pretext or other. In this instance the government was accused of not having acted quickly enough.

Carysfort was sold for £6.25 million to an individual businessman, Pino Harris. Critics insinuated that the government could have bought it for that price. But would the owners have sold it to the government for the same price? After all, the price dropped because the government was not interested in the property. In such dealings, people frequently wonder whether they might have done better with other tactics, and this case was little different, except that the Opposition introduced what might be called the sleaze factor into the affair.

On previous occasions some elements of the media would have come to Haughey's defence by pointing out the inconsistencies in the arguments of his opponents. Even during the GUBU period of 1982, when some of his harshest critics – people like Geraldine Kennedy and Vincent Browne – accepted that the media had been unfair to him, there were a number of editors from whom Haughey could at least expect a sympathetic hearing – people like Douglas Gageby of the *Irish Times*, Tim Pat Coogan of the *Irish Press* and Michael Hand of the *Sunday Independent*.

Gageby had insisted on balancing his newspaper's political comments by employing John Healy as a regular columnist. But after Gageby retired, he was replaced by Conor Brady, who had been in charge of the *Sunday Tribune* during the GUBU period, and Healy quit the *Irish Times*. Since then, there had also been a major shake-up in the Irish Press group, headed by Vincent Jennings, who had caused a sensation in 1982 with his signed editorial in the *Sunday Press* castigating Haughey following the Dublin West by-election defeat. There was no longer any national editor sympathetic to Haughey.

Columnists like Bruce Arnold and Conor Cruise O'Brien were particularly critical of Haughey. Things became so bad at one point that Vinny Doyle, the editor of the *Irish Independent,* asked Cruise O'Brien to lay off. 'Enough is enough,' Vinny told him one day. 'If you cannot do a positive piece on Charlie Haughey, which I am sure you can't, can you pick another subject?'

Cruise O'Brien promptly submitted another scathing attack, and it was duly spiked. 'Vinny, I'm deeply disappointed you spiked my column,' he complained.

'Conor, I told you enough was enough. You were not being fair to Haughey,' the editor told him.

Doyle warned Cruise O'Brien that he would be in breach of contract and the *Independent* would probably sue him if he sent the article to the *Sunday Tribune*. But Cruise O'Brien sent the column to the *Tribune* anyway, and it gladly published it.

When four Fianna Fáil backbenchers issued a joint statement criticising Haughey on 27 September, they received extensive national publicity. Had twenty-four backbenchers come out in a similar way in support of him, their actions would probably not have received nearly as much coverage. Indeed, only the previous weekend the *Sunday Tribune* had had a banner front-page headline that ran, 'Fianna Fáil Backbenchers Want Haughey to Resign as Leader.'

This was the lead for a story about a survey of fifty-one backbench deputies by the newspaper on the leadership question. Twenty-four said Haughey should stay and thirteen said he should go, while the remainder refused to comment. Even if only two deputies had called for Haughey's resignation, the headline would have been technically correct, but there could be little doubt that it was misleading. Distortions were to be found not only in misleading headlines and the undue prominence given to critical reports, but also in the biased analyses of political commentators, as well as the uncritical reporting of unsupported – and sometimes unsustainable – accusations made by opponents.

The publication of Garret Fitzgerald's autobiography in the midst of the scandals also hurt Haughey. As the first autobiography published by any former Taoiseach, it attracted enormous media attention and comparisons were inevitably made between Fitzgerald and Haughey, who was depicted in a less than flattering light. When Fitzgerald appeared on *The Late Late Show,* for instance, there were a number of pointed references by people in the audience to Haughey's 'lust for power' and the mysterious way in which he had 'acquired enormous wealth'. Although his name was never actually mentioned, there was no doubt that those people were referring to him, and their snide insinuations on the most popular Irish television programme had an insidious impact by subtly projecting the feeling that there was an air of unspeakable sleaze around Haughey. In response to a question from Gay Byrne, Fitzgerald explained that his 'flawed pedigree' remark in 1979 had been taken out of context. He noted that he had merely been observing that questions had been raised about Haughey that had not been raised about any of his predecessors.

In a veiled allusion to the Carysfort controversy, Fitzgerald complained that the government's decision had been taken without any cabinet memorandum on the subject. He characterised this as a complete departure from normal procedure, even though his own government had acquired the old School of Engineering from UCD without presenting a memorandum to the cabinet. It was his government which had initiated the move to acquire a new office for the Taoiseach. But Haughey had been pilloried ever since he moved his office in January 1991 because the whole thing had cost so much money at a time when hospital wards were being closed throughout the country due to financial constraints. The building, on which a very impressive job was done, was dubbed the 'Taj Mahaughey' or 'Chas Mahal' by some in the media. (For all its splendour outside, Haughey was reportedly unhappy that the Taoiseach's toilet was unheated and not en suite. He was told by an official of the Office of Public Works that radiators in the hall would heat the area. 'There you are,' Haughey said, throwing his key on the desk. 'Try it on the way out, and I hope it freezes the balls off you.')

Many of the accusations being made against Haughey could just as easily have been directed against Fine Gael. At the centre of those allegations was the implication that his friends had ripped off the state. This involved all kinds of unwarranted assumptions.

No evidence had been produced that Bernie Cahill or Michael Smurfit had personally done anything wrong. Moreover, it should be noted that both had been appointed to their public positions by Fitzgerald's government. In addition, the fraudulent claims – made by the Goodman company for export-credit subsidies – that led to the Beef Tribunal had been made while Fitzgerald was in power, and his Minister for Agriculture had helped set up the Egyptian deal involving the initial fraud. It should also be noted that Dermot Desmond's company was first hired as a consultant by Aer Lingus while Jim Mitchell of Fine Gael was the relevant minister. Of course, it would be grossly unfair to accuse any of the Fine Gael ministers of wrongdoing in these matters; it was just as unfair to make such allegations against Haughey without producing evidence of wrongdoing.

In Irish society people are entitled to a presumption of innocence, but now virtually all of the media were presuming Haughey's guilt and ignoring all other possibilities. If Fine Gael deputies were guilty, they would have had a vested interest in setting Haughey up as a scapegoat. Likewise, if businessmen in the so-called golden circle had been ripping off the country, they would have had good reason to get him out so they could have his successor play down the scandals on the pretext that the man responsible for them had been ousted and further publicity would be damaging to the country.

The media people should have stuck to the facts and not allowed themselves to be stampeded into a highly personalised campaign. Instead of presenting an unbiased account of events, they went whoring after false demons. Haughey was essentially tried and convicted by the media, who produced no firm evidence against him. In a review of the year, Gerald Barry, the political correspondent of the *Sunday Tribune,* noted that 'no single piece of directly incriminatory evidence has been produced against the Taoiseach.' But the media treated the absence of hard evidence as if it were an irrelevant technicality.

On 16 October 1991 the Taoiseach opened the confidence debate in the Dáil with a strong defence of his government. 'Irish political life is going through a traumatic period with many disturbing features,' he said. The 'disclosure of reprehensible behaviour of a small number' of businessmen had been 'added to, hyped up and exaggerated by a massive campaign of vilification and character assassination of unprecedented intensity without regard to evidence, proof or justification,' he argued.

'We have had a campaign of personalised attack by way of unfounded allegation, innuendo, accusations of guilt by association and all the other traditional despicable weapons of such campaigns,' he continued. 'The object of the campaign was nothing less than to undermine and destablise this government and to damage the credibility of individual members, particularly myself.'

The purchase of Carysfort was 'an entirely praiseworthy and progressive step,' he maintained. 'The transaction was carried out in a perfectly straightforward manner and I was not involved in it. I gave it my full support.'

'I think you gave it more than support,' Ruairi Quinn interjected.

'I defy the deputy to prove anything of that kind,' Haughey snapped back.

Before the debate was even over, however, Mary O'Rourke, the Minister for Education, admitted that she had made the initial approach in the matter to the President of UCD on her own initiative. But Haughey had played a more active role than even she realised: he had had a couple of private meetings with the head of the UCD School of Business to discuss the acquisition.

Some opponents charged that there was no need for the state to have subvented UCD in the whole matter because arrangements had already been made with business interests to have a graduate business school built, at no cost to the taxpayer. Ultimately, of course, the taxpayer would probably have ended up paying a great deal more, if only by way of taking up the shortfall as a result of tax concessions given to the businessmen. Building a new graduate school from scratch would undoubtedly have cost considerably more than the £9.7 million that it cost the state to purchase and renovate Carysfort. Moreover, this would have been a disgraceful waste of resources, both financial and physical.

On the basis of the evidence produced, Haughey's biggest mistake in the whole Carysfort controversy was his denial that the government had taken the initiative in the project. He should instead have admitted it. Indeed, he could have been proud of the fact that he had sliced through the bureaucratic red tape.

When Fianna Fáil and the Progressive Democrats went into coalition, it was decided that their programme for government would be renegotiated after two years, and the Progressive Democrats were now threatening to withdraw their support if agreement was not reached before a vote of confidence was taken. There had been intermittent negotiations throughout the summer and an agreement had appeared imminent when Albert Reynolds walked out of the talks and baulked at some final concessions. Haughey had apparently been prepared to concede these, and as a result Reynolds was credited with forcing the Progressive Democrats to back down when they gave in on some of the Fianna Fáil demands at the eleventh hour.

Bertie Ahern was credited with having concluded the negotiations with the Progressive Democracts. As Ahern was explaining the deal to journalists in Government Buildings, a buoyant Haughey briefly interrupted the proceedings. 'He's the man,' the Taoiseach said, pointing at Ahern. 'He's the best, the most skilful, the most devious and the most cunning.'

'God, that's all I need,' Ahern exclaimed.

Although the government then survived the confidence

motion, there were rumours in Leinster House that Reynolds would lead a heave against Haughey for the leadership of Fianna Fáil within a week. The plan was for Reynolds, Ahern and Flynn to go to him and ask for his retirement. If he refused, as expected, they would show him a motion of no-confidence that they would table for the next parliamentary-party meeting.

Haughey was worried enough to hold extensive consultations. 'Why are they trying to humiliate me?' he asked. On 22 October Ahern advised him to indicate that he had a retirement date in mind. Haughey heeded the advice.

The next day he appealed at the weekly meeting of the parliamentary party to be allowed to quit the leadership with dignity at a time of his own choosing. He talked about a 'time-frame' for his departure. He led deputies to believe that he wished to complete a scheduled meeting with Prime Minister John Major of Britain in December and attend the EC summit at Maastricht later in the month, as well as overseeing the introduction of the budget in January. 'I will know when it is time to step down,' he said.

This situation was reminiscent of his appeal to a similar meeting on 27 January 1983. As then, his remarks were interpreted as an indication that he intended to go in the near future, and as on the previous occasion, Ray Burke openly said that he believed that Haughey was about to step down.

Ahern assured deputies that the Taoiseach would go after completing his political agenda, but the Reynolds camp saw the appeal as a sign of weakness. Haughey was mortally wounded and supporters of Reynolds were moving in for the political kill, just as Haughey would have done himself in similar circumstances.

They argued that it would be best if he were forced out before there were any more damaging disclosures, but Reynolds was being outmanoeuvred by Haughey. Deputies were moved by his private entreaties to be allowed to go with dignity and not to be kicked out ignominiously after thirty-five years of 'service to the party'.

There were also similarities between the present situation and events leading up to the abortive heave by O'Malley in February 1982. Deputies who had privately expressed a desire for change began to waver, and Ahern now seemed to be playing the role that Martin O'Donoghue had played in calling on O'Malley not to go through with the challenge almost ten years earlier. Ahern told Reynolds that he would not back a heave at this time. 'He brought us right up to the brink,' one Reynolds supporter complained, 'and then he opted out.'

Friday 25 October was to be the day for the challenge. When Haughey went to open a new shopping centre in his constituency that morning, he looked like a very worried man. His voice quivered with emotion as he began to address the gathering. 'It's always good to be among your own when the going gets tough,' he said. Everyone knew what he meant when he said that this was likely to be one of the more pleasant duties he would have to perform that day. If Reynolds challenged him, he was obviously going to have to call for his resignation, but Reynolds lost his nerve. He announced that the challenge was being shelved to give Haughey an 'honourable time-frame' to complete his political agenda.

'I am not interested in any way in bitter divisions opening up within Fianna Fáil,' Reynolds said. 'I have long experience and sharp memories of that situation and I want no part of it ever again.' This was like an echo of what Dessie O'Malley had said when he talked to the press after calling off his challenge on 25 February 1982. Haughey had then been given a breathing space of some seven months before the McCreevy challenge, but this time he was not even given two weeks. By the following

Wednesday he was back in the middle of a political storm.

The previous week he had indignantly refuted an intimation by Dick Spring that Bernie Cahill had not been asked to step aside from Greencore because he knew too much about Haughey. Spring contended that it was Haughey who had suggested to Cahill that NCB and his friend Pat O'Connor should be appointed as advisors to Greencore on its privatisation.

'I reject that with contempt,' Haughey replied. 'That is totally untrue and it does the deputy no credit to make those sort of unfounded allegations. I suggest to him on that score that he too await the outcome of the present investigation when he will find – '

'The Taoiseach had no meeting?' Spring interjected.

'I had no meetings. I suggest to him on that score that he too await the outcome of the present investigations, when he will find that he will owe me an apology.'

At the end of a further exchange, Haughey reaffirmed that 'no such meeting took place.' It quickly became apparent, however, that he had met Cahill and that there was evidence to prove that on 26 May 1990 Cahill had flown by helicopter from his home in west Cork to Kinsealy. What was more, the Irish Sugar Company had paid for the trip.

Cahill admitted this at an extraordinary general meeting of Greencore shareholders on Wednesday 30 October. He said he had shown Haughey the list of companies from which a stockbroker would be chosen to advise on Greencore's privatisation, but he denied that 'any undue pressure' had been put on him to support the appointment of NCB. It was already on the list. Although pressed a number of times, he persistently sidestepped questions about whether Haughey had recommended NCB.

Cahill's confirmation appeared to prove that the Taoiseach

had lied to the Dáil, but Haughey denied this. 'I did not say, as is now being suggested, that I had no meetings with Mr Bernard Cahill,' he explained. 'What I said was that no meeting of the kind suggested by Deputy Spring took place.' In the context of his initial remarks, however, what Haughey had initially denied was the suggestion that he had recommended the appointment of NCB to Cahill. If he had, so what?

Haughey was Taoiseach and there was nothing wrong with recommending the best people for any position. Politicians of all parties regularly make representations on behalf of people or companies. So long as no undue pressure was applied, there was nothing wrong with making recommendations, and Cahill had confirmed that no undue pressure had been exerted on him in this instance.

In typical fashion, Haughey had walked into trouble by denying involvement, though he could have provided a rational explanation for that involvement. Whether he had actually lied may be open to question, but there was no doubt that he had deliberately tried to mislead the Dáil.

In the past this kind of dispute in the Dáil would have been quickly forgotten, but now there were television cameras in the chamber. The earlier part of his initial remarks, in which he had denied meeting Cahill, had been shown that night on television and were now repeated. Taken by themselves, these seemed to offer conclusive proof that Haughey was saying that he had not met Cahill, but he subsequently qualified his initial denial by stipulating that there had been 'no such meeting'.

Deputies know that the use of qualifying words like 'such' is pregnant with significance. But he should have remembered that he was going into homes all over the country through the medium of television. His subtle nuance was lost because it was not included in the edited highlights. Whether or not deputies had been deceived, there is no doubt that the viewing public was.

As a result there was further speculation about a heave within Fianna Fáil. It was ironic that such a fuss should have been kicked up over this affair. Haughey had misled the whole country between 1983 and 1987 with his criticism of health cuts, the Hillsborough Agreement and the Single European Act, when most of the party had gladly gone along with him. He was playing the political game as both sides had played it for generations.

McCreevy challenged Haughey to ask for a vote of confidence in his leadership at the next parliamentary-party meeting. The challenge was brushed aside, however, as the Taoiseach took the offensive by suggesting that Spring was deliberately deflecting attention from the Greencore scandal by attacking the government.

P. J. Mara then pulled a little stunt on Haughey's behalf. He set the press up by suggesting that Spring had been associated with the property developer Pat Doherty, who claimed to be the principal owner of Hoddle Investments, the company which ultimately sold the controversial building to Telecom Éireann. 'If we are going into guilt by association,' Mara told reporters, 'one of the things that will emerge in the Dáil will be the association between Mr Pat Doherty and Mr Dick Spring.' He was very careful with what he had to say. In order that there would be no confusion, he read the single sentence from a piece of paper.

The press swallowed the bait hook, line and sinker. The whole thing made front-page headlines, with articles suggesting that Haughey believed he had the dirt on Spring, who was worried enough to go scurrying through his diaries. The ruse worked. The press turned the spotlight on the Labour leader, though there was nothing to the whole thing. Doherty announced that Spring had once been introduced to him at a function in the Irish embassy in London, but he doubted that the Kerryman even remembered the introduction. Haughey was making no apologies. He asked how many questions the Opposition would have tabled if somebody had told the press that the Taoiseach had once met Pat Doherty. Nobody needed to answer that!

The media were outraged. They had been made to look foolish. They ignored their own unprofessional gullibility and accused Haughey of having misled the people, whereas the media had in fact misled them. Mara was denounced for 'acting as a professional character-assassin'.

The next day, Sean Power – one of the 'gang of four' backbench dissidents who had criticised Haughey back in September – proposed a formal motion calling for Haughey's removal as leader at the next meeting of the Fianna Fáil parliamentary party. Reynolds announced his support for the motion the following day. The sense of drama was heightened as Reynolds was about to be interviewed on RTÉ television's evening news. Gerard Collins seemed near to tears during an interview in the Dáil studio. He accused Reynolds of 'frightful political immaturity' and made an emotional appeal to him not to go through with the challenge. 'You will wreck our party right down the centre and bust up the government,' Collins said. It was a ridiculous performance, in which Collins effectively destroyed whatever chance he had had of succeeding Haughey himself.

This had been the first real political crisis since the introduction of television cameras in the Dáil. The highlights of parliamentary proceedings in recent days had been depicting a most unruly setting in which politicians were merely trying to score cheap points off each other. On top of all this came the tear-jerking appeal by Collins. The whole thing was beginning to look like a bad political play in which ham actors were turning a tragedy into a farce.

'For some time now there has been considerable political instability, which has led to an erosion of confidence in our democratic institutions,' Reynolds declared. 'This uncertainty must not be allowed to continue.' He added that the country needed 'strong and decisive leadership', with the result that he would be supporting the motion. He had every right to disagree with the government but, since Article 28 of the country's Constitution enshrines the concept of collective cabinet responsibility, he should have resigned if he wished to disagree publicly. Haughey was obliged to demand his resignation, but Reynolds refused. The Taoiseach therefore asked the President to remove him.

Reynolds was possibly hoping that his dismissal would provoke the kind of sympathy that Lenihan had received a year earlier. Pádraig Flynn adopted the same course in forcing Haughey to have the President dismiss him, too, after he had come out in support of Power's motion, but eleven other ministers – together with Brian Lenihan – came out strongly for Haughey.

On Friday, the eve of the parliamentary-party meeting, Haughey denounced the whole thing as a 'power grab' during an extended lunchtime interview on RTÉ radio. 'When Albert talks about political stability and wishing to avoid political instability, that seems to be very much like a bookie complaining about gambling,' he said. 'This is just a new type of campaign, directed, I believe, quite simply, not so much at getting rid of me as a campaign to install Albert Reynolds as Taoiseach.

It was ironic that Haughey's opponents should be turning to Reynolds. After all, he was one of the gang of five who claimed credit for having pushed Jack Lynch and having organised Haughey's rise to power in 1979. Indeed it would seem that he was more than just one of the gang, given that he was the only one of the five who had been immediately appointed to the cabinet in 1979.

Reynolds appeared to be moving with precipitous haste by being unwilling to await the results of the various investigations. His supporters argued that it was necessary to get Haughey out before there were any more embarrassing disclosures. Everyone expected political sparks from the Beef Tribunal, but Reynolds was more liable than any other politician to be dragged into this controversy because it was he who had ignored the strong advice of his civil servants to reintroduce insurance cover on beef exports to Iraq. This monumental blunder was probably going to cost the state well over £100 million. When the money involved in all the other scandals was added together, it amounted to only a fraction of that squandered on exports to Iraq. The whole thing would inevitably raise questions about Reynolds's much-vaunted fiscal prowess, with the result that there was an element of 'now or never' in his challenge to Haughey.

On the day of the challenge, 9 November 1991, Haughey was confident enough to have his own people put forward an amendment calling for a vote of confidence in his leadership, which was something he had pointedly refused to do when challenged by McCreevy earlier in the week. The media, which had been predicting his demise, suddenly began to hedge. Having got things wrong so often in the past, the political pundits did not actually write him off this time. They said he might survive in an open vote but would be defeated in a secret ballot.

The first part of the parliamentary-party meeting was taken up with a procedural debate on whether the vote on the motion should be secret or open. Haughey's opponents contended that it should be secret, as he had been elected by secret ballot. He had also had his position confirmed by a secret vote during the last heave, in February 1983. Haughey argued that he had been a member of the Opposition the last time. When he had been in government at the time of the McCreevy motion, his election had been by open vote, which Reynolds and Flynn had supported. Moreover, Lynch had demanded an open vote of confidence in 1970.

The public was bombarded with the usual clichés about democracy and the secret ballot, but a secret vote on the leadership issue would have been patently undemocratic in this instance. While it is vital that people should have a secret vote in choosing their representatives, it is equally important that these representatives should then vote openly so the people can assess how they are being represented. This is why all votes in the Dáil are taken openly.

After more than three hours of debate, the party voted openly by forty-four to thirty-three for a roll-call vote on the actual motion. Thereafter, the eventual outcome was virtually a foregone conclusion. When the meeting reconvened after a short break, Reynolds was among the first to speak. He complained that 'disinformation' had been circulated about him. There had been an unfounded story, for instance, that Larry Goodman had loaned him £150,000 to keep one of his business interests afloat. In addition, he said that 'a very prominent businessman' from Dublin had been investigating his business dealings going back to the late fifties. His home in Longford had been under surveillance by people in a white Hiace van, and somebody had been acting suspiciously near his Dublin apartment. Jim Tunney, the chairman of the parliamentary party, promptly proposed that a committee be set up to investigate the charges. This was agreed.

The atmosphere was electric as Reynolds went on to accuse Haughey of having instigated the campaign of misinformation through the Government Information Service because of the rumours that Reynolds was preparing to challenge for the leadership. He denied that he was making a grab for power. Indeed, having lost the procedural vote, he clearly recognised that he was now involved in a lost cause. He said that he was throwing away power because of his principles. There was a deathly silence as he wound up. 'It is enough for evil to prosper that good men do nothing,' he concluded.

The discussion on the actual motion dragged on for a further ten hours, well into early Sunday morning. Much of the initial tension dissipated as critics were allowed the opportunity to let off steam. Several people complained about Haughey's arrogance. Senator Don Lydon complained that he had been summoned to the leader's office and bawled out for having made a public speech on Northern Ireland without permission. Lydon had then been contemptuously dismissed from the Taoiseach's office, but in his stunned state he could not find the door in the midst of all the wood-panelling. After some time, Haughey looked up to find the bemused senator still in his office.

'What are you doing here?' he asked.

'I can't find the door, Taoiseach,' Lydon replied.

'Then why don't you jump out the fucking window?' Haughey retorted.

If Lydon had expected people to be outraged at the Taoiseach's conduct, he must have been sorely disappointed, because the meeting erupted with laughter.

Pádraig Flynn waited until after midnight to speak. He reminded the gathering that it was now a quarter of a century to the day since Haughey's father-in-law, Sean Lemass, had stepped down as Taoiseach. Lemass had been party leader for seven years. Haughey had been leader for almost twelve years, but he still had no intention of accepting the invitation to quit.

Before the vote Haughey called on his supporters to ensure that there would be no triumphalism. He clearly did not want a repetition of the disgraceful scenes outside the Dáil in the aftermath of the McCreevy motion in October 1982. As expected, the vote on the amendment expressing confidence in Haughey's leadership was easily carried, by fifty-five votes to twenty-two. There was no triumphalism on the part of Haughey's supporters, but there was a disingenuous display by his ousted opponents, who congratulated themselves on having supposedly made a principled stand.

'I made the ultimate sacrifice to be able to be free to go into the parliamentary party and say what I wanted to say and to vote no confidence in Mr Haughey,' Reynolds declared on returning to his constituency. 'Everybody can take their own message out of that.' If principle had been the motivating factor, however, surely he would have gone ahead with his challenge a fortnight earlier. His timing and tactics suggested that his move had more to do with ambition and poor political judgement than with principle. He did not even have that modicum of self-sacrifice which should have required him to resign from the cabinet rather than force the Taoiseach to dismiss him in order to preserve the principle of 'collective responsibility' required by the Constitution.

Haughey used the dismissal of the two cabinet ministers to effect the most extensive cabinet reshuffle of the four different governments which he had set up. Along with the two new ministerial appointments – Noel Davern as Minister for Education and James McDaid as Minister for Defence – he announced six other changes. This turned out to be one of the greatest blunders of his career.

The nomination of McDaid, a relative newcomer to the Dáil, provoked a storm and landed Haughey in an unprecedented controversy. Some twenty months earlier McDaid had been photographed coming out of the Four Courts with James Pius Clarke, a convicted member of the Provisional IRA. The Supreme Court had just ruled against a request for Clarke's extradition to Northern Ireland.

McDaid had taken a personal interest in the case because he knew that Clarke had not been involved in an attempted murder for which he had been convicted in Northern Ireland. Clarke and McDaid had both been members of the same Gaelic football club, and on the night of the crime they had both been at a stag party in Letterkenny. Under the circumstances McDaid felt a moral duty to defend Clarke, but he obviously got caught up in the euphoria of the moment after the Supreme Court found in Clarke's favour. One of the photographs taken outside the Four Courts showed McDaid smiling broadly, with his hand on Clarke's shoulder.

Neither John Bruton nor Dick Spring made any reference to the press photographs in their addresses. It was Proinsias de Rossa, the leader of the Workers Party, who first raised the issue of McDaid's presence outside the court. This was like throwing a bone to Fine Gael wolves. Jim O'Keeffe and Michael Noonan launched into bitter attacks on McDaid. The latter produced newspaper clippings of the Clarke case with a photograph of McDaid in the background. Looking directly at Dessie O'Malley, Noonan intimated that O'Malley should have followed George Colley's example by insisting on a veto over the appointments of Ministers for Justice and Defence before agreeing to serve in Haughey's government. O'Malley, who had raised no objection to McDaid's appointment when informed about it by Haughey, had not been aware of the incident outside the Four Courts. He withdrew from the chamber to read up on the Clarke case.

As the storm began to gather momentum, McDaid went to Haughey's office at about 6.45 that evening. 'He said that he had expected the attack but didn't expect anything as abusive as this,' McDaid said afterwards. The *Irish Times* took this as an admission that Haughey had been aware of the photograph before making the nomination. But what he had actually been expecting was the normal critical reaction from the Opposition. Whoever he selected – even a member of Fine Gael – was likely to be criticised in the charged personalised atmosphere prevailing in Leinster House.

McDaid naturally felt aggrieved. 'I explained my involvement in the James Pius Clarke case and suggested that any other TD in the same circumstances would have done the same for a constituent, especially for somebody he believed to be totally innocent,' he explained.

Haughey arranged for McDaid to meet O'Malley and Molloy. McDaid told them what had happened and emphasised that he had no sympathy whatever for the Provisional IRA. 'I sincerely believe he is in no way supportive of the Provisional IRA or any other violent organisation,' O'Malley explained afterwards. 'But I had to say to him that he had compromised himself, unfortunately.' Molloy, a former Minister for Defence, explained that somebody wishing to join the army as a mere private would not be accepted if he had been photographed with a member of the IRA.

'You didn't have to be a psychiatrist to realise that they were having a major problem with the situation,' McDaid said afterwards. 'They made it clear that in any other portfolio, except Justice, there would have been no problem at all. Making a long story short,' McDaid continued, 'when I was going out the door I was under no illusion but that they could not see to my appointment.' He went back and reported what had happened to Haughey, who said that he would talk to the Progressive Democrats again himself. McDaid then withdrew to his office to prepare a statement for the Dáil to explain his involvement in the Clarke case. 'It was at that point I made my mind up there was never going to be any peace for me in the role of Minister for Defence and took the decision to go into the Chamber and announce my withdrawal,' he explained. 'I went back to the Taoiseach and told him. He agreed my decision was the correct one and I went into the chamber.'

Before McDaid could make his statement, however, he had to endure a vitriolic attack from the Fine Gael spokesperson on Defence, Madeleine Taylor-Quinn. 'I wonder now, given the proposed appointment,' she asked at one point, 'will the terrorist organisations of this country be privy to very secret matters?' There was outrage in the Dáil. The word was already out that McDaid was withdrawing, but Taylor-Quinn had not heard it. Her attack added considerable insult to the injury already felt on the Fianna Fáil side.

McDaid made a dignified statement: 'In view of the attacks made on me and to avoid the slightest suspicion, however unwarranted, attaching to the Minister for Defence, and in the broader national interest, I have requested the Taoiseach to withdraw my nomination as a member of the government.' There was uproar on the Fianna Fáil benches. Some deputies were incensed that Haughey had again bowed to the wishes of the Progressive Democrats, though in this case McDaid had withdrawn himself, if only to spare the Taoiseach the indignity of having to surrender to the Progressive Democrats again. People had never before seen such indignation in the chamber. Many deputies demanded a meeting of the parliamentary party the following morning. Haughey was willing but Jim Tunney insisted that time was needed to allow tempers to cool, as such a meeting would, in the circumstances, be much too divisive.

Haughey undoubtedly made a mistake in selecting McDaid

as his Minister for Defence. He essentially admitted as much himself the following day when he said that it would not have been 'appropriate, in the circumstances, to proceed with the appointment'. There is no room in that sensitive ministry for even the slightest suspicion of ambiguity towards the Provisional IRA. McDaid had compromised himself outside the Four Courts, though not to the extent of justifying the deluge of invective that ensued. He had been a victim of character-assassination.

Of course, Fine Gael was not really going after McDaid at all. The whole thing was part of the ongoing effort to gut Haughey, and they did not give a damn whom they hurt in the process. What was Haughey's mistake this time? That he had not seen or remembered a face in the background of a photograph on the front pages more than a year earlier? Neither had O'Malley, Bruton or Spring. Haughey knew McDaid was not an IRA sympathiser, and his failure to remember the incident was therefore as understandable as it was unfortunate. The Taoiseach was castigated not only from the Opposition benches but also in the lobbies by his Fianna Fáil critics, who accused him of 'gross misjudgement' because of his failure to stand up to the Progressive Democrats.

For them it was another case of the tail wagging the dog. Lyndon B. Johnson, the former American President, was fond of a particularly crude saying: 'When you've got 'em by the balls, their hearts and minds will follow.' The Progressive Democrats had Haughey, and when they put on the squeeze he submitted, while Reynolds and 'the country-and-western gang' screamed.

While the drama of the McDaid affair was being played out in the Dáil on 13 November, Ben Dunne got three cheques in false names for £70,000 each for his brother and two sisters. He still had those in his pocket shortly afterwards when he went to visit Haughey in Kinsealy on his way home from a golf game in County Louth. He said that Haughey 'looked down – a broken man'. Dunne, whose son had recently had a liver transplant, was very touched when the Taoiseach inquired about his boy's health. As he was leaving after a short chat, Dunne was so appreciative and felt so sorry for the Taoiseach that he spontaneously took out the three cheques and gave them to him.

'Look, that's something for yourself,' Ben said.

'Thanks, big fella,' Haughey replied.

This was the first time that Haughey had received money directly from Dunne. On all previous occasions Des Traynor had acted as the go-between. If his finances had been totally controlled by Traynor without Haughey knowing anything about them, as he later tried to pretend, those three cheques, totalling £210,000, should have prompted Haughey to ask questions about the arrangement. The cheques effectively blew his cover story.

Following the McDaid debacle, Haughey's days as Taoiseach were obviously numbered, especially with the Beef Tribunal gathering momentum. On 15 January 1992 Donal Creedon, the Secretary of the Department of Agriculture, told the inquiry that when he had first told Haughey about the beef fraud at one of Goodman's plants, the Taoiseach had seemed not to want to know. 'My view is that he wanted to get rid of me as quickly as possible,' Creedon testified.

The big news on television that night was not Creedon's testimony, however, but a report that RTÉ's *Nighthawks* programme would be carrying an interview in which Sean Doherty would suggest that other members of the cabinet had known about the tapping of Geraldine Kennedy's and Bruce Arnold's telephones in 1982. Even before the programme was aired, Doherty's remarks were being highlighted on news bulletins.

This was news-orchestration of the most blatant form. People were being given news of forthcoming news, and then what they actually got was not news at all but a rehash of an old story in which Doherty was complaining about having been left to carry the can for what had happened in 1982. He had said much the same thing in a 1984 interview with *Magill* magazine. 'I felt let down by the fact that people knew what I was doing,' he said.

The media assumed that Doherty was insinuating that Haughey had authorised the taps. In the following days reporters pressed Doherty to be more specific, but he refused to comment on the matter. It may have been more than a coincidence that Albert Reynolds and his supporters suddenly raised the tempo of his campaign for the Fianna Fáil leadership. On Marian Finucane's *Liveline* programme on RTÉ radio, Reynolds suggested that Haughey had no intention of stepping down and that Doherty should be more specific. That weekend the *Sunday Tribune* played up the Doherty story with a picture of the former minister on the colour wraparound with a large, bold caption: 'GUBU or GAGA?' Inside there was an extended profile of Pádraig Flynn.

Was it just a coincidence that these events were being orchestrated by some of the same people who had been active in the push to oust Jack Lynch in 1979? Reynolds and Doherty had been members of the gang of five who had led that campaign, and Flynn had been one of their most active supporters. Moreover Vincent Browne, the editor of the *Sunday Tribune*, was the first journalist with whom they had entrusted their story back in 1979.

After having fended off reporters for almost a week, Doherty gave a press conference on 21 January at which he announced that he had been lying over the years when he said that Haughey did not know about the wire taps before the story broke in December 1982. 'I am confirming tonight that the Taoiseach, Mr Haughey, was fully aware in 1982 that two journalists' phones were being tapped and that he at no stage expressed a reservation about this action,' Doherty stated. 'As soon as the transcripts from the taps became available, I took them personally to Mr Haughey in his office and left them in his possession.

'When I indicated on RTÉ's *Nighthawks* programme that I felt let down by lack of support from people who had known what I was doing, I was referring exclusively to Mr Haughey,' Doherty added. He was speaking out after nine years, he said, because Haughey had succumbed to pressure from the Progressive Democrats to introduce phone-tapping legislation 'at a time when it could only do maximum embarrassment to me as Cathaoirleach of the Seanad'.

Doherty's announcement that he was resigning his Senate position probably had a great deal more to do with the leadership struggle with Fianna Fáil than with the phone-tapping legislation. He had the power to deliver a fatal political blow by telling what he knew about the events of 1982. He declared that he had not only lied for Haughey but had surrendered his front-bench position and had given up the party whip voluntarily in 1983. 'Why should we believe Sean Doherty now?' he asked, rhetorically.

'Because,' he explained, 'I am resigning my post. You only do that for the truth.' His concern for the truth was rather touching, but he had just said that he gave up his position in 1983 to foster a lie. There were contradictions and serious flaws in his statement, but these were initially ignored by the media.

The whole thing had been carefully organised: Doherty's press conference was timed to secure maximum media impact. It began late in the evening so that journalists had barely enough time to file their stories before their deadlines. Printed copies of the text of Doherty's statement were handed to the journalists, so there was no need for him to read it before the television cameras, especially when he was refusing to answer questions. The whole thing was being done for effect.

Faced with pressing deadlines, there was little opportunity for journalists to reflect. They had to write virtually by instinct, and the natural instinct of most of the media was to be critical of Haughey. As well as being an attack on Haughey, Doherty's statement was a defence of his own actions in connection with the tappings. He said that the tappings had originated after he went to Deputy Garda Commissioner Joe Ainsworth to complain about cabinet leaks and that it was Ainsworth who had proposed the tap on Bruce Arnold's telephone.

Nine years earlier, however, Ainsworth had stated that it was Doherty who requested the taps, and no reference to cabinet leaks had been made then. Arnold had been writing primarily about the infighting within Fianna Fáil and foreign policy in relation to the Falklands War, not about cabinet matters. Nobody ever identified any item in his articles that might conceivably have been considered a cabinet secret. At the time the justification for the tap was that Arnold was considered 'anti-national', whatever that meant. Later, in his biography of Haughey, Arnold suggested that George Colley had informed him about a cabinet meeting in 1979. This emerged long after Haughey had retired from politics, however.

Haughey denounced Doherty's allegation as 'absolutely false' at a press conference the next day. 'I wish to state categorically that I was not aware at the time of the tapping of these telephone conversations. I also wish to say that I have always abhorred the principle of phone-tapping, except where absolutely necessary to prevent serious crime or subversion by paramilitary organisations.'

It was not, he said, until January 1983 that 'Mr Doherty came to see me in the company of another colleague and revealed to me his involvement in these events.' Reading from a carefully prepared text, the Taoiseach referred to a number of discrepancies in Doherty's latest statement. Doherty had said, for instance, that he forwarded the transcripts to Haughey over a period of several months, but this was impossible, according to the Taoiseach, because Doherty had only been given transcripts on one occasion. Haughey proceeded to quote from several of Doherty's earlier, contradictory statements. 'Mr Haughey did not know that I was tapping these journalists' phones,' Doherty told Gerald Barry in an RTÉ interview on 24 January 1983. Barry asked Doherty why he had not told Haughey about the taps. 'Because he would have stopped it,' Doherty replied.

Unlike his accuser, Haughey fielded questions from reporters. It was one of his more impressive performances, but his opportunity to shine was undermined by an RTÉ strike. The radio and television audiences missed much of what went on because the dreadful sound quality failed to pick up most of the questions.

In response to one question, Haughey said that Ray MacSharry was the colleague who had been present when Doherty first told him about the taps, but MacSharry said that, although he had indeed been present, he had not heard what was said between the two. People were therefore going to have to decide for themselves on Doherty's version of the story.

Haughey tried to blame Doherty for the mess, but in the final analysis it was the Taoiseach's own responsibility because he had appointed Doherty as Minister for Justice. This was a blunder, but Haughey had made no effort to remove him, even though he now said that he had already made some preparations to set up a judicial inquiry into Doherty's conduct before leaving office in 1982. Yet the Taoiseach made no effort to prevent Doherty being elected Speaker of the Senate in 1989.

'Why did you support his elevation to the position of Cathaoirleach of the Seanad?' one reporter asked.

'I didn't support [it], I left that to the Senate group,' Haughey replied. 'In fact, for the first time I did not nominate anybody to the Senate group. I let them take their own decision.'

As it was, Doherty only won when his name was drawn after he had tied with Des Hanafin, so Doherty would never have been elected if the Taoiseach had opposed him. At any rate, if he had opposed Doherty's elevation to Speaker, Haughey would have been able to maintain that he had acted consistently with his supposed disapproval of Doherty's earlier behaviour.

Over the years Haughey's problems stemmed not so much from his actions, or alleged actions, as from his denials. In the context of his whole career it seemed that he was conveniently ignorant about too many things – whether in relation to the Arms Crisis, the financing of *Voice of the North*, the fraud within the Goodman organisation or the reintroduction of insurance coverage on beef exports to Iraq – and later there would be his professed ignorance about his own finances. When things went wrong, Haughey tended to deny responsibility and blame somebody else. He would maintain that he had acted with total propriety himself, but even giving him the full benefit of any doubts, it was difficult to avoid the conclusion that he could be very economical with the truth.

His credibility, which had been damaged by the earlier controversies, was further undermined after his return to power in 1987 when he made policy U-turns on the Anglo-Irish Agreement, the Single European Act, health spending, extradition, birth-control legislation and coalition. He was further hurt by evidence that, when he was saying that he had no intention of asking Brian Lenihan to resign, he had already asked him – and was in fact putting pressure on him – to do so. On top of these matters were his denials that he had been involved in the Carysfort deal, and the controversy over his meeting with Bernie Cahill.

If it had not been for all the other contradictions over the years, people might not have been as ready to believe Doherty as they were. For the Progressive Democrats, however, it no longer mattered whether Haughey or Doherty was telling the truth: the persistent controversies were undermining the work of the government and it was obvious that they were not going to stop as long as Haughey was Taoiseach. The Progressive Democrats therefore issued a thinly veiled ultimatum warning that they would withdraw their support for the government if Haughey did not step down.

Haughey had sacrificed too many of his political supporters in the past. He had dropped McDaid and had sacked Lenihan at the behest of the Progressive Democrats. Now, as Sean Power had predicted, it was his own turn and his colleagues were no longer ready to risk their political careers to save him. His past had finally caught up with him.

In November he said he would go in his own time after he had completed his agenda, which included a meeting with the British Prime Minister, the EC summit at Maastricht and the introduction of the next budget, on 29 January 1992. With the Progressive Democrats unwilling to back down, he announced on 30 January that he would be retiring as leader of Fianna Fáil on 7 February 1992.

Many people thought he might try to hold out and pull off one more escape, but he decided to go with grace and dignity. Suddenly his opponents were saying things about him that had not been said for decades. 'He could not have inspired so much loyalty in his own party for so long,' Garret Fitzgerald wrote, 'if he did not possess some remarkable qualities which are inherently difficult to pin down – a magnetism and capacity to relate to people which made it difficult for even his bitterest political enemies to dislike him personally and an instinct for generosity which made him something of a soft touch.'

'Over the more than twenty years I have known him, I could never fault him for his courtesy and commitment to working in the Dáil,' John Bruton said. 'Charles Haughey would probably not thank me for fulsome tributes; neither would his supporters or mine. But I must say I would be sorry to see him leave the Dáil. We would miss his style and shafts of wit.'

Haughey's political style got him into endless trouble. Some of his principal opponents had great style. They were good, decent men who got on very well with the media, but there was little substance to their political achievements. Haughey, on the other hand, had a brilliant legislative record, but he was the man the media loved to hate. 'He did more than his critics ever did,' former Taoiseach Liam Cosgrave remarked.

In his final address to the Dáil as Taoiseach on 11 February 1992, Haughey quoted from *Othello*: 'I have done the state some service, and they know't,' he said. 'No more of that.'

'It's going to be a damned boring scene without Charlie to kick around,' his long-time critic Charlie McCreevy said.

# 17

## 'My glory was I had such friends'
## Haughey in Retirement, 1992–1999

Although Haughey remained a member of the Dáil for the next ten months, he essentially retired from active politics. He was indirectly in the news in August when it was reported that his son Conor had been given a £60,000 loan to pay for the refurbishment of the yacht *Celtic Mist,* which was in Conor's name. The loan had been authorised by Dermot Desmond, who had power of attorney over the account of the Isle of Man company Freezone, which had been involved in selling the controversial Johnston, Mooney and O'Brien building to Bord Telecom.

That story was a portent of things to come, but it did not set any alarm bells ringing at the time. Haughey was gracefully slipping into retirement. Even Bruce Arnold had some nice things to say about him. 'Charlie Haughey achieved a great deal. And it is grossly unfair to him that there should now be a sense of relief at his not being there,' Arnold wrote in the *Irish Independent* on 22 August 1992. He noted that the former Taoiseach had vast experience, dating back to the time of the first Programme for Economic Development, in 1958. 'He was brilliant on that and on the economy generally over the years since then, and the legacy lingers on, marred by other things,' Arnold continued. Nobody could doubt that Haughey had left a flawed legacy, but some of his critics seemed unwilling to give him credit for anything he had done.

The Fianna Fáil National Executive hosted a dinner in Haughey's honour on 1 October 1992. He was presented with oak carvings of Leinster House, Government Buildings and Dublin Castle to mark his years as a Dáil deputy, as Taoiseach and as President of the European Council of Ministers in 1990. In his address he paid tribute to his friends by quoting from Yeats:

*Think where man's glory begins and ends*
*And say my glory was I had such friends.*

His failure to mention his successor, Albert Reynolds, even once during the speech seemed rather pointed. Reynolds referred to Haughey in his speech, but there was no danger that he would be accused of being effusive. 'The greatest tribute we can pay to the achievements of Charles Haughey is to be able to say in a few years' time that his government laid the basis for a long period of Fianna Fáil rule, even if there had to be a few years of Fianna Fáil-led coalition in the middle,' he said.

Reynolds was obviously still smarting over Fianna Fáil's coalition with the Progressive Democrats, which he had dismissed as a 'temporary little arrangement'. Just how temporary it was would become apparent little over four weeks later, in the drama of the Beef Tribunal. Haughey began four days of testimony at the tribunal on 13 October 1992. For the first time in 133 days of testimony, the hearing room was full at Dublin Castle.

The proceedings turned into virtual theatre as the former Taoiseach was tough and combative, much to the amusement of the spectators. He seemed to relish the opportunity to be the centre of attention again. The proceedings were compared to a testy Dáil question time.

'This is not Dáil Éireann,' the chairman, Liam Hamilton, remarked at one point.

'Although some may be forgiven for thinking that now,' Haughey replied, provoking laughter from the public gallery. 'May I say, sir, that you would have made a big contribution to Dáil Éireann,' he said to Hamilton, who had been an unsuccessful candidate for the Labour Party many years earlier.

'If that was the case you might not have been Taoiseach,' Hamilton replied.

'And if I had chosen the courts, I might have ended up as President of the High Court,' said Haughey.

The main issues that Haughey had to deal with were his involvement in both the abortive Goodman Plan and the reintroduction of the export-credit insurance scheme. This involvement had been only peripheral, he said.

Haughey reaffirmed his complaint that the former deputy leader of the Labour Party, Barry Desmond, had tried to sabotage the Irish beef industry. He said that the allegations made against himself by Desmond and Tomás Mac Giolla of the Workers Party 'were absolutely absurd and recklessly made'. He was equally caustic about the Progressive Democrats, who, he said, were accurately anticipated in the poem 'Leaders of the Crowd', by W. B. Yeats:

*They must keep their certainty, accuse*
*All who are different of base intent,*
*Pull down established humour, hawk for news:*
*Whatever their loose fantasy invent.*

When someone pointed out that Haughey himself had appointed Des O'Malley as Minister for Industry and Commerce, the former Taoiseach conceded with mock humility, 'Nobody's perfect.'

Adrian Hardiman, a well-known member of the Progressive Democrats, and Diarmuid McGuinness were representing Des O'Malley at the tribunal. As McGuinness was cross-examining, Haughey asked him, 'Are you a PD?'

'Unlike Mr Hardiman, who underwent a voluntary conversion, and my client, who underwent a forcible conversion,' McGuinness replied, 'I am not a PD.'

Although Haughey was often entertaining in the witness box, he was only minimally revealing. He was intent on belittling the allegations made against him. 'At the end of the day,' he argued, 'they don't amount to a row of beans.' The allegations against the Irish beef industry did not amount to much more, in his view. 'If there had been breaches of regulations in the Irish beef trade, they are only trotting after what has been perpetrated in other countries,' he said. 'I don't know what we're all doing here.'

He was especially critical of the 'yellow-press type of television programme' which suggested that he and Goodman were long-standing friends, whereas in fact he had not even met Goodman until 1987. In all, Haughey had had fourteen meetings with him between then and 1990. 'We met exclusively to deal with official matters,' Haughey explained. But he had taken no notes at any of those meetings and he was particularly vague about what they had discussed, he said. On the other hand, he said there were documents to suggest that there was 'a very substantial correspondence' showing that Goodman had been much closer to Fitzgerald than he had been to Haughey. But the tribunal was told at that point that Fitzgerald wished it to be known that, notwithstanding a report on the files by one of his staff that he had met Goodman 'on a regular basis', he had in fact met him on 'at most' three occasions.

The main thrust of Haughey's evidence was that Goodman

had come up with a plan that had great economic potential for the beef industry in Ireland. 'It was not a question of the government wanting to advance Mr Goodman's companies, rather that it wanted to advance the interest of the economy and the Goodman company would be the vehicle for that,' the former Taoiseach explained. 'Here was a proposal based on an indigenous industry, based on the beef industry and on a company with a proven record of success. It would have been lunacy not to decide yes,' he asserted. He provided a somewhat contradictory explanation for his involvement in compelling the IDA to drop the performance clause that would have required the Goodman companies to produce a certain number of jobs before receiving any grant. He admitted that he was 'almost certain' that he had discussed the performance clause with Goodman four days before it was modified by the government, but he denied having instructed the Secretary of his department, Pádraig Ó hUiginn, to intervene. Ó hUiginn had already testified that he had indeed talked to the IDA on his own initiative. It was pure coincidence that he had made the call shortly after Goodman's meeting with Haughey. James Nugent, counsel for John Bruton, was sceptical about this testimony of Haughey and Ó hUiginn.

'I have to put it to you that his evidence and your evidence are not credible,' he said.

'I don't think defending your client justifies your right to make such an allegation,' Haughey snapped. 'I won't take it from you.'

'Don't try to bully me,' said Nugent.

'And don't you try to bully me,' Haughey shot back.

'Don't think you can question my credibility. I won't take it,' retorted Nugent.

The two men clashed a number of times during the former Taoiseach's testimony. Nugent seemed to be playing to the media. At one point he appeared to be addressing the reporters even though he was questioning Haughey. 'I don't like talking to the back of your head,' the former Taoiseach protested.

'I am here to ask the questions,' Nugent snapped at another point. 'You are here to answer them!'

'You are trying to make mysteries out of straightforward facts,' Haughey protested.

'If you are intent to lecture me on my role, I may presume to lecture you,' Nugent shot back.

Haughey was particularly dismissive when he was asked what he thought of Bruton's accusation that he had put pressure on the IDA to give Goodman the deal of a lifetime. 'I would be inclined to be apoplectic if I were not a sane person,' Haughey replied to that question, and he went on to characterise the Fine Gael leader as 'the Admiral Stockdale of Irish politics'. When he was complimented afterwards on using this comparison, Haughey reportedly asked, 'Just who is this Stockdale character?'

Admiral James Stockdale was Ross Perot's running mate in the ongoing American presidential election campaign. Stockdale had recently shown himself to be a bumbling individual who was almost totally out of his depth in a television debate with the other two vice-presidential candidates, Dan Quayle and Al Gore.

During his testimony Haughey seemed to admit that he might have gone too far in putting pressure on the IDA but he argued that, if this were the case, the situation should have been rectified by the civil servants. 'The government from time to time takes decisions and afterwards departments point out, "Look, you can't do that",' he explained. 'So formulae are found which make them workable – that's the job of good officials.'

'We took our decision at government and that was the end of the matter as far as we were concerned,' he continued. 'But in all these circumstances, it is the duty of the officials and Secretaries of the government departments to clear up any of these sort of legal difficulties, which government decisions may give rise to.' He was contending, true to form, that if he had made a mistake, it was somebody else's fault! By law the IDA had the right to determine the extent to which it would help to facilitate the Goodman plan, and undue government pressure would have been not only improper but also illegal. Although he was cross-examined by seven barristers, none of them was able to make more than a coincidental link between the timing of Haughey's meetings with Goodman and the subsequent pressure that had been put on the IDA to adjust its terms for supporting the company's plan. Yet the weight of those coincidences became overwhelming.

'It was obvious that the Authority would not have deleted the clause were it nor for the intervention of the government,' Liam Hamilton concluded in his report. The government had 'wrongfully and in excess of its powers' directed the IDA to remove the performance clause, and 'this direction was made either at the instigation of the then Taoiseach or the Secretary of his department.' Although the government bent over backwards to facilitate it, the Goodman plan was never implemented because Goodman did not get things all his own way. Thus the whole affair did 'not cost the exchequer a penny', Haughey argued. In a sense he may have been right, but it cost the country a small fortune in the legal fees required to investigate the whole thing in order to placate his critics.

On the reintroduction of the export-credit insurance scheme for beef exports to Iraq, which was probably the most costly faux pas in the history of the state, Haughey sought to dump all the responsibility on the head of Albert Reynolds, whom he accused of having reintroduced the scheme without his knowledge or approval. 'All I can say to you is that Mr Reynolds was an experienced businessman aware of the complexities of international markets and trading and aware of all the pitfalls,' Haughey said. 'It was just another ongoing departmental scheme administered by the minister in the department, without reference to me.'

Hamilton noted in his report that 'Goodman states that he would have discussed all matters that were of importance to him whenever he got the opportunity but had no clear recollection of discussing export-credit insurance with the Taoiseach on any specific occasion but emphasised that he would have discussed it whenever he got the opportunity.' Haughey could not remember discussing it, but he appointed Reynolds as Minister for Industry and Commerce, with the result that he bore ultimate responsibility for the mistakes made by Reynolds, whether the then Taoiseach had discussed the scheme with him or not.

At the end of his testimony, Haughey announced that he was leaving to return to his 'books and bucolic pursuits'. He slipped gracefully into official retirement on 5 November 1992 when the government came crashing down after Reynolds accused O'Malley of being 'dishonest' in his testimony at the Beef Tribunal. On formally retiring, Haughey indicated that he would not write his memoirs and would not be making any further public statements. He declined to be interviewed by RTÉ when it made a television programme on the twenty-fifth anniversary of the Arms Crisis. 'I will comment on the fiftieth anniversary,' he said.

Haughey became involved in some charity work and seemed to be enjoying his retirement. While at Kinsealy he went riding regularly on Portmarnock strand on his hunter, Gatsby, and he took a keen interest in his racehorses, especially Flashing Steel, which won the Irish Grand National on Easter Monday 1995, when the Taoiseach, John Bruton, was presenting the trophy.

Haughey continued to perform the official opening of the Dingle Regatta. There was an extraordinary story about the regatta in the *Irish Independent* on 27 August 1997. In her coverage of the opening of the regatta the previous day, Miriam Lord reported that Haughey had 'fallen off *Celtic Mist*' in Dingle harbour and had to be rescued by a marine-rescue helicopter. 'That's what happens when you are enjoying your retirement and have no responsibilities,' she wrote. 'You fall into the sea.'

It was Miriam Lord who had gone overboard, because there was no truth in the report. She had apparently been joking, but the story obviously became garbled. If Haughey had fallen into the sea and been rescued in that way, it would have been front-page news and would not have been buried in the middle of the newspaper.

Lord telephoned Haughey to apologise profusely about the story the next morning. He undoubtedly had grounds for legal action against the newspaper, but he graciously accepted her apology. When she asked how he would like her to apologise in print, he told her to do it in whatever way she wished, or not to bother at all. He was content with her telephone call and he told her she could forget it.

'Sorry. Sorry. Sorry. I'm as sick as a pig,' she began an open letter to Haughey the next day. 'I have done you a dreadful disservice.' She admitted that he had never fallen off *Celtic Mist* and had not been rescued by the Air Corps. It was Lord who was rescued by Charlie Haughey on that occasion.

Haughey was hardly a week out of the Taoiseach's Office when an incident occurred in Miami, Florida, that was to have profound long-term repercussions. The police arrested Ben Dunne as he threatened to jump from a high-rise building. He was high on cocaine and apparently thought he could fly. The saga of his involvement with Haughey would gradually unravel as an indirect consequence of his erratic behaviour that night.

In the aftermath of the Miami incident, Dunne was ousted as chief executive of the family business by his sister Margaret Heffernan. A bitter family feud followed as he sought to break up the family trust. She was horrified to learn from a company accountant in July 1993 that Dunne had given Haughey over £1 million of company money. It was bad enough giving the money to a politician, but giving it to Haughey was the last straw because her father had detested him ever since an incident that had occurred between them at a trade exhibition in New York in the 1960s. Dunne was unwilling to provide his sister with details of the cheques he had given to Haughey.

'If you don't tell me,' she warned, 'I'm going to keep digging.'

'You can look all you like,' he replied. 'You'll never trace them.'

She confronted Haughey personally. 'I said it had come to my knowledge that my brother had given him £1.1 million,' she recalled. He had actually given Haughey at least £1.3 million.

'I can't be responsible for what your brother says,' Haughey had replied. He went on to say that Dunne 'was unstable'. When she tried to press him about the money, he avoided the issue. 'He kept going back to the stability of my brother,' she said. 'I was as non-committal as I could be to Mrs Heffernan because that's the first time I heard this rumour about this million pounds,' Haughey later contended. He said he had only referred to Dunne as being unstable in the light of her remarks. 'I may have said "From what you describe, Margaret, it would seem that your brother is acting in an unstable way",' he explained.

In March 1994 Noel Smyth, Dunne's lawyer, told Haughey that the story of the money might be made public. Haughey's response was to lie and say that he had never received any money from the businessman. In fact, throughout his numerous meetings and some forty telephone conversations with Smyth during the next couple of years, Haughey never admitted that he had received money from Dunne, but Smyth did not need an admission. 'If Mr Haughey wanted to make some other case, I was leaving that really to him,' Smyth explained. 'I knew I had sufficient documentary evidence.'

The Dunne family feud was resolved in November 1994. Dunne was bought out for some £100 million, but solicitors for Dunnes Stores still tried to recover the money from Haughey. On 13 November they wrote to him with details of the payments that they contended had been 'improperly diverted' to him.

'As no such moneys had ever been paid to me by Mr Ben Dunne or any of the companies mentioned, no question of repayment arises,' Haughey replied the next day. 'I take grave exception to the use of the words "improperly diverted" and the implication that I was aware of such conduct by or on behalf of Mr Ben Dunne.'

Haughey's stonewalling tactics began to unravel in December 1996 when the Dáil requested that Judge Gerard Buchanan investigate payments made by Dunne to Michael Lowry after Lowry was forced to resign as a minister in the rainbow coalition. Haughey's name became linked with the disclosure that £20,000 had been paid to his wife for his election expenses in 1989. It was also disclosed that Haughey's son Ciarán had been paid £10,000 for helicopter services and that his brother, Fr Eoghan Haughey, had been paid £2,000 for Masses. But then *Phoenix* magazine broke the story that Haughey had been given over £1 million. As a result of the Buchanan Report, the government established a tribunal under Mr Justice Brian McCracken to investigate Dunne's payments to politicians. The tribunal had already been set up when Noel Smyth showed Haughey three bank drafts that Dunne had given him at

Abbeville in November 1991. Viewing the drafts as 'lethal', Haughey admitted to Smyth that they 'could be a cause of some embarrassment'.

'I think he said, "Is there any way we can get rid of these?"' Smyth later testified. This was reminiscent of Haughey's question to Des O'Malley about Peter Berry's forthcoming testimony shortly before the Arms Trial.

Haughey had told Smyth in 1993 that he had not availed of the tax amnesty, with the result that Smyth concluded that he was likely to have trouble with the Revenue Commissioners. Dunne had therefore authorised Smyth to offer Haughey 'up to £1 million' more towards the cost of settling his tax affairs. Smyth urged Haughey to make a full disclosure about the money. Although he acknowledged the 'very gracious offer', Haughey said that it was 'impossible' for him to accept it, even though Smyth warned that the tribunal, with its very extensive powers, was likely 'to get all the information sooner rather than later'. He again advised Haughey to do himself a 'huge favour' by making a clean breast of things. But Haughey tried to brazen it out.

Throughout most of the time that the McCracken Tribunal sat, he denied that he had received any money. On 7 July 1997 he submitted an eight-page statement denying that any meetings had taken place between Ben Dunne and himself at Kinsealy or that he had received three cheques totalling £210,000 from him in person. This time he had gone too far, though. He stated that he had first heard of the Dunne money when Margaret Heffernan confronted him in July 1993. He had then telephoned Des Traynor, who said that he would be meeting her himself to 'hear what she had to say but that I need not be concerned about these rumours as they were without foundation,' Haughey added.

This was an unbelievable statement. The tribunal had enough

evidence to convince Haughey's own lawyer that his client's position was untenable. The tribunal was suspended for the day and the next morning Haughey submitted a revised statement accepting that he had indeed received the money and had misled the tribunal. 'As a result of reviewing the excellent work of the tribunal and considering the very helpful documentation recently received from Mr Ben Dunne's solicitor, I now accept that I received the £1.3 million from Mr Ben Dunne and that I became aware that he was the donor to the late Mr Traynor in 1993, and furthermore, I now accept Mr Dunne's evidence that he handed me £210,000 in Abbeville in November 1991,' Haughey declared. 'In making this statement, I wish to make it clear that until yesterday, I had mistakenly instructed my legal team.'

Haughey testified before the tribunal in Dublin Castle on 15 July 1997. Members of the public had been gathering in the early hours of the morning to gain access to the tribunal chamber. Haughey arrived before 7.30 am, eluding reports and photographers. He was no longer the same combative witness who had appeared before the Beef Tribunal less than five years earlier. At the outset he read a prepared statement in which he expressed regret for his behaviour in not cooperating with the tribunal 'in the manner which might have been expected of me'.

He insisted that he did not know where any of the money had come from until July 1993, but he admitted that his statement that Traynor had dismissed the story as a rumour when he first talked to him about it 'was incorrect. I can only suggest that I was reluctant to face the inevitable consequences of disclosure,' he explained.

He clearly tried to dump the responsibility for all his finances on Traynor, who had died in 1994. 'I never had to concern myself about my personal finances,' Haughey said. '[Traynor] took over control of my financial affairs from about 1960 onwards. He sought, as his personal responsibility, to ensure that I would be free to devote my time and ability to public life and that I would not be distracted from my political work by financial concerns.'

'Traynor had complete discretion to act on my behalf without reference back to me,' Haughey continued. 'In hindsight, it is clear that I should have involved myself to a greater degree in this regard . . . My private finances were perhaps peripheral to my life,' he contended. 'I left them to Mr Traynor to look after.' Of course this was not the case with the three cheques worth £210,000 that Ben Dunne had handed to Haughey, who said that he could not remember that incident. But he accepted Noel Smyth's documentary evidence and Dunne's word that he had handed him the cheques.

It was pointed out that a sizeable loan taken out by Celtic Helicopters was paid off from Haughey's Ansbacher account. Haughey said that he was unaware of this transaction but that Traynor would have known that it was acceptable to him to use offshore funds for family-related business. Although Haughey had been spending much more than his official salary, he denied that he lived extravagantly. 'I didn't have a lavish lifestyle,' he told the tribunal. 'My work was my lifestyle and when I was in the office I worked every day, all day. There was no room for any sort of an extravagant lifestyle.'

He had to concede, however, that as recently as 7 July he had been 'persisting in accounts of events which were short of the truth'. Yet while he was on the stand, neither he nor any of the lawyers had referred to his deception as lying.

'It wasn't a full explanation,' he insisted.

'It was pretty economical?' counsel asked.

'I hate to use that phrase,' Haughey replied.

'It was not true, Mr Haughey, isn't that right?'

'It was not a full explanation.'

When he emerged from the tribunal, a crowd of up to 1,000 people had gathered outside Dublin Castle. There was a smattering of applause, but his loyalists were quickly drowned out by booing.

On 25 August 1997 the tribunal report was published. In it McCracken concluded that it was 'quite unacceptable that a member of Dáil Éireann, and in particular a cabinet minister and Taoiseach, should be supported in his personal lifestyle by gifts made to him personally'. The report was a devastating indictment of Haughey in which the judge made little or no effort to hide his annoyance at the way in which the former Taoiseach had prevaricated and lied. He had wasted the time of the tribunal by repeatedly ignoring requests for information. Then, when he had provided answers, he had lied in three separate written submissions. The judge also concluded that Haughey had not been honest in his testimony either. 'The tribunal considers Mr Charles Haughey's evidence to be unacceptable and untrue,' he wrote, citing eleven different instances in which he described the former Taoiseach's evidence as 'not believable', 'quite unbelievable', 'most unlikely', 'beyond all credibility' or 'incomprehensible'.

Since Haughey had admitted that he knew about his £105,000 loan from the ACC during the late 1980s, for instance, McCracken found it strange that he 'did not admit to being aware of any other loans'. He did not believe the story about not remembering the three cheques given to him by Ben Dunne in November 1991. 'It is not believable that a person could not remember an event such as this, which was quite bizarre,' McCracken contended. 'It is also most unlikely that if Haughey gave those bank drafts to Des Traynor, Traynor did not reveal that other moneys had been received from Dunne at an earlier date.'

The judge refused to believe several aspects of the former

Taoiseach's story involving his relationship with Traynor. For instance, McCracken found it 'unbelievable' that all of Haughey's financial affairs had been managed without reference to him by Des Traynor since around 1960. Moreover, it was 'quite unbelievable that Traynor would not have told him in some detail of the difficulties and it is equally unbelievable that Haughey would not have asked'. It was incredible that he would not have discussed the tax implications of this situation with Traynor. McCracken argued that it was 'far more likely' and 'far more consistent with his subsequent actions' that the tax implications were discussed and 'that it was decided that the money should be kept offshore and that its receipt should never be acknowledged.' Since Traynor had apparently been 'a meticulously careful person', it was unlikely, according to the tribunal report, that he would 'have used any money in the Ansbacher deposits, which were held for the benefit of Haughey, to support Celtic Helicopters unless he had the authority of Haughey to do so.'

After Traynor's death in 1994, it was 'beyond all credibility' that the former Taoiseach 'would not have become very concerned as to his affairs, and particularly concerned to ensure his assets were secured'. At one point during Haughey's testimony, McCracken noted that the former Taoiseach admitted that he had received financial statements from Traynor. 'The clear impression is that, despite his earlier denials, Haughey had in fact received statements dealing with his accounts which he read and noted, and therefore he did not ask about his affairs, because he was already aware of them.' The judge went on to state that 'the tribunal thinks it probable that he was at all times aware that money was being held for his benefit in Ansbacher Cayman Limited.' Moreover, McCracken argued that 'While he may not have known the exact sums of money which he was spending, he must have known that large sums of money were being spent on his behalf, despite his denial of having a lavish lifestyle.'

Although the judge stopped short of accusing Haughey of perjury, the implications of the report – that Haughey had obstructed the work of the tribunal and perjured himself – were unmistakable. 'It is not for the tribunal to determine whether Mr Charles Haughey should be prosecuted,' McCracken wrote. 'This is a matter for the Director of Public Prosecutions.' He added, rather pointedly, 'that the circumstances warrant the papers in the matter being sent to the Director of Public Prosecutions for his consideration as to whether there ought to be a prosecution, and the Tribunal intends to do so.'

In the aftermath of the McCracken Report two more judicial tribunals were set up under High Court judges to investigate allegations of political corruption. One tribunal, under Michael Moriarty, was to investigate the Ansbacher accounts and related payments to politicians, while the other, under Fergus Flood, was to investigate corruption in relation to the planning process; this corruption included allegations of payments to politicians.

As the inquiries proceeded, other people were gradually dragged into the story. It transpired that Haughey was not the only Taoiseach for whom AIB had written off part of a loan. The bank had also written off £200,000 owed by Garret Fitzgerald, who had borrowed money to buy stock in Guinness Peat Aviation before its planned flotation, which turned into a financial disaster that cost the former Taoiseach a fortune.

Of course, Fitzgerald's case was different from that of Haughey. First, Haughey had borrowed money to finance his lavish lifestyle, whereas Fitzgerald had borrowed to gamble, albeit by investing in the flotation of a company of which he was a director. Second, the bank had written off much of the interest that Haughey owed, whereas it had written off all the interest and some of the principal in Fitzgerald's case.

Ray Burke resigned from the cabinet in 1998 after it was disclosed that he had received over £30,000 in 1989, and he later said that he was still holding in his own name around £118,000 that he had collected on behalf of Fianna Fáil some years earlier. A British-based property developer stated publicly that he had given £50,000 to Pádraig Flynn for Fianna Fáil in 1989. These issues, which are being investigated by one tribunal or another, still remain to be explained.

Haughey was billed for £2 million by the Revenue Commissioners, but he appealed the assessment. The case was heard in camera in October 1998 before Ronan Kelly, an appeals commisioner. Kelly's task was to sit independently of the Revenue Commissioners in order to evaluate the assessment and decide whether it should stand, be reduced or be dismissed.

The Revenue Commissioners insisted that the McCracken Report identified Ben Dunne as the donor of £1.3 million to Haughey. The money was paid by offshore companies – Equifex Trust Corporation, registered in Zug, Switzerland, which forwarded £621,000 sterling to Haughey, and Tutbury, a company in the Isle of Man which provided £410,000 sterling. A further £182,650 sterling was provided by Dunnes Stores in Bangor, Northern Ireland. Haughey's legal team contended that in law the actual donors were the offshore companies from which Dunnes Stores had withdrawn the money for the benefit of the former Taoiseach. The shareholders of the companies were thus the actual donors, but, as these people were not identified, Kelly had no real option but to conclude that the money had come from outside the state and was therefore not liable to income tax under existing laws.

When it was announced on 15 December 1998, this decision was greeted with a storm of protests. The Revenue Commissioners indicated that they would be appealing the finding to the circuit court, where the proceedings would be open to the public. The Luton-based property developer Tom Gilmartin was so irate about the decision that he announced that he 'couldn't be bothered' testifying before the Flood Tribunal. He had reportedly given £50,000 to Pádraig Flynn back in 1989. Some weeks later Flynn referred to Gilmartin in rather patronising terms during an interview on *The Late Late Show,* and the property developer changed his mind and decided to testify after all. Although the payments to Haughey's ministerial colleagues Ray Burke and Pádraig Flynn are beyond the scope of this study, when the full story of all the payments to politicians comes out, it will probably detract from Haughey's accomplishments as Taoiseach and cast a further shadow over his political legacy.

It was Gay Byrne's last season as host of *The Late Late Show,* the longest-running program of its kind in the world. His penultimate show, on 14 May 1999, featured Terry Keane, who raised many eyebrows by talking openly about her twenty-seven-year affair with Haughey. By then even the 'dogs in the street' knew about the affair, according to Byrne. Keane had been making snide references to the affair in her column in the *Sunday Independent* over the years, and the couple's relationship had been parodied week after week on *Scrap Saturday,* a popular radio comedy programme. She said she was telling her story because Kevin O'Connor was bringing out a book, *Sweetie,* which she said would distort the affair. She said she was motivated by a desire to ensure that the relationship was accurately depicted as 'a genuine love affair'.

'I hear from people who had seen the script that it was a very loveless relationship, punctuated only by expensive dinners or trips on yachts,' she explained. 'It wasn't like that. I wanted to show that it really was love.'

Although she also praised Haughey's achievements, the studio audience did not seem inclined to believe that he had ever done anything worthwhile. 'They have forgotten all the good things he has done,' she said. 'When Ireland was a begging bowl, Charlie went out and eyeballed people in Europe and the world.'

She felt he was being treated unfairly and was revolted when somebody on television suggested that he had done as much damage to politics as the paedophile priest Fr Brendan Smyth had done to the Catholic Church in Ireland. 'Brendan Smyth buggered little boys,' Keane said. 'Charlie has never done that.'

'Charlie took money from people who were very willing to give it to him so that he would go out and not have to worry about his own finances, that he could go and run the country, which he did brilliantly and brought us the Celtic Tiger and the prosperity we have today,' she argued. She was crediting him with too much, but then others do not give him any credit at all.

Over the years there had been so many rumours about Haughey that turned out to be untrue that there were still people who doubted Keane's story. For instance, there was the totally unfounded rumour that Haughey had had an affair with Emer O'Kelly of RTÉ. O'Kelly had first heard this story in 1980 and used Keane's revelations as an opportunity to deny that she herself had been romantically involved with the former Taoiseach.

There was another false story that did the rounds for decades about Éamonn Andrews supposedly having beaten Haughey up one night in the 1960s. One version of the story was that Haughey had made a pass at Éamonn's wife, Gráinne. This incident was meant to have happened either at Haughey's home, the Gresham Hotel or Jury's Hotel, depending on who was telling the story. Andrews and his wife had attended a party at Haughey's home before he moved to Kinsealy. 'Charlie received us personally and graciously, as was his wont,' Andrews recalled. 'And he did make an innocent pass at Gráinne, who was looking particularly fetching. Both she and I would have been somewhat peeved had he not. But it was hardly the sort of pass to warrant a punch on the nose.'

The story persisted until Andrews finally became exasperated when it was repeated in the *News of the World.* He sued for libel and secured 'a few thousand pounds and an apology in open court,' he said. On returning to Dublin, Andrews invited Haughey to his house for a champagne celebration.

'I'll come,' Haughey said, 'provided it's Dom Perignon!'

It was, and Haughey came. Andrews had purchased some sixty copies of the offending newspaper and he made a carpet of them from the doorway all the way into the house. The rumour persisted, but at least it had financed a good party.

There were other groundless rumours about Haughey. For example, unfounded stories about his famous fall from his horse in 1970 persisted. Over a quarter of a century later twisted versions of that story were still being told. It was also reported that Haughey had been beaten almost to death by the father and brother of a young woman after they supposedly caught him in bed with her, upstairs in the Grasshopper Inn in Clonee, County Meath. But there was no truth to the story.

Haughey's behaviour tended to encourage some of the rumours. In 1991, when he officiated at the start of the Dingle Regatta, he was still Taoiseach. He arrived in Dingle on *Celtic Mist,* clearly in a happy mood. There was a women's team in the first race. Before starting the race the Taoiseach shouted down to the women, 'Are yer knickers wet?'

He later gave an interview to a young female reporter from the *Kerryman*. 'I suppose,' he said at the end of the interview, 'a ride would be out of the question!' There were witnesses there, so this was obviously not a proposition. It was Haughey's way of saying to the young people that he was still 'with it'. Some people would say, no doubt, that his behaviour was confirmation of the old Irish adage, 'the older the goat, the giddier!'

'He is not an oil painting – never was,' Joanne McElgunn wrote in the *Sunday Independent*. 'Women were metal and he was a powerful magnet.' He tended to flirt shamelessly, and they loved it. 'Once C. J. patted my bottom,' McElgunn continued. 'The company and the consumption of two gin and tonics might just have saved him from the sharp edge of my tongue. In retrospect I was strangely flattered. I know many women with whom he had only shaken hands.'

Terry Keane was certainly proud of her dalliance with the short fellow, which she went on to detail in a series of articles in the *Sunday Times*. These details included a photograph of the couple kissing while she was stretched out on the floor. Any lingering doubts about the existence of the affair were dispelled by that photograph. But she was taken aback by the intensity of the public reaction to her articles. 'I certainly was surprised by the fallout after the first extract from the *Sunday Times*,' she said. 'Perhaps naively, I didn't expect such a shock wave of reaction.'

For a while she tried to defend Haughey, especially over the financial allegations against him. 'All Ben Dunne got for the million pounds-plus that he gave to Charlie Haughey was an invitation to a few parties at Abbeville and some family weddings,' she told Marian Finucane in an RTÉ interview. 'If anybody is foolish enough to give a million pounds to be included in someone's social circle, that's up to them.'

Although Ben Dunne continued to assert that he had never got nor sought any favours from Haughey, the Moriarty Tribunal uncovered further cheques totalling £180,000 that Dunne had given Haughey in November 1992. This was after the short fellow had lost his political clout. In fact, he had quit politics, so those cheques would tend to support Dunne's contention that he was not looking for political favours.

Between 1987 and 1997, when the story of the Dunne money first broke, Haughey spent far more money than he earned. Just where he got all this money is still not clear. The Ansbacher accounts controlled by Des Traynor, which the McCracken Tribunal suspected might contain up to £40 million, were actually much more extensive than that. In all about a hundred Irish residents had such accounts and the total amount of money in the accounts ran into the hundreds of millions of pounds. Despite reckless remarks by some politicians suggesting that all those who had Ansbacher accounts were criminal tax evaders, some of the accounts were perfectly legal and were being used for legitimate business reasons.

In the midst of these further Ansbacher disclosures, in September 1999 Terry Keane was back in the news when she auctioned off some paintings of Haughey and some other memorabilia of the couple's affair. The news that she was auctioning these items was first published in various Irish newspapers on the Haugheys' forty-eighth wedding anniversary.

A whole plethora of issues about Haughey's financial affairs were meanwhile being raised by Moriarty Tribunal, especially in relation to his handling of the party leader's allowance, which was provided by the state. This allowance was initially established by Éamon de Valera's government in the 1930s to provide for a party secretariat and fund political research. This account was run out of the AIB branch in Baggot's Street, Dublin, but Haughey had other money also deposited in the account. Between 1984 and 1991 over £540,000 extra was deposited in the account, in addition to the £945,000 contributed by the state, but there are questions about the use of the money. For instance, £100,000, contributed to Fianna Fáil by the Irish Permanent Building Society, was deposited in the leader's account during 1986, but in the same period £75,000 was apparently transferred out of the leader's account to another account used to pay Haughey's domestic bills. One might reasonably wonder whether this was a legitimate use of that account?

The Irish Permanent Building Society made further contributions of £10,000 to Haughey's personal political fund and £20,000 to help defray the cost Brian Lenihan's liver transplant at the Mayo Clinic in the United States in June 1989, but those two cheques were 'inadvertently' lodged in the account of Celtic Helicopters. Haughey insisted that his son Ciarán had withdrawn a similar amount from the company's account on the same day and 'an examination of the available bank records indicates that this cheque, for £30,000, was in fact lodged to the party leader's account'. But lawyers for the Moriarty Tribunal contended that the £30,000 cheque was apparently cashed at the bank rather than being deposited in the leader's account. There was a lodgement for £36,000 on 20 June 1989 but that included a £25,000 cheque from Larry Goodman towards Lenihan's medical expenses. What happened to the £30,000 contributed by the Irish Permanent Building Society in June 1989 is a matter which has yet to be resolved.

A considerable amount of money collected on Lenihan's behalf in 1989 was deposited in the leader's account. Although Lenihan was a member of the Voluntary Health Insurance scheme, his expenses were not covered because he was having the operation outside the country. Following a personal request from Haughey to Tom Ryan, the chief executive of VHI, the board of the company decided to make a special contribution to help defray Lenihan's medical expenses. Lenihan's widow, Anne, told the Moriarty Tribunal in October 1999 that the only cash her family received was £200 that Haughey's driver delivered as Brian about to go to the United States for the operation. That would not have paid for even one of Haughey's French shirts, but most of the media ignored the fact that £54,498.58 was paid from the party leader's account to the Mayo Clinic towards Lenihan's medical costs in 1989, and a little over £10,000 was paid to Department of Foreign Affairs on Lenihan's behalf that year, while over £5,700 was used to pay off further bills at the Mayo Clinic, a hotel, and a limousine Service in the United States, the following March. A further £12,900 was reportedly paid from the account to the Department of Defence in February 1991, 'in discharge of sums incurred in connection with the travel arrangements' of the Lenihans. Thus, over £80,000 was paid out of the leader's account towards Lenihan's bills, not just the £200 highlighted by the media. In total £188,000 was paid into the party leader's account around the time of the appeals for funds for Lenihan's operation in 1989, but this would have come in at about the same time as money collected for that year's general election campaign. How much was collected for Lenihan and what happened to it all are questions that remain to be answered.

Many other questions remain unanswered about the handling of the party leader's account. In 1990, for instance, Haughey gave Fianna Fáil Deputy John Ellis £26,000 from the fund to help stave off bankruptcy; if he had been declared bankrupt, he would have had to vacate his Dáil seat, and the government would have lost its majority. The National Irish Bank was even persuaded to write off a debt of £263,540 owed by Ellis at about the same time.

The party leader's account was also used to pay two bills

totalling £15,832 for Charvet shirts from Paris and £15,084.44 to Le Coq Hardi restaurant in Dublin, where Haughey and Terry Keane had many intimate dinners, according to Keane. It is difficult to understand how anyone could justify using this account to pay such bills.

Rather than answer the various questions, however, Haughey has appeared to prevaricate and even try to frustrate the investigation. He challenged, on constitutional grounds, the right of Moriarty Tribunal to investigate his bank accounts and those of wife, daughter and two sisters. In April 1998 the High Court held that the failure to give the members of his family advance notice of the discovery orders executed on their accounts was unfair but not sufficient to void the proceedings of the tribunal. On the other hand the court ruled that Haughey's own complaints against the tribunal itself were 'bordering on the absurd'. The judge, Hugh Geoghegan, concluded that 'some invasion of Mr Haughey's constitutional rights, such as his right of privacy et cetera, is justified, having regard to the legitimate public concern': valid questions were raised by his acceptance of gifts.

'Ethical behaviour in public office surely incorporates more than simply refusing to take bribes,' the judge contended. An office holder was obliged to behave in a way that did not give rise to a public apprehension or inference of impropriety. In Geoghegan's judgement there was already evidence that Haughey's conduct had given rise to such apprehension because he had accepted money from Ben Dunne. The judge concurred with the conclusion of his colleague Brian McCracken that 'Haughey's whole lifestyle' would appear to have been 'dependent upon such gifts'.

Justice Geoghegan ruled that Haughey had to pay half the cost of the High Court hearing. The former Taoiseach appealed this to the Supreme Court but lost in 1999. As a result he was saddled with half the High Court costs, and the whole cost of the Supreme Court hearing. It was estimated that the total bill could run as high as £500,000. This was only one of his growing number of financial problems. The Revenue Commissioners have lodged an appeal to the Circuit Court against the verdict of the Appeals Commissioner in essentially dismissing the £2 million tax assessment against Haughey. Moreover, he has been returned for trial in March 2000 on charges of obstructing the McCracken Tribunal. If convicted, he could be fined £10,000 and sentenced to two years in jail.

Haughey's charisma was based on his ability to survive a whole series of political scandals and escape from tight, seemingly inescapable, political corners. The perception of his personal invincibility has already been tarnished, maybe irrevocably.

Time and again Haughey confounded his critics and bucked the system. If he bucks it this time, he will be remembered as the greatest bucker of all time.

# Bibliography

Allen, Gregory. *The Garda Síochána: Policing Independent Ireland, 1922-81.* Dublin: Gill & Macmillan, 1999.

Andrews, Éamonn and Grainne. *For Ever and Ever, Éamonn: The Public and Private Life of Éamonn Andrews.* London: Grafton Books, 1989.

Arnold, Bruce. *Haughey: His Life and Unlucky Deeds.* London: Harper–Collins, 1993.

____________. *What Kind of Country: Modern Irish Politics, 1968–1983.* London: Jonathan Cape, 1984.

Bell, J. Bowyer. *The Secret Army: a History of the IRA.* London: Anthony Blond Ltd., 1970.

Bloch, Jonathan and Fitzgerald, Patrick. *British Intelligence and Covert Action: Africa, Middle East and Europe Since 1945.* Dingle: Brandon Press, 1983.

Boland, Kevin. *the Rise and Decline of Fianna Fáil.* Cork: Mercier Press, 1982.

____________. *Up Dev!* Dublin: Private, 1977.

____________. "We Won't Stand (Idly) By." Dublin: Private, 1974.

Bowman, John. *De Valera and the Ulster Question, 1917-1973.* Oxford: Clarendon Press, 1982.

Brady, Conor. *Guardians of the Peace.* Dublin: Gill & Macmillan, 1974.

Brady, Seamus. *Arms and the Men: Ireland in Turmoil.* Dublin: Private, 1971.

Bugliosi, Vincent with Gentry Curt. *Helter Skelter: The True Story of the Manson Murders.* New York: Bantam Books, 1974.

Byrne, Gay with Deidre Purcell. *The Time of My Life: an Autobiography*. Dublin: Gill & Macmillan, 1989.

Collins, Tom. *The Irish Hungerstrike*. Dublin: White Island Book Co., 1986.

Collins, Stephen. *The Cosgrave Legacy*. Dublin: Blackwater Press, 1996.

_______________. *The Haughey File: the Unprecedented Career and Last Years of The Boss*. Dublin: The O'Brien Press, 1992.

_______________. *Dick Spring and the Labour Party*. Dublin: The O'Brien Press, 1993.

Coogan, Tim Pat. *Ireland Since the Rising*. London: Pall Mall, 1966.

Coombes, David, ed. *Ireland and the European Communities: Ten Years of Membership*. Dublin: Gill & Macmillan, 1983.

Courtney, John. *It Was Murder*. Dublin: Blackwater Press, 1996.

Cruise O'Brien, Conor. *States of Ireland*. London: Hutchinson & Co., 1972.

____________________. *Memoirs: My Life and Themes*. Dublin: Poolbeg Press, 1998.

Curtis, Liz. *Nothing but the Same Old Story: the Roots of Anti-Irish Racism*. London: Private, no date.

Downey, James. *Lenihan: His Life and Loyalties*. Dublin: New Island Books, 1998.

______________. *Them & Us: Britain Ireland and the Northern Question, 1969-82*. Dublin: Ward River Press, 1983.

Drower, George. *John Hume: Man of Peace*. London: Vista, 1995.

Duignan, Sean. *One Spin on the Merry-Go-Round*. Dublin: Blackwater Press, 1995.

Dwyer, T. Ryle. *De Valera's Darkest Hour: In Search of National Independence*. Cork: Mercier Press, 1982.

_______________. *Michael Collins and the Treaty: His Differences with de Valera*. Cork: Mercier Press, 1981.

Edmonds, Sean. *The Gun the Law and the Irish People: From 1912 to the Aftermath of the Arms Trial 1970.* Tralee: Anvil Books, 1971.

Feehan, John M. *An Apology to the Irish People.* Midleton, Cork: Royal Carbery Books, 1988.

______________. *Operation Brogue: a Study of the Vilification of Charles J. Haughey Code-named "Operation Brogue" by the British Secret Service.* Cork: Mercier Press, 1984.

______________. *The Statesman: a Study of the Role of Charles J. Haughey in the Ireland of the Future.* Cork: Mercier Press, 1985.

Finlay, Fergus. *Snakes & Ladders.* Dublin. New Island Books, 1998.

Griffith, Kenneth and O'Grady, Timothy E. *Curious Journey: an Oral History of Ireland's Unfinished Revolution.* London: Hutchinson & Co., 1982.

Hannon, Philip and Gallagher, Jackie, eds. *Taking the Long Five: 70 Years of Fianna Fáil.* Dublin: Blackwater Press, 1996.

Haughey, Charles J. *The Spirit of the Nation* . Cork: Mercier Press, 1986

Horgan, John. *Sean Lemass: the Enigmatic Patriot.* Dublin: Gill & Macmillan, 1997.

Joyce, Joe and Murtagh, Peter. *The Boss: Charles J. Haughey in Government.* Dublin: Poolbeg Press, 1983.

Kelly, James. *Orders for the Captain?* Dublin: Private, 1971.

Kennedy, Kieran A. and Dowling, Brendan R. *Economic Growth in Ireland: the Experience Since 1947.* Dublin: Gill and Macmillan, 1975.

Kennedy, Tadhg. *Charles J. Haughey: Kinsealy.* Dublin: Atlantic Press, 1986.

Kenny, Shane. *Go Dance on Somebody Else's Grave.* Dublin, Kildanore Press 1990.

Lenihan, Brian. *For the Record.* Dublin, Blackwater Press, 1991.

MacIntyre, Tom. *Through the Bridewell Gate: a Diary of the Dublin Arms Trial.* London: Faber and Faber, 1971.

Maher, D. J. *The Tortuous Path: the Course of Ireland's Entry into the EEC, 1948-73.* Dublin: Institute of Public Administration, 1986.

Mallie, Éamonn, and McKittrick, David. *The Fight for Peace: the Secret Story Behind the Irish Peace Process.* London: Heineman, 1996.

Maloney, Ed and Pollak, Andy. *Paisley.* Dublin: Poolbeg Press, 1986.

Manning, Maurice. *James Dillon: a Biography.* Dublin: Wolfhound Press, 1999.

O'Byrnes, Stephen. *Hiding Behind a Face: Fine Gael under Fitzgerald.* Dublin: Gill & Macmillan, 1986.

O'Conner, Kevin. *Sweetie.* Dublin: Private, 1999.

O'Malley, Padraig. *Uncivil Wars: Ireland Today.* Belfast: Blackstaff Press, 1983.

O'Reilly, Emily. *Candidate: the Truth Behind the Presidential Campaign.* Dublin: Attic Press, 1991.

O'Sullivan, Michael. *Sean Lemass: a Biography.* Dublin: Blackwater Press, 1994

Prior, Jim. *Balance of Power.* London: Hamish Hamilton, 1986.

Ryan, Tim. *Albert Rynolds: the Longford Leader.* Blackwater Press, 1994.

_________. *Dick Spring: a Safe Pair of Hands.* Dublin: Blackwater Press, 1993.

_________. *Mara, P. J.* Dublin: Blackwater Press, 1992.

Smith, Raymond. *Charles J. Haughey: the Survivor.* Dublin: Aherlow Publishers, 1983.

_______________. *Garret: the Enigma of Dr Garret FitzGerald.* Dublin: Aherlow Publishers, 1985.

_______________. *Haughey and O'Malley: the Quest for Power.* Dublin: Aherlow Publishers, 1986.

Smyth, Clifford. *Ian Paisley: Voice of Protestant Ulster.* Edinburgh: Scottish Academic Press, 1987.

Smyth, Sam. *Thanks a Million Big Fella.* Dublin: Blackwater Press, 1997.

*Sunday Times* 'Insight' team, The. *Ulster.* Harmondsworth, England: Penguin Books, 1972.

Thatcher, Margaret. *The Downing Street Years.* London: Harper Collins, 1993.

Tobin, Fergal. *The Best of Decades: Ireland in the 1960s.* Dublin: Gill & Macmillan, 1984.

Walsh, Dick. *Des O'Malley: a Political Profile.* Dingle: Brandon Books, 1986.

___________. *The Party: Inside Fianna Fáil.* Dublin: Gill & Macmillan, 1986.

Watts, David. *The Constitution of Northern Ireland: Prospects and Problems.* London: Heinemann, 1981.

White, Barry. *John Hume: Statesman of the Troubles.* Belfast: Blackstaff Press, 1984.

Whyte, J. H. *Church and State in Modern Ireland, 1923-1979.* Dublin: Gill & Macmillan, 1980.

Wilner, Ann Ruth. *The Spellbinders: Charismatic Political Leadership.* New Haven and London: Yale University Press, 1984.

Young, John N. *Erskine Childers: President of Ireland.* Gerrards Cross: Colin Smythe, 1985.

# Index